MODERN LEGAL STUDIES

The Relational Theory of Contract:
Selected Works of Ian Macneil

D1615243

AUSTRALIA
LBC Information Services Sydney
Sydney

CANADA and USA
Carswell
Toronto, Ontario

NEW ZEALAND
Brooker's
Auckland

SINGAPORE and MALAYSIA
Sweet & Maxwell Asia
Singapore and Kuala Lumpur

MODERN LEGAL STUDIES

THE RELATIONAL THEORY OF CONTRACT: SELECTED WORKS OF IAN MACNEIL

Ian R Macneil, John Henry Wigmore Professor of Law Emeritus, Northwestern University School of Law

edited by David Campbell, Professor of Law, Cardiff Law School

with introductory essays by David Campbell; Jay M Feinman, Distinguished Professor of Law, Rutgers School of Law, Camden; and Peter Vincent-Jones, Professor of Law, Lancashire Law School

London
Sweet & Maxwell
2001

Published in 2001 by
Sweet & Maxwell Limited of
100 Avenue Road London NW3 3PE
http://www.sweetandmaxwell.co.uk
Typeset by YHT Ltd,
London
Printed in England by MPG Books Ltd., Bodmin, Cornwall

A CIP catalogue record for this book
is available from the British Library.

ISBN 0421 722401

No natural forests were destroyed to make this product,
only farmed timber was used and re-planted.

Acknowledgments

Grateful acknowledgment is made to the following, for permission to quote from the works of Ian R. Macneil:

A Brief Comment on Farnsworth's "Suggestions on the Future" (1988), 38, *Journal of Legal Education* 301–303. Reprinted by permission of Journal of Legal Education, the American Association of Law School's.

A Primer of Contract Planning (1975), 48, *Southern California Law Review* 627–704. Reprinted by permission of Southern California Law Review.

"Barriers to the Idea of Relational Contract" p. 31–49, The Complex Long-Term Contract: Structures and International Arbitration (1987), F Nicklisch ed. Reprinted by permission of Ian R Macneil and Hüthig GmbH + Co. kG.

Bureaucracy and Contracts of Adhesion (1984), 22, *Osgoode Hall Law Journal* 5–28. Reprinted by permission of Ian R Macneil and the Osgoode Law Journal.

Bureaucracy, Liberalism, and Community—American Style (1985), 79, *Northwestern University Law Review 900–948*. Reprinted by special permission of Northwestern University School of Law Review.

Contractland Invaded Again: A Comment on Doctrinal Writing and Shell's Ethical Standards (1988), 82, Northwestern University Law Review 901–903. Reprinted by special permission of Northwestern University School of Law Review.

Contracts: Adjustment of Long-Term Economic Relations Under Classical, Neoclassical, and Relational Contract Law (1978), 72, *Northwestern University Law Review*. Reprinted by special permission of Northwestern University School of Law Review.

Contracts: Exchange Transactions and Relations (1971, 1st ed. 1978, 2nd ed), p. xlix, 1320, Foundation Press. Reprinted by permission of Foundation Press.

Contracts: Instruments of Social Co-Operation—East Africa (1968), p. xiii, 758, Fred B Rothman. Reprinted by permission of Ian R Macneil.

Contract Remedies: A Need for Better Efficiency Analysis (1988), 144, *Journal of Institutional & Theoretical Economics* 6–30. Reprinted by permission of Ian R Macneil and J.C.B. Mohr (Paul Seibeck).

Economic Analysis of Contractual Relations: Its Shortfalls and the Need for a 'Rich Classifactory Apparatus' (1981), 75, *Northwestern University Law Review* 1018–63. Reprinted by special permission of Northwestern University School of Law Review.

Efficient Breach of Contract: Circles in the Sky, (1982), 68, *Virginia Law Review* 947–969. Reprinted by permission of Virginia Law Review.

Essays on the Nature of Contract (1980), 10, *North Carolina Central Law Journal* 159–100. Reprinted by permission of Foundation Press.

"Ethics" p. 567–593. Exchange Revisited: Individual Utility and Social Solidarity (1986), 96,. Reprinted by permission of the University of Chicago and Ian R Macneil.

Political Exchange as Relational Contract, in Generalized Political Exchange (1991), B Marin & A Pizzorno eds., 154–172, Westview Press. Reprinted by permission of Ian R Macneil and Westview Press.

Power of Contract and Agreed Remedies (1962), 47, *Cornell Law Quarterly* 495–528. Reprinted by permission of Cornell Law School.

Reflections on Relational Contract (1985), 141, *Journal of Institutional & Theoretical Economics* 541–546. Reprinted by permission of Ian R Macneil and J.C.B. Mohr (Paul Seibeck).

Relational Contract: What We Do and Do Not Know (1985), *Winsconsin Law Review* 483–525. Reprinted by permission of Winsconsin Law Review and Ian R Macneil.

Relational Contract Theory as Sociology: A Reply to Professors Lindenberg and de Vos (1987), 143, *Journal of Institutional & Theoretical Economics* 272–290. Reprinted by permission of Ian R Macneil and J.C.B. Mohr (Paul Seinbeck).

Restatement (second) of Contracts and Presentation (1974), 60, *Virginia Law Review*. Reprinted by permission of The Virginia Law Review.

The Many Futures of Contracts (1974), 47, Southern California Law Review 691–816. Reprinted by permission of *Southern California Law Review* and the American Association of Law Schools.

The Masters of Arts in Law (1965), 17, *Journal of Legal Education* 423–431. Reprinted by permission of Journal of Legal Education.

The New Social Contract—An Inquiry into Modern Contractual Relations (1980), p. xiii, 164, Yale University Press. Reprinted by permission of Yale University Press and Ian R Macneil.

Values in Contract: Internal and External (April 1983), 78, *Northwestern University Law Review* 340–418. Reprinted by special permission of Northwestern University School of Law Review.

"When Acceptance Becomes Effective" Formation of Contracts: A Study of the Common Core of Legal Systems (1968), R.B Schlesinger et al eds., 2v, p. xv, 1727, Oceana Publications & Sweet & Maxwell. Reprinted by permission of Oceana Publications.

Whither Contracts? (1969), 21, *Journal of Legal Education* 403–418. Reprinted by permission of Journal of Legal Education and the American Association of Law Schools.

While every care has been taken to establish and acknowledge copyright, and contact the owners, the publishers tender their apologies for any accidental infringement. They would be pleased to come to suitable arrangement with the rightful owners in each case.

Contents

CONTENTS

Preface

In this book, I have attempted to present a comprehensive selection of Ian Macneil's writings on the relational theory of contract and a representative selection of that theory's background social philosophy in Macneil's relational theory of exchange. I have ignored Macneil's work in other areas, although that work is often of great value, including authoritative works on arbitration and, my favourite amongst these omitted works, a highly interesting paper on Fuller's jurisprudence. Faced with the large corpus of Macneil's work just on contract, in order to produce a book of reasonable length I have had to take a number of editorial decisions which I fear are controversial. I will now attempt to justify or at least explain three of them.

First, there is the selection itself. Though the selection is comprehensive, and a number of entire papers have been included, this is principally a set of excerpts from Macneil's work rather than reprints of entire works. This has been done to eliminate instances of outright repetition and to focus on those themes which seem to have proven most lasting in the reception of Macneil's work.

Secondly, there is a bias towards more recent works. I have ignored those of Macneil's works prior to "The Many Futures of Contract" in which he can be seen struggling with the shortcomings of the classical law of contract before stating his own rival, relational theory in "The Many Futures". I have also largely omitted Macneil's direct criticisms of the more sophisticated forms of classical contract, which he calls "neo-classical" contract, in order to concentrate on the resulting statement of the relational theory. (The process by which Macneil reached his own position is briefly described in his biographical statement in this volume). The reception of Macneil's work has focused on "The Many Futures", although Macneil has subsequently restated the central themes of that paper as his views have developed, and these restatements have in many cases anticipated or responded to common criticisms of "The Many Futures". The bias towards more recent works has been intended to direct the reader to these restatements, some of which will, I think, startle readers familiar only with "The Many Futures". (That many criticisms of Macneil have failed to take account of developments in his thought is pointed out in the introductory essays to this volume). To, as it were, hammer the point home, "The Many Futures of Contract" itself has been completely excluded. This, of course, may be going too far and I am unsure about what I have done. In my defence, I can say that this very long paper proved extremely resistant to abridgement and, under any sort of constraint of space, in the light of its subsequent restatements, I would not now wish to reprint it all. I am also very pleased to be able to say that its complete exclusion has been approved by Macneil himself.

Thirdly, there has been a *drastic* reduction in the number of footnotes so that the footnotes kept are almost all instances of direct quotation by Macneil. The Harvard style of referring to books and articles has been adopted to minimise even further the number of footnotes as such. I have chosen to sacrifice Macneil's footnotes to allow more excerpts to be included in the space allowed, and I believe their elimination sometimes usefully focuses attention on the main things Macneil is saying. There is, however a cost. Macneil has often put a lot of interesting observations in footnotes, particularly in his articles in US law reviews, the format of which, of course, encourages this. The elimination of these footnotes is the editorial decision about which I am most uncertain. Macneil does not approve of it and has asked me to include the following warning: "Rightly or wrongly, wisely or unwisely, Macneil often writes in two closely related streams at the same time—text and textual notes. Thus, the text can be incomplete and/or distorted in the absence of the latter. Economy has, however, made it necessary to omit most of the notes. Readers in the slightest doubt about the message Macneil intended at any given point are thus strongly advised to examine the original writing with its textual notes".

In the light not merely of this but of all my editorial decisions, it is as well for me to state outright what is anyway my principal hope, that this book will stimulate its readers to turn to Macneil's original works, something which, I am obliged to say, has not been done to anything like the extent that the number of citations of his work would lead one to believe.

In the course of editing this book I have incurred a number of debts. The first is to Ian Macneil himself, for his always generous reception of my interest in his work which has now culminated in his allowing me to edit this book. Ian's kindness towards me has been rather stretched in the course of the production of this book, in which he has taken a full part. I am also indebted to the editors of *Modern Legal Studies*, and especially to Hugh Beale, for their brave decision to allow a book of this format to appear in their series. I thank Jay Feinman and Peter Vincent-Jones for their introductory essays. The production of this book has been financially supported by grants from the Cardiff Law School and the Socio-legal Studies Association. These grants have funded the work of Rachel Davies, who graduated from Cardiff Law School in 2000, on the book. Ms Davies has, in commendable fashion, done most to deal (following my instructions) with the footnotes to Macneil's original pieces.

David Campbell
Cardiff
July 18, 2001

Biographical Statement

Ian Macneil was born in New York City in 1929, growing up in suburban Long Island and rural Vermont, sometimes with, and sometimes without, a silver spoon in his mouth. His schools ranged from the fabled one-room schoolhouse of rural America (two of them, both excellent), to more or less posh private day schools, to large public schools (American meaning), to Castlebay Primary School, and finally to a small coeducational boarding secondary school—now long deceased—then in the throes of transformation from progressive to more conventional education.

Macneil went to the University of Vermont because he loved Vermont, the University was inexpensive, and he had the naive idea that he would become a Vermont politician. After receiving his BA and commission in the USAR and spending a year at Harvard Law School, he was called to active duty during the Korean War.

While in the army Macneil married Nancy Wilson and they lived happily ever after. None of the various infantry outfits with which he served found their way to Korea while he was with them, and in 1953 he returned to Harvard Law School. A short preliminary stint with the Law Review reminded him too much of the Army, so he quit and spent much of the next two years happily with his family, although he did manage to secure an LL.B. with reasonably respectable credentials.

After a year of clerking for the Honourable Peter Woodbury, US Court of Appeals for the First Circuit, and three years of law practice in Concord, New Hampshire, Macneil joined the law faculty of Cornell University. He taught there from 1959 to 1972 and from 1974 to 1980, in the later years as the Frank B. Ingersoll Professor of Law. In between he was a Professor of Law and a member of the Center for Advanced Studies at the University of Virginia.

In 1980 Northwestern University School of Law made an offer Macneil could not refuse, and he became the John Henry Wigmore Professor of Law, a position he held until becoming Emeritus in 1999.

Along the line, Macneil spend two years teaching at the University of East Africa in Dar es Salaam, and one each at Duke and Harvard Law Schools. Also the Law Faculty at the University of Edinburgh was kind enough to let him be a visiting fellow, as was Oxford University. Throughout, personal legal work and later consulting and arbitration, took him out of the Ivory Legal Tower.

In 1970 Macneil succeeded his father as Macneil of Barra, hereditary chief of the Clan Macneil, and he then became an active proprietor of a Hebridean crofting estate. Macneil has long been a member of the Barra community—to the limited extent possible for anyone not born there.

The rich social complexities of his life probably contributed to Macneil's escape from the narrow ruts of classical and neo-classical contract into the openness of relational contract. There, relatively discrete transactions are important but only as part of a broad landscape.

A more direct influence was Lon Fuller, whose half-escape from classical and neo-classical contract begged for something more. Even more direct was immense frustration generated by participation in Rudolph Schlesinger's study of the comparative law of offer and acceptance.

Perhaps the final straw was Macneil's spending most of the summer of 1964 trying to find coherent principles consistent with neo-classical law in hundreds of American "agreement to agree" cases—a fool's errand. Agreements to agree make sense only in terms of relations *outside* any theoretical structure—economic or legal—where consent is always either 100 per cent on or 100 per cent off. In real-life, on-off consent (in contrast to apparent expressions of such consent) is virtually if not totally non-existent. This experience led Macneil to realise that only a fully relational approach can deal adequately with *either* relations *or* the relatively discrete transactions embedded in them. He has been working out the ramifications of this ever since.

Ian R Macneil
Edinburgh
January 29, 2001

PART 1

INTRODUCTION

Chapter 1

Ian Macneil and the Relational Theory of Contract

David Campbell[1]

Contents

---

[1] A seminar based on this introduction was given to the Faculty of Management, Erasmus University Rotterdam, The Netherlands, April 2000. I should like to thank participants in that seminar for their comments. I should also like to thank Hugh Beale, Kevin Dowd, Donald Harris, Peter Vincent-Jones and Bill Whitford for their extensive comments.

1. Introduction

In 1999, the career of Ian Macneil was celebrated by Northwestern University Law School, where Macneil did the largest part of his teaching, which held a Symposium in his honour on "Relational Contract Theory".[2] Though Macneil has done much other valuable work, particularly in arbitration (Macneil 1992; Macneil, Speidel and Stipanowich 1994) and legal (Macneil 1981c) and political philosophy (Macneil 1990), his principal achievement has been that in 30 or so of the more than 50 books and articles he has published since 1960 he has set out the principal formulation[3] of what has come to be known as "the relational theory" of the law of contract. That theory is the most promising basis for the construction of the alternative jurisprudence of market transactions now widely recognised to be necessary following the "death" of "the classical law of contract." Macneil's accounts of those extensive elements of contract which cannot be brought under any other than his relational view are the fundamental achievement of his work. Their empirical plausibility and depth of comprehension of the law provide the major resource for the reconstruction of contract jurisprudence. They are coupled to a sophisticated social philosophy

---

[2] (2000) 94 (3) *Northwestern University Law Review*.
[3] The other formulations which might be thought comparable to Macneil's are those of Goetz and Scott (Goetz and Scott 1981; 1983; Scott 1987; 1990) and, less clearly, Goldberg (1980) and Schwartz (1992).

which Macneil calls "the relational theory of exchange" which is itself of great originality. In this introduction, I hope to guide the reader through this selection of Macneil's works by describing his critique of the classical law of contract (and, later, his critique of the contract scholarship influenced by Chicagoan law and economics after Posner), his alternative, relational theory of contract, and his background relational theory of exchange.

In so doing, I hope to stress the following point. There is a sharp contrast between the profundity of Macneil's work and the, as he himself recognises, still disappointing reception of that work. So far as this is an intellectual matter, it can largely be put down to the widespread interpretation of Macneil that he claims there is a separate "relational" category of contracts. This is, at best, thought to be a claim about a perhaps interesting but certainly marginal category of contracts other than classical or discrete contracts. Macneil is widely thought to have described a "spectrum" on which relational contracts are placed at the opposite pole to classical or discrete contracts. But though there certainly is warrant for this interpretation of Macneil, the main intended thrust of his work is not so much to distinguish the relational from the discrete contract but to reveal the relational constitution of all contracts.

2. The Critique of the Classical Law of Contract

Macneil's first publication (1960a) gave clear notice of what was to follow. It was a review of what would now be called a socio-legal work on freedom of contract in which he noted that maintaining the existence of that freedom "in an age of [standard] forms and concentration of economic and social power" was "surely one of the most pressing of all contract problems" (Macneil 1960a, 177). Macneil's other writings on contract prior to 1968 focused on the specific problems, particularly the (lack of) reality of the "agreement" secured by the rules of acceptance (Macneil 1968q, 1395–433), agreement of remedies (Macneil 1962) and hire-purchase (Macneil 1966b; 1966c), in which the failure of the classical law of contract (Macneil 1968b-d, f-q) was then being acutely manifested. He later summed up the position that can be taken from these early works thus:

the limited extent to which it is possible for people to consent to all the terms of a transaction, even a relatively simple and very discrete one, soon forces the development of legal fictions expanding the scope of "consent" far beyond anything remotely close to what the parties had in mind. The greatest of these . . . is the objective theory of contract. The classical . . . contract is founded not upon actual consent but upon objective manifestations of consent. Moreover, in [the] classical law[,] manifestations of intent include whole masses of contract consent one, or even both, of the parties did not know in fact (Macneil 1978a, 883–4).

In 1968, Macneil published his first casebook, which he began with a statement of what had become his general dissatisfaction with the classical law. Having referred his students to the principal standard English contract textbooks, he continued:

it is not unfair to say that all the standard texts on English law reflect a notion that the law of contract litigation is a relatively neat and logical structure of rules. The author of this book believes this idea to be inaccurate . . . Contract law is hardly a neat and logical structure of rules, but like all law a social instrument designed to accomplish the goals of man (Macneil 1968e, 2).

He further observed that:

this book deals with contracts, and the standard texts deal largely with the law as defined by the outcome of contract litigation (and by statutes), or more specifically with the outcome of appellate decisions in contract litigation. Contracts and contract litigation are not the same thing (Macneil 1968e, 1)

Macneil accordingly uses the term "contract" to embrace the formal doctrine condensed in textbooks or derived from the proper study of cases and statute, but only when these sources of the law are placed within the social normative structure of "contract" as a legal institution which has the economic "function of projecting exchange into the future" (Macneil 1980, xiii).

Macneil's emphasis here on English, rather than U.S., textbooks arose in that this casebook was written for the purposes of his teaching at University College, Dar Es Salaam, Tanzania, where he took sabbatical leave from Cornell between 1965–7.[4] The contract law of East Africa, including Kenya and Uganda as well as Tanzania, was derived from the English law, and students from all three countries studied law at Dar Es Salaam. The even then more critical attitude to the classical law of contract in U.S. jurisprudence (in which realism has played a far larger part than in the English) had led to wide currency being given to the argument, which Gilmore (1995) expressed most forcefully (Macneil 1978a, n. 101), that there was no law of "contract" at all. Rather, the complexity of exchanges meant that there had to be a set of different laws of "contracts" adequate to that complexity. In a paper on the teaching of contracts addressed to a student audience at the 1967 meeting of American Association of Law Students, Macneil acknowledged the power of this argument but ultimately rejected it:

> Is there such a thing as contracts? My friends teaching such courses as Contracts 201 (Sales), Contracts 202 (Negotiable Instruments), Contracts 307 (Creditors' Rights), Contracts 312 (Labour Law), Contracts 313 (Corporations) and Contracts 319 (Trade Regulation) delight in telling me there is no such thing as contracts. There are, they say, sales contracts, negotiable instruments, secured transactions and bankruptcy, collective bargaining agreements, insurance contracts, real estate transactions and a host of other contract-types, but contracts-in-gross there ain't. Having earlier rejected childhood beliefs in the higher abstractions of Samuel Williston's metaphysics, I almost came to believe them. But a personal vested economic interest in the existence of contracts-in-gross caused me to search further. Since you too share that vested interest you will be pleased to know that I have reached the conclusion that contract exists (Macneil 1969b, 403. *cf.* 1987c, 374).

Of course this makes it imperative to show that "a reunification of contract law ... is possible [which] might lead to more effective administration of justice than is presently achieved" (Macneil 1974a, 816). Macneil was of the opinion that this was possible:

> I am not convinced that the disappearance of a generalised course in contracts from the law school curriculum would be a disaster on

---

[4] For details of Macneil's life see the Biographical Note in this volume.

the scale of Waterloo. Nor do I think the Western world would collapse if the generalised concept of contracts ceased altogether to be a way of organising statutes, judicial decisions, administrative action, textbooks, legal digests, etc. I do think, however, that we would lose some of our understanding of the functions and techniques of contracting and of contract law in the various transaction-type areas themselves. In short, recognition that the various transaction types do have common elements of behaviour can lead lawyers, judges, legislators, administrators and even law teachers to a better grasp of and better dealing with each transaction-type itself. To the extent that this is true a generalised contracts course becomes justified, not on the ground that there is a "law of contracts" but on the ground that the common elements in contracts-in-gross present problems and challenges for the legal system which widely cut across transaction-type lines (Macneil 1969b, 408).

Macneil has never denied that the classical law of contract has been of enormous, and continues to be of substantial, value (Macneil 1987a, n. 19), and he finds "very powerful" the argument that "[w]hat we have works reasonably well, and we have no assurance that after much expenditure of time and other resources any general law of contract relations we might produce would be better from a practical standpoint" (Macneil 1987a, 36). However, though he is very generous in his evaluation of innovative work broadly within the classical law, such as that of Eisenberg (Macneil 1985a, 544–5), his own work is driven by the belief that a more attractive rival theory of contract is both possible (Macneil 1974a, 807–8; 1985a, 544–5) and necessary to displace the classical law (Macneil 1985a, 542). Certainly, whatever the failings of the classical law, it will not be falsified until the superiority of such a rival is established (Campbell 1992).

Though in his later work Macneil continued, when necessary, to lay bare the classical law's failings as effectively as anyone (Whitford 1985, 546–8),[5] his particular contribution has not so much been to the exposure of the doctrinal incoherence of classical law, exemplified by Gilmore (1995) in the USA and Atiyah (1990, chs. 1–11) in the UK, or

---

[5] I shall discuss a special case of this below, Macneil's criticism of the formalistic understanding of contract in Chicagoan law and economics after Posner.

to the exposure of the empirical "non-use" in business of the formal contract remedies (Macaulay 1963a; 1963b). Rather, taking these to be the case (Macneil 1969b, 408; 1987a, 35–6), he has sought to reveal the shortcomings of the philosophy articulated by the classical law that produces incoherence and empirical irrelevance. By doing so, he has attempted to construct a coherent and relevant rival law of contract. (Of course, by deepening our understanding of the contract phenomena which the classical law cannot explain, Macneil has increased our perception of the extent of the existing explanatory failures.) It is tremendously to his credit that Macneil saw that, as it is the social philosophical underpinning of the classical law that is ultimately at issue, his attempt to construct a rival theory could not be a matter of narrow, legal scholarship but required him to draw on the resources of other disciplines:

> just as contractual relations exceed the capacities of the neo-classical contract law system, so too the issues exceed the capacities of neo-classical contract law scholars. They must become something else—anthropologists, sociologists, economists, political theorists, and philosophers—to do reasonable justice to the issues raised by contractual relations (Macneil 1978a, n. 137).

3. Co-operation and Norm in the Identification of Relational Contracts

3.1. Co-operation in Macneil's Early Writings

Although Macneil's work has come to based on the concept of the "relation," he began to develop his rival account of contract not around that concept but around "co-operation." It is instructive to chart the development of his thinking, not least because co-operation has remained central to his work. This development can be seen as an attempt to flesh out his early belief that contracts are, as he put it in the sub-title of his first casebook, *Instruments for Social Co-operation*. Fundamentally, he maintained in his early writings, contracts are co-operative:

> The first thing to note about contract is the fact that it concerns social behaviour ... The next thing to note is that the kind of social

> behaviour involved is co-operative social behaviour, behaviour
> characterised by a willingness and ability to work with others ...
> contract involves people affirmatively working together (Macneil
> 1968e, 14).

He established the existence of this element of co-operation through a
sort of lawyer's phenomenology of contract. Empirical examination of
contracting revealed that co-operation was the most important common
characteristic, one of the five "basic elements" of contract identified in
his earlier writings[6]:

> There are ... five basic elements of contracts: 1. co-operation; 2.
> economic exchange; 3. planning for the future; 4. potential
> external sanctions; and 5. social control and manipulation (Macneil
> 1969b, 407).

For Macneil, the recognition that "all mutual planning in transactions ...
is conflict laden", and indeed may involve "the most brutal kinds of
infighting" (1974a, 780), is coupled with a description of co-operation
which gives it a rather more central place than that of "external material
... of little interest" (1980c, 91) typical in the classical law.

Macneil's insistence that "the first thing to note about contract ... is
that it concerns social behaviour," though sociologically commonplace,
has a most serious implication for the classical law of contract, for it runs
against the radical individualism of the will theory of contract. As it has
been put as recently as 1993: "The distinguishing feature of contractual
obligations is that they are not imposed by the law but undertaken by the
parties" (Smith 1993, 2). This is right in a sense which must be stressed,
for it goes to the heart of the freedom provided by the market. But it is
also wrong in a sense, and this sense is far less well understood. It is the
explanation of this aspect of contract that is at the heart of what now is
interesting in contract scholarship. For parties can make contracts only in
certain ways—not by claimed telepathic communication, or through
exercise of physical force or fraud, etc.—and this is because they must
express their undertakings through social institutions. As Macneil put it
in 1960: "contract is an edifice partly built by the parties but also partly

---

[6] In his later writings these were treated as four "primal roots" (Macneil 1974a, 696–712;
1980b, 1–4) and in his most recent reflection on his work as contract's "essence" (Macneil
2000a, 432).

built by society, by the law" (Macneil 1960a, 177). To the extent that it remains committed to the pure will theory, the classical law has inevitably become a few remote core principles surrounded by a plethora of exceptions because contract has social features which the will theory ignores. Those social features, however, have explanatory primacy over the individual features on which that theory concentrates. This becomes obvious when the law refuses to give effect to some agreements which it was the will of one or both of the parties should be enforceable, as when agreement was obtained by undue influence or involved a willing party who did not have capacity. But, crucially, this negative aspect is merely the other side of the positive fact that it is the law that makes possible any contractual agreement at all. After noting some refusals to give effect to agreements, Macneil said:

> These ... appear as exceptions to some general rule permitting the parties fully to define their legal status [but] if the role of the law in creating contracts were more completely presented this distortion would not occur, and these matters would be seen not as exceptions to freedom of contract but as simply part of the law's definition of contract (Macneil 1960a, 177. cf. 1990, 154).

Over the almost 40 years since this was written, Macneil has been one of the few who have pursued the coherent, inclusive concept of contract this statement indicates is possible.

3.2.   MACNEIL ON THE NORMATIVE CONSTITUTION OF CONTRACT

In his later work,[7] Macneil explains the existence of the five basic elements or four primal roots or the essence of contract, and particularly co-operation, through an extremely exhaustive catalogue of the social norms or values which operate in contract. Following *Webster* by taking a norm to be "a principle of right action binding upon the members of a group and serving to guide, control, or regulate proper and acceptable behaviour" (Macneil 1980c, 38), Macneil says of contract that:

> [in] the process of projecting exchange into the future ... people

---

[7] Macneil's earlier work distinguishes three forms of co-operation in terms of the orientations of action that produce those distinct forms (1968b, 14–6) in a way obviously reminiscent of Weber (Weber 1978, 24–6), but this seems to play no role in his later work.

specialise and exchange, exercise choice, plan to exercise power, and fit all these things together in the society of which they are members. This behaviour gives rise to prescriptive norms, to standards of proper conduct (Macneil 1980c, 36).

Macneil developed his perception of the role of "society" in building the "edifice" of contract into a system of what he came to call the common contract norms. It is, I believe, vital to Macneil's criticism of the classical law that three levels of these norms be distinguished in his developed argument for the existence of co-operation in contract.

The first level is of the ontologically fundamental social relations within which all human action is constituted, the "social structure" of shared meanings, language, normativity, etc. within which all action is framed. This is the basic sense in which society "is the fundamental root, the base, of contract:"

> Contract without the common needs and tastes created by society is inconceivable ... contract without language is impossible; and contract without social structure is—quite literally—rationally unthinkable (Macneil 1980c, 1).

These relations shade into a second level, that constituted by the background polity of bourgeois society which provides the political boundaries for the market economy:

> contract between totally isolated, utility-maximising individuals is not contract, but war ... contractual solidarity—the social solidarity making exchange work ... at a minimum holds the parties together so that they will not kill and steal in preference to exchanging [This is a matter of the] external god providing social stability, enforcement of promises, and other basic requirements. Within these rigid confines, the parties are free to maximise their individual utilities to their hearts' content (Macneil 1980c, 1, 14).

The "Sovereign imposition of norms" by the "external god" Leviathan (Macneil 1983b, 370) furnishes political and legal security in order that the generalised market might operate.[8] Macneil insists on the necessity of

---

[8] The particular form of this imposition will, of course, substantially affect the way the market operates (Macneil 1980c, 38–9; 1985b, 491–3).

a background social matrix (Macneil 1974a, 710–2) composed of first and second level relations for contracts to take place, and contrasts this to the way the classical law and neo-classical economics take this matrix for granted. The latter:

> assumes the existence of very complex relations between the parties—relations established through society generally, language, law, and societal economic organisation. But once such relations are assumed, the impact of those relations on the analysis is typically ignored. *Ceteris paribus* conquers all . . . Because economic analysis is analysis of social behaviour, economic man is necessarily in society at all times . . . potential fallacy lurks in all social analysis starting from the non-social, relation-omitting model of neo-classical economics (Macneil 1982, 961. *cf.* Macneil 1983b, 377).

When one recalls the silly rhetoric in which populist neo-liberalism insisted "there is no society," and the cast of mind of and to which it spoke, this point arguably needs to be made. However, we should allow that the existence of these first and second level relations is not in itself necessarily embarrassing for the classical law, which has adopted (at least some statements of) such relations as boundary statements for the operation of its neo-classical economic assumptions. The perennial problem, indeed paradox (Hegel 1967, secs. 182–208), of bourgeois political theory—generally referred to as the Hobbesian problem of order (Parsons 1968, 89–94)—follows from the very positive valuation that capitalism places on individual acquisitiveness. Neo-classical economics assumes that rational economic action is motivated by a form of pure selfishness which it terms rational individual utility maximisation (Gossen 1983, 3–4). The individuals motivated in this way nevertheless must co-exist, but, of course, the positive attitude towards others necessary for co-existence is undermined by generalised, selfish motivation. However, the central claim of economic liberalism (Nozick 1974, 155–60) is that, when confined within certain conditions broadly of peacefulness (von Mises 1981, 36) guaranteed by Leviathan (Hobbes 1968, ch. 13), economic action, though motivated by individual utility maximisation, spontaneously will produce social order (Hayek 1976, ch. 9). The concept of general competitive equilibrium at the heart of neo-classical economics (Arrow and Debreu 1983) is a highly sophisticated methematical demonstration that an optimally efficient allocation of goods (Pareto 1971, ch. 6, sec. 33) will tend to be produced by a market conforming to the assumptions of those economics (Walras 1977, lesson 12). However, the sociological point at issue has never been better expressed than it originally was (Keynes 1973, 358–9) as the transformation of "private vices" into "public benefits" (Mandeville 1970) through the operation of the "invisible hand" (Smith 1976, 412). The invisible hand is, it is important to recognise, a tremendously powerful argument that unconscious but nevertheless effective co-operation will, as it were naturally, be produced by economic action.

Macneil has indeed acknowledged (1969, 405) that the self-interest of the rational utility maximiser must bring about a certain element of co-operation between the parties if their separate goals are to be realised through mutual performances. However, such "co-operation" does not require commitment to the goal of the other party and indeed may, within prudential limits, be inimical to it. But it is not the first and second level relations which carry the thrust of Macneil's criticism of the classical law (Macneil 1985b, 491–3). Rather it is a third level, that of relations articulating co-operation external and internal to the conduct of contracting parties. It is the way these relations express the co-operative influences of the first two levels and also themselves generate co-operation *within the fundamental unit of economic analysis of contract* that supplants neo-classical assumptions (Macneil 1980c, pref). It is this alteration of the "fundamental unit" of the analysis of contract that is the core of the relational theory of contract.

Having described the common sociality essential for all human activity (Macneil 1980c, 1) and the political limits to self-interest which prevent economic competition from decaying into war (Macneil 1980c, 1) or parasitism (Macneil 1980c, 42) as the background social matrix of contract, Macneil crucially then goes on to argue that "law contributes more than general stability, it is directly facilitative in [that] it provides for the accomplishment of co-operation [and the] continuation of interdependence" (1980c, 93) through external and internal (1980c, 36–7; 1983b, 367; 1987a, 31–2) "values of contract behaviour ... generated ... in billions of contractual relations" (Macneil 1983b, 351).

External norms are imposed, not only, nor even necessarily (Macneil 1980c, 37), by "the positive law of the sovereign, but also from many other sources [including] private law, such as that imposed on ... businesses by trade associations." Not only are there such relatively "vertical impositions", but there is also the "more horizontal imposition of external values, such as those arising from ... customs of a trade" (Macneil 1983b, 367–8). These foster co-operation by reducing the "choice of a party which is reciprocating too little, is too powerful, is terminating relations, or is following arbitrary or other procedures viewed as inadequate" (Macneil 1983b, 379).

Finally, and most importantly, *internal* norms intimately linked to the external ones orient "both [the] actual behaviour and [the] principles of right action" (Macneil 1980c, 38) of contracting parties. Macneil describes, in his last formulation, ten common contract norms which underpin all contracting by generating a (to various degrees, as will be seen below) co-operative attitude which respects "solidarity and reciprocity" (Macneil 1983b, 348):

> The ten common contract norms are (1) role integrity ... (2) reciprocity (simply stated as the principle of getting something back for something given), (3) implementation of planning, (4) effectuation of consent, (5) flexibility, (6) contractual solidarity, (7) the restitution, reliance and expectation interests (the "linking norms"), (8) creation and restraint of power (the "power norm"), (9) propriety of means, and (10) harmonisation with the social matrix (Macneil 1983b, 347. *cf.* Macneil 1974a, 808–9; 1978a, 895; 1980, 40).

This normative schema is rather elaborate and expressed in terms to which Macneil typically gives rather unconventional meanings, and I will not set it out fully here. Though it has been used by others than Macneil for detailed analysis of specific contracts (Brown and Feinman 1991, 350–1), its detail would seem mainly to hold interest for the sociologist (Lindenberg and de Vos 1985) seeking to flesh out how the law of contract represents what Durkheim (1984, ch. 3) calls the "organic" solidarity of modern societies (Macneil 1980c, 93–102; 1986, 583–8). For present purposes, one need focus only on the very idea of identifying a normative structure in relation to contract.

3.3. Complexity, Duration and the Concept of the Relational Contract

Though I will argue that the first impression he gives is rather misleading, Macneil's work does, in the first instance, draw our attention to the highly planned, very extensive inter-firm contracts between large, legally independent but economically interdependent firms which have become far more significant with the increase in the scale of production over the course of capitalist economic development (Macneil 1974a, 694–6. *cf.* Gottlieb 1983). Contracts of this sort involve substantial "asset specific" (Williamson 1985, 52–6) or "idiosyncratic" (Williamson 1986, 105–10) investment which cannot be reallocated to other contracts without uncompensatable loss. It is exemplified by buyers having taken great pains to bring their suppliers up to standard by extensive (and expensive) joint quality assurance programmes. Such investment is, by definition, non-transferable in the event of complete termination of contractual relations, but it would be extremely difficult to claim adequate compensation in damages for its loss as it is very likely to be substantially uncertain and remote. Such contracts also are too complex (including what would be an infinite number of terms were an attempt made *ex ante* to express those terms, being of long duration under uncertain circumstances, etc.) to be fully specified during pre-contractual negotiations and so require the parties to be prepared to adjust, *ex post*, in ways unspecifiable in advance, both their expectations and obligations during and at the conclusion of performance. Any substantial building works contract produced by any of the trade bodies, in which the precise quantification of the amount of work, time taken, and materials needed can really be revealed only in the course of actually doing the work, contains extensive price and time adjustment provisions in recognition of this.

Contracts of this nature are not efficiently governable by the classical law of contract. That law typically turns on the imposition of strict liabilities. Breach leads to the award of purportedly precisely quantified damages in compensation of certain, foreseeable losses. This remedy cannot efficiently govern contracts characterised by complex (*ex ante* unspecifiable) obligations and asset specific (*ex post* non-compensatable) investments (Campbell and Clay 1995, 3–19). Rather, they can be governed efficiently only if the parties adopt a consciously co-operative attitude (Campbell and Harris 1993; Deakin *et al.*, 1997). The norms Macneil identifies create such an attitude, setting the boundaries within which legitimate negotiation and competition are allowed. Any legitimate competition is bounded by an integral acceptance of co-operation as operative within the contract:

> The word "solidarity" (or "trust") is not inappropriate to describe this web of interdependence, externally reinforced as well as self-supporting, and expected future co-operation. The most important

aspect of solidarity . . . is the extent to which it produces similarity of selfish interests, whereby what increases (decreases) the utility of one participant also increases (decreases) the utility of the other . . . Seldom, if ever, is this merger of interests complete, but it is omnipresent, immensely significant, and, in a vast range of circumstances, complete for most practical purposes . . . [S]imilarity of interests may be produced by external forces such as sovereign law. But . . . solidarity may and does arise internally in relations (Macneil 1981, 1034).

This co-operative attitude makes the notion of the individual utility maximiser inappropriate to certain contracts which, as they turn on co-operative awareness of the value of the relation legally expressed in the contract between the parties, Macneil calls *relational contracts*:

An individual utility maximiser may be perfectly well aware of the fact that the deal he makes creates exchange-surplus, but his *sole* concern about that utility is to grab as much of it for himself as he can. He will feel nothing but regret at whatever amount is snared by the other party and nothing but happiness that the other failed to secure more of it. That is not, however, the case in relational exchange . . . Relational exchange . . . creates circumstances where the long-run *individual* economic (material) interests of each party conflict with any short run desires to maximise individual utility respecting the goods in any particular exchange; the more relational the exchange, the more artificial becomes the idea of maximisation. The capacity of an exchange to produce exchange-surplus . . . constitutes a pool of wealth which can be shared as well as grabbed, shared not to make a gift but out of deep economic self-interest . . . Over time, exchanges made with . . . long-run motivations produce norms to which the participants expect to adhere and to which they expect adherence from other parties (Macneil 1986, 578–9).

In relational contracts, we should note:

there can be present a "sense of productive increase from the relationship which can dwarf variations in expectation, or of long-term anticipations of mutual benefit that dwarf variations in shares received by parties." This anticipatory, commonly held "sense" of the parties may virtually obliterate any present separation as maximisers, thereby making them effectively a single maximiser (Macneil 1981b, 1023–4).[9]

It is Macneil's major achievement (Eisenberg 1995, 303; Gordon 1985; Whitford 1985) to have shown that open minded analysis of contracting reveals a class of relational contracts in which action predominantly is so oriented in the minds of the parties towards conscious co-operation that a contract of this class "no longer stands alone as in the discrete transaction, but is part of a relational web" (Macneil 1974b, 595). All the negotiating tactics adopted by parties, concerning formation (Macneil 1974a, 726–35, 753–80; 1975b, 666–76; 1981b, 1044–6), performance (Macneil 1974a, 780–2; 1975b, 651–6; 1981b, 1047–8), variation (Macneil 1978a, 886–98), termination (Macneil 1974a, 750–3; 1978a, 899–900; 1981b, 1041–3) and application of remedies (Macneil 1975b, 676–702), can be explained only as being informed by this co-operative attitude. Therefore, at the heart of the analysis it is no longer possible to work with the assumptions of classical contract, for they cannot plausibly be thought to describe the attitudes of the parties to relational contracts and it is those contracts which now are most significant forms of market exchange:

> Somewhere along the line of increasing duration and complexity, trying to force changes into a pattern of original consent becomes both too difficult and too unrewarding to justify the effort, and the contractual relation escapes the bounds of the [classical] system. That system is replaced by very different adjustment processes of an on-going administrative kind ... Moreover, the substantive relation of change to the status quo has now altered from what happens in some kind of market external to the contract to what can be achieved through the political and social processes of the relation, internal and external. This includes internal and external dispute resolution structures. At this point, the relation has become a mini-society with an array of norms beyond the norms centred on exchange and its immediate processes (Macneil 1978a, 901).

---

[9] Macneil is quoting from a letter sent to him by S. T. Lowry (Macneil 1981, 1020 n. 3).

Macneil gives the following hypothetical example[10] which it is worthwhile to quote at length of how "a smelting operation—Smelter— might secure the coal needed for its operations." Smelter might, of course, make a "[s]pot purchase from a stranger of 500 tons in a market of many sellers, Seller's agents delivering the coal by truck dumped at Smelter's yard, cash paid on delivery of each load." Of course, Smelter has no security of future supply under this arrangement and, if this valued, a more complex, long-term arrangement is needed, though it will have to deal, *inter alia*, with variations in price and possible problems with delivery over the term specified. At the other extreme to the spot contract is the vertical integration in which Smelter integrates supply into its own firm by buying a coal mine (or other source of secure supply). Between these extremes, however, is a range of alternative, relatively complex, relational contracts:

[1] Smelter contracts with Coal Mine to buy all the coal it requires during one year; the specified price is subject to a quarterly escalator clause based on a designated market. [2] Same ... except that in addition to the escalator clause there is a provision: "Should a party become dissatisfied with the price, the parties agree to negotiate about a new price and, in the absence of agreement, to refer the matter to X as arbitrator to determine a fair and equitable price." [3] Same ... except that the latest contract, entered into this year, is for 20 years rather than one; requires Coal Mine periodically: to provide Smelter with extensive cost information; to allow Smelter's experts to monitor mining operations; and to receive from Smelter recommendations respecting new equip-ment, improved methods of management and the like. Smelter and Coal Mine also agree to build and operate a conveyer belt system from minehead to smelting plant, sharing the capital costs equally and operating the conveyer system jointly. As part of the deal Smelter gives Coal Mine a five-year loan to cover part of Coal Mine's costs of the conveyer system and, in order to satisfy other lenders, guarantees Coal Mine's half of a 20-year mortgage loan on the conveyer system. [4] Same ... except that the payment by Smelter to Coal Mine is in return for 20% of Coal Mine's shares

---

[10] For empirical examples see Macneil (1978b).

rather than a loan; Smelter is guaranteed two seats on Coal Mine's Board of Directors (Macneil 1981b, 1025–6).

Macneil's account of such relational contracts is, as I have said elsewhere, "a most substantial contribution to the economic and social theory of the capitalist economy" (Campbell 1990, 82). It is interesting to compare its reception to that of an oeuvre of similar status in another discipline. A. D. Chandler's (1962; 1976; 1990) authoritative descriptions of the actual form of the most important business organisations as giant administrative hierarchies rather than transparent processors of market signals have had an enormous impact on business history and management studies. In his descriptions of the relational contract, Macneil has given a similarly authoritative account of the growth of what Chandler has called "the visible hand." Macneil parallels Chandler's description of the way "that modern business took the place of market mechanisms in co-ordinating the activities of the economy and allocating its resources" (Chandler 1976, 1) within firms with an account of the relational market exchanges that are the means of planned production between firms. One should not be unduly surprised that Chandler's (and similar) empirical findings remain marginal to the core of neo-classical economics, but Chandler has at least been given appropriate recognition in his own discipline. Macneil as yet has not.

4. The Discrete and Relational Contract Norms

4.1. CO-OPERATION AND COMPETITION

Of course, this account of co-operation in relational contracting makes it imperative to give a compatible account of competition, and in his developed work Macneil does so in two ways (which I will distinguish though he runs them together (Macneil 1980c, 59–61)) based on his concepts of the discrete and the relational contract norms and of presentation. I shall take up the former here and the latter in a later section. I have so far discussed relational contracting in the way it most obviously strikes the reader of Macneil's work—as a specific class of contracts. "Relational" is, however, a very complicated (and, it must be said, overall confusingly expressed) term in that work. It must be understood—though it forgivably has not—that Macneil's developed view of contractual relations does not identify the relational elements in only one particular class of contracts (Feinman 1987, n. 56. *cf.* Macneil 1988a, n. 5. *Pace* Collins 1999, 140–3; Eisenberg 2000; McKendrick 1995). Competition plays almost as important a role as co-operation in Macneil's full account of the relational aspect of contracting, for the full sense of "relational" contracting cannot be appreciated in isolation from its opposite in Macneil's thinking, "discrete" contracting.

Though, as we have seen, Macneil rests all contract on the common contract norms, some of these norms are, as it were, relatively "particularistic" or "discrete" (Macneil 1980c, 59–60) and some relatively "common" or "relational" (Macneil 1980c, 65). Relatively discrete and relatively relational forms of contract can be devised within the common norms depending on the differing emphasis which is given to particular norms in particular contracts. Discrete contract emphasises the common norms of a competitive character (Macneil 1983b, 360), such as the attempt closely to specify (and impose strict liability for) performance which Macneil calls the "implementation of planning" (Macneil 1980c, 47). Relational contract emphasises the common norms of a co-operative character (Macneil 1983b, 363–4), such as preservation of the relation in "contractual solidarity" (even to the point of adjusting obligations by waiving strict liabilities).

In order to realise the efficiencies which may follow from concentration on detailed, specialised tasks, it may, Macneil argues, be appropriate to ignore the wider ramifications of an exchange, including aspects of the personalities of the parties involved (other than those essential to their being a buyer and a seller), and create a discrete exchange, discreteness being "the separation of a transaction from all else between the participants at the same time and before and after" (Macneil 1980c, 60). To do this, the parties orient their action to enhance the relatively discrete norms:

> Enhancing discreteness requires ignoring the identity of parties to a transaction, lest relations begin to creep in ... discreteness [also] calls for avoiding multiple parties ... Since the ideal subjects of the discrete transaction are money on the one hand and an easily measured commodity on the other, discreteness is enhanced by treating the subject of exchange as much like commodities as possible ... In determining the content of a transaction, discreteness calls for strictly limiting the sources of communication and the substantive content of the transaction, in order to sharpen

the focus as much as possible. Ideally, planning and consent should occur only through formal, specific communication; non-linguistic communication or the setting in which the transaction occurs should be considered as irrelevant as the identity of the parties. Clear recognition of when a deal is on and when a deal is not on is required, with no halfway stations, such as that created in law by doctrines like promissory estoppel (Macneil 1980c, 61–2).

On the other hand, in circumstances where contract takes place through "behaviour that does occur in relations, must occur if relations are to continue, and hence ought to occur so long as [the relations'] continuance is valued" (Macneil 1980c, 64), contract action will enhance the relatively relational norms. Typically:

> relations are of significant duration (for example, franchising). Close whole person relations form an integral aspect of the relation (employment). The object of exchange typically includes both easily measured quantities (wages) and quantities not easily measured (the projection of personality by an airline stewardess). Many individuals with individual and collective poles of interest are involved in the relation (industrial relations). Future co-operative behaviour is anticipated (the players and management of the Oakland Raiders). The benefits and burdens of the relation are to be shared rather than divided and allocated (a law partnership). The bindingness of the relation is limited (again a law partnership in which in theory each member is free to quit almost at will). The entangling strings of friendship, reputation, interdependence, morality and altruistic desires are integral parts of the relation (a theatrical agent and his clients). Trouble is expected as a matter of course (a collective bargaining agreement). Finally the participants . . . view the relation as an ongoing integration of behaviour which will grow and vary with events in a largely unforeseeable future (a marriage, a family business) (Macneil 1974b, 595).

In such a case, contracting is, as we have seen, guided by the relational norms which emphasise preservation of the relation and co-operative adjustment of obligations in order to do so.

4.2. THE DISCRETE CONTRACT

Given that even discrete contract rests on the common norms, the possibility of treating an exchange as discrete can "properly arise only after a recognition ... that a decision is being made to treat the pertinent aspect of exchange relations as if it were discrete, although in fact it is not, in short to ignore the non-discrete aspect of the relation" (Macneil 1987, 277). Macneil is perfectly well aware that, as a technique, neo-classical economics makes such defensible, indeed highly useful, decisions (Macneil 1988b, 9). To insist on awareness of relations:

> is not to say that some kinds of limited social analysis based on Hobbesian assumptions can never be correct. For example, if all a social inquirer cares about is what will happen to the consumption of milk in a chain of supermarkets if there are price changes of a fairly normal sort, the assumption of a 100% selfishness respecting price in sales of milk will not distort the results of the analysis sufficiently to be of concern. The reason is not that consumers act entirely selfishly in going through a supermarket and buying milk. It is because their particular forms of self-sacrificing behaviour, such as refraining from shoplifting or changing price labels, co-operating with other customers by queuing, etc., do not happen to be affected by normal price changes in that product (Macneil 1990, 152–3).

The point is that discrete contract has a coherent place within Macneil's theory. Though I believe it fair to say that any sophisticated contract scholar would now allow that there must be some acknowledgement given to co-operation in contracting (Adams and Brownsword 1995, ch. 9), resistance continues to be made to that acknowledgment because it is felt that allowing it will undercut the role of competition, and, it is correctly felt, competitive contracting is too valuable an institution to lose. As Lord Ackner has put it in relationship to the concept of a general duty of good faith:

> the concept of a duty to carry on negotiations in good faith is inherently repugnant to the adversarial position of the parties when involved in negotiations. Each party is entitled to pursue his (or her) own interest, so long as he avoids making misrepresentations ... A duty of good faith is ... inherently inconsistent with the

position of a negotiating party (*Walford v. Miles* [1992] 1 All E.R. 461).

Were relational contract identified with trying to impose highly co-operative forms of negotiation on all contracts, it would be wrong. However, Macneil does *not* want to do this and has strongly attacked that critical legal scholarship in which it arguably is the case that discrete contract is rejected merely for being discrete:

> the Critical Legal Studies movement ... has avoided facing up to what it means to incorporate the discreteness universally found in material relations into [the] general principles and law of such relations. They seem most often to prefer pointing out the obvious limitation of the discrete general law of contract only in terms of a limited set of relational concerns. These are mainly concerns relating to equality and participation of individuals in relations affecting their lives [but] we must have *some* law dealing with discreteness in contractual relations (Macneil 1987a, 37).

It would seem clear that some exchanges are best carried out through highly competitive negotiation, for it would undercut the efficiency of some commercial bargaining were there to be no incentive to enter into negotiations with superior information (Kronman 1978). It is very arguable that a general duty of complete disclosure would logically mean that exchanges had to take place on standard terms ultimately set by the state, and no-one wants this. Share dealing seems as clear an example of arguably productive highly competitive contracting as we are going to find (Macneil 1986, 593). The valuation of corporate securities in "risk arbitrage" works only by the adoption of the narrowest view of returns to an individual investor. Securities' prices can be determined according to the "fundamental theorem of asset price," on which the "efficient stock market hypothesis" is based (Black and Scholes 1973), only on radically simplifying maximising assumptions (Black 1989, 67) and, by implication, by allowing trade on this basis.[11] The normative permission of narrowly selfish behaviour is, then, integral to the working of a stock exchange. But this is (or should be seen to be) normatively constituted

---

[11] Actually productive industrial investment decisions are far more complex than merely speculative financial ones.

behaviour which has clear limits. To the extent it can be said to work, risk arbitrage works only by reliance on a system of communication the integrity of which is extensively (if manifestly inadequately) protected (Carlton and Fischel 1983). Investors or dealers interfering with the accuracy of the information system, say by insider dealing or publication of misleading information about a company, theoretically should incur a severe sanction from the same trading system that encourages them to seek no other end but the purely speculative expansion of capital with no regard to its social consequences (Macneil 1987a, 33–4).

The point emerges clearly, I think, from one of Macneil's common examples, the football game (Macneil 1980c, 59). The football game requires behaviour according to the, by analogy discrete, norm of physical competitiveness, and it would appear that a considerable part of American wealth is devoted to the production of young men who are trained to act most destructively in the game. But the 350lb tackle who legitimately may throw his entire body weight at an opponent in broken field play cannot even shrug at that opponent at the line of scrimmage. The very possibility of competitiveness emerges only because of the common norms which constitute the game. Most tellingly, a player who consistently cheats out of unrestrained will to win defeats the object, and should incur a sanction, for failure to follow the rules in the correct spirit is *not to play the game*.[12] As Wittgenstein (1968, sec 564) has it, a game "has not only rules but also a *point*," and, we would add, the point is constituted by a common norm.

When he stresses that his relational view does not preclude relatively discrete exchanges (Macneil 1983b, 364–6), Macneil is trying, quite properly, to guard his view from being regarded as inevitably leading to an emphasis on macro-economic planning by hierarchical bureaucracies (Macneil 1984; 1984–5), about which he is rightly profoundly suspicious.[13] Macneil tells us that: "those who read relational contract

---

[12] I drafted this shortly after a driver escaped meaningful sanction for attempting to win the Formula 1 World Motor Racing Championship by deliberately crashing into an opponent, arguably the second time he has done so. Of course, such is the commodification of this and other sports that they are under constant threat of becoming, as a distinguished sports journalist has it, "non-sport."

[13] *E.g*: Human beings have an inordinate love of power, of being able to move their brethren and sistren in directions other than those in which the siblings would otherwise go. At no time is this love more dangerous than when it is meshed with pure reason. And of all the human social institutions in existence, bureaucracy most exemplifes—even though it corrupts—pure reason (Macneil 1984–5, 26–7).

theory as necessarily or presumptively supporting great sovereign intervention are mistaken" (Macneil 1983b, 410). Even in the fully relational view, there will, as we have seen, be room for relatively discrete contracts. A consistent emphasis on relations does not necessarily involve the rejection of broadly market solutions to economic allocative issues (nor of libertarian solutions to political ones). Equally, of course, we should choose more co-operative forms of contracting in the right circumstances (Eisenberg 1982a; Trebilcock 1993), and Macneil's schema allows us to do so (Campbell 1996b).

4.3. THE PERCEPTION OF DISCRETENESS IN THE CLASSICAL LAW

By distinguishing the discrete and the relational norms, Macneil offers an account of contract which allows us to place the various forms of contract action, ranging from the highly competitive to the highly co-operative, within one integrated framework based on the common contract norms. To be frank, one feels that the normative schema ultimately becomes somewhat convoluted and pleonastic (Williamson 1986, 103), but the fundamental point is that it is basically sound and is able to incorporate all the various forms of contract action, including those with which the classical law signally has not been able to deal. Focused as it is on the discrete contract, the will theory is faced with a truly vast number of exceptions. That number is most obviously represented in the astronomical growth in the size of the textbooks that has been needed to accommodate all these exceptions. To take what admittedly is the worst example, the discussion of consideration in the latest edition of *Treitel* is 85 pages long, but not 10 of these are occupied with the positive statement of the doctrine (Treitel 1999, ch.3 para 3).[14] It should, of course, be remembered that this growth has taken place over the same period in which the proper treatment of "the exception" of consumer law (and many related topics) has been hived off from the "general principles" of contract and placed in separate books!

A doctrine which can be expressed only through the simultaneous expression of its myriad exceptions is one characterised by the quite unprincipled "reasoning" needed to accommodate those exceptions (Macneil 1987c, 373). The post-war history of the classical law of

---

[14] I do not include the 12 pages given to intention to create legally binding relations, itself an exception to the claim that sufficient consideration identifies enforceability.

contract can, indeed, be seen as a continuous but desperate attempt to incorporate doctrinal refinements which will allow it to deal with the awkward facts presented by relational contracting (Macneil 1974a, 815. *cf.* Campbell 1992). Macneil has, as I have said, not paid particular attention to these doctrinal shifts, which he clearly regards as superficial responses to the failures of the classical law, or, indeed, as counter-productive. However, Macneil has always insisted upon the value of good doctrinal work (Macneil 1988c, 1195), and, significantly, has said that legal education develops "an increased capacity for sustained rational thought:"

> Some of the purposes of the case method were summarised recently as "training students to think clearly and exactly, to analyse and synthesise, to sift the relevant from the irrelevant, to beware of overgeneralising." I ... suspect that nowhere else in American education can as sustained, across-the-curriculum demands for this kind of thinking be found as in the first year of law school (Macneil 1965, 427).

But all this, of course, assumes that the doctrinal work is taking place within a basically sound framework. In such a framework, it can confine itself to the type of broadly deductive task it can best perform. Outside such a framework, it is prone to reduction either to "mindless bureaucratic formalism" (Macneil 1992, viii) if it rests content with itself, or is driven to perform self-ridiculing miracles of logomachy in order to address most real problems from within its present unrealistic framework.

Macneil has, however, spent a great deal of time engaging one form of the refinement of the classical law, one which most directly has posed questions about the doctrinal framework of that law. This is the discussion of contract within Chicagoan law and economics after Posner, which undoubtedly has been the most significant theoretical intervention in the subject since realism. I will now turn to Macneil's evaluation of this intervention.

5. Macneil and the Law and Economics of Contract

5.1. THE DISCRETE CONTRACT IN NEO-CLASSICAL ECONOMICS

As a body of law with fairly directly "economic" concerns, contract, and particularly remedies, is particularly amenable to discussion within law and economics, and it is only right to say at the outset that law and economics recently has produced at least as many insights into the law of contract as any other form of general jurisprudence, including the sociology of law to which Macneil should be seen as having made one of the most substantial post-war contributions.

Macneil has been at pains to acknowledge the value of contract scholarship within law and economics when surveying the contract literature in a highly original way which turns on the concept he has developed of a "spectrum" of contracts. He has argued that discrete exchanges and relational contract form an axis (Macneil 1974a, 736–7), and along this axis runs a spectrum (Macneil 1978b, 12) of contractual phenomena. At one pole (Macneil 1978a, 902) is the discrete transaction exemplified by the spot sale (Macneil 1975b, 594; 1978a, 855 n. 2), and at the other the intertwined relation (Macneil 1981b, 1021; 1987b, 276) exemplified by a web of long-term commercial relations between a number of parties (Macneil 1974a, 738–40).[15] Particular contracts can, of course, fall at particular points along the spectrum depending on, to put it this way, how relational they are: "Exchange occurs in various patterns along a spectrum ranging from highly discrete to highly relational" (Macneil 1987b, 275). I will discuss the spectrum as such later. For the moment, let us look at how he uses it to analyse the contract literature.

Macneil has claimed that different theories of contract are appropriate to the different types of contract found at various points along the spectrum. At the extremely discrete end of the spectrum is the classical law; at the extremely relational end is the relational theory. The relational theory bids fair to so extend along its axis as to take over much the greater part of the spectrum, leaving only what we shall see is the vexed possibility of the purely discrete contract to the classical law, and that it does not do so is because in later work Macneil distinguishes a third form

---

[15] In earlier versions of the spectrum, the discrete pole was called the "extreme transactional" pole (Macneil 1978b, 14–6. *cf.* 1974a, 738–40).

of contractual theory, the "neo-classical law" (Macneil 1981b, 865–86).

Macneil somewhat confusingly uses the term "neo-classical" to capture both the neo-classical economics that are the foundation of the classical law of contract and the neo-classical law that he believes is an improvement on that law (*i.e.* it is a distinct form of traditional contract law from the classical law (Macneil 1978b n. 2)). The classical law is, of course, typically expressed in formal doctrinal terms to which, as has been said, Macneil does not pay particular attention. However, he describes writing on contract by law and economics scholars as the elaboration of the economic foundation of the classical law. The individualism of the will theory of contract (the classical law) (Macneil 1983b, 390–7) is the individualism of rational individual utility maximisation (neo-classical economics and Posnerian law and economics) and is exemplified by the discrete contract:

> It is quite true that the discrete [contract] fits very well the concepts of efficiency developed in the neo-classical microeconomic model. Indeed, that is a tautology, since the discrete transaction is the basis of that model (Macneil 1980c, 63).

In a way which we will see is not without its difficulties, Macneil criticises not so much the model of the discrete contract as the way that law and economics believes this model can cover all contracts on the spectrum of contract, tending to identify the discrete contract as contract as such, when this identification is indefensible:

> The existence of relations ... raises theoretical problems for the neo-classical microeconomic model founded on the discrete transaction. Even putting aside the theoretical difficulties, however, a range of practical problems precludes effective, simple application of the model to relations of any complexity. At the very least this includes a large percentage of real-life contractual relations (Macneil 1981b, 1062).

Macneil's theoretical criticism of this view of contract is that it does not take into account the co-operative, relational phenomena to which he draws our attention. As well as taking up the social philosophical issues involved in this, he makes this point in respect of many contract doctrines, such as the regulation of penalty clauses (Macneil 1981b, 1056–62) and (other) standard terms (Macneil 1984–5, 917–9), the

29

adjustment of formally strict liabilities (Macneil 1983b) and the nature of breach. The last of these is particularly instructive, for it does not turn on any welfarist considerations but solely on "economic efficiency."

It has been argued that a contract can "efficiently" be breached if doing so realises sufficient profit in excess of that expected under the original contract. Resources freed by the breach can be used to compensate the non-breaching party whilst leaving leaving a larger than originally expected profit for the party in breach. In what Macneil calls the "simple" version of this notion exemplified by Posner (Macneil 1982, 949. *cf.* Posner 1998, 130–40) all this is set out as analytically true, as indeed one may, for the purposes of argument, allow it is.[16] But to turn this into a policy prescription for real world situations, as Posner unproblematically does, is quite absurd. One needs to know a great deal about the transaction costs of switching allocations in the given situations of both parties before one can say anything about the efficiency of such a breach. Important considerations include whether the breach is easily recognisable and a remedy for it will easily be forthcoming, whether damages will fully compensate the non-breaching party (or will there be certainty or proximity problems, etc.), whether there will be a reputational effect, and so on. Macneil puts the point this way:

[T]he broad scope of the inquiry required before even slightly definitive conclusions could be suggested should be stressed. The pertinent transaction costs cannot be limited to one or two supplemental matters. Rather the inquiry must be addressed to *all* transaction costs ... This includes some costs of initial planning in the *first* contract (including negotiations essential to the mutual planning required in contracting), costs of planning (again including negotiations) after the new opportunity comes along, costs of potential or actual litigation (including costs of delay), information costs, costs of inertia, costs of uncertainty, relational costs, such as damage to reputation and loss of future opportunities to deal, and undoubtedly others (Macneil 1982, 957–8).

From this he draws the following conclusion (which he later applied to a range of other abstract "efficiency" analyses of remedies rules (Macneil 1988b)):

---

[16] Macneil himself (1982, 950–3) does not allow this.

The microeconomic model assumes the existence of very complex relations between the parties ... But once such relations are assumed, the impact of those relations on the analysis is typically ignored. *Ceteris paribus* conquers all. Thus, it is extremely easy to introduce selected transaction costs to show that the model "proves" what the modeller wants it to prove, while ignoring countless other transaction costs of equal or greater pertinence in the real world ... the ease of slipping in some but not all, transaction costs is a problem ... within the model. There is a fundamental intellectual flaw in using a model based on man-outside society to analyse the behaviour of man-in-society ... The particular fallacy of the simple-efficient-breach theory is relatively easy to uncover but potential fallacy lurks in all social analysis starting from the non-social, relation-omitting model of neo-classical economics (Macneil 1982b, 961).

5.2. Posner's Evaluation of Macneil

Macneil has not been completely ignored by the proponents of the law and economics of the classical law, who have made two distinct responses to his views, though both amount to a rejection of those views. The first is to deny that Macneil's view of contract is accurate. As Posner has put it: "I do not think ... Professor Macneil a reliable guide to the nature and problems of modern American contract law" (Posner 1993, n. 20). What really is at issue here is the extraordinary extent to which law and economics after Posner works with the most formal notions of contract doctrine, ones which by no means would now be maintained in the best black-letter scholarship. Macneil has recounted the following event which, on the basis of my own experience, I suspect captures a quite common experience:

> To refer to someone as a Willistonian is to describe them as addicted to discrete general contract law. In January 1986 at a panel of the Association of American Law Schools, I referred to a particular view as Willistonian, and for the first time in decades heard a defence of Williston! Although I was taken aback at the time, I also recall musing on many occasions about the failure of those law and economic scholars habitually defending what are in

31

fact Willistonian views to resurrect his sainthood (Macneil 1987a, n. 19).

Comment here is superfluous on criticisms of Macneil that are not informed by an awareness of the difficulties of the classical law. To critics without such an awareness, his work must, indeed, seem outlandish (Feinman 1990, 1299–1300).

A second response has been to register some of the difficulties of the classical law but to say that Macneil's work does not assist in coming to terms with them. Posner puts the point this way:

> Macneil believes that contract law has been too much concerned with spot contracts to the exclusion of contracts embedded in an ongoing relationship between the contracting parties ... unfortunately, although all too commonly when one is speaking of legal "theories" that lack a foundation in economics, Macneil's theory of contracts has very little content ... If [Macneil] means that we must recognise the problems and opportunities that arise when parties have a continuing relation rather than merely meeting in a spot market, I agree. Such a relation may make contracts self-enforcing, because each party stands to lose if the relation terminates. Conversely, it may create temptations to opportunistic[ally] breach—maybe one party's performance precedes the other's—or problems of bilateral monopoly, which can be acute in cases in which one party seeks modification of a contract, because the parties can deal only with each other. These are problems on which economics has a strong grip; so far as I am able to determine, neither Macneil nor any other "legal theorist" has anything to contribute to their solution (Posner 1993, 84).

All one can say is that one is obliged to follow the line indicated by Macneil if one seeks to frame one's answers to such problems as they are understood by the parties and dealt with by empirical contractual practices. Of course, one can substitute for these facts formal economic assumptions of remote relationship to the understandings of the parties and formal contractual doctrines which are quite inaccurate accounts of business practice. One really must make a choice about the approach one finds superior. More fairly, Trebilcock allows that "Macneil's approach ... accurately ... describes reality" but "does not yield determinate legal principles for governing the allocation of unassigned risks" (Trebilcock

1993, 141). By "determinate" Trebilcock means tractable in terms of neo-classical economic principles and, presumably, therefore ultimately translatable into classical contract doctrine. The circularity of his position surely is manifest. The strength of the grip such principles provide is indeed strong. It has the strength which can follow from being formally abstract, and the clarity of explanation this furnishes is valuable. But it therefore is a grip which, if maintained insensitively, can fasten on very little that exists in the real world of contract.[17]

In what Macneil calls "neo-classical contract," the account of legal doctrine is very much refined to take account of the problems of the classical law. The most live current example in the UK is the recognition of "practical benefit" in the case of use of an existing obligation as consideration. That "practical benefit" flatly contradicts the existing obligation rule is the truth that cannot be admitted in such scholarship. But allowing practical benefit is undoubtedly superior, in the practical sense of resolving disputes if not in the theoretical sense of developing coherent law, to insensitive maintenance of the classical law of insufficiency. Such neo-classical law is the law of any decent legal scholarship, and, as we have seen, it has a very clear and defensible place in such scholarship.

5.3.   WILLIAMSON'S EVALUATION OF MACNEIL

The economic corollary of such scholarship is the "new institutional economics". It has been mentioned that neo-classical economics has, at its core, a demonstration that a market in which economic action conformed to the assumptions of rational individual utility maximisation is perfectly efficient. However, general economic equilibrium requires economic actors to have complete knowledge of the state of the world in which they make their exchanges and that those exchanges are perfectly easy to make. That is to say, exchange must be completely costless or, following Coase (1986, 114–9), involve zero transaction costs. Of course, any empirical exchange involves positive transaction costs, and the new

---

[17] Trebilcock's (1993) book on *The Limits to the Freedom of Contract* in which this criticism of Macneil is maintained is, accordingly, one in which the basic principle of freedom of contract is maintained by the argument that the exceptions to it in modern contract as merely that principle's "limits." As Trebilcock is knowledgeable and fair, the overwhelming accumulation of exceptions dwarfs the indeed limited principle.

institutional economics seeks to identify the institutions which facilitate exchanges by keeping those costs as low as possible (though they cannot be driven to zero) (Coase 1994, ch. 1; North 1990; Williamson 1996, Pt. 1). In capitalist economies, the principal such institutions are the various legal frameworks of enterprise. In institutional economics (which, of course, are congruent with good law and economics), the conditions of the application of neo-classical economic analysis are carefully specified by descriptions of the economic institutions within which economic action takes place. The market (at various levels of competitive organisation) is one such institution. So, however, is the firm and the state (and a range of "hybrid" institutions).

It is obvious that if one is at all prepared to draw on social sciences other than neo-classical economics to undertake the description of the various institutional settings of economic action, then Macneil's work can serve the same function with regard to understanding the realities of contract as, say, H. A. Simon's (1976) work can with regard to the "black 1997 box" conception of the structure of the firm. Williamson has been generous in his reference to the influence Macneil's work has had in the formulation of his conception of the internal and external determinants of a firm's decision making:

> Although the law was obviously relevant to what I was doing . . . its more general significance was not obvious to me until Victor Goldberg . . . suggested that I examine some of Ian Macneil's recent work on contract law. Macneil's treatment of contract was much more expansive, nuanced, and interdisciplinary (mainly combining law and sociology) than I had seen previously . . . This invited a more general formulation in which law, economics and organisation were joined in the effort to assess the governance of contractual relations (Williamson 1996, 355–6).

Williamson has made repeated productive use of Macneil's distinction of different types of contracts at different points of the spectrum (Williamson 1985, 68–73; 1986, 102–5). He has identified many issues in the discussion of what Macneil would call relational contracting by drawing on his (Macneil's) work to show that "contracts are a good deal more varied and complex than is commonly realised [and] that the institutional matrix within which transactions are negotiated and executed [varies] with the nature of the transaction" (Williamson 1986, 105). The subtitle of what remains Williamson's most ambitious work—*The Economic*

Institutions of Capitalism—is *Firms, Markets, Relational Contracting.*
Macneil has welcomed the development of transaction cost analysis in
new institutional economics for the obvious reason: "Because it is
impossible to conduct exchange without transaction costs ... Any
sensible application of these costs requires the inclusion of these costs"
(Macneil 1981b, 1022). He has particularly welcomed Williamson's
contributions. At one point, Williamson criticised one of Macneil's
comparisons of discrete and relational contract as so "rich" as to be
difficult to apply (Williamson 1986, 103). As this particular "classificatory
apparatus" involved 12 "concepts" (and as many sub-concepts) as points
of comparison (Macneil 1978a, 902–5. Cf. 1974a, 738–40), this was a
perfectly fair point. Macneil has been good enough to acknowledge this
(Macneil 1981b, n. 26). However, he ultimately has sought to argue that
the richness of his work follows from his attempt to capture the sense of
co-operation that will always escape even Williamson's reasoning from
what remain neo-classical assumptions of individual utility maximisation,
even though Williamson may attempt to model such co-operation in
broadly game-theoretical, and increasingly complex (Macneil 1981b,
1062), terms:

> A key element in neo-classical microeconomic analysis is exchange
> between maximising units. In his discussion of transaction costs and
> their effect on choice of contract governance structures, William-
> son [in cases of "asset specific" or "idiosyncratic" investment
> creating opportunities for opportunistic behaviour] treats the
> parties not as separate exchangers, but as if they comprised a *single*
> *maximising unit* ... This, according to Williamson, leads in such
> circumstances to the parties making arrangements for either
> trilateral governance, such as contractual enforcement in courts,
> or to unified governance—the firm. This is not neo-classical
> microeconomic analysis, since there is by hypothesis no exchange
> transaction to analyse ... That Williamson is treating buyer and
> seller as a maximising unit, and not making a neo-classical analysis
> of their separate individual choices of governance structures, may
> be obscured by ... his concern [with] the prevention of their
> subsequently acting as separate maximisers [by] the limiting of
> opportunism. But his treatment of transaction costs and govern-
> ance in a non-neo-classical manner bears out [the] point [that in]
> relational exchange there can be present a "sense of productive
> increase from the relationship which can dwarf variations in

expectation, or of long-term anticipations of mutual benefit that dwarf variations in shares received by partie." This anticipatory, commonly held "sense" of the parties may virtually obliterate any present separation as maximisers, thereby making them effectively a single maximiser (Macneil 1981b, 1023–4).

Macneil's relational theory turns on the suggestion that a different view of the nature of economic action than that assumed in neo-classical economics and in the new institutional economics which more accords with the reality of contract. Certainly, though I hope I have made it clear where Macneil's work is so elaborate as to be confusing, it deals with that reality with considerably more explanatory economy than does Williamson's own work, the most marked characteristic of which is an even greater degree of terminological elaboration (Campbell and Harris 1993, 175). In terms of Macneil's distinction of three types of contract theory, the neo-classical and the relational very substantially overlap,[18] for the new institutional economics is at one with the relational theory in attempting to explain "relational" phenomena rather than Posnerite law and economics, which attempts to explain them away. However, there is, at bottom, a profound difference over what the "phenomena" described as transaction costs are:

> The only way anything more of material relations [than is seen by concentration on the discrete contract] is seen by analysis related to microeconomics is by looking through a relatively new and very different lens called transaction costs. If taken seriously, transaction costs could, of course, theoretically become so all encompassing as to constitute a genuine examination of solidarity and reciprocal material relations. But they are seldom taken with such seriousness, and if they were, would soon cease to be denominated "transaction costs" (Macneil 1987a, n. 11).

Though Macneil does not tell us what they would be called, it is, I suggest, clear enough that, if we look only at market transactions, they would be called something like the social relations constituting economic action. The securing of social and political stability, the ability to

---

[18] Indeed, the metaphor of the spectrum with different types of contract and contract theory at different points along its axes breaks down.

communicate, the ability to rely on promises, etc. are all costs of market exchange. But they are also the social relations which indispensably facilitate those exchange. Such relations cannot be viewed *only* as costs, for, the point is, they are not so much the friction which impedes fully contingent contracting but the relations which make any contracting possible. In Macneil's terms, they are the first and second level relations which constitute the social matrix and the third level relations based on the common contract norms through which parties are able to agree (discrete) competitive contracts or (complex) consciously co-operative contracts. In the light of this insight of Macneil's, the technical function of transaction cost analysis must be subsumed to, and reinterpreted in the light of, understanding the relations which the costs represent. If I may be allowed to quote myself:

> Coase (and Williamson *et al*) readily concede—in fact it is more fair to say that they centrally urge the recognition—that transactions at zero cost will never empirically obtain, but the point is to approximate towards that ideal [of a fully contingent contract]. However, this is a paradoxical and confusing goal because they do not fully understand why the goal is unrealisable. The negotiating, information gathering, organising, etc. within which transactions take place are not *only* costs, they are also the social relations which are essentially facilitative of the transaction. Negotiation is a cost, but what contract could be made without language? Information gathering is a cost, but what contract could be made in complete ignorance? All actions, including all transactions, can take place only within constitutive social relations. The stress on the reduction of transaction costs has a *technical* function but inevitably is carried too far if that technical function is confused, as it typically is in law and economics, with a basic analysis of the ontological character of economic action. If one really took away *all* the costs of exchanging, the exchange would not take place cost free, it would not take place; and this should tell us that though the transaction cost approach certainly has a very important *technical* function, it cannot *begin* to stand as an *understanding* of economic actions (Campbell 1997a, 230–1).

Macneil's work is by far the most substantial working out of a theory of contract in which this point is taken, and in any reputable social theory of which I am aware other than neo-classical economics, that point is allowed to be sound.

6. The Discrete Contract and the Critique of Presentiation

6.1. THE CONCEPT OF PRESENTIATION

The argument that the classical law articulates a "market-individualist ideology" now enjoys a wide currency in critical contract scholarship (*e.g.* Adams and Brownsword 2000). This is right, and that the classical law *is* market-individualist is not worth disputing. When they can be pressed to move away from technical formalism and discuss their values, those committed to the classical law themselves insist upon the market-individualist character of at least the core of their subject (*e.g.* Beatson 1998, ch. 1, sec. I(a). *cf.* Atiyah 1990, ch. 12). However, the use of the word "ideology" typically is intended to connote that market-individualism is wrong,[19] and something of this sort obviously is Macneil's position (Macneil 1987a, 37). This is, of course, a matter of legitimate dispute, and Macneil's position on this is rather complex.

The crucial point about the invisible hand is that it is invisible. It works by ordering the actions of individuals who are not conscious of it, and so, of course, do not frame their agreements to express it. Consequently, the classical law of contract's principal doctrines articulate a denial of the parties' co-operation at exactly the same time as those doctrines bring that co-operation about. It is Macneil's argument that though:

> We ... think of economic exchange as being extremely individualistic and selfish, rather than co-operative [it] is the fact that exchange represents a species of human co-operation. In the first case it is a kind of social behaviour—the true lone wolf has no

---

[19] So, having told us in their contracts casebook that "Contract ideas form part of the ideology of capitalism," Macaulay and his colleagues in the Wisconsin Contracts Group, then say "We use the term 'ideology' rather than political philosophy because ideology connotes a system accepted and assumed rather than a thought-out view" (Macaulay *et al* 1995, 19 n. 9).

one with whom to exchange goods or services ... exchange involves a *mutual* goal of the parties, namely the reciprocal transfer of values. And this is true however strongly the "economic man"—the "as-much-as-possible-for-as-little-as-possible-in-return-man"—may dominate the motivations of both parties to an exchange (Macneil 1969b, 405. *cf.* 1968e, 14).

Any purported refutation of an incorrect belief must, to hope for complete success, account for that belief's enjoying sufficient currency to make it worth refuting (Campbell 1996a, ch. 3), and so a rigorous insistence on the relational basis of all contract must involve giving a relational explanation of the existence in contracting of perceptions of complete discreteness and of narrowly individualistic conduct based on those perceptions. Macneil, most perceptively, attempts to explain how the classical law's mistakenly individualistic understanding of contract could arise. He says the following of parties' subjective understandings of their contract behaviour in terms of narrow individualism:

> The discrete transaction is the perfect setting for maximising recognition of exchange and its motivations. The narrow focus of the ... transactional planning, the monetisation and measuring of what is exchanged, the minimum need for co-operation in planning and performance, the discreteness of the incidence of benefits and burdens, the specificity of obligation and the nature of potential sanctions, all go to guarantee the absence of room for anything but exchange and its motivations ... Recognition by the parties of the prevalence and exclusivity of exchange motivations is inevitable in such ... circumstances (Macneil 1974a, 795).

The way in which the discrete view emerges is through "presentiation," a rendering of past and particularly future events or structures influencing present allocative decisions as if they were present. By this Macneil means, in the context of contract negotiation, the pursuit of an "ideal" (Macneil 1980, 60), of which "traditional contract systems are among the greatest intellectual expressions" (Macneil 1974b, 590–1). It entails bringing all relevant dimensions of a contract to the notice of the parties at the time of making the contract so that that contract can properly be said to be the product of the parties' intentions:

> The aim was to establish, in so far as the law could, the entire

relation at the time of the expressions of mutual assent. Total presentiation through 100% predictability was sought as of the time of something called "acceptance of the offer" (Macneil 1974b, 593).

This is a strikingly accurate fleshing out in contract doctrine of the assumption of a complete knowledge of the state of the world at the time of the contract necessary for the fully contingent contract of general equilibrium theory which is the more remarkable in that Macneil seems to have developed it through a sense of the practice of contracting rather than by drawing on information economics.

Of course, the ideal of "100 per cent consent as well as 100 per cent planning" is "never achieved in life" (Macneil 1980c, 60–1). This is manifest in longer-term contracts which of necessity postulate continuing, consciously co-operative relations to deal with the impact of future developments on present allocations of resources. To try to bring these sophisticated relational plans within the concepts of the classical law is, as Macneil overwhelmingly demonstrates, manifestly absurd (Macneil 1975; 1978a). Macneil's most substantial achievement in contract scholarship narrowly understood is his second casebook, *Contracts: Exchange Transactions and Relations* (1978b), in which his early expansion of the meaning of "contract" to include far more than contract litigation is developed into an ordering of the material found in a contract course around the concept of contract planning. This ordering places that material in a practically determined sequence dealing with negotiation of terms of performance, provision of contractual mechanisms for assuring performance, and arranging ways of dealing with failure to perform (both of the last two including adjustment of performance).

This ordering principle is concisely stated in a 1975 paper which uses the organisation of, and linking passages from, the casebook (Macneil 1978b, 16 n. 1) to provide, "A Primer of Contract Planning" (Macneil 1975b).[20] In this inclusive, empirically and practically plausible description of the functions of contract, the pursuit of a remedy through

---

[20] The bridging sections of *Contracts, Exchange Transactions and Relations* which bear more on the social theory of relational exchange than on the analysis of contract more narrowly understood are reworked as an integrated essay in "Essays on the Nature of Contract" (Macneil 1980a). This relatively little known piece is the most complete statement of Macneil's views prior to 1979, when he then gave the Rosenthal lectures which were written up as *The New Social Contract*.

litigation has a subordinate but integrated part in contract planning. This approach is of incomparably more practical value[21] than the concentration on logical problems and on litigation typical of casebooks and textbooks. Litigation appears only as the third possible way of resolving disputes after self-help (itself divided into refusing to perform and suspending or stopping performance, forfeit of securities (of various forms), and seeking assurances), and forms of alternative dispute resolution. Planning for dispute resolution itself appears only last in a list of topics that good legal advice should seek to incorporate in a complex contract to avoid such disputes. That all these matters are essential to contract would not be denied by those who promulgate the classical law (especially if they practise). But it is principally in Macneil[22] that one finds these matters not stated as ancillary material to the formal and, it transpires, rather irrelevant general principles, but rather integrated into an overall account of contracting.

6.2. THE NON-EXISTENCE OF THE DISCRETE CONTRACT

It is precisely here, however, that, over the course of its development, Macneil's relational theory of contract seems to have displayed an ambiguity (Macneil 1987b, 276–7) which, in my opinion (Campbell 1990), has handicapped the admittedly restricted reception (Macneil 1985a, 541; 1987a, 36; 1988a, n. 5) of his work. Throughout that work there are statements in which Macneil has stressed the "existence of relations in all real-life transactions" (Macneil 1981b, 1062), and that, consequently, it is an error to believe that "entirely discrete transactions ... could occur at all" (Macneil 1978a, 856) because "pure discreteness is an impossibility" (Macneil 1978a, 857 n. 10). This is to say, Macneil repeatedly denies that there are *any* truly discrete contracts (Macneil 1980c, 11). In a 1987 retrospective paper, having flatly stated that "All exchange occurs in relations," Macneil amplified the point in this way:

---

[21] Assuming that the function of the commercial lawyer is to assist, in an economic, efficient and effective fashion, in the prevention or resolution of disputes. There is considerable empirical evidence that this assumption does not necessarily hold (*e.g.* Wheeler 1991).

[22] Though see the review of the "contracts casebooks ... that changed the very definition of the field" by the Wisconsin Contracts Group (Macaulay *et al* 1995, 25–8). The Group's own effort should be included in this set of mould-breaking American works. On the British work to similar effect, see Campbell (1997b).

Even the purest discrete exchange necessarily postulates a social matrix providing at least the following: (1) a means of communication understandable to both parties; (2) a system of order so that the parties exchange instead of killing and stealing; (3) typically, in modern times, a system of money; and (4) in the case of exchanges promised, an effective mechanism to enforce promises (Macneil 1987b, n. 5).

On the other hand, there are also passages in which he does seem to allow that one could conceive there are discrete exchanges as such:

A *truly* discrete exchange transaction would be entirely separate not only from all other present relations but from all past and future relations as well. In short, it could occur, if at all, only between total strangers, brought together by chance ... Moreover, each party would have to be completely sure of never again seeing or having anything else to do with one another ... Moreover, everything must happen quickly lest the parties should develop some kind of relation impacting on the transaction so as to deprive it of discreteness (Macneil 1978a, 856).

In this passage Macneil is at pains to stress how abstract and fanciful this notion of the purely discrete exchange is, but I do believe it is right to say that he *has* allowed a theoretical limiting case of a transactional exchange which is discrete (Macneil 1978a, 856–7), and gives an example of this in modern contract:

The gas purchase is a transactional event in the sense that, except for the expectation of the driver that the station would have gasoline available and the expectation of the station that any driver stopping would have some means of paying, the exchange has no past. There are no precedent relations between the parties. Nor will there be any future relations between the parties. As to the present, two general characteristics dominate the transaction: it is short; it is limited in scope. A few minutes measure its duration, and no one, even the most gregarious, enters into anything approaching a total human relationship in such a situation. In such a transaction the measured exchange, gallons/dollars, is what matters. Without it, the pleasantries, the little extras of service and courtesies have no real meaning; with it those immeasurables are an added fillip and no more (Macneil 1974a, 720-1).

I emphasise that Macneil stresses that a social matrix *is* necessary for even this transaction (Macneil 1978a, n. 10), which therefore in an important sense only *seems* discrete (Macneil 1983b, 344). But this matrix is constituted only of first and second level relations and not, he allows, third level ones. In terms of the third level, *internal* relations, Macneil seems to allow the possibility of a discrete exchange between persons so unrelated, so much "total strangers," as each to have "as much feeling for the other as a Viking trading with a Saxon" (Macneil 1974b, 633).

These two positions carry very different implications for the analysis of discreteness and presentiation. The first, that there are *no* discrete contracts, is obviously most consistent with the claim for the existence of the common contract norms if the internal aspect of those norms is accepted (Feinman 1990, 1301). On this first position, the discrete contract of neo-classical economics and the classical law of contract *is* an ideology. It contains a misdescription of itself in the sense that it denies the relational dimensions which it *does* possess:

> Although the intellectual concepts of the market exchange economy took—and still have—a stranglehold on Western thinking, it is a mistake of incredible magnitude to think that any economy has ever been a market exchange economy in the sense suggested by formal economic analysis, a mistake regularly made by the intellectual left, right and middle. Market exchange in the utilitarian model is exchange in discrete transactions in which relations between the parties are seemingly assumed not to exist. This is as empty a social set in a nineteenth century market economy or modern twentieth century economy as it is in primitive economies. Not only has market exchange always been heavily embedded in social relations, but discrete (relatively) exchange patterns have always occupied only limited sectors of market economies as well (Macneil 1986, 591–2).

This position is a radical one, for in an important way it involves denying that there ever has been a truly laissez-faire economy (Campbell 1987, 213–7). Such an economy *must* (Macneil 1985b, 485–91; 1986, 591) have been relationally constituted, though perceived, for reasons which must be explained, as composed of discrete exchanges. In essence, "[n]o one can ever understand discrete elements in contractual relations without understanding the relations themselves" (Macneil 1988a, 302).

Macneil does allow that something can be gained in the explanation of the ideology of discrete contract from recognition of the interests that ideology serves: "the market-oriented political right ... finds the ideology of the discrete transaction useful in achieving its goals" (Macneil 1987a, 37), and he has made strenuous efforts (Macneil 1981b, 1049–62) to include analysis of the power exercised through patterns of exchange in his later work (Macneil 1987b, n. 4). This, as we shall see, has led to some powerful critiques of forms of exchange which basically are opportunities for the exercise of inequalities of bargaining power. Though such critiques clearly have their origin in his early perception of the implausibility of classical contract's notions of agreement, this focus on power and ideology is not really, however, the characteristic direction of Macneil's thought. He seeks to show why perceptions of discreteness *are* plausible, and incorporates the reasons for that plausibility in his relational theory largely through his concept of presentation.

It seems that the interpretation of Macneil's work has not so much been guided by working out the implications of the common contract norms but by a rather literal reading of the spectrum of contracts. The problem with the metaphor of a spectrum is that it allows, as Macneil has recognised (Macneil 1987b, 276), an interpretation which tends to confine relations to only the relational end, and this is not easily reconcilable with Macneil's general relational claim about contracting. We have seen that Macneil argues that the contracts to be found at particular points on this spectrum have attracted one of three types of legal and economic theory. Towards the discrete exchange end, the explanation has tended to be the classical law of contract and neo-classical economics (and simple law and economics). Neo-classical contract, including new instititonal economics, forms an intermediate category which we will not discuss again. At the other end of the spectrum, Macneil says fully relational law is appropriate, and claims that this latter theory is of the greater importance because it covers more of the spectrum.

Central to Macneil's work is the claim that "discrete exchanges are always relatively rare compared to patterns of relational exchange" (Macneil 1985b, 487) and that therefore relational contracting rather than discrete exchanges should be the central unit of the economic analysis of contract. The classical law of contract underpinned by neo-classical economics systematically fails to recognise that "contractual relations, not discrete contract, always have and always will be the dominant form of exchange behaviour in society" (Macneil 1985a, 451), and it therefore should be superseded by a relational view able to slip "the bounds of the classical contract system altogether [by] reducing [norms of] discreteness ... from dominant roles to roles equal or often subordinate to relational norms" (Macneil 1978a, 886). Macneil has weighed the amount of attention which must be paid to relational as opposed to discrete aspects in the explanation of contract, correctly argued that the former is far greater than the latter, and concluded that we must stress the relational dimension in contract. It is a question of balancing discrete exchange and contractual relations, but only in the sense of balance which follows after one accepts the manifest empirical evidence (Macneil 1985b, 487 n. 21) that there is a great imbalance in favour of the latter between the importance of these two elements in determining contract (Macneil 1985b, 498–508).

I have claimed above that the relational aspects of contract are more apparent in contracts at the relational pole of the spectrum (Macneil 1981, 1040–1). Long-term, variable and open-ended contracts clearly display their relational character (Macneil 1974b, 595), and this encourages the perception of relations in all contracts right down to spot sales. Equally, such long-term contracts tend strictly to prohibit opportunistic behaviour (Macneil 1986, 578), and this leads towards grasping the element of co-operation in all contracts. It is the growth of these relational phenomena that has mainly imposed the stresses on the classical law that has caused the law so unacceptably to twist and turn to try to accommodate that growth (Macneil 1974a, 815).

But how accurate is the presentiated perception of discreteness for the short-term exchange exemplified by the spot sale? Dwelling on the common contract norms would lead one to conclude that it is not accurate, for there are no truly discrete contracts. However, one can, as we have seen, also find various passages in which Macneil holds that "[a] high degree of presentation is possible in truly discrete transactions" (Macneil 1974b, 524). I am afraid one must conclude that he cannot consistently be saying both of these things.

It obviously does not help that Macneil has used the key term "relational" in two different ways. He means it to encompass the relational aspects of all, including discrete, contracts, and also to mean relational as opposed to discrete contracts. That he has done this is surprising as one complaint a reader may make about his writing with some justice is that his imagination is very fecund indeed when it comes to inventing schemes of classification and terms to fill them out. In his later writing, he has advanced the term "intertwined" to deal with relational in the sense of contracting under the relational norms (Macneil 1987b, 276–7). I personally believe that "complex" is a better term for this (Campbell 1996b, 59–61). Whatever one's opinion of this, the coherent use of either term in preference to the second of Macneils's uses of "relational" avoids a substantial confusion. One then can clearly see that, as his work matured, Macneil's essential claim about the co-operative function of contract came to be stated as the claim that relations underpin all exchanges in order to embrace competition within the relational framework by explaining it as discrete contracting.

One concerned with the law of contract more narrowly understood could leave the matter here. Unfortunately, the ambiguity is not merely terminological, contrary to what appear to be Macneil's own views (Macneil 1987b, 276–7). To assess both why this ambiguity arose and how far it can be removed, we must turn from relational contract to the social philosophy Macneil intends to underpin it, his relational theory of exchange.

7. Macneil's Social Theory

7.1. THE RELATIONAL THEORY OF EXCHANGE

The ambiguity over Macneil's account of the nature of the discrete contract arises because, though his contract work overall requires some sort of denial that there are any truly discrete exchanges, he also wishes to find a central place for both exchange and discreteness in his social theory of relational exchange. As we have seen, Macneil's stress on contract as an instrument for social co-operation is intended to reject the individualist understanding of exchange. But, it is essential to note, he also wishes to retain the classical category of exchange itself (cf. Feinman 1983, 833), and indeed it plays an even larger role in his work than in law and economics.

It will be recalled that the early Macneil identified "economic exchange" as the second basic element of contract, and, in his mature work, it features as the second primal root. He defines exchange in a most general fashion, as "simply the way . . . specialists distribute their work products among themselves in a reciprocal manner" (Macneil 1980b, 160). This is to say, on Macneil's view, any "[s]pecialisation of labour presupposes exchange" (Macneil 1974a, 697), so that, certainly, the modern "division of labour always does presuppose exchange" (Macneil, 1980c, 2 n. 6). Macneil defines the very general idea of exchange this implies as "the giving up of something in return for receiving something else" (Macneil 1986, 567). The only really essential element of this concept of exchange is "reciprocity," but as reciprocity was given just the same definition as exchange when set out as the second common contract norm (Macneil 1983b, 347), this obviously is reciprocity understood in a somewhat special way.

By reciprocity, Macneil does not mean what he calls "monetised exchange," that is to say, the generalised commodity exchange mediated by the universal commodity of money developed under capitalism:

> let me emphasise that "exchange" as used here is most certainly not
> "measured reciprocal payment," a common usage of the term by
> both Marxist and non-Marxist writers. "Exchange" here encom-
> passes much more. In particular it does not necessarily require
> measurement of reciprocity or conscious desires to gain by
> exchange, all of which are patent or latent elements of "measured
> reciprocal payment." Nor is payment necessarily involved if that
> word implies the use of money (Macneil 1974a, 700).

All that is left of reciprocity is "not equality" but "some kind of evenness" (Macneil 1980,44). Under this definition, if someone threatens forcibly to take a good from another, and the good is surrendered without actual conflict, this is an exchange, for there has been an exchange of a possibility of injuring in return for a good. This specifically is not what is meant by capitalist exchange. Nor is it an exchange in the capitalist sense if one gives up something of great value in return for something of little value, or even for nothing in return but the pleasure of another's gratification. These phenomena are robbery, fraud and sentimentality, not exchange. Macneil looks all this in the face and accepts it:

> [I insist] upon including in the concept one-sided and abusive
> exchange relations ... the presence of such characteristics in
> relations does not somehow magically wipe out the element of
> exchange ... seldom are such relations so rigidly coercive, one-
> sided and abusive "as to leave no realm whatever for the apparent
> exercise of some moderately pressured choice" ... the failure to

include highly coercive, one-sided, and abusive relations creates the need for an entirely arbitrary dividing line between what is sufficiently coercive to exclude the relation from the realm of exchange relations and what is not (Macneil 1990, 154–5 (quoting from Macneil 1974a, 703)).

It is obvious that such a concept of exchange will "apply to all societies," and this is so over the widest moral range, including "plantation slavery" and "Stalin's labour camps" (Macneil 1990, 155); the widest geographical range, "including the nineteenth-twentieth century market economies and all segments of today's world economy" (Macneil 1986, 570); and the widest historical range, including primitive as well as all traditional and modern societies (Macneil 1986). Indeed, Macneil also often intimates that animal societies—from primate (Macneil 1981b, n. 44) to insect (Macneil 1974a, 697–8)—come under the scope of his concept of exchange.

With reciprocity and exchange defined in this way, it cannot easily be said that what Macneil brings under "exchange" is a smaller set than what is usually understood as social action. In Weber's definition, for example, action is behaviour to which "the acting individual attaches a subjective meaning," and action is social "insofar as its subjective meaning takes account of the behaviour of others and is thereby oriented in its course" (Weber, 1978, 4). (Indeed, if we take Macneil's remarks about animals at face value, his concept is far wider than Weber's, obviously approximating to sociobiology after Wilson (1975)). This is to say, the social theory of relational exchange is a general social theory in the widest sense (Elliot 1981, 351. *Pace* Macneil 1983b, n. 5. *cf.* Macneil 1990, 161–2).[23] Macneil does allow that people may be placed under such total compulsion as to negate their real participation in an exchange, but the type of utter powerlessness which he thinks necessary for this would reduce that action to (a low species of) "merely reactive behaviour" in Weber's terms (Weber 1978, 4). There is something "economic" about

---

[23] Macneil has continually (*e.g.* 1969, n. 3; 1974a, nn. 78, 92, 797; 1986 n. 42) shown an interest in the "exchange theory" literature traceable to Becker (1956) and Homans (1958) but of which Blau's (1964) *Exchange and Power in Social Life* is now the best remembered example. This literature also seeks to expand exchange into a ubiquitous human phenomenon (Macneil 1978b, 177–81). Of course, attempts to give a central importance to reciprocity in social relations, which in some sense it undoubtedly has, predate Becker and Homans, and indeed are to be found in antiquity. Gouldner (1975, ch. 8).

Macneil's exchange (Macneil 1986, 570), but it is much wider than Weber's concept of economic action, for the latter turns on rational calculation in pursuit "the satisfaction of a desire for 'utilities' " (Weber 1978, 63). Macneil's concept of exchange is explicitly intended to include reciprocity calculated much less precisely and involves a much wider range of concerns than utility (Macneil 1974a, 797–8).

It has been objected that all this is so wide as to lose determinate content (Campbell 1990, 87–8; Foster 1982, 146). But if the generality of Macneil's concept of exchange is its principal feature, this does not mean that it lacks some determinate features, and these are the heart of the social theory of exchange. It is, indeed, the extreme width of Macneil's notion of reciprocity through exchange that is itself intended to convey what "surely must be the most forgotten fact in the modern study of contracts" (Macneil 1980c, 1), the fact that human life is social. The basic claim is that co-operation is an integral part of any sort of society displaying an at all settled diversity of roles (*i.e.* leaving aside essentially hypothetical pathological forms (Macneil 1986, 567) such as prolonged utter isolation or (approximations to) the war of all against all):

> One form of exchange, the measured reciprocal exchange ... is clearly an exchange under anyone's definition. But discrete exchange is *not* the primal root of contract. Whilst it has far deeper historical and prehistorical antecedents than is sometimes recognised, discrete exchange is but one of the subspecies forming the exchange part of this second primal root [of contract]. The broad generic concept of exchange traceable far back into history and prehistory simply recognises that specialisation requires some process of reciprocal distribution of product for the specialisation to be worthwhile ... *How* such exchange occurs is irrelevant to this foundation notion of the concept and to understanding it as a basic root of contract. Exchange can happen in countless ways other than measured reciprocal exchange, ways such as following custom, the Pharaoh's feeding of the pyramid-building slaves, a socialist centralised rationing system, or the intricacies of complex employment relations. But whatever the particular technique of exchange, without it the system of specialisation will come to a grinding halt (Macneil 1980c, 2–3).

More than this, some types of exchange will more adequately express the basic reciprocity of exchange than others. Macneil is anxious to allow conflict ridden exchange into the domain of exchange, but only there to condemn it as bad exchange. Having argued for the inclusion of "highly pressured situations within the domain of contract," Macneil goes on to say that this:

> should not, of course, be taken to suggest that a highly coerced pattern is ... the ideal prototype of contract ... Clearly slavery in an Arabian satrapy is not as "contractual" a relationship as is a contract to work in an American corporation (at whatever level), nor is an adhesion contract for goods sold by a high-pressured door-to-door salesman in the ghetto as "contractual" as a contract to sell a used car between one consumer and another. But all have significant contractual elements. Twisted 18 inch specimens near the final tree line are usefully called "trees" just as are their straight 150 foot cousins on the lower slope; so too with twisted little specimens of contract living too close to the harsh winds of tyranny (Macneil 1974a, 705).

Macneil's initial emphasis on the co-operative dimension of contracts had the (natural) corollary that consideration of the asymmetries of power in contract was relatively underemphasised. When later taking up questions of power (Macneil 1981b, n. 44), Macneil used the distinction his concept of exchange generates, between good contract expressive of reciprocity and bad contract expressive of coercion, to categorise exchanges marked by asymmetries of power as bad or, as he very tellingly puts it, "inadequate" (Macneil 1983b, 379) or "inappropriate" (Macneil 1986, 568). His most substantial work in this vein has been on the use of standard forms by large firms is such a way as to turn them into contracts of adhesion and thereby make consumers' "agreement" "a very poor joke" (Macneil 1984, 6. cf. Macneil 1984–5). At one point Macneil seems to contradict himself by denying that slave labour camps (which we have seen him insist are examples of exchange) are contractual, but, without denying the slip, the way he frames this denial is instructive:

> One example of how sovereign [interference] destroys contract is the generally conceded inefficiency of slave labour camps; the levels of reciprocity in such camps are simply too low for effective contractual relations to exist (Macneil 1983b 369).

Such exchanges are inadequate to the ideal exchange Macneil has fashioned.

This, I think, brings us to the key to Macneil's thinking, which is his view that, properly understood, the concept of exchange is *the* key to a grasp of the core of human character and social institutions. To be such, it must be freed from the previous misunderstandings which have either given monetised exchange either too much or too little importance:

> our thinking ... is also influenced by the deification of exchange by Nineteenth (and Twentieth) century laissez faire political economists, and the countervailing consignment of exchange to the works of the devil by Karl Marx and at least some of his successors (Macneil 1969b, 405).

For Macneil, exchange (and with it the spectrum of contractual phenomena) is the fundamental feature revealed by philosophic analysis of the nature of human beings. Its general quality is the product of the contradictory yet ineluctable presence of what he describes as the individualist (discrete) and the communalist (relational) elements in the character of humankind:

> men are individuals born and dying one by one, each suffering his or her own hunger pains and enjoying his or her own full stomach, yet each individual absolutely requiring other human beings even to exist physically and psychologically, much less to become an ordinary, whole human being. The consequence is that humans are—cannot otherwise be—inconsistently selfish and socially committed at the same time. No amount of close community can ever do away with this fundamental individuality; and no separation can ever do away with this living through others (Macneil 1986, 568).

The way in which Macneil understands this, to my mind perfectly accurate, description, is somewhat singular. He takes it as evidence of an irrational schizophrenia at the core of human nature, which attempts to understand that nature must accept and come to terms with:

> As students of man in society, we are faced with an illogicality. Man is both an entirely selfish creature and an entirely social creature in that man puts the interests of his fellows ahead of his

own interests at the same time that he puts his own interests first. Such a creature is schizophrenic, and will, to the extent that it does anything except vibrate in utter frustration, constantly alternate between inconsistent behaviours—selfish one-second and self-sacrificing the next. Man is, in the most fundamental sense of the word, irrational (Macneil 1983b, 348).

Exchange, with its combination of discrete and relational elements, is the institution which can express this schizophrenia, whereas the extreme individualism of neo-classical economics and the extreme communalism of command economics both extinguish it (though each in a different way). Against unduly individualist perceptions of exchange, Macneil's polemical point is that: "*no* pattern of exchange merely enhances individual utility ... and *all* patterns of exchange accepted by all parties enhance social solidarity" (Macneil 1986, 568). He equally insists that the logical endpoint of unduly communalist perceptions, with their implications of technically determined perfection in the arrangement of human affairs is unacceptable totalitarianism:

> Technical Man is inevitably a perfectionist. Whether it is objects, institutions, or people, nothing Technical Man touches can escape the aim of perfection ... Perfection in humans naturally varies with the tastes of Technical Man; in Stalinist Russia it was Stakhanov, the coal mining dynamo; in America it is the flawless, unblemished centrefold Playmate of the month; in China it is the perfect co-ordination of 10,000 gymnasts in a stadium. In an imperfect world where most miners, most women and most gymnasts have the usual quota of imperfections, Technical Man is constantly frustrated with actual human beings. But if he cannot perfect them—at least not yet—then he can try to perfect their institutions ... Our glimpses into the misty future of Technical Man are often nightmares. Two apocalyptic visions occur, the constructive and the destructive. The destructive ends ... in a bang ... The constructive variation is far more frightening—the system continues with the crushing of all that is human in man, 1984 or worse. Given either of these apocalyptic visions, there is no sense in talking about relational contract law (Macneil 1980c, 109–12).

As it is more or less fully developed by the time of *The New Social Contract*, Macneil's argument, that beneath the perceptions of self-interest which motivate exchange, contracts fundamentally effect co-operation, is built up into the claim that, *properly regarded,* exchange is an adequate form of human co-operation. Exchange is regarded as a proper expression of human nature because it deals with the contradictory character of that nature, combining both individualism, by fostering individual utility maximisation, and communalism, by fostering solidarity.

Macneil's critique of the very form of the classical law of contract is shaped by his perception of the productive schizophrenia of exchange. We have seen above how Macneil rejects the formalism of the classical law because "contract law is hardly a neat and logical structure of rules, but like all law is a social instrument designed to accomplish the goals of man." However, this is not merely a most useful insistence on the weakness of treating social problems as matters of deracinated deduction but turns on the belief that, as human life is irrational, then it is mistaken to "believe that useful, complete, and internally logical systems can ever be developed respecting human behaviour or human societies" (Macneil 1983b, n. 5):

> Man is, in the most fundamental sense of the word, irrational, and no amount of reasoning, no matter how sophisticated, will produce a complete and consistent account of human behaviour, customs, or institutions (Macneil 1983b, 348).

On this basis, Macneil's view of contract reasoning is as follows:

> Once you see the law as a useful social instrument for accomplishment of human goals you will see clearly why it is not a neat and logical package. It is because neither individuals nor their societies are neat and logical packages. Man is full of conflicting motives and conflicting actions. He seeks security and yearns for adventure. He wants companionship and privacy at the same time. He seeks peace and he makes war. He punishes those he loves and weeps over the graves of his enemies. How, except by a denial of human nature, could any legal system devised and used by such a creature be a neat and logical structure? (Macneil 1968e, 2).

7.2. THE RELATIONSHIP OF MACNEIL'S THEORIES OF CONTRACT AND EXCHANGE

I do not wish to say anything about the social theory of exchange as such here but would like to say something about its relationship to the relational theory of contract. It will be recalled that the principal ambiguity of the latter theory turns on whether Macneil allows that there are such things as actually discrete contracts, and that, consistently, he should deny that there are. This would set up one relational theory of contract rather than a theory which seems not to apply to all contracts. In a retrospective essay, he captured the issue strikingly by insisting that he had sought to identify "a *Grundnorm* recognising the imbeddedness in exchange of all relations." However, on the very next page, returning to the metaphor of the spectrum and of theories appropriate to the different parts of the spectrum, Macneil gives up the unified approach turning on a *Grundnorm*:

> Let me add that both neo-classical economic analysis and neo-classical contract law have proper, although limited, roles in social analysis ... (These limited roles are intellectually difficult to deal with, because both are closed systems which deny, yet inconsistently postulate, an external social structure in which they operate) (Macneil 1985a, 543).

Analytically, there cannot be two *Grundnormen*. *Why* Macneil effectively says here that there is hopefully now is clear. He ultimately does not want to eliminate the incoherence produced by retention of the concepts of the classical law which he identifies as appropriate to discrete contracts, for the relational theory of exchange needs to keep these if it is to set up the description of human nature as illogical. The position which is revealed at the bottom of the theory of exchange is a celebration of contradiction, an insistence on the "fundamental fact [of] the essential logical inconsistency of man", the "very contradiction" which means that "we are, in part, eternally absurd" (Macneil 1986, 568–9). What Macneil means by this is that human beings are the products of the individualism of neo-classical assumptions and the communalism of some hellishly egalitarian anti-individualistic utopia (Macneil 1984–5, 919–29). He wishes to claim that a "tension arises from the inevitable conflicts between participants' desires to enhance individual utilities ... and their desires to enhance social solidarity" (Macneil 1986, 580). That is to say, he wishes to emphasise the tension between individuality and sociality which is an unquestioned aspect of all interesting modern political theory.

But a tension is not an "illogicality", a "contradiction" or an "absurdity". These are the properties of a theory which describes tension as the product of an individualism which denies sociality and a communalism which denies individuality. Macneil intends to bring neo-classicism and communalism into his theory, and to combine them to produce a contradiction both in his general social theory and, in the form an intertwining of discreteness and relations along the spectrum of contractual phenomena, in his core work (Macneil 1987, 276). However, *these specific constructions* of individuality as individualism and sociality as communalism, cannot be combined, even to produce a contradiction.

"Man," we have seen Macneil tell us, "is both an entirely selfish creature and an entirely social creature," but, of course, what Macneil shows us is that human beings are *never* entirely either. To take only individualism, it knows no contradiction for it denies all sociality. To be sure, it very quickly runs out of explanatory productivity because of this denial. Recognising this, Macneil then purports to include individualism in a contradiction with communalism. But in so doing he has thereby begun to change complete individualism into an individualism which, by holding that "the idea of man-the-atom is always 50 per cent utter nonsense" (Macneil 1984–5, 934), acknowledges the tension involved in recognising sociality. This nonsense is the very idea that he purports to work with. However, to use it he has to change it. In changed form, it invites the development of possible political philosophical ways of handling the tension with communalism, such as the community in which "the non-existent Hobbesian atomistic individual becomes the real-life human being ridden with the conflicts of desires for self-gain and self-loss at the same time" (Macneil 1984–5, 935) which Macneil himself suggests.

The denial of this shift from the extant individualism of discrete exchange to an individuality produced by ideal exchange produces the confusion we have seen in Macneil's theory of contract, for the reworking of individualism into socially conscious individuality is necessarily only partial in a purportedly "half-Hobbesian" (Macneil 1987a, 42; 1988b, 6) theory which retains certain characteristics of individualism to produce an existential contradiction. As we have seen Macneil say, "[t]here is a fundamental intellectual flaw in using a model based on man-outside-society to analyse the behaviour of man-in-society" (Macneil 1982, 961). The individualism of the assumptions of neo-classical economics is not reconcilable with relations; it is an individualism which, as we have seen Macneil repeatedly state throughout his work, denies relations. If individuality is (as it has) to be brought into a relational account, it cannot be as this individualism, for there cannot be a "half-Hobbesian" account.

The point emerges when one considers a specific example of encouraging discrete contracting as an economic and legal policy. For example, one can agree, as I do, with Coase's belief (Coase 1994, 62–3) that general planning structures have been extended too far and conceive of spheres of allocation which could more efficiently be handled by a market of private (if regulated) producers selling to consumers—in essence, allowing the case for the privatisation of some of the formerly nationalised utilities. However, on a relational view, to base policy on this belief is not a question of freeing the innate efficiency of a deregulated and therefore assumedly optimal market. It requires rather the improvement of the social structures of consumer education and protection, of product availability and comparability, and corporate accountability. This will facilitate the necessary micro-level transactions by making choice and consumer sovereignty real rather than, as we have seen him memorably put it, "a very poor joke." Such success and failure as privatisation has encountered very much turn on whether the necessary relations (and the institutions which embody them) have or have not been established; as in the U.K. they arguably have over the competitive selling of telephone services but as they manifestly have not over the remuneration of the senior management of the privatised utility companies. This lesson has truly been learned the hard way in the former communist countries, which have recklessly smashed their command economies in pursuit of capitalist reconstruction which has been conceived merely negatively as a process of deregulation. As a consequence of their scant regard for the positive development of the normative institutions necessary for a welfare enhancing market, there has been a disastrous growth in gangsterism to the point where it dominates the now decentralised economies of these countries.

The conception of consumer sovereignty outlined above is not really akin to the perception of discreteness in classical law and neo-classical economics. Although it is discussing the micro-economic allocations they take as paradigmatic, it understands those allocations in an entirely different way. The understanding is that even these allocations are relationally constituted, and this is specifically what is denied in the legal and economic analysis which works with the discrete exchange as a fundamental unit of analysis. When Macneil speaks of micro-allocation through the operation of a discrete norm within the range of common contract norms, he is not talking of a discrete transaction as viewed by neo-classicism. This view entirely denies relations. In Macneil's terms it ignores the common contract norms, and indeed, unless we stretch the sense of "normative" a great deal, its attitude to discrete exchanges is not normative at all. It is a view based on pure individual utility maximisation. The presentiated view, as Macneil says, cannot ever actually presentiate, but those holding it believe that it does, and it is this mistake that Macneil has intended his entire work on relational contracts to correct. That Macneil has had to allow that that view is accurate for some phenomena along the contractual spectrum has diluted the most important thrust of his work.

The fundamental reason this dilution has occurred is one to which Macneil himself alluded when making some perceptive remarks on the philosophy of science in one of his retrospective papers (1985a, 542). There he correctly insisted that no theory can embrace two mutually exclusive approaches, and that any theory which appears to do so really calls for its own replacement by a more adequate one. Building on these remarks, we can see that this is because the two approaches call for a third which can specify the conditions under which either of the first two come into play. When this is developed, the first two are shown to be reconcilable and their antagonistic features rejected as errors, leaving the third, now all-embracing, theory (*cf.* Lakatos 1980, ch. 1).

The curious feature of Macneil's work has been that he has, in the above terms, at different times been committed to one of the two mutually exclusive approaches *and* the third reconciling approach. When counterposing relational to truly discrete contracts as ends of the spectrum of contracts, he has put forward the relational (as opposed to the classical) law as one of two mutually exclusive approaches. When stressing the common contract norms, and the relational constitution of relational (in the sense of complex or intertwined) *and* discrete contracts, he has put forward the third approach. In his own essays reflecting on his work, he undoubtedly has attempted to sort this out. How far he can be successful whilst he remains committed to the schizophrenic positions of the relational theory of exchange must be open to doubt, for schizophrenia requires incoherence, not the removal of incoherence.

All this is of little account, however. In the positions he has clearly established, Macneil has taken the law of contract to a simply qualitatively different level of social theoretical profundity than can be found in the bulk of the scholarship. The principal task facing contract scholarship now is to come to terms with what he has done.

Chapter 2

The Reception of Ian Macneil's Work on Contract in the USA

Jay Feinman

In his 1985 "Reflections on Relational Contract," Ian Macneil lamented that "there never [was] any race to [create] a relational theory of contract, nor have the succeeding years seen either widespread acceptance of (or indeed much challenge to) my particular theory or the development of other relational contract theories" (Macneil 1985a, 541). As usual, Macneil is both a perceptive analyst of the state of American contract law scholarship and too modest. Relational contract theory has had a significant impact on the understanding and teaching of contract law, though not as much impact as it deserves. A version of the most basic insight of relational contract theory—that contractual relations are different than discrete transactions and merit separate treatment under a different form of analysis—has been absorbed into the mainstream of contracts scholarship and teaching in the United States. Macneil's richer analysis, which Campbell has summarised earlier in this 'Introduction,' has been widely misunderstood and, as misunderstood, has not been embraced by mainstream scholars (Feinman 2000).

Relational contract is the latest step in the scholarly project of responding to the inadequacies of classical contract law (Eisenberg 2000; Feinman 1983; 1990). Classical contract law—the body of law usually associated in the United States with Holmes, Williston, and the original *Restatement of Contracts*—was motivated by an image of the isolated bargain between independent, self-interested individuals. Hard bargainers carefully calculated their interests in a particular exchange, gave a promise or performance only to receive a precisely measured return promise or performance, and embodied their transaction in an agreement that carefully defined the terms of performance and therefore could provide the basis for a determinate remedy in the event of breach.

Almost immediately after classical contract's enshrinement in Williston's (1920) treatise and the *Restatement* (American Law Institute 1932) in the 1920s, scholars began to criticise it and attempt to reconstruct it. The essence of the criticism and reconstruction through several generations was contextualisation. Scholars first situated contract law doctrine in the decisions of courts in many cases, demonstrating that the abstract rules of the classical structure were inaccurate, misleading, or indeterminate. Corbin's (1952) treatise was the apotheosis of this critical project, showing that facts were more important in determining legal results than rules. By focusing on facts, one could begin to construct principles and policies—but not abstract, formal rules—that guide contract law decisions. Subsequent generations, especially after World War II, then situated the cases within the commercial contexts of contracting practices. This later work never heavily influenced the central tendencies of contract law, but it provided a consistent counterpoint to the attempt to construct doctrinal structures that were relatively removed from the reality of day-to-day contracting.

Relational contract theory is a continuation of this project of contextualisation (Gordon 1985) Macneil's starting point is the same as that of many leading post-classical scholars: "social relations matter" (Macneil 1987b, 278). Most scholars, however, have treated relational contract as an excessively abstract, modest extension of the project. In this mainstream view, the core assertions of relational contract theory are that the dominant form of contract, relational contract, "occurs over time through continuous interactions between parties," so that "one must investigate the social conditions that form the foundation of parties' bargains in order to comprehend the relational norms and hence to understand contract" (Hillman 1988, 124). Classical contract, with its focus on a distinct moment of contract formation, could not accommodate these concerns. The recognition of this characteristic has had a profound effect on modern contract law. However, mainstream scholars assert that, contrary to the opinion of relational extremists such as Macneil, modern contract law recognises the existence of relational contracts, though not their dominance, and is well equipped to investigate the social contexts of such agreements to determine their legal effect. For example, the use in the Uniform Commercial Code of resort to course of performance, course of dealing, and usage of trade as sources of contract interpretation (§2–208) and good faith as a baseline obligation (§§1–201(19), 1–203, 2–103(1)(b)) situate contracts to a sufficient degree in their relational settings. Thus neo-classical contract already embodies the important parts of relational contract; the rest consists of unnecessary flights of theoretical fancy.

Macneil's relational contract theory is different and much richer than the mainstream interpretation of it. Relational contract begins at a different point. Any society in which specialisation of labour exists will include exchange, and exchange always occurs in a relational context. In any society, even the most capitalistic, individualistic one, the production and distribution of goods and services is carried on through a variety of exchange mechanisms, of which discrete, self-maximising exchange on a market (the paradigm of neo-classical contract) will be a very small part. More commonly, exchange occurs within relations that involve more elements and are of longer duration than does an isolated, discrete exchange. Moreover, even the most discrete contract is an event that is always situated within a framework of non-discrete relations which must be examined to understand the discrete contract. Accordingly, as an initial empirical and conceptual matter, thinking about contract ought to begin with relational exchange, not discrete contract. Recognising, as neo-classical contract does, that some contracts are more extensive than discrete bargains is not enough; relational contract theory stresses that all contracts are relational to some extent, and truly relational contracts predominate.

When one examines in more detail the behaviour exhibited by parties along the spectrum of discrete and relational exchange, it become apparent that all exchanges require certain kinds of behaviour, such as a common means of communication between the parties, a minimum amount of solidarity, and some reciprocity. Some exchanges are relatively discrete, involving short duration, limited party interactions, and precise measurement of the value of the objects exchanged. Other exchanges are more relational, involving significant duration, many facets of the parties' lives, and the exchange of values that cannot easily be quantified. The distinction between discrete and relational exchanges is perhaps the most important way of categorising exchanges.

The different types of exchange behaviour observed give rise to norms, "a case of an 'is' creating an 'ought' " (Macneil 1987b, 274). The norms parallel the categories of behaviour that have been conceptualised; some norms are common to all exchanges, while others are associated more strongly with discrete and relational exchanges, respectively. Solidarity and reciprocity, for example, are norms that are common to all contracts. In discrete contracts the norms of implementation of planning and effectuation of consent are intensified by the distinctive elements of discrete exchanges. On the other hand, in relational contracts other common contract norms, such as maintaining the integrity of one's role within the relation and harmonising the relation with the surrounding social matrix, are more important because of the more extensive characteristics of relational exchanges.

Two points are most striking about this conception of contract as a contrast to the mainstream neo-classical view. First, wealth maximisation becomes only one among many factors motivating people to engage in contractual relationships and to be considered by courts in evaluating those relationships (Gordon 1985; Whitford 1985) In the neo-classical view, contracts are exchanges entered in to for gain. In the relational view, contracts are social relationships in which economic gain is an important factor but, particularly in intertwined relationships of long standing not the only factor. As a consequence, relational analysis certainly emphasises different elements than does neo-classical law and provides a more complete analysis. In addition, the framework brings to light certain features of many exchanges that neo-classical law under-values or ignores because of its emphasis on relatively discrete, value-maximising agreements. Sometimes relations are not mutually favourable to all parties because they arise out of social situations of inequality, so the values may include elements of coercion and dependence, contrary to the neo-classical assumption of rough equality. In other situations, values such as trust, co-operation, reciprocity, and role integrity are essential to the relationship.

Secondly, the process of definition and application of contractual norms provides a "rich classificatory apparatus" (Williamson 1986, 103. *cf.* Macneil 1981b, n. 14) for the analysis of contracts, far richer than that provided by neo-classical contract law. Neo-classical law is directed ultimately at the production of doctrine and the resolution of cases: a lawyer's project, though one often carried out by academics at a considerable remove from the daily concerns of lawyers and their clients. Relational contract theory arises from law, but is a highly theoretical project that takes a much broader scope for legal study than is traditionally accepted, developing an understanding of contractual practices and then abstracting from that understanding to create ideal types, hypotheses, and generalisations of the kind more familiar to social scientists than to legal academics.

The broad orientation of Macneil's work suggests reasons why the work has not become as widely adopted as it otherwise might. As a broad project, Macneil's relational contract theory requires a different vocabulary and style of presentation than traditional scholarship which is focused on the development of legal doctrine. Much of the work is difficult to read, requiring the reader to absorb unfamiliar vocabulary ("common contract norms," "solidarity," "reciprocity," and "harmonisation with the social matrix," to mention only a few of the newly-coined or applied terms). The work also is complex, in that it begins with highly abstract observations about society and exchange behaviour within it, proceeds to the categorisation of exchange behaviour, describes many contract norms applicable to different contexts, and explores the realisability of legal doctrine. The style and complexity have put off many contract scholars, and certainly have prevented the work from being widely read by practising lawyers and judges.

The style of Macneil's work is a reflection of its substance, however. "Relational contract theory is not intended . . . to be a complete theory of human relations, an impossibility in any event," but it is "concerned with seeing exchange whole, *i.e.* as an integral aspect of relations, rather than isolated"(Macneil 1981b, 277, 279). Not only is this level of inquiry unfamiliar to scholars primarily occupied with the production of legal doctrine, but it is less immediately useful to that task. American legal scholars always have perceived a conflict in their dual role as true academics in a university setting and servants of the practising profession. By training and inclination, most scholars are bound to approaches to contract law not too far removed from what is useful to lawyers and judges everyday. It is not immediately obvious how Macneil's more abstract work translates into that forum, and Macneil himself has not devoted much effort to that side of the project, considering how the work might be applied to doctrinal problems. Because of the complexity and orientation of the work, few other scholars have attempted that type of application, either.[24]

Another factor limiting the impact of the work, in addition to style and orientation, is its substance. One way of describing the core observations of the work is that discrete contracts are a limited way of viewing exchange behaviour, and that in contracting parties are influenced (explicitly and implicitly) by a multiplicity of values. Those two propositions are at odds with the prevailing views of contracts

---

[24] For some attempts see Brown and Feinman (1991); Feinman (1995; 1996); Rubin (1995) and Speidel (2000).

scholarship. For more than a hundred years, the basic assumptions of contract law and scholarship have been the discrete transaction as the paradigm of contracting and economically defined self-interest as the primary motivation of contracting parties. Although recently these assumptions have been tempered by the recognition of the existence of relational contracts and the presence of values other than short-term economic interest, they remain at the core of thinking about contract. Macneil's work has not been able to overcome the power of these entrenched ideas, so the acceptance of the work has been limited.

The power of this conflict can be shown by the extent to which an analogous body of work has been more widely commented on, if not wholly accepted. There is in American scholarship another body of relational contract theory besides Macneil's, generated by scholars including Robert Scott (Goetz and Scott 1981; Scott 1987) and Alan Schwartz (1992). It recognises relational contracts to be long-term contracts that are incomplete as to their terms at the time of formation. This body of work is within the tradition of law and economics scholarship, broadly construed to include game theory and decision analysis. As such, the problems it looks at and the analysis it uses in considering those problems is far narrower than Macneil's. Nevertheless, because it is more congenial to prevailing notions of discreteness and self-interest, it has engendered more scholarly attention, but no more apparent influence on the courts.

As is commonplace in legal education in the United States, Macneil embodied his theoretical views in a set of teaching materials as well as in his expository writings. His casebook for use in a first-year contract law course went through two editions, in 1971 and 1978. The casebook was as extraordinary for its novelty as are the scholarly writings. As with the scholarly writings, though, the uniqueness of the book contributed to its lack of popularity.

Macneil summarised the difference in scope of the casebook, compared to the usual materials in the field, in the "Preface" to the second edition:

> The fundamental assumption is that contract encompasses all human activities in which economic exchange is a significant factor—marriage as much as sales of goods, the complex web of relations constituting a major corporation as much as a sale of commodity futures, collective bargaining as much as a two week engagement to star in a Law Vegas night club ... Thus the range of

activities treated goes beyond those traditionally associated with the doctrinally structured first year contracts course. And when subjects such as collective bargaining and franchise agreements are treated, the focus is less on neo-classical doctrine as it applies to them, than it is on those relations as generators of contract principles, structures and processes going beyond the limits of neo-classical doctrine (Macneil 1978b, xvii).

The casebook was organised functionally, beginning with an inquiry into "The Foundations and Functions of Contract," then continuing with "Exchange, Society, Contract and Law," "Contract and Continuing Relations," and "Social Control and Utilisation of Contractual Relations." Not until after this extensive, unusual introduction to contract understood broadly did the book introduce many of the basic contract law concepts that are the staple fare of the ordinary contracts course.

The second half of Macneil's casebook focused on "Planning Contractual Relations." Although Macneil rightly resisted the characterisation of the first half of the book as "theoretical" and the second half as "practical," the materials on planning paradoxically provide a better introduction to contract law as it is used by lawyers than do the approaches of more traditional courses. These materials are collected together as Macneil's 1975 article "A Primer of Contract Planning" (Macneil 1975b). The article and the course materials provide a theoretical framework that links the understanding of contract in context with lawyer tasks of counselling, planning, and drafting.

The Macneil casebook was never very widely adopted by law teachers, for reasons that parallel the lack of widespread acceptance of the scholarly work. The approach was so different than that employed by most teachers, particularly in its pervasive emphasis on abstraction and contextualisation and its resistance to making legal doctrine the centrepiece of the course, that teachers were unprepared to make the leap to Macneil's approach. Some teachers did, particularly those who were receptive to the underlying theory, and they often encountered resistance from students, who did not see the approach as "real law."

Macneil's work did have significant influence on legal pedagogy on two respects, though. The casebook organisation became a model for a book produced by the contracts faculty at the University of Wisconsin School of Law (Macaulay 2000; Macaulay et al 1995). This work is more accessible and therefore has become more popular. Also, at least some of the basic insights of relational theory have been absorbed into many contracts courses. The ideas that long-term contracts and complex contracts demand attention in the first-year course and that context has become an essential element of study have become widespread, if not universal.

Chapter 3

The Reception of Ian Macneil's Work on Contract in the U.K.

Peter Vincent-Jones

1. Introduction

The beginning of the new millennium is likely to prove particularly significant in any long-term evaluation of the reception of Ian Macneil's work in the U.K. Apart from this edited collection, the appearance in 2000 of articles drawing more or less substantially on Macneil's ideas in *Feminist Legal Studies*, the *Oxford Journal of Legal Studies*, and *Social and Legal Studies*, is indicative of their contemporary relevance and breadth of appeal. The view that "people should not attempt to write about contracts until they have studied Macneil" (Macaulay 2000, 776) may be expected to become more widely accepted in future than it is at present.

Macneil's recent clarification and extension of essential contract theory (so-called to distinguish it from other relational theories), in his contribution to the Symposium on relational contract theory held in his honour at Northwestern University (Macneil 2000c), provides a useful basis for mapping the reception of his work in Britain. Implicit in this account is the fundamental distinction between contract *behaviour and norms* on the one hand, and *law* concerning such observed social phenomena on the other. This distinction is emphasised here because the behavioural dimensions of Macneil's writings on contract have frequently been underplayed. According to Macneil, any adequate relational analysis (including descriptions of how law governs and prescriptions as to how the law ought to govern) must be founded on an understanding of the ways in which social exchange behaviour both gives rise to and is supported by the ten "common contract norms" of role integrity, reciprocity, implementation of planning, effectuation of consent, flexibility, contractual solidarity, the protection of restitution, reliance and expectation interests, the creation and restraint of power, the propriety of means, and harmonization within the social matrix (879–80). These basic patterns of behaviour and associated contract norms supply the framework for relational analysis of transactions in the context of all their essential elements and enveloping relations (893).

The central importance of the common contract norms in Macneil's relational theory is arguably only now becoming apparent. It is more than coincidental that a number of recent applications and accounts of this theory, including Campbell's introduction to this volume, have either begun with the common contract norms or accorded them special prominence (Macneil 2000a; Vincent-Jones 2000; Wightman 2000). Campbell further implies, however, that a major factor contributing to the misinterpretation and general misunderstanding of Macneil's theory of contract concerns his attempt to develop, in conjunction with the common contract norms, an analysis based on the polar types of "discrete" and "relational" contracts. The substance of this long-standing critique (Campbell 1990; Campbell and Clay 1992) is acknowledged at least in part by Macneil, who nevertheless regards the problem as terminological rather than fundamental, and continues to defend the idea of the discrete-relational spectrum (Macneil 2000c, 894). Macneil "resolves" the theoretical tension accompanying the dual claims that all exchange occurs in relations so there is no such thing as a discrete contract, while at the same time discrete contracts may be found at the opposite end to relational contracts on a spectrum, by re-labelling the poles of the spectrum "as-if-discrete" and "relational" (895).[25] The common contract norms and patterns of behaviour are to be found all along this spectrum. Transactions at the "as-if-discrete" pole are characterised by an intensification of the norms of implementation of planning and effectuation of consent, which together serve to enhance discreteness and presentation, while contracts at the "relational" pole involve intensification of the norms of role integrity, contractual solidarity, flexibility, power, and harmonization with the social matrix (896–7).

---

[25] The alternative having been the earlier attempt, now abandoned, to re-label the relational end of the spectrum as "intertwined" (Macneil 1987b, 276).

One of the major issues to be explored in assessing the impact of Macneil's writings concerns the uses made by commentators of the discrete-relational spectrum, in the light of Macneil's own acknowledgement that this has become the most widely recognised aspect of his work on contract (2000c, 894). The present account will consider Macneil's influence on UK scholarship in the distinct but inter-related areas of the analysis of contract law and the study of contract behaviour, including the role of contract as a regulatory instrument in the restructuring of public services.

2. The Law of Contract

The widespread acceptance of the basic insights of relational theory has led to the observation that "we are all relationalists now" and that "the debate, rather, is over the proper nature of contract law" (Macneil 2000c, 901). Contemporary debates over contract doctrine in the U.K. have made use of Macneil's ideas in three main ways. First, there are interpretations that focus on the discrete-relational spectrum to the exclusion of the common contract norms, so involving a distortion of Macneil's position. Secondly, there are analyses that focus on the common contract norms but draw also on the discrete-relational spectrum, representing Macneil's true position. Finally, in the most radical interpretation, Macneil's discrete-relational spectrum is rejected completely in favour of an analysis based on the common contract norms. These positions will be considered in turn.

2.1. ANALYSES FOCUSING ON "DISCRETE" AND "RELATIONAL" CONTRACTS TO THE EXCLUSION OF THE COMMON CONTRACT NORMS (A DISTORTION OF MACNEIL'S POSITION)

The "minimal" neoclassical interpretation of the significance of relational theory for contract doctrine accepts the need for rules promoting fairness and co-operation, and subordinating short-term to longer-term interests, but only as part of a framework of classical principles relating to contract formation, performance and remedies. Here Macneil is read as suggesting that relational contracts should be treated as different from more discrete contracts, or in other words that "there exists a class of relational contracts that deserve treatment as a special subcategory of the general contract law" (Feinman 2000, 740; Bell 1989, 198). On the basis of such a reading, Eisenberg (1995; 2000) concedes that the relational literature has performed a valuable role in correcting the erroneous premise of the classical law that most contracts are discrete, but maintains that the case for a special law of relational contracts has not been made out.[26] Rather, "the general principles of contract law can and should be formulated to be responsive to relational as well as discrete contracts. By and large, that is just the position to which modern contract law has been moving" (Eisenberg 1995, 304). The task becomes, then, to distinguish in the relational contract literature those rules that are good for all or most contracts and should therefore be principles of general contract law, from those that are not good for any contracts (299). This interpretation leads Eisenberg to a neoclassical defence and refinement of the classical principles of contract law that denies the viability of a relational alternative. Similarly for McKendrick, while the courts should recognise the need for flexibility in adjusting long-term contracts to meet changed circumstances, there is nothing special about such contracts that would merit distinctive regulation. Consistent with the classical notion of freedom of contract, the onus is on the contracting parties to take legal advice and to incorporate into their bargain suitably drafted clauses that provide for contingencies (McKendrick 1995, 314–6).

In contrast to these writers, Collins is well known for his argument that contract doctrine needs to overcome fundamental obstacles presented by the classical law, for example by upholding consensual modifications made following changed circumstances, by enabling the courts to consider long-term interests as a guide to requirements of co-operation in particular contexts, and by giving effect to unwritten expectations of co-operation such that economic opportunities can be maximised (Collins 1997, 309). Collins' critique of the classical law draws only marginally on Macneil, however, and is confined to pointing up the artificiality of the common law's assumption that risks can be fully allocated through presentiation (Collins 1996, 76). Again Macneil is read as advocating a spectrum of contracts ranging from discrete or spot contracts characterised by rational utility-maximising behaviour on the one hand, to relational long-term contracts characterised by co-operative

[26] cf. *Total Gas Marketing Ltd v. Arco British Ltd and Others* [1998] 2 Lloyd's Rep 209, 218 per Lord Steyn: "(This is) a contract of a type sometimes called a relational contract. But there are no special rules of interpretation applicable to such contracts". I am grateful to Andrew Harries for drawing my attention to this judgment.

behaviour on the other. Collins discovers little evidence of distinctive features of contractual behaviour in connection with long-term contracts that would support the proposition that they rest on a different logic from spot contracts (83). While Macneil is portrayed as arguing that the source of co-operative behaviour lies in a particular type of long-term contract, Collins is anxious to show that co-operation of the sort illustrated in *Williams v. Roffey* is rooted in the "extra-contractual context" of the business relation—the length of the commercial dealings between the parties—irrespective of the particular contractual form (long-term finite, long-term indefinite, or series of spot contracts) or its duration (87).

Although these neoclassical and "co-operative" positions have very different implications for the nature and scope of contract law, they presuppose in common that Macneil's relational theory posits a relatively clear distinction between discrete and relational contracts and their corresponding forms of contract law. Ironically, Eisenberg's conclusion that a single law of contract should apply to all contracts, while presented as a rejection of Macneil's claims for relational law, is arguably true to Macneil's real position—that relational contract law must apply to all contracts since even the most apparently discrete contract behaviour is underpinned by the common contract norms, some of which are inherently relational.[27]

A similar irony is evident in Collins' "alternative" explanation of the *Williams v. Roffey* phenomenon of consensual modification: "As well as the terms of the contract, which seek to close down and specify the commitments of the relationship, there are other norms which govern the parties' behaviour which compel them to have regard to each other's interests. These rival norms are grounded in the business relation itself, as opposed to the particular instance of that relation created in the contract" (Collins 1996, 70). Collins' claim that the reason why one party places the other party's interest above her own is because "contractual behaviour is invariably referable to more than the norms set by the contract" is entirely consistent with a relational analysis in terms of the common contract norms. The argument that the contrast between discrete and relational contracts is inadequate as a tool for analysis because of its implication that these dimensions present oppositions, and that "all

---

[27] "Eisenberg seems to envision a relatively static, black-and-white division between relational contracts (and the law that fits them) and discrete contracts (with their corresponding law). Having set up this straw man, he knocks it down by asserting that a single law of contract must apply to all contracts" (Mertz 2000, 914 n. 29).

71

transactions have discrete and relational elements" (Collins 1999, 142), is unexceptionable from Macneil's true perspective.[28] The misunderstanding here stems from the erroneous belief that Macneil divorces particular contracting practices from their behavioural context, a misinterpretation that accompanies the tendency to reification of "types of contract" in the discrete-relational spectrum.[29]

2.2. ANALYSES FOCUSING ON THE COMMON CONTRACT NORMS AND DRAWING ALSO ON THE DISCRETE-RELATIONAL SPECTRUM (MACNEIL'S POSITION)

Macneil's relational theory implies analysis based on the common contract norms in conjunction with the spectrum of discrete and relational contracts: "The common contract behavior and norms are the end of neither the descriptive nor the theoretical story. I also combined these behavioral patterns and norms with something else, namely the idea of two polar types of contracts, discrete and relational" (Macneil 2000c, 894). In contrast to the interpretations considered in the previous section, however, Macneil envisages these analytical elements working in conjunction, rather than one being subordinated to the other.

Macneil's position is well represented by Feinman's exposition of relational method as involving the elucidation of the context of exchange by assessing the relative values attaching to each of the common contract norms: "For example, implementation of planning and effectuation of consent are especially important in contracts with strong discrete elements, while role integrity, preservation of the relation, and harmonization of relational conflict are particularly important in contracts with especially relational characteristics" (Feinman 2000, 742). The normative context of the exchange is external as well as internal to the contract, including positive law, industry customs, and the rules of trade associations and professional organisations (742). In this interpretation, the fundamental difference between neoclassical and relational analysis is methodological. Whereas traditional doctrine

---

[28] The linking of contractual behaviour to "communication systems" in autopoietic theory, in order to analyse the "normative points of reference that guide behaviour" (Collins 1999, 143), adds little that could not have been achieved through Macneil's relational theory.

[29] Reification inevitably results from the question 'What is a relational contract?', posed explicitly by McKendrick (1995, 307) and implicitly by Collins.

consists of rules and principles taking a deductive form, relational analysis is inductive, directed at consequences and based on the contextual assessment of the structure of norms internal and external to relations: "The use of this normative structure in analyzing contracts leads substantially, if not totally, to a rejection of the doctrinal method as it is ordinarily practised, in favor of a method that looks much more like policy analysis" (743). On this reasoning Feinman abandons the general project of redefining the core of contract doctrine in terms of the categories of the common contract norms, arguing instead for a more modest extension of relational analysis in particular sub-fields such as commercial construction contracting, long-term relationships involving large economic entities, and family economic relations (746–7).

Relational analysis may be applied in this vein not just to "monetised" relations but to any social interaction in which reciprocity is the dominant element, including family relations (Feinman 2000, 741; Kingdom 2000; Belcher 2000; Wightman 1996; 2000). In welcoming the interest shown by feminist and gay and lesbian theorists in Macneil's work, Wightman has considered some of the problems involved in applying the relational approach to intimate relationships outside marriage and other types of formal cohabitation or pre-nuptial contract. One of the obstacles to this task concerns the relative absence of established normative reference points (customs, standards) that in commercial settings produce patterns of regular behaviour which can be used to help ascertain the parties' expectations. A further difference with commercial contracting is that in intimate relations the parties' motivations are not so amenable to analysis in terms of the attenuation of self-interest, and concepts such as co-operation and altruism therefore also carry different meanings. Nevertheless, Wightman contends that such "contractual" relations, although not enforceable under any current contractual or reliance-based doctrine, might be distinguished from purely gratuitous promises and be legally recognised where the relationship is characterised by a sufficient degree of inter-dependence and reciprocity. The enforcement of non-bargain agreements on these grounds is argued to be preferable to other types of legal response based on more conventional doctrines such as promissory estoppel. Here a relational argument linking the case for legal reform to the normative context of the parties' behaviour is developed in conjunction with an analysis drawing also on the classification of types of contract (Wightman 2000, 102–5).

2.3. ANALYSIS BASED ON THE COMMON CONTRACT NORMS AND
REJECTING COMPLETELY THE DISCRETE–RELATIONAL SPECTRUM
(CAMPBELL'S DEVELOPMENT OF MACNEIL'S POSITION)

In contrast to Feinman's pessimism over the possibility of advancing
Macneil's project for a general relational theory of contract, Campbell has
argued consistently over the past decade that the development of such a
rival to the classical law is possible, but only on the basis of a radical
resolution of the ambiguity that is argued to lie at the heart of Macneil's
statement of that theory. Since Campbell's position has been spelt out in
this introduction and elsewhere, it will not be resumed here in detail. In
brief, Campbell acknowledges Macneil's outstanding contribution to
contract scholarship as the relational critique of the classical or neo-
classical law, but argues that this critique has been "insufficiently
forcefully expressed" (Campbell 1990, 76). The precondition for the
development of an adequate relational law of contract is the complete
rejection of the "discrete contract" as the fundamental unit of legal
analysis, together with the associated neo-classical economic concepts of
individual self-interest and utility-maximisation. From this viewpoint,
the idea of a discrete-relational spectrum of contractual phenomena, with
contracts ranged at various points along it being analysed according to
different discrete and relational legal and economic theories, is
fundamentally flawed. Obviously long-term contracts cannot be fitted
within the classical model of contract (Campbell and Harris 1993), but
neither can any type of exchange, even the most apparently simple and
discrete. "What is essential is that relational theory be not confined to
complex contracts but show its superiority for all contracts, a superiority
manifested across *all* contracts by theoretical integrity and explanatory
economy" (Campbell 1996, 61). The challenge is "to fashion a modern
form of contract which consciously expresses relationism even in the
setting up of micro-level allocations" (Campbell 1990, 90). The way
forward in accomplishing this task lies not in the misleading polar
opposition of discrete and relational contracts, but in detailed contextual
analysis according to the common, discrete and "complex" norms of
contract (Campbell 1996, 59–61).

3. Analyses of Contract Behaviour

The influence of Macneil's relational theory may also be seen in the U.K. in analyses of contract behaviour, including studies of the role of contract as a governance mechanism in the restructuring of public service provision. As has been demonstrated, the explanation of contractual phenomena proceeds through the analysis of transactions and their enveloping relations according to the "checklist" supplied by the common contract norms (Macneil 2000c, 893). This is the basis on which contract law may then be described and analysed, and prescriptions for the better governance of contract behaviour generated. However, while references to Macneil's writings are commonplace in studies of contract behaviour across a wide range of private and public sector contexts, much of the research has again focused on the idea of polar types of discrete and relational contract to the exclusion of the common contract norms.

3.1. ANALYSES BASED ON THE TYPOLOGY OF DISCRETE AND RELATIONAL CONTRACTS

One of the most frequent uses of Macneil's ideas in the analysis of contract behaviour has been in connection with Williamson's influential interpretation of the link between relational theory and transaction cost economics (Williamson, 1986, ch. 7; Macneil 1978a; 1981b). In his development of Macneil's spectrum of contract, Williamson relates the basic concepts of classical, neoclassical and relational contracting respectively to economic institutional forms of market governance, trilateral governance, and bilateral (obligational contracting) and unified governance (internal organisation). Williamson's hypothesis—that the various types of contract should be "matched" to different types of transaction according to the economic conditions of asset specificity, frequency, and uncertainty—has been tested in studies of long-term contracting in international iron ore and other natural resources markets (Daintith 1986, 1987), and in the U.K. manufacturing and public transport sectors (Lyons and Mehta 1997; Wistrich 1998).

While this research has cast light on the institutional conditions that create and sustain relational contracting in the areas studied, it has been more concerned with the corroboration or qualification of the basic postulates of transaction cost economics than with the development or application of relational contract theory (see Daintith 1986, 185; 1987, 207; also Sako 1992). From the latter viewpoint, a more productive strand of recent research, and one more subtly influenced by Macneil, has involved the comparative study of contract law, social norms and co-operative business relations in Britain, Germany and Italy (Deakin et al. 1997). In exploring in depth the social, institutional and organisational contexts in which contract behaviour in the different countries is embedded, this research reveals how trust and co-operation are sustained by a variety of relational influences in the "contractual environment" including trade associations, government standards, and a wide range of formal and informal norms at national and local levels (Deakin and Wilkinson 1996). As a counter-balance to the view attributed to previous empirical studies regarding the marginal importance of law in business practice, the use of formal agreements and the presence of legal enforceability as a form of security are regarded as highly compatible with relational contracting (Arrighetti et al. 1997). Again, however, while these studies pursue research questions in a manner consistent with the methodology suggested by Macneil's relational theory, there is no attempt to develop the analysis in terms of the internal and external dimensions of the common contract norms such as reciprocity, solidarity and role integrity.

Studies of the operation of the NHS internal market following the reforms introduced in the National Health Service and Community Care Act 1990 have also drawn on the Williamson-Macneil typology, but with less of a focus on transaction costs (but see Ferlie 1994) and greater attention to evaluating the nature and impact of the new structures of contractual governance.[30] Hence the general question addressed in one study concerned whether the model of contracting developing in the NHS was relational rather than classical (Bennett and Ferlie 1996; cf. Allen 1998). Another study analysed the contracting behaviour of contrasting health authorities according to their adoption of different styles of "classical" or "relational" contracting, placing the authorities towards opposing ends of a corresponding continuum of "adversarial" and "partnership" dealing (Hughes et al. 1996; see also McHale et al.

---

[30] For a different interpretation of the link between relational contract theory and transaction cost economics, in the attempt to theorise public sector transacting in terms of a continuum of contractual and non-contractual relations rather than according to a spectrum of discrete and relational contracts, see Vincent-Jones (1994b), Vincent-Jones and Harries (1996a).

1997). The categorisation of classical and relational contracts has proved similarly attractive to researchers examining the impact of public management reforms in local government, where restructuring has taken the form of the splitting of purchaser and provider roles and the introduction of contracts and competition into arrangements for the delivery of professional and public services. In this setting too, classical contracts are rejected in favour of the development of a framework for relational contracting which seeks to minimise the costs of transactions by developing trust-based relationships (Walsh 1995, 40–45). The findings that "contracts are more to do with relationships than with what is being exchanged" (Walsh *et al* 1996, 214), and that "the stronger the supporting institutional social framework of norms and relationships, the easier it will be to manage through contracts" (Walsh 1995, 41), are presented as bearing out Macneil's general thesis (see also Walsh *et al* 1997).

The use of the Macneil's discrete-relational continuum as an analytical tool has been taken to a logical conclusion in an empirical study of local authority contracting (Walker and Davis 1999). Interviewees in ten English local authorities were asked to indicate scores on the continuum for various dimensions of the client-contractor relationships in which they were involved (such as the type of communication, degree of initial planning, expectations as to bindingness, the distribution of benefits and burdens, and the anticipation of problems), in order to determine whether the relationships were primarily "transactional" or "relational" in character (Walker and Davis 1999, 25). Respondents were asked further to compare their assessment of *existing* relationships with a score indicating where on the scale they thought the relationships *ought* to be situated. While there were differences in the responses of clients and contractors, the overall findings revealed preferences for a combination of transactional and relational aspects: "Both clients and contractors value the certainty that clear initial specification of the contract with its attendant duties, obligations and expectations can provide. Subject to this, some flexibility and altruism is preferred, and it is felt to be necessary to trust the other party to perform appropriately on those aspects of the contract which cannot be measured . . . Both clients and contractors wish to engage in the sort of extensive co-operation, communication and mutual planning that can only arise under a relational, trust-based contracting relationship" (Walker and Davis 1999, 29).

Such studies in the commercial, health and local government sectors have confirmed the findings of previous research demonstrating the importance of trust and co-operation in exchange relationships, and have contributed to our overall understanding of relational contracting. However, in comparison with the potential scope of relational theory as set out in Macneil's recent clarification, the analyses appear unduly limited by an ideal-type methodology based on the polar opposition of discrete and relational contracts.[31] They have achieved little (unsurprisingly given the limited interpretation of Macneil) in the way of application or development of relational theory.[32]

3.2. ANALYSES FOCUSING ON THE COMMON CONTRACT NORMS AND BEHAVIOUR

The proper way to conduct relational analysis of contract behaviour, it is suggested, is not in terms of its conformity to models or types of discrete or relational contract, but through a methodology exploring the various institutional factors in the contractual environment of particular exchanges. The corollary of the postulate that "where the common contract norms are inadequately served, exchange relations of whatever kind fall apart" (Macneil 2000c, 893) is that the key to understanding the efficient operation of exchange relations lies in the analysis of the configuration of the common contractual norms in the institutional environment.

Implicit in Macneil's relational theory is a methodology that may be used to assess the state of contractual relations with reference to the condition of contract norms in a variety of economic and social settings (Vincent-Jones 2000, 325). Where contractual relations are operating effectively the contract norms are likely to be in "robust" condition and to be supported by additional relational norms. Where however relations are "in trouble" the contract norms are likely to be revealed "in varying

---

[31] This is so even though the researchers attempt to escape these limits with reference to additional categories of "administered contract" (Hughes *et al.* 1996, 163–5) and "regulated contract" (Bennet and Ferlie 1996, 51).

[32] The reification of contracts as "things" has tended to impede the analysis of complex behavioural phenomena. In some instances, findings have appeared either vacuous, as in the suggestion that full relational contracting is not necessarily desirable in the context of the public service on the ground that "the closer the partnership or relationship, the greater the potential for corrupt practice" (Walker and Davis 1999, 33), or misleading, as in the policy prescription that local authority managers will have to choose between "transactional" or "relational" contracting models according to the nature of the service (31). The point here is not that the issues raised are unimportant, but that they cannot fruitfully be addressed with such limited theoretical resources.

degrees of disarray" (Macneil 1983b, 351–2). "A sufficiently serious defect in any one of the contract norms will bring a contractual relation down over time". It is theoretically possible that all but one of the norms could be working well; however, "like a spiderweb, if one pulls on one bit, the whole web will be changed" (Macneil 1990, 168). Contractual relations in unhealthy condition will be characterised by disproportionate intensification of the planning and consent norms that serve to enhance discreteness and presentiation.

The radical restructuring of the U.K. public sector over the past 20 years, involving the splitting of responsibilities for purchasing and provision and the introduction of contracts and competition across a wide range of local authority, health and social services, may be regarded as having created ideal "laboratory" conditions for the testing of Macneil's relational theory. The "discretist" character of many of the public management reforms in this period is revealed in government policy documents and consultants' reports, which appear to have been heavily influenced by "classical" conceptions of the role of contract in private business relations (Vincent-Jones 1994a, 226–7; Vincent-Jones and Harries 1996b, 194). The disruption of pre-existing bureaucratic norms and patterns of behaviour by new forms of contractual arrangement was accompanied in many instances by a relative vacuum in the institutional environment necessary for relational contracting.

In local government the organisational response on the part of client and contractor managers was frequently to attempt to compensate for the lack of established patterns of co-operative behaviour and their supporting norms through detailed contract planning. In one study of local authority contracting under compulsory competitive tendering (CCT), detailed presentation was shown to have negative consequences, in supplying the parties with pretexts for the opportunistic pursuit of objectives unrelated to the main purpose of the exchange (Vincent-Jones and Harries 1996a, 183). In this adversarial climate, conflicts over contract monitoring and adjustment led increasingly to intractable disputes that unsurprisingly proved incapable of resolution by reference to written plans and contract documentation. Similarly in the health and social care sectors, research has shown that immediately after the introduction of a contract regime there is a tendency for relationships between purchaser and provider to deteriorate, and for there to be an emphasis on sanctions for poor performance (Deakin and Walsh 1996). Here and in local government, contract behaviour has become more relational as trust and other normative supports in the institutional environment have developed (Deakin and Walsh 1996, 41; Flynn and Williams, eds 1997). While contractual procedures and documentation may serve to enhance trust by giving information, clarifying responsibilities, improving accountability, and providing channels for problem solving, this role is contingent: "Co-operation is achieved overwhelmingly by formal and informal processes which bypass or supplement the contract. Most fundamentally, contract cannot secure co-operation where its underlying institutional conditions do not exist, or have been undermined, or have not had a chance to develop" (Vincent-Jones 1997, 158–9).

With regard to competitive tendering, Macneil has pointed to the inherently transactional or unrelational properties of this mode of contracting: "What is the most transactional of transactional ways to create contracts and their content? What else but competitive price bidding on unilaterally formed plans sent out for bids?" (Macneil 1974a, 756 n. 192). The verb "transactionise" describes the "conversion of behavior, social patterns, etc., into discrete transactional patterns" while "transactionising" refers to "the consequences of such conversion" (693 n. 4). The tender invitation sets out the detailed specification of client requirements in response to which competing potential providers bid a price at which the work can be done. Price is a key feature in the evaluation of bids, indeed the fundamental purpose of competitive tendering is to drive down costs through competition. The relationship between the parties at the planning stage becomes focused on the discrete question "how much?" (777). The emphasis on price may create problems in the course of the contract due to under-bidding. The "take it or leave it" form of the tender process may undermine the bargaining function of "establishing agreed terms which adhere to some kind of norm … convincing the parties not only that each is willing to deal on the terms mutually agreed to, but also that by some additional standard the terms agreed to are just" (778 n 247). Competitive tendering may have other transactionizing tendencies. The advance specification of obligations has a static quality. Extremely detailed specifications may actually tend to discourage the development of relations (761), and may provide hostages to fortune by creating the potential for excessively literal or pedantic contract interpretation. The prospect of re-tendering may create insecurity in the relationship where the present contractor is not confident of winning any further bid. These tendencies may be most acute where services rather than goods are concerned, since such exchanges are by nature (and need to remain in reality) particularly relational.

While competitive tendering for public services under the rigid constraints of CCT may be regarded as having been particularly prone to these tendencies, empirical research has shown the ways in which such transactional elements were counter-balanced in many instances by relational techniques involving the award of contracts to the same provider over a number of tendering rounds, the negotiation of details after the decision to award the tender, and the use of approved lists and knowledge of the tendering parties through reputation and past dealings (Vincent-Jones et al; 1998). The significant difference between voluntary and compulsory competitive tendering is that, in the former case, the client authority exercises greater choice, and the procedure is more flexible as to time-frames and selection criteria. It has been the *compulsory* nature of competitive tendering and the climate of mistrust accompanying this form of regulation that have given rise to contractual problems (Vincent-Jones and Harries 1998). Voluntary tendering allows greater scope for dialogue, with more face-to-face negotiation and give-and-take bargaining (sharing risks, identifying potential problems) in contract making, and for this reason is more likely to result in mutually satisfactory arrangements. Even under CCT, case studies of internal provision of housing management and legal services show that co-operative relationships can be established (Vincent-Jones et al. 1998; Vincent-Jones and Harries 1998; Harries and Vincent-Jones 2001). Competitive tendering, appropriately implemented, does not in practice pose an insuperable barrier to the development of relational contracting. Consistent with such empirical findings, government policy is moving towards more flexible and less prescriptive regulation in the local authority and other public service sectors, for example in the Best Value regime that has replaced CCT as a method of enhancing efficiency and effectiveness in the performance of local government functions.

4. Conclusion: Some Futures of Relational Contract

Macneil's relational contract theory has been influential in the U.K. within a variety of disciplinary perspectives and in the analysis of a remarkably wide range of contemporary contract phenomena. However, the statement that "while Macneil's work is widely cited, the level of engagement with its details has not been commensurate with its contribution, and the work is frequently misread by scholars" (Feinman

2000, 737) is as true of this country as the USA. Most interpretations of Macneil have drawn excessively on the several articles appearing in the 1970s and early 1980s, in which the discrete-relational spectrum features prominently but in which there is comparatively little reference to or development of the common contract norms.[33] While relational theory provides a solid foundation on which to ground both arguments for the reform of contract doctrine and prescriptions for the more efficient and effective use of contract, its full potential is only likely to be realised on the basis of a far deeper understanding of relational method than is currently generally evident in the literature.[34]

The interest expressed in Macneil's writings across the disciplinary boundaries of law, economics and socio-legal studies in the U.K. belies the claim that the relational approach is narrow in scope, or that it juxtaposes economic and sociological notions of contract such that "economics stands for self-interest, rational choice and market exchange, and sociology for solidarity, co-operation and community" (Teubner 2000, 405). The notion of relational contract as "the warm, co-operative interpersonal relation that overcomes the cold economic instrumentalism with a communitarian orientation" (405) owes nothing to Macneil, who has rejoined that "conflict is rife" both *within* the common contract norms (such as role integrity, reciprocity, and power) and *among* them (for example, between flexibility and planning/consent, and between propriety of means and the other norms) (Macneil 2000a, 433). The "normative permission of narrowly selfish behaviour" is a necessary feature of certain types of transaction such as the valuation of corporate securities in risk arbitrage (Campbell 1996b, 60). Similarly in the case of contracting for public services, the precarious nature of certain types of exchange relationship (expressed in the unsettled condition of the contract norms) may be reflected in relatively discrete client planning, without damaging the fundamentally relational nature of the transaction. Given these preliminary observations, and the reception of Macneil's work so far in the U.K., relational contract theory might be expected to develop productively in three main directions.

---

[33] The articles most commonly cited are (1974a), (1978a), and (1981b). Only five "principles or norms" were identified in (1974a), and then only in the Postscript.

[34] Both the theoretical debate over Macneil's relational theory, and the operationalization of the contract norms in empirical research, are much further advanced elsewhere. See Paulin *et al.* (1997) for a discussion and review of the extensive marketing and business and management studies literature.

First, with regard to reform of the contract law, Campbell has argued that a credible socio-legal rival to the classical doctrine now exists in the various strands of socio-legal scholarship that in different but complementary ways are beginning to constitute a co-operative or relational theory of contract (Campbell 1997b, 259). As has been shown above, however, only a relatively small proportion of this scholarship has paid much regard to Macneil, whose ideas have tended to be distorted by excessive attention to the discrete-relational spectrum at the expense of the broader behavioural context of the common contract norms. Nevertheless, this review has shown how classical doctrine is being contested in two ways drawing on Macneil, one involving the application of relational method in specific sub-fields as indicated by Feinman and illustrated by a number of writers exploring the scope of the law of obligations in intimate relations (Wightman 2000), and the other involving the more ambitious project for a general relational theory of contract as represented by Campbell. A central question for those seeking a better law of contract by either route concerns the relationship between the common contract norms and behaviour on the one hand, and specifically legal norms on the other. The need to reform contract law doctrine better to reflect and therefore to support commercial practice is widely accepted as a central task of contemporary socio-legal scholarship (Brownsword 1996; 2000, 55; Campbell 1997b, 252). In his recent clarification, Macneil is careful to distinguish *descriptions* of contract behaviour and law from *prescriptions* about the law that should govern (2000c, 877): "In essential contract theory there is a somewhat general assumption that typically the law will more or less track the common contract behavior and norms. This should not, however, be overread. There may often be good reasons why the law should not track the common contract behavior and norms" (893). Despite this caveat, Macneil remains broadly committed to the idea that the law should generally track the relational behaviour and norms found in the relations to which it applies (900).

Secondly, with regard to the study of contract behaviour, relational contract theory has the capacity to be developed further in the analysis of "non-monetised" social and political relations.[35] Macneil has argued

---

[35] Macneil criticises the view that a sharp distinction may be drawn between monetised exchange and all other types of exchange. Such a view "leaves economic exchange relations in one field, and social, including political, exchange relations in a different one" (Macneil 1990, 162). "What makes economic relations different is not that they are discrete

that, whatever the form in which human beings interact in modern societies as a result of the division of labour, "all common contract norms are essential to the processes of projecting exchange into the future; no exchange activity can continue for long absent of any of them" (Macneil 1983b, 366). Teubner's passing reference to Macneil in his analysis of the threat to modern democracy posed by privatisation and the decline of the nation state has created an opportunity for exploring the relevance of relational theory to the macro-phenomenon of "globalisation." In one view, the reduction in the "conscious co-ordination" of the world economy and the growth of private governance regimes may indicate a need radically to re-think our notions of contract and the role of the state, but this task may be addressed within relational theory, and nothing but confusion is added by the language of autopoiesis and "polycontextuality" (Campbell 2000, 444–5). Macneil argues that the world socio-economy is a "massively large and complex ongoing relational contract" that can be analysed through essential contract theory with particular reference to the norms of harmonization and the creation and restraint of power (Macneil 2000a, 433). Relational theory may have a role also in the analysis of non-monetised relations at a more micro-level, for example in assessing the effectiveness of the use of contract as an instrument of regulation of social relations between the state and citizens in the fields of welfare, education and criminal justice (Vincent-Jones 2000, 344–9).

Thirdly, relational contract theory might be developed further in analysing the new forms of quasi-market relationship accompanying the continued restructuring of public service provision. Contractual arrangements in these instances (for example under the Access to Justice Act 1999 or the Private Finance Initiative) are increasingly the product of specific central government policy frameworks involving multiple regulatory tiers and linkages, all of which are dependent in some sense on the quality of the common contract norms (Vincent-Jones 2000, 339–44). The increase in substantive policy-driven regulation of this kind, however, raises issues concerning the nature and legitimacy of government policy that cannot easily be addressed exclusively within

---

transactions and other social relations are not. The difference is that economic relations are ... social relations in which monetised exchange is particularly dominant, whereas that element is less dominant, conceivably lacking altogether, in other social exchange relations, such as political relations ... But political relations often do involve monetization" (160). Nevertheless the distinction remains useful and will be adopted for present purposes.

the framework of relational theory. Having observed that "where the common contract norms are inadequately served, exchange relations of whatever kind fall apart", Macneil is careful to note that "essential contract theory does not postulate that exchange relations should never fall apart" (Macneil 2000c, 893). The negative impact of government reforms on stable patterns of relational norms within inefficient and unaccountable public bureaucracies, for example, might be justified by organisational reforms that increase effectiveness and the quality of services to consumers. The absence of answers to the question of when it might be legitimate to encourage exchange relations to fall apart suggests that the limits of the relational approach may have been reached, and that resort to other theoretical concepts in the regulation literature may be required (Vincent-Jones 2000, 330–4).

In final conclusion, the best prospects for the future development of Macneil's ideas, whether in the analysis of contract behaviour or in respect of contract doctrine, appear to lie in the interpretation of relational theory as a methodology focusing on the common contract norms. Rather than counterposing "discrete" and "relational" contracts, each with its own distinctive mode of legal reasoning, the better view is that discreteness and relationality are products of the interplay of norms in the contractual environment of all exchanges. It is not that some contracts are discrete and some relational, but rather that discrete and relational norms are involved to a greater or lesser degree, and in a variety of combinations, in all human interactions.

PART 2

THE RELATIONAL THEORY OF CONTRACT

Chapter 4

Exchange and Co-operation

4.1. "Exchange Revisited: Individual Utility and Social Solidarity" (Macneil 1986)

4.2. "Political Exchange as Relational Contract" (Macneil 1990, 151–152, 152–154, 154–155, 155–156, 156–158)

The selections in this chapter set out Macneil's explicit attempt to construct a social philosophy of exchange as a background to the understanding of modern contract as specific form of exchange, displaying both features specific to itself, such as highly regularised proportionality, and general features of exchange, including an essential reciprocity expressive of co-operation. In "Political Exchange as Relational Contract", the statement of the ubiquity of exchange in "The Many Futures of Contract" is repeated.

4.1   Exchange Revisited: Individual Utility and Social Solidarity

Exchange—the giving up of something in return for receiving something else—is one of the most ubiquitous of all human behaviors. Indeed, in all societies only the most aberrant social behavior, if that, ever appears altogether lacking in some element of exchange, direct or indirect, short-term or long-term. As many views of exchange and its nature exist as there are viewers, but two in the non-Marxist world stand out as apparent polar opposites. One is the utilitarian position that exchange enhances the individual utilities of the participants respecting the goods being exchanged. The other, illustrated by Marshall Sahlins's (1974) *Stone*

Age Economics, is that certain patterns of exchange—categories of reciprocity—enhance social solidarity and *not* individual utility respecting the goods being exchanged, whereas other patterns enhance such individual utility and harm solidarity.

The thesis of this paper is that *no* pattern of exchange merely enhances individual utility respecting the goods being exchanged, and *all* patterns of exchange accepted by all parties enhance social solidarity. (Healey 1984, 43) (The acceptability qualification is necessary because, as will be seen, patterns of exchange viewed as inappropriate to the circumstances *are* destructive of solidarity.)

The foundation of this thesis lies in the fact that men are individuals born and dying one by one, each suffering his or her own hunger pains and enjoying his or her own full stomach, yet each individual absolutely requiring other human beings even to exist physically and psychologically, much less to become an ordinary whole human being. The consequence is that humans are—cannot otherwise be—inconsistently selfish and socially committed at the same time. No amount of melding into a sense of close community can ever do away with this fundamental individuality; and no separation can ever do away with this living through others. The upshot is that

> we are faced with an illogicality. Man is both an entirely selfish creature and an entirely social creature, in that man puts the interests of his fellows ahead of his own interests at the same time that he puts his own interests first. Such a creature is schizophrenic, and will, to the extent that it does anything except vibrate in utter frustration, constantly alternate between inconsistent behaviours— selfish one second and self-sacrificing the next. Man is, in the most fundamental sense of the word, irrational, and no amount of reasoning, no matter how sophisticated, will produce a complete and consistent account of human behavior, customs, or institutions—(Macneil 1938b, 348)

The importance for social analysis of recognizing this existential fact is immense. It is the failure of utilitarian models to incorporate the social aspect and of much Marxist dogma adequately to accept human separateness as a fact that at the end of the day prevents either from coming to grips with the issues bedeviling economics and anthropology.

It seems to me also that it is the failure of a great deal of social analysis to accept as a fundamental fact the essential logical inconsistency of man that makes so much of it fundamentally useless except as an intellectual game. The human love of consistency and order—perhaps originating in this very contradiction—makes it exceptionally difficult for us to live with the fact that we are, in part, eternally absurd. Hence our intellectually brilliant members often try desperately to develop systems of thought to show how our absurdity can be washed away. The task is impossible of achievement. We must instead accept the absurdity. (But most certainly not by descending into the theater of the totally absurd: that, too, is to deny the illogical *duality* of man.) Then we can talk about sensible things, such as how we must constantly resolve the inconsistencies, not in a truly orderly fashion, but in the only way we can, always temporarily in repeated ongoing interchanges with each other. In these, order and disorder, selfishness and sacrifice, will be resolved, but never in an entirely logical and consistent manner.

The alternative to recognizing the contradiction is to hope the hopeless. Consider, for example, Alan Hunt's (1981) criticisms of four pairs of contradictions by which theories have attempted to depict the social world. These contradictions—freedom-unfree, consciousness-being, determinism-voluntarism, and consent-coercion—simply reveal the difficulties of founding social analysis on the tension created by real contradictions. That social theory may misuse them goes without saying; but their use reflects the illogic of human nature rather than necessary defects in the contradictory concepts. To wish them away is simply one more cry to God to change the universe in which we find ourselves.

Of significance for the thesis advanced in this paper is the consequence of this selfish-social contradiction for patterns of reciprocity and solidarity:

> Two principles of behavior are essential to the survival of such a creature: solidarity and reciprocity. Man, being a choosing creature, is easily capable of paralysis of decision when two conflicting desires are in equipoise. The two principles of solidarity and reciprocity, neither of which can operate through time without the other, solve this problem. Getting something back for something given neatly releases, or at least reduces, the tension in a creature desiring to be both selfish and social at the same time; and solidarity—a belief in being able to depend on another—permits the projection of reciprocity through time (Macneil 1983b, 348–349)

It is out of the contradictory duality of selfishness and sociality and the reciprocity and solidarity required for achievement of human desires that the thesis of this paper grows: no pattern of exchange solely enhances individual utility respecting the goods being exchanged, and all patterns of exchange accepted by the parties enhance social solidarity.

Because I came to these issues via reading anthropological materials—particularly Sahlins—the illustrations in the paper center on primitive societies, but the conclusions apply to all societies, including the nineteenth-twentieth-century market economies and all segments of today's world economy.

Three patterns of exchange are explored in this paper: generalized reciprocity, the gift route to social solidarity; nonspecialized reciprocity, the low exchange-surplus, mechanical route; and specialized reciprocity, the high exchange-surplus, organic route.

Terminology

In this highly ideological area, inadvertent, but great, differences between the writer's meaning and the reader's understanding of common words are especially difficult to avoid. Strict definition and confinement of each term to the definition will be followed here to reduce that risk.

Goods are anything people want. Since it is necessary in understanding social analysis of exchange to distinguish other goods from the good of solidarity, the word "goods" does not, for the purpose of this paper, include solidarity itself. Although most often "goods" refers to material goods, the word can refer to relatively nonmaterial things such as a smile or a compliment.

Economic refers to meeting the material needs of people. In this it departs from both Sahlins (1974, 185–187) and modern utilitarian usage equating economic with scarcer (Prattis 1982) being much closer to usages of what Cooter and Rappoport (1984) refer to as the material welfare school of economics. (Sahlins 1974, 192)

Exchange is any "vice-versa movement" between or among individuals. The vice-versa movement of goods may occur in either "specialized exchange" or "nonspecialized exchange." These terms refer to the division (or specialization) of labor.

Specialized exchange is the product of division of labor—the inevitable product. An example is the exchanges occurring in the Huon Gulf

Trade, where the Tami islanders make wooden bowls, the southern villagers make pottery, the Busama are large food producers, and each exchanges its speciality with the others. (Sahlins 1974, 285–291) Another example is exchange between a husband and wife to the extent that a sexual specialization of labor exists. In specialized exchange the vice-versa flow is necessarily of different goods, although eddies may occur.

Nonspecialized exchange is any vice-versa movement among people *not* resulting from specialization of labor. An example of nonspecialized exchange is the giving of a present, say a pig, to a kinsman, with the understanding that at some appropriate occasion in the future a pig will be returned. Such exchange would remain nonspecialized if the understanding was that the kinsman could return at his option either a pig or some other commodity of roughly the same scale of value. It might or might not be nonspecialized exchange if the understanding was that not a pig, but some other commodity of equivalent value, for example, taro, would be returned. In the latter case one would need to know more, for example, does the donor concentrate on raising pigs and the donee on raising taro, so that pig-taro exchange is a common pattern, or is it merely an isolated one? (Repeated movement of one commodity in one direction and another in the opposite [directly or indirectly] normally indicates the occurrence of specialized exchange.) Nonspecialized exchange also occurs when similar tasks are shared, for example, when people pair off to do each other's haying. (Hawkes 1977)

Both specialized and nonspecialized exchange often occur at the same time or relative to connected events, for example, reciprocal feasts as part of a trading relation, where both traders raise their own food but where the main purpose of the relation is to exchange wooden bowls for pottery.

Individual utility means individual benefit from having particular goods for one's use. A participant in an exchange is a *"maximizer"* of individual utility when no other goal conflicts with his desire to secure the most goods in return for giving the least *in the exchange in question*. (This is a fictional situation.) A maximizing participant would, if he could, take what he seeks for nothing. A maximizing participant may, nevertheless, have other nonconflicting goals, such as the desire to increase his own power through driving the toughest possible bargain. But if an exchanger has a goal conflicting with his desires to secure the most economic (material) goods in return for giving the least *in the exchange in question*, for example, the desire to appear generous by giving favorable terms or the desire not to violate the law against theft, he ceases to be a maximizer. He may remain an *"enhancer"* of individual utility wishing to give the least goods in return for the most, but only to the extent possible within bounds created by the conflicting goals. In the examples given this would mean without appearing ungenerous or without becoming a thief. (The words "enhancer" and "enhancing" are used here to avoid becoming involved in the debate about satisficing vs. maximizing.)

Solidarity or social solidarity is a state of mind or, rather, a state of minds. It is a belief not only in future peace among those involved but also in future harmonious affirmative cooperation. (An equally good word for solidarity is "trust.") Solidarity by no means requires liking the one trusted nor is it dependent upon a belief that the other is altruistic; nor does solidarity necessarily imply friendship, although friendship often is a manifestation of solidarity. From the viewpoint of an individual, he may sacrifice solidarity, enhance it, or even, in theory, maximize it if he has no conflicting goals.

Exchange-surplus is used in this paper to describe the enhanced utility enjoyed *by a society* as a result of an exchange between members of the society. The modifier "exchange" distinguishes this kind of increase in utility from utility produced in other ways, such as an increase in the total stocks of food in the society resulting from the efforts of a single fisherman. The following illustration shows how exchange-surplus is generated.

If A and B, the sole members of a hypothetical society, each motivated to enhance his individual utility, exchange meat for fish, the total stocks of meat and fish in the A B society are unaffected. But the utility of the stock of provisions *as viewed by the members of the society* has risen, because each member has evidenced more desire for what he received than for what he surrendered. Nor does this surplus result merely from the prospect of happier taste buds; a better balanced diet also is in view. Thus, exchange-surplus has been created. (It is merely added to the already existing utility: the main source of utility was the hunting and fishing rather than the exchange. Nevertheless, to produce greater utility this economy evidently requires distributional exchange as well as production.)

If in the foregoing example A is generally a hunter and B generally a fisherman, and if this meat-for-fish exchange is common and generally in the same directions, then the example is one of specialized exchange. Such exchange is a prerequisite to continuing the division of labor. Without it A must become also a fisherman or go without fish, and B must become also a hunter or go without meat. In sum, specialized exchange always produces an exchange-surplus and the continuance of a division of labor depends on its occurring.

Nonspecialized exchange may also produce exchange-surplus. A and B may be nonspecialists; each hunts and fishes. But suppose A has, through good luck, been relatively more successful in the latest hunting and B relatively more successful in the latest fishing. The fortuitous character of the exchange does not prevent it from enhancing the individual utilities of both nor from producing exchange-surplus for the AB society. But there is a significant difference, namely, that failures to carry out nonspecialized exchange do not prevent continuance of a division of labor, there being none to start. Nonspecialized exchange is thus not, for direct material purposes, as essential as specialized exchange. (It may be and often is vital for other purposes, including achieving the solidarity necessary to continue economic activities, as will appear.) Nevertheless, extensive fluctuations of various kinds of stocks of goods among nonspecialists are bound to happen in any given society in ways leading to exchanges creating significant exchange-surplus. In technologically advanced societies the widespread existence of markets for used goods among ultimate consumers is a good example.

Gift is here used to describe an apparently unidirectional transaction, or part of a transaction, where the element of *economic* (material) exchange is so attenuated that resulting economic surplus, if any, is more properly called *donative surplus* than exchange-surplus. Nevertheless, to whatever extent the donee is perceived as having a greater material need for what is given than does the donor, the goods have a greater economic utility for the society after their transfer than before. This may be one reason why generalized reciprocity—close to, but not quite, one-way transfers—may be one way for long periods of time, perhaps indefinitely. Neither party will view the transfer as materially wasteful but as economically productive.

Sahlins, (1974, 149ff) following in the tradition of Mauss, argues that gifts are made to create social solidarity, a proposition accepted in this paper. The following section deals with the relation of this proposition to exchange and particularly to the enhancement of individual utility.

Gifts, Individual Utility, and Social Solidarity

These subjects may be explored by starting with two unrelated individual utility maximizers (necessarily fictional) of equal fighting power seeking

95

the most goods and giving the least in this exchange. One is a farmer and one a hunter. F has a supply of potatoes, and H has a supply of meat, each supply being well guarded. F wants meat; H wants potatoes. Each, being rational in the neoclassical microeconomic sense, would prefer to kill or disable the other quickly, or at least easily and safely, and take what is desired. But the balance of fighting power makes this an unpromising course for either; hence exchange is the only way they may satisfy their respective desires. But is exchange possible?

If F will part with no more than two pounds of potatoes for one pound of meat, and H will part with no more than half a pound of meat for two pounds of potatoes, no exchange will take place; each will go off grumbling, carefully looking over his shoulder to avoid any sudden change for the worse in the military situation.

But suppose that F would, if necessary to get meat, give as much as five pounds of potatoes for one pound of meat; and suppose that H would, if necessary to get potatoes, trade as low as pound for pound. Now exchange may take place, at ratios from 1 to 5 pounds of potatoes for 1 pound of meat. An exchange at *any* of these figures will improve the positions of *both* F and H relative to not having any exchange. Thus, if exchange occurs (at any of the ratios), each will be conferring a gain on the other.

As F and H slowly and reciprocally shove the agreed amounts toward each other with one hand, while clutching a club in the other, no one would perceive this as an exchange with an element of gift. Thus, in this prototype of the neoclassical microeconomic model no gift-induced social solidarity is created between these fictional stranger-enemies.

Now place F and H in a social setting, a limited one recognizing and protecting property rights in various ways and creating internalizations precluding F and H from using force or theft. Little changes. Mutual gain through exchange remains possible, again at ratios ranging from 1:1 to 5:1. But, since F and H remain individual utility maximizers, again no gift will result irrespective of the actual ratio of exchange, and again no gift-induced social solidarity is created.

To avoid misunderstanding, an aside is in order about the ratio at which the foregoing exchange would occur. Assuming equal knowledge about each other, equal ability at concealing feelings, equal and symmetrical intensity of desires as each moves from his most favorable ratio to his least, and the like, the exchange will tend to approximate 3:1 potatoes to meat. No sense of equity is required to cause this, only maximizing behavior in the face of mutual knowledge that each is a maximizer with no reason to move off dead center in favor of the other, and with reasons not to do so (Cook, Emerson and Gilmore 1983; Cook and Emerson 1978). (The result described assumes that some knowledge of the desires of each slips by the shield of guile each tries to erect. If zero knowledge throughout is postulated, probably no exchange will occur at all, and if it does it could occur anywhere from 1:1 to 5:1 on a random basis. In real life zero knowledge will not be the case. Other assumptions about the relative information and power of the parties may be made with different exchange ratios resulting. But whatever ratio results, in these artificial circumstances, they will reflect no sense of equity.)

Now enrich the sociality of the FH society. A belief prevails that the value of potatoes and meat is in the ratio of around 3 or 4:1. (Conscious valuing of this kind appears to smack of an individualism less than universal in human behavior, especially in highly communal societies. But it in fact occurs even where the primary aims of exchange are the achievement of social solidarity through economic exchange.) F and H remain individual utility maximizers, although the artificiality of this supposition constantly increases as they become increasingly social. If either succeeds in pressing the other outside the 3:1 or 4:1 ratio to his own advantage, it will be solely because of some inequality in their information and power. There will be no gift and no gift-induced social solidarity. Nor will an exchange within the 3:1 or 4:1 ratio itself involve any gift; the result remains motivated by a desire to maximize on each side, not by a desire to follow the social norm.

Next make F and H kin, and, more realistically, merely enhancers of utility, not maximizers. H has been having a hard time of it lately. To help H, F offers six pounds of potatoes for one pound of meat, even though he knows that, if pressed, would settle for as little as 1:1. No one conversant with these facts would doubt that F has made H a gift of at least one pound of potatoes. This is the amount by which his offer exceeds the highest he would possibly make on the basis solely of enhancing his individual utility. The transaction thus can produce gift-enhanced social solidarity. (It is an especially gentle, undemanding form of gift in that its form, economic exchange, obscures the obligations of reciprocity imposed on the donee.)

Finally, suppose that F, under some economic pressure himself, or perhaps not caring quite so much about H, instead offers H 4.5 (rather than 6) pounds of potatoes for one pound of meat. This is less than he would have given if really necessary in order to secure the meat, but it is half a pound more than the upper value the FH society places on meat.

97

At least half a pound of the potatoes will be understood as a gift. In fact, in such a case, some of the potatoes *within* the 3 or 4:1 range may be viewed as a gift, since usually there would be no reason to think that H, in a bargain not influenced by these special circumstances, could necessarily have convinced F to give 4 pounds rather than somewhere between 3 and 4.

Where F gives 4.5 pounds, he is motivated in the exchange *both* to enhance his individual utility and to make a gift. An example of this sort of behavior is described by Sahlins (1974, 268) from Ewers's account of the Blackfoot Indians. Where the average man gave two horses for a shirt and leggings, the rich man gave three to nine horses. Keeping in mind that individual utility means individual benefit from having particular goods for one's use, a maximizer of individual utility cannot, but an enhancer of individual utility can, do this sort of thing. Gift-enhanced solidarity can be and is, therefore, brought about by exchange which is significantly, but not entirely, motivated by desires for individual utility. Much of Sahlins's assemblage of anthropological knowledge suggests that this behavior is very common, and little, if any, contradicts that conclusion.

Sahlins himself supports the foregoing argument in his discussion of the difficulty of deducing standard going rates of exchange: "Even if a table of equivalences is elicited—by whatever dubious means—actual exchanges often depart radically from these standards, tending however to approximate them in socially peripheral dealings, as between members of different communities or tribes, while swinging wildly up and down in a broad internal sector where considerations of kinship distance, rank and relative affluence are effectively in play. This last qualification is important: the material balance of reciprocity is subject to the social sector. (Sahlins 1974, 279)

The existence of exchange-surplus is the factor permitting a range in which these dual motives can operate. In its absence a participant in an exchange has to choose *between* making a gift by engaging in a losing exchange (in terms of his own utility) or deriving a benefit to himself at the cost of a net loss to the other. (A third alternative, dead even, would have no *economic* reason for occurring, although it can and does occur for other reasons.)

Gift giving in a utility-enhancing exchange is but one way by which enhancement of individual utility through exchange can contribute to social solidarity. The following section focuses on strengthening of social solidarity by utility-enhancing exchange itself, exchange not putatively altruistic.

STRENGTHENING SOCIAL SOLIDARITY THROUGH EXCHANGE AIMED AT
ENHANCING INDIVIDUAL UTILITY

If one starts with the neoclassical utilitarian model, it is easy to slip into
the fallacy of thinking that utility-enhancing exchange contributes
nothing to social solidarity, or worse, harms it (Sahlins 1974, 195). This is
because in the model the participants lack all relations apart from
whatever transaction is being analyzed (Macneil 1981b). A transaction
"opened and conducted toward net utilitarian advantage" (Sahlins 1974,
195) is, then, one between those two individual maximizers and total
strangers of equal fighting strength, our old friends, F and H. Even
though their exchange produces exchange-surplus, no solidarity results,
no more than if two unrelated rogue male lions happen to corner a
wildebeest that would have escaped either alone.

But exchange simply does not happen this way. All real life exchange
takes place in the context of relations more extensive than the exchange
itself, relations preventing individuals from being individual utility
maximizers respecting the goods of each exchange. At the very least their
desires to maximize individual utility from *this* exchange are likely to
conflict with desires to maximize individual utility from anticipated
future exchanges with the same or a related party. This interdependence
for the future gives each a real *present* need for social solidarity. Moreover,
"the very least" is rarely all there is to an exchange relation; most
certainly that is true not only of kinship relations analyzed by Sahlins, but
also up to and including intertribal trade and most—in many ways, all—
exchanges in technologically advanced societies (Macneil 1981b).

It is thus a mistake to think of "net utilitarian advantage" in its outside-
of-society context involving fictional maximizers of individual utility,
equally powerful or not. In the real world there are only enhancers of
individual utility immersed in relations creating countless contramotives.
Exchange is virtually always *relational* exchange, that is, exchange carried
on within relations having significant impact on its goals, conduct, and
effect. (Relational exchange includes Sahlins's category of generalized
reciprocity.)

The contramotives have a bearing on the importance of exchange-
surplus as a contributor to social solidarity. An individual utility
maximizer may be perfectly well aware of the fact that the deal he
makes creates exchange-surplus, but his *sole* concern about that utility is
to grab as much of it for himself as he can. He will feel nothing but regret
at whatever amount is snared by the other party and nothing but

99

happiness that the other failed to secure more of it. That is not, however, the case in relational exchange. It has already been seen how relational exchange can be conducted to confer gifts, not in complete substitution for enhancing individual utility, but as an additional goal. Such an exchange is "opened and conducted toward net utilitarian advantage" *and* toward making a gift. But this is far from the whole story.

Relational exchange also creates circumstances where the long-run *individual* economic (material) interests of each party conflict with any short run desires to maximize individual utility respecting the goods in any particular exchange: the more relational the exchange, the more artificial becomes the idea of maximization. The capacity of an exchange to produce exchange-surplus now takes on further importance, beyond that of simply making an exchange possible and providing opportunities to make gifts. That utility constitutes a pool of wealth which can be shared as well as grabbed, shared not to make a gift but out of deep economic self-interest. Without recognizing this precise point, Sahlins sums up the consequences: "When people meet who owe each other nothing yet presume to gain from each other something, peace of trade is the great uncertainty. In the absence of external guarantees, as of a Sovereign Power, peace must be otherwise secured: by extension of sociable relations to foreigners—thus the trade-friendship or trade-kinship—and, most significantly, *by the terms of the exchange itself*. The economic ratio is a diplomatic manoeuvre ... The rate of exchange takes on functions of a peace treaty (Sahlins 1974, 302–303).

Because solidarity is essential to harmonious *affirmative* cooperation as well as to peacemaking, more must be said. The allocation of the exchange-surplus in *this* exchange must be viewed in terms of allocation of exchange-surplus in future exchange. This becomes especially important in specialized exchange, upon which continuance of the division of labor depends. The husband, for example, who fails to bring home to his wife fair amounts of his fish catch, may find less plantain in his bowl or pleasure in his bed in the future. These affirmative aspects of future cooperation are just as fundamental as peacekeeping. (Sahlins seems generally to think of solidarity primarily in the negative sense of peace. While his views of humanity are not as bleak as those of the utilitarian, this negative approach to solidarity does seem unrealistically stark. Only the incorporation of affirmative aspects of cooperation and social harmony rescues humanity from being summarized as quite brutish and not very social brutes at that.)

Over time, exchanges made with these long-range motivations

produce norms to which the participants expect to adhere and to which they expect adherence from other participants. These norms generated between the parties in relational exchange cannot be truly separated from norms generated by the society of which they are a part, for example, kinship obligations and modern contract law. But whatever their source, departure from the norms will harm, social solidarity. Even more important, however, is the affirmative aspect. Since any repeated behavior creates norms and strengthens existing norms (Lewis 1969; Ullman-Margalit 1977), making exchanges in accordance with relational norms strengthens them. Since the norms themselves are important aspects of social solidarity, simply conducting the exchanges in accordance with them thus contributes to solidarity.

Thus far I have made no distinction between specialized and unspecialized exchange, except indirectly in that the former always produces exchange-surplus, whereas the latter may not. But specialized exchange is a creator of social solidarity in a further way. It is a prerequisite to the continuance of a division of labor. And participants in the division of labor are inevitably—always potentially and usually in outcome—inter-dependent in that continuance of labor specialization by one depends upon continuance by the other. Thus relational specialized exchange is always dependent exchange in the sense that each participant, to the extent he wishes to continue specialization, is dependent on the other for future exchanges, to whatever extent alternative specialists of the same kind are unavailable. Given this, wherever future exchange is anticipated, specialized exchange is interdependent exchange. At the very least this restrains tendencies toward fraud, sharp practice, and the like. Each specialized exchange in such circumstances is a major contributor to a continuing web of interdependence. Thus even though the motivation for the specialized exchange may largely be enhancement of individual utility, its mere occurrence is a contributor to social solidarity.

CONFLICT OF MOTIVES IN RELATIONAL EXCHANGE: EXCHANGE-TENSION

Participants in relational exchange are under a great tension. See, for example, Sahlins's summary of Radcliffe-Brown's account of the Andamans: "[It] suggests a higher level of generalized reciprocity within the local group, . . . and more balanced forms of reciprocity between people of different bands, particularly in durables. The exchange of presents is characteristic of interband meetings, an exchange that could amount to swapping local specialities. In this sector. '*It requires a good deal of tact to avoid the unpleasantness that may arise if a man thinks he has not received things as valuable as he has given.*'" (Sahlins 1974, 234 emphasis added) Such difficulties are by no means limited to interband exchange but occur also in kinship exchange, as the proverbs and behavior patterns Sahlins describes illustrate (1974, 124–127), although he would reject the analysis made here. (1974, 126–127, n 12) Instead, he analyzes the situations treated on those pages in terms of kinship distance. That analysis does not, however, resolve the basic question of the existence of such tension.

A similar tension also exists in Sahlins's generalized reciprocity, as is demonstrated by the wheedling, evasion, et cetera involved in it, (Sahlins 1974, 268ff) although there the donor is getting back so little materially that it would be silly to attribute to him *any* motive of *gaining* in economic utility by the exchange. Instead his tension arises from conflicts between his desires to be generous (for whatever reason), but not too generous, that is, to limit his material costs, as well as other possible conflicts, for example, wishes not to reward excessive laziness or concern that a particular gift will produce scorn rather than deference (Sahlins 1974, 246).

Exchange-tension is endemic in relational exchange of all kinds and, particularly, in specialized exchange with its inherent exchange-surplus. Such tension arises from the inevitable conflicts between participants' desires to enhance individual utilities from the exchange in question and their desires to enhance social solidarity. Whether the conflict arises almost entirely from narrow desires to enhance individual utility in the future or from countless possible broader desires, it is there. One desire calls for getting everything possible from each exchange; the other calls for the opposite, sacrifice in each exchange.

Summary

The position to this point may be summarized as follows: (1) The nature of man—at once a part of society and yet separate from it, inconsistently selfish and socially committed at the same time—creates a permanent tension of motives whenever his narrow self-interest varies from his interest as a part of society. In the realm of exchange this tension manifests itself in exchange-tension, a conflict between desires to enhance individual utility respecting the goods in the exchange and desires to enhance social solidarity. (2) Social solidarity is a state of harmonious affirmative co-operation as well as of peace. (3) Specialized exchange produces exchange-surplus, as may some nonspecialized exchange. (4) Relational specialized exchange, that is, virtually all real life specialized exchange, even where heavily motivated by desires to enhance individual utility, creates social solidarity through a sharing of exchange-surplus, through repeated following of norms, and through the web of interdependence resulting from the division of labor. The norms are generated both between the participants inter se and in the larger social relations, for example, kinship, village, company, in which the smaller one occurs, (5) Gift making enhances social solidarity. (It may also have the effect of creating a donative surplus.) (6) Exchange can be, and often is, the consequence of dual motives: making a gift and enhancing individual utility respecting the goods of the particular exchange; when so made the gift motive serves to enhance solidarity. (7) It is the existence of exchange-surplus that permits motives to enhance both solidarity and individual utility to be satisfied by the same exchange.

Types of Reciprocity

Three kinds of reciprocity emerge from the foregoing, all leading to social solidarity: generalized reciprocity—the gift route to solidarity; non-specialized reciprocity—the low exchange-surplus, mechanical route to solidarity; and specialized reciprocity—the high exchange-surplus, organic route to solidarity.

GENERALIZED RECIPROCITY—THE GIFT ROUTE TO SOLIDARITY

The definition here of generalized reciprocity follows Sahlins: "Transactions that are putatively altruistic, transactions on the line of assistance given, and *if possible and necessary*, assistance returned (1974, 193 emphasis added). He suggests that a "good pragmatic indication of generalized reciprocity is a sustained one-way flow" of materials (1974, 194). It is thus economically largely a one-way street. with a very loose reciprocity, reserved for better times for the donee, greater needs of the donor, and the like. Although it is putatively altruistic, in fact reciprocity occurs but primarily in terms of reputation, prestige, and power rather than in economic returns. Generalized reciprocity is heavily oriented toward maintenance of social solidarity. Sahlins, for example, labels it the "solitary extreme" and puts it at the top of his hierarchy of solidarity-building types of reciprocity. This placement is justified only if such gifts, disconnected from real economic exchange, are somehow *more* productive of social solidarity than are other types of reciprocity. As will appear, I do not believe this is to be the case.

NONSPECIALIZED RECIPROCITY—THE LOW EXCHANGE-SURPLUS, MECHANICAL ROUTE TO SOLIDARITY

Nonspecialized reciprocity—exchange *not* resulting from the division of labor—is typically characterized by a very low, or even nonexistent, exchange-surplus. An example of nonspecialized exchange is what Sahlins calls "balanced reciprocity." Its epitome, perfectly balanced reciprocity, is the simultaneous exchange of the same kinds of goods in the same amounts. But it also extends to include "transactions which stipulate returns of commensurate worth or utility within a finite and narrow period." (Sahlins 1974, 194–195) Here, according to Sahlins, the material side of the transaction is at least as critical as the social. (This is questionable indeed, respecting perfectly balanced reciprocity, since *no* economic [material] change occurs; the material aspects, *i.e.*, exchanging of economic goods, thus serve *only* symbolic roles.) The pragmatic test of balanced reciprocity is the inability to tolerate one-way flows of materials and disruption of relations by failures to reciprocate within leeways of limited time and equivalence, essentially the same requirement for the continuing of social exchange (Blau 1964, 88ff). In both primitive (Sahlins 1974, 215–219) and modern societies exchange of food and entertainment is often this type. In Durkheim's (1984, 31–67) terms, nonspecialized reciprocity creates mechanical solidarity.

Given the low exchange-surplus in nonspecialized reciprocity, the only apparent reason for engaging in it—and it is very common—is to enhance social solidarity. Thus, although Sahlins puts it only at the midpoint of his hierarchy of solidarity-building techniques, it in fact appears to be at least equal to all the others.

A word about symbolism is in order here. Obviously, much complicating symbolism occurs in nonspecialized reciprocity. By definition, nonspecialized reciprocity involves like producers and like consumers, yielding segmental, mechanical solidarity. Yet the actual exchange behavior simulates partially that occurring in specialized exchange, that is, exchange resulting from the division of labor, which produces organic solidarity. What is the symbolism here? Is it, as Sahlins implies, aimed at simulating gifts, that is, generalized reciprocity, to knit solidarity? Or is it, as Durkheim might argue, aimed at simulating specialized exchange, with its implications of the organic solidarity of the division of labor? In fact, both simulations are probably occurring at the same time, with low exchange-surplus exchange symbolizing for exchangers in larger groups both the organic solidarity of the household resulting from the sexual and other divisions of labor and the mechanical solidarity of similar households linked into a tribal band or, in the modern context, in a condominium association. for example.

SPECIALIZED EXCHANGE—THE HIGH EXCHANGE-SURPLUS, ORGANIC ROUTE TO SOLIDARITY

Specialized reciprocity—exchange resulting from the division of labor— is characterized by a large exchange-surplus, a direct consequence of the interdependence created by that division. Such interdependence may be individualized, as in the case of the sexual division of labor within the household. That is to say, the interdependence is between individual A (wife) and individual B (husband). Or it may be generic, as in the case of trade where people in category A (wooden bowl makers) are *as a class* interdependent with the people in category B (pottery makers) *as a class*. (Differences between individualized and generic interdependence will be explored later.)

The *size* of the exchange-surplus does not depend upon which of these categories encompasses a particular exchange. Size of the exchange-surplus depends instead upon such factors as the economic and social importance of the subjects of exchange and the importance of the existing division of labor in maintaining production of the goods in question. Suppose, for example, that a hunter-gatherer band trades nuts gathered in the forest for plantation coconuts with a farming tribe. The exchange-surplus may be very low if each group lacks very intense desires for the other's product, either because nuts and coconuts are seen as really quite interchangeable or because the farmers could quite easily gather the nuts for themselves, and nonplantation coconut palms are relatively common in forest glades, or both. If, however, each group sees each product as quite important to a proper diet, *and* the costs of abandoning the specialization of labor are high, the exchange-surplus will be high as well. Jean Peterson's (1978) description of protein-carbohydrate exchange between Agta and Palanan provides an example.

The allocation of a large exchange-surplus always raises difficulties. How do the parties to the exchange go about the allocation? And what preserves solidarity while they engage in this conflict-laden task?

We can begin to answer these questions by examining the most important division of labor in primitive societies, the sexual division. So solidary is the domestic relation that Sahlins refuses even to admit it to his scheme of reciprocities. "But reciprocity is always a 'between' relation: however solidary, it can only perpetuate the separate economic identities of those who so exchange." (Sahlins 1974, 94) He sees household distribution instead as a pooling of resources, pooling being "socially a *within* relation, the collective action of a group." (188) (It may be noted that pooling or redistribution, as Sahlins describes it, also occurs extensively in modern contractual relations and in many ways, *e.g.*, flat hourly wages for workers with differing production levels.) Sahlins adopts Morgan's label "communism in living" to describe the domestic economy, and goes on: "Householding is the highest form of economic sociability: 'from each according to his abilities and to each according to his needs'—*from the adults that with which they are charged by the division of labor, to them, but also to the elders, the children, the incapacitated, regardless of their contributions, that which they require.*" (94 emphasis added)

Sahlins's description of the household and its exclusion from his scheme of reciprocities suggests a melding of human individuality into a social structure that does not occur in ordinary human existence. The household is as close to communism in living as humans are ever likely to get for any length of time, but they nevertheless remain individuals eternally—inconsistently selfish and socially committed at the same time. Not only is reciprocity essential to the household, the household economy is the very seedbed of human reciprocity, a seedbed stretching back to our evolutionary primate roots.

If we restore the household to schemes of reciprocity, much of what Sahlins describes in the household falls in the category of generalized reciprocity, for example, one-way material flows to children and the incapacitated. But between husband and wife specialized—high exchange-surplus—exchange occurs. Nevertheless most of it is conducted without careful or conscious measuring of the allocation of exchange-surplus. Rather, it is conducted through the ordinary day-to-day ebb and flow of effort and consumption. Thus the exchange between husband and wife is in the *form* of generalized reciprocity, while in substance it is not one-way, the test of *real* generalized reciprocity. If we reject Sahlins's idea of a melding of individual personalities within the household, why and how does this happen?

The answer lies in recognition that intense division of labor yields intense interdependence—in the case of the household, individualized interdependence. Intense interdependence creates an intense need for solidarity, not only its negative side, peace, but even more important, its affirmative side, active cooperation. Workable ways of sharing the large exchange-surplus become vital to continuance of the relation. The more intense is this kind of individualized interdependence, the more likely it is that norms will emerge of a sharing, noncalculating, putatively altruistic character. The goals of the individual become primarily those of enhancing solidarity rather than enhancing individual utility respecting the goods in any given exchange. Indeed, one of the characteristics of such relations is avoidance of "given exchanges"; it is likely to be virtually impossible to say what was given in return for what. This essential fuzziness is enhanced by distributions through generalized reciprocity to children, the infirm, etc.

Since it is postulated here that the individuals in the household do not lose their individual selfishness, the question is, what, if anything, based in whole or in part on self-interest, sustains their solidary beliefs? At root the answer is expectations of continued interdependence. Those expectations lead each to trust that the self-interest of the other will lead to adequate future concern for the interests of the one trusting. Generally, each can have this trust only if he also believes the other has such a trust in him. What keeps it all going is the reinforcement resulting from regular and sufficient realization of those expectations. Such reinforcement permits continuance in the household of forms of reciprocity not requiring constant conscious concern about modes of enforcing reciprocation or specifying in detail the terms of exchange. At their strongest such solidary beliefs become almost entirely unconscious and habitual. And that is our closest approach to "communism in living."

Thus in the household we find intensely specialized exchange, generating a high exchange-surplus, but taking place in the form of generalized reciprocity, the gift route to solidarity. We may speculate about why this occurs—efficiency, a drive toward altruism etc.—but the fact of its occurrence in the prototypical household seems beyond dispute.

Now contrast specialized exchange in the household to that between relative strangers, and we arrive at such terms as "haggling" and "barter." Sahlins's baleful view of these processes puts them in negative reciprocity, "the unsociable extreme"—"the attempt to get something for nothing with impunity, the several forms of appropriation, transactions opened and conducted toward net utilitarian advantage." (Sahlins 1974, 195) But Sahlins is simply wrong; these too are processes for building the solidary belief, for building trust. Consider the situation. Each of the participants knows that an exchange will create an exchange-surplus. Each, within the bounds that make this a trade, rather than murder and theft, would like to grab as much of that exchange-surplus as possible. Each knows that he cannot get it all, since the other will not trade for zero gain. Each is distrustful of the other. So they haggle.

Haggling is a social process, and it is one that cannot help but convey information—information about the goods, about their value, both in terms of costs of production and in terms of "market" (what others might give for them), and, above all, information about how each views the exchange-surplus. The upshot is—must be if a trade occurs—some kind of convincing each that he is not being ludicrous in giving up an undue share of the exchange-surplus. (Between strangers generosity readily becomes either guile or gullibility or both.)

The edifice of trust built by haggling as described above hardly compares with that of husband and wife, of kinship or simulated kinship trading partnerships or even of countless modern trading relations, to say nothing of employment relations. But such haggling is building trust in an otherwise nonsolidary desert. It is working in an environment of an "unsociable extreme;" nonetheless it is a sociable process, a builder of solidarity, and as "extremely sociable" as the circumstances permit.

The foregoing view is contrary to Sahlins's, who implies that haggling and barter tear solidarity apart. Refuting his position requires dealing with his extensive and convincing evidence that haggling is widely viewed in primitive societies as antisocial. This is, however, easy enough: haggling *is* socially destructive when used where an edifice of trust sufficient to obviate its need already exists or should exist. To haggle with a kinsman is to tell him he cannot be trusted to look out sufficiently for your interests. It is to insult him and treat him as a stranger. Haggling also emphasizes one party's desire to enhance individual utility at the expense of the other. Haggling is also antisocial in another sense whenever it is applied to nonspecialized exchange. Since haggling normally suggests a fairly high level of exchange-surplus, using it where the level is low displays a willingness to try to persuade the other to enter a transaction at net economic disadvantage, to make a gift. But it will be a gift appearing to be a trade. This will deprive the donor of the opportunity to bind the haggler through the gift route to solidarity, the normal element of reciprocity in gifts. Such a transaction makes a contribution neither to the donor's economic utility nor to solidarity. In short, haggling in such circumstances is a sneaky, antisocial way to solicit a gift, a gift lacking altogether in reciprocity of any kind, indeed even in appearance.

Specialized exchange has now been examined in two relational contexts—minimum solidarity, transactions between strangers, and maximum solidarity, the household. In each the processes used build solidarity. Much specialized—high exchange-surplus—exchange occurs, however, neither within households nor among strangers but in a wide variety of circumstances of in-between intimacy. We must, therefore, ask how solidarity, beyond the limited solidarity haggling can produce, is built in such circumstances.

The key to this question is found in the difference between individualized and generic interdependence mentioned earlier. To explore this, suppose that the interdependence is quite intense, that is, the division of labor produces a large exchange-surplus if exchange occurs. Thus continuance of both the division of labor and successful exchange relations is important to everyone concerned. Suppose further that individualized interdependence does not exist. While category A (wooden bowl makers) is very interdependent with category B (pottery makers), each individual member of category A is merely dependent on those in category B, without being able to count on any of them being dependent on him. Similarly, each individual in category B is merely dependent on those in category A, without being able to count on any of them being dependent on him. Thus each individual in each category is highly vulnerable. (It is very easy in such circumstances to starve to death while sitting amid a large pile of wooden bowls or pottery as the case may be.)

The individuals have two routes to safety, not necessarily mutually exclusive. One is the market route, depending on competition among the other category of specialist to provide a supply of its product on reasonable trading terms. The second is to create conditions of individualized interdependence. Both kinship and quasi-kinship trading partnerships (Sahlins 1974, 279–314), as well as modern corporations and socialist state enterprises, can, for example, be understood as ways of creating and maintaining individualized interdependence in conditions where otherwise the interdependence would be only generic. To some extent this individualized interdependence may arise "naturally" from simple "net utilitarian advantage," that is, once the relation is underway, ordinary economic forces would make changing to alternative sources costly. To some extent it may be created purposely (as in marriage) by deliberately making it difficult to slip away to alternative sources. To some extent balanced nonspecialized exchange, for example, feasts, may be used to create obligations to maintain interdependence. To some extent "external" relational ties may bind, such as legal obligations, oath taking, etc. Finally, one of the most important factors is that actually operating in a state of interdependence begets norms reinforcing it (Macneil 1983b). Since a trading partnership is aimed at creating solidary beliefs, it will not do, for example, to haggle as if no trust existed. And repeated, fair, nonhaggled exchanges in turn beget more trust.

Trading partnerships are, of course, but one of myriads of possibilities for creating conditions of individualized rather than generic interdependence outside of kinship structures. In modern societies virtually every contract—from the smallest short term deal to the largest contractual relation of indefinite length (such as General Motors)—is an effort to accomplish this result. But in all of them, primitive or modern, a spectrum of social solidarity may be seen in specialized reciprocity ranging from a low level in barter between strangers through a medium level in an arrangement such as a trading partnership on to a high level in husband-wife relations within the household. Within that spectrum various patterns of exchange and processes of solidarity are at work, all aimed at least in part to establish and maintain trust. Interdependence always tends toward solidarity.

Conclusion

This paper advances the following theory: (1) because exchange requires sacrifice and entails gain, exchange enhances both individual utility and solidarity; (2) the two elements—desires to gain individual utility and enhance solidarity—are always at least partially in conflict, thereby creating exchange tension; (3) the conflict and the tension reflect a basic, immutable human characteristic: a dualistic nature inconsistently selfish and socially committed *at the same time:* (4) this particular inconsistency in human nature can be resolved only imperfectly and in ongoing patterns by principles of reciprocity, of which three types emerge from the study of primitive societies: generalized, nonspecialized, and specialized. Each of these creates solidarity, the first via gifts, the second mechanical solidarity via low exchange-surplus exchange, and the third organic solidarity via high exchange-surplus exchange. All may also be seen in modern technological, heavily capitalized societies. (5) The social processes appropriate to maintain or increase solidarity vary depending upon the level of solidarity already prevailing and the type of reciprocity being effectuated. Processes suitable at one level or for one type may be useless or destructive of solidarity at other levels or for other types. None of the types of reciprocity is, contrary to Sahlins's argument, inherently more or less productive of solidarity than the others.

This hypothesis has significance respecting formal economic analysis, the exchange theory-production theory polemic. (Prattis 1982, 222) Polanyian analysis, and our understanding of exchange in market economies.

ECONOMIC ANALYSIS

Although not specifically argued earlier, it follows from the foregoing that any model purporting to be a complete, internally consistent model of human behavior is unsound. Nowhere is this more true than in the case of economic behavior, whether by economic is meant material, as here, or scarce, as in neoclassical economics, since solidarity is always a scarce element in material exchanges. The constant conflict between the utility maximizer and the solidarity enhancer in each person always creates two-dimensional social relations. Any single-dimension model can have no legitimate claims to social completeness. Thus typical utilitarian models purporting to be complete analyses of behavior— whether micro or macro—are not merely unsound at the periphery, but at the center as well since the conflict in human nature itself is not logically reconcilable within one consistent system. This is true whether the model is used merely as a guide to description of behavior, as a predictive model, as an explanation of actual behavior, or as a basis for normative evaluation.

Holmstrom's discussion of the problem of free riding in team behavior illustrates the distortion which can result when one-dimensional analysis is applied to two-dimensional exchange: "The fact that capitalistic firms feature separation of ownership and labor implies that the free-rider problem is less pronounced in such firms than in closed organizations like partnerships." (Holmstrom 1982, 325) This statement is correct only to the extent that teams of laborers make identical sacrifices for solidarity in their exchange behavior as do teams of laborer-owners. There is, of course, no reason to assume this; many factors may incline the latter to sacrifice for solidarity more than, or even differently from, the former. Until we know that this is not the case the statement remains problematic whether we take it as a description of the way teams do behave, a prediction of the way they will behave, an explanation of why they behave as they do, or as a normative conclusion as to how entrepreneurs ought to deal with the free-rider problem in teams.

The most we can come up with are models based on reciprocity, and these will have irreconcilable inconsistencies between individual utility enhancement on the one hand and solidarity enhancement on the other. Such models will inevitably be richer classificatory apparatuses than utilitarian models. Moreover, to the extent that solidarity may be psychologically more complex than desires for getting the most in any particular exchange and also culturally more diffuse, utilization of the hypothesis in model building would lead to greater recognition of cultural diversity in economic behavior than does the current formal economic model.

EXCHANGE THEORY—PRODUCTION THEORY

The theory advanced here can provide a starting point for a synthesis of exchange theory—formal economic theory based on scarcity—and production theory. Iain Prattis summarizes the latter: "The production theorists claim theoretical primacy over exchange theory in economic anthropology on the grounds that the analysis of the regularities and processes of interpersonal exchange has little scientific value. Furthermore, as exchange relations are held to take their definition from the relations of production, an understanding of the structure of exchange only follows upon a prior analysis of the relations of production. In other words exchange theory in its present form is simply a redundant and inaccurate explanatory mode." (Prattis 1982, 222) The theory advanced in this article makes unnecessary the exchange theory—production theory polemic altogether. This is true, although it does nothing directly to resolve any of the differences underlying those theories in the form of diverse views of the nature of man, or of history, or of political or social desires of the theorists. It does, however, deprive each side of one its weapons in that underlying debate. Production theory at its most vulgar deterministic best asserts that "the economic base—that structured antagonism between forces and relations of production"—is the only determinant of social formation. (Prattis 1982, 226) But exchange behavior under a view of exchange encompassing not only maximizing (really enhancing) of utilities respecting goods being exchanged, but also solidarity, *is* the structured antagonism between forces and relations of production. In other words, exchange relations are the relations of production. Introducing solidarity into exchange necessarily introduces all elements of the society—including most certainly history—into the picture both infrastructure and superstructure, however they may be defined. (In one sense then, to accept the two-dimensional exchange theory advanced here is to abandon the infrastructure-superstructure dichotomy altogether, leaving social analysts free to choose what aspects of social relations they deem fundamental and what more peripheral, either generally or respecting particular situations.) Thus, to accept the theory advanced here is to accept a merger of exchange theory and production theory.

Polanyian Analysis

How the present theory departs from formal economic models of utilitarianism is already apparent. Its departure from the Polanyian school is also apparent in that it rejects the sharp distinction between reciprocity and market exchange to be found in Polanyi (1944) and Sahlins. Both are fundamental departures, the latter not only for reasons already addressed, but also because it ends up at odds with the Polanyian thesis that nineteenth-century market economies became disembedded from social relations. They simply became embedded in different ways.

Exchange in Modern Economies

Although the intellectual concepts of the market exchange economy took—and still have—a stranglehold on Western thinking, it is a mistake of incredible magnitude to think that any economy has ever been a market exchange economy in the sense suggested by formal economic analysis, a mistake regularly made by intellectual right, left, and middle. Market exchange in the utilitarian model is exchange in discrete transactions in which relations between the parties are seemingly assumed not to exist. This is as empty a social set in a nineteenth-century market economy or modern twentieth-century economy as it is in primitive economies (Macneil 1981b; 1985b). Not only has market exchange always been heavily embedded in social relations, but discrete (relatively) exchange patterns have always occupied only limited sectors of market economies as well (Macneil 1985b). Utilitarian theory, with its focus on discrete exchanges, obscures the fact that production and most aspects of distribution have always been carried on almost entirely in ongoing relationships—family in the case, for example, of cottage industry: relatively long-term employment relations in factory, farm, transportation, and office; ongoing relations among capitalists within the corporate structure; and countless others. It is only at certain stages, largely in distribution and in some kinds of capital transactions, rather than in production, that this pattern is avoided with the interposition of markets in which discrete transactions are the rule. And prevalence of even this is easy to exaggerate. The transformation of precapitalist economies to market exchange economies is *always* an extremely incomplete one insofar as the organization and conduct of reciprocal processes are concerned. This is to deny neither the impact of the cash nexus nor of capitalism itself in terms of (1) increases in capital, (2) separation of capital ownership from labor, (3) creation of market mentalities at all levels of and affecting *all* relations in society, and (4) class structures. It is simply to recognize that these and other consequences occurred while market exchange in the form of discrete transactions was a relatively small part of the entire economy and was itself thoroughly embedded in the remainder of an economy organized in relational patterns.

The market economy requires solidarity every bit as much as any other economy. Indeed, it has acute problems respecting solidarity because the embeddedness of exchange in the social structure very often requires particularly complex legal structures in many ways remote—although nonetheless essential—from the exchanges themselves. The solidarity of market exchange is built on the belief that property law (and its underlying social acceptance) permits effective present exchanges and that property law plus contract law (and their underlying social acceptance) permit effective exchange of obligations. In a very real sense, the exchange of obligations to exchange goods for money in the future is the epitome of social solidarity. That the solidarity is more measured than in nonmarket exchange enhances rather than reduces the need for its existence.

Prattis has recently focused on the embeddedness of the market economy in social relations in both the transition from precapitalist modes of production to capitalist and in peripheral rural areas of advanced capitalist societies (1982, 218–219). He describes the former: "The persistence of precapitalist value systems and modes of transaction has two related functions. It provides a basis for reproducing capitalist relations of production, and at the adaptive level (for households and communities) this persistence has the function of providing necessary support structures for populations as they adapt to the uncertainties and relative disadvantages of participating in the market economy on unequal terms. Furthermore, traditional modes of production are retained as necessary subsistence adjuncts for the maintenance and reproduction of household units." (219) Prattis is correct but fails to go far enough. The embeddedness is not limited to transitions to capitalism and to communities peripheral to advanced capitalism; it exists everywhere to this day. Household subsistence production—production for self-use—has always been and continues to be a major "precapitalist value system" and "mode of transaction" continuing in the capitalist era. Although it is common to overlook such production, increasing levels of capital invested in the home and its contents which steadily produce consumer goods for the occupants in advanced societies reveals it to be very much on the increase. Consider also the degree to which self-service retailing and the automobile have shifted a very significant part of distribution from nonsubsistence patterns to subsistence patterns. That modern subsistence patterns are vastly different from primitive subsistence, precapitalist patterns—distorted by capitalism, if one will—prevents them neither from being subsistence in nature nor from constituting a foundation upon which capitalism depends; we forget this at our peril.

In addition, countless other kinds of relational patterns permeate virtually all levels of capitalist organization. The only near exceptions are the relatively rare (especially in the latter twentieth century) markets which utilize discrete transaction techniques at particular points in distribution and for some kinds of capital transactions. And even these are deeply embedded in economic and social relations without which they could not exist.

Nor is it enough to speak only of the embeddedness of the market economy in its own production relations, even including household production as a fundamental part of those relations. The market economy is equally embedded and dependent on every aspect of the particular cultures in which it exists—the social relations of language, of custom, of religion, of family, of ethnicity, of consumption, of employment, and of everything else in human life. And to whatever extent exchange is involved in such relations it is relational exchange, not discrete market exchange.

Although everything the market touches is transformed, it nevertheless remains always dependent for its existence on all the complex and particular social relations in which it exists, relations which always remain partially independent of the market economy. Thus, the need for "a basis for reproducing capitalist relations of production" partially external to those relations is not limited to the transition from precapitalist modes of production to capitalist but remains throughout the era of capitalism, whether "private" or "socialist."

4.2 Political Exchange as Relational Contract

Introduction

Reading papers on political exchange—an intellectual area of economic and social exchange almost new to me—has once again brought home forcefully the great difficulty we have in avoiding a Hobbesian view of man-as-the-individual-atom, rather than man-as-the-individual-in-community. What most fascinates me about this difficulty is that it has nothing to do with the real world of human existence and behavior. Nothing in our past or present history justifies thinking of men as individual selfish atoms. We did not evolve from sharks or tigers or other loners. We evolved from social primates and we have never ceased being social primates nor ever lost their peculiar tensions between self and others. Indeed, far from losing them, we have developed them to a richness far beyond the realm of even our brightest cousins, the chimpanzees and gorillas; our immense capability for feeling guilty is an example of our progress. Thus the Hobbesian view has little to do with reality. Rather, it is imposed entirely by culture, ironically enough by a culture priding itself on empirically and rationally sound investigation of the physical and social world.

I have expressed the consequence of this human nature elsewhere:

> Man is both an entirely selfish and an entirely social creature, in
> that man puts the interests of his fellows ahead of his own interests

at the same time that he puts his own interests first. Such a creature is schizophrenic, and will, to the extent it does anything except vibrate in utter frustration, constantly alternate between inconsistent behaviors—selfish one second and self-sacrificing the next. Man is, in the most fundamental sense of the word, irrational, and no amount of reasoning, no matter how sophisticated, will produce a complete and consistent account of human behavior, customs, or institutions. (Macneil 1983b, 348)

I should point out that whether the self-sacrificing side of this peculiar creature is thought to be *really* selfish in origin or *really* rooted in true altruism of some kind, or both, is generally quite irrelevant to the social analysis of human behavior and human institutions. What matters in considering behavior and norms of behavior is that the self-sacrificing side as well as the selfish side always be taken into account.

Thus what the duality means, *inter alia*, is that sound social analysis purporting to be comprehensive in any sense can be founded only on the assumption of a tension between selfishness and self-sacrifice. It is this combination which occurs in cooperative behavior of any kind, although all too often the root "cooperat-" is used to delineate only self-sacrificing or non-conflicting behavior.

This is not to say, of course, that some kinds of limited social analysis based on Hobbesian assumptions can never be correct. For example, if all a social inquirer cares about is what will happen to the consumption of milk in a chain of supermarkets if there are price changes of a fairly normal sort, the assumption of a 100 per cent selfishness respecting price in sales of milk will not distort the results of the analysis sufficiently to be of concern. The reason is not that consumers act entirely selfishly in going through a supermarket and buying milk. It is because their particular forms of self-sacrificing behavior, such as refraining from shoplifting or changing price labels, co-operating with other customers by queueing, etc., do not happen to be affected by normal price changes in that product.

The narrowness of the exception should be noted. Whenever patterns of self-sacrifice will be affected by the factors being studied—in the foregoing example, price changes for milk—that aspect of man must be treated. For example, if the price rise is so great that customers begin to be quite desperate in their desires for milk they now find too dear to buy, their existing levels of self-sacrifice may be eroded and the level of shoplifting of milk may increase. Food riots are a good example of this

117

phenomenon. Similarly, if the price falls far enough, those who currently sometimes steal milk may, for many possible reasons, decide no longer to do so. In either case, failure to take into account the necessarily self-sacrificing nature of the customers will result in inaccurate analysis.

One may have difficulty in seeing adherence to social or legal norms as a form of self-sacrifice, since entirely selfish fears of punishment might conceivably be the sole reason for obedience. (This is probably true, if at all, only of extreme sociopaths.) This point is closely related to whether self-sacrifice is true altruism, or merely a form of selfishness. The fact is that, whatever the motivation, the rules force people, if they wish the gains from exchange, to sacrifice other selfish desires in favor of the interests of other people. This creates the tension discussed above, whether it is a tension between selfishness and true altruism or between two conflicting kinds of selfishness. In addition to the foregoing, exchange itself always involves sacrifice. See (Macneil 1981b; 1986)

But how does one go about building tools of social analysis on a tension rather than on a Hobbesian rock such as selfishness? The answer is simpler than might at first appear (although its consequences are far from simple, and it will never permit the simple analytic models emerging from Hobbesian utilitarianism). The answer lies in the ways this odd creature we are goes about resolving the tension.

Two principles of behavior are essential to the survival of such a creature: solidarity and reciprocity. Getting something back for something given neatly releases, or at least reduces, the tension in a creature desiring to be both selfish and social at the same time; and solidarity—a belief in being able to depend on another—permits the projection of reciprocity through time. (Macneil 1983b, 348)

It may be noted that any analysis recognizing the necessity of reciprocity and solidarity must *never*, except for extremely limited purposes, treat separately either exchange or the relations in which it occurs. The extremely limited purposes are those where the analyst is interested solely in the immediate terms of the exchange *and* where those terms are unaffected by the relations. About the only situation where this is the case is the study of *variations* in the terms of exchange from a real or supposed status quo, variations too small to change the remainder of the relation in any significant manner. Other than that, both exchange and the relation in which it is embedded must always be considered together. Indeed, I believe that a proper analysis of exchange and social solidarity makes it impossible, with such very limited exceptions, ever properly to treat them separately. That is to say, the demands of solidarity are built into exchange itself; the very ways by which people engage in exchange are principal ways of building solidarity. Nor is it possible to continue exchanging without building solidarity. (Since solidarity requires sacrifice, it is this fact which, *inter alia*, permits the description above of obeying laws respecting shoplifting as a form of self-sacrifice.)

Reciprocity and solidarity are the first among equals in exchange relations, but they by no means constitute the only principles essential to such relations. Others include using roles, planning, consenting, achieving flexibility, protecting restitution, reliance, and expectation interests, creating *and* restraining power, following accepted ways of doing things, and harmonizing the relation with its internal and external social matrix. Obviously these categories of behavior conflict (as well as overlap) in many ways, but some minimum level is required of *each* of them, else the relations will cease to exist.

It should also be noted that behavioral patterns of exchange inevitably produce behavioral norms. Since these norms of exchange relations are inextricably interwoven with the behavior in those relations. I do not believe that any analysis ignoring the norms can be sound even respecting the behavior itself.

It follows, in my view, that any analysis of exchange relations which omits not only either reciprocity or solidarity, but also any of the other factors essential to their success, can at best be of only extremely limited value. It follows equally that no positive, nonnormative analysis of exchange relations can ever be realistic. Only when one has *no capability of exercising any choice whatever* can one properly be described as powerless. Such situations are extremely rare, even among prisoners and slaves in the most horrible circumstances.

The importance of the foregoing assertion is vital respecting the analysis of exchange relations. Years ago I wrote as follows of my insistence upon including in the concept of contract one-sided and abusive exchange relations.

[That inclusion] should not, of course, be taken to suggest that a highly coerced pattern is either the ideal prototype or current stereotype of contract. What is suggested is merely that inclusion of all choice situations, however truncated or twisted the choice may be, within the definition of contract may be useful in developing an understanding of the many futures of contracts. Clearly slavery in an Arabian satrapy is not as "contractual" a relationship as is a contract to work in an American corporation (at whatever level), nor is an adhesion contract for goods sold by a high-pressured door-to-door salesman in the ghetto as "contractual" as a contract to sell a used car between one consumer and another. But all have significant contractual elements. Twisted 18-inch specimens near the final tree line are usually called trees, just as are their straight 150 foot cousins on the lower slopes; so too with twisted little specimens of contract living too close to the harsh winds of tyranny. (Macneil 1974a, 705)

The price of excluding from our concept of exchange relations highly coercive, one-sided, and abusive relations is, I believe, an almost certainty of failing to understand exchange relations of any kind. The reasons for this are many fold. First, the presence of such characteristics in relations does not somehow magically wipe out the element of exchange; to be of any value to the master slaves must be fed, clothed and housed, however crudely. Secondly, seldom are such relations so rigidly coercive, one-sided, and abusive, "as to leave no realm whatever for the apparent exercise of some moderately pressured choice." (Macneil 1974a, 703).

A third reason is that the failure to include highly coercive, one-sided, and abusive relations creates the need for an entirely arbitrary dividing line between what is sufficiently coercive to exclude the relation from the realm of exchange relations and what is not.

[A]s we move from the [armed] holdup to primitive patterns of raid-or-trade (where the price paid in trade, if any, is strongly affected by the military situation) to the contract of adhesion in the oligopolistic market, there is no point at which it is clear that we have passed from the realm of noncontract to the realm of contract. This is a spectrum, and however inutile it may be to include the extreme coercive end—the holdup—it will be more inutile to draw an artificial boundary or area somewhere along the way towards the non-coercive end ... As we move from slave labor camp to plantation slavery to household servant slavery to serfdom (of varying degrees of liberality) to indentured service to employment contracts of American athletes containing reserve clauses, at no point is it clear that we have just moved from noncontract to contract. And once again, although it may seem bizarre to include the operation of Stalin's labor camps as within the realm of contract, it would be more distorting to try to eliminate them. (Macneil 1974a, 703–704.)

A fourth reason for not hiving off such exchange relations from our concepts of contract is the wide range of differences in kinds of coercion, differences which may nonetheless in the end turn out in some respects to be superficial or even non-existent.

1. Nature of Power in Exchange

While on a panel at a meeting of the Association of American Law Schools a year or so ago, I made the following statement relating to doctrines of duress and inequality of bargaining power—popular concepts in modern American neoclassical contract law:

> Neither [duress nor inequality of bargaining power] copes adequately with the fact that the exercise of choice is never voluntary, but always compelled by circumstances. The important compelling circumstances in exchange relations in this society are that everyone has property and liberty rights, and that anyone making an exchange is motivated to do so to secure a surrender of such rights in his or her favor. These rights in others create "duress" in every exchange, and, since these rights are both unequally distributed and of differing value to different people, they create "unequal bargaining power" in most if not all exchanges. Because of this these neoclassical concepts either eliminate legal contract altogether or must be narrowly defined. In the latter case they are simply empty buckets collecting instances of particular kinds of behavior which will result in the law's superseding the consent principle.

That consent in human relations is not voluntary, but always results from power of others, is really quite indisputable. The fact is, nonetheless, not only relatively rarely recognized but often denied, usually tacitly. It is, therefore, necessary to explore the matter in a bit more detail. Robert L. Hale has put the point about as clearly as one can.

> [L]egal rights and duties [of contract] are created at the initiative of private individuals. But they are created (or modified or extinguished) by virtue of the power of mutual coercion (in the form of pre-existing rights) vested by the ordinary law in the two contracting parties. It will not do to say that the party to a contract is a voluntary agent merely. He makes the contract in order to acquire certain rights he does not now possess, or to escape certain legal obligations with which he is now burdened. Were his liberty not restricted by these obligations imposed on him by the law and enforced in the ordinary courts, he might never submit himself to

the new obligations of the contract. Thus in a sense each party to the contract, by the threat to call on the government to enforce his power over the liberty of the other, *imposes* the terms of the contract on the other. (Hale 1920, 452)

Two decades later Hale enlarged on these ideas. After noting the limited availability of a subsistence economy, the collective production of goods, the division of labor, and the resulting need for exchange, he goes on:

The owner of the shoes or the food or any other product can insist on other people keeping their hands off his products. Should he so insist, the government will back him with force. The owner of the money can likewise insist on other people keeping their hands off his money, and the government will likewise back *him* up with force. By *threatening* to maintain the legal barrier against the use of his shoes, their owner may be able to obtain a certain amount of money as the price of not carrying out his threat. By threatening to maintain the legal barrier against the use of his money, the purchaser may be able to obtain a certain amount of shoes as the price of not withholding the money. A bargain is finally struck, each party consenting to its terms in order to avert the consequences with which the other threatens him.

This does not mean, of course, that in each purchase of a commodity, there is unfriendliness, or deliberation and haggling over terms ... Nevertheless the transaction is based on the bargaining power of the two parties. (Hale 1943, 604) Hale goes on

[W]hile there is no explicit legal requirement that one enter into any particular transaction, one's freedom to decline to do so is nevertheless circumscribed. One chooses to enter into any given transaction in order to avoid the threat of something worse— threats which impinge with unequal weight on different members of society. The fact that he exercised a choice does not indicate lack of compulsion. Even a slave makes a choice. The compulsion which drives him to work operates through his own will power. He makes the "voluntary" muscular movements which the work calls for, in order to escape some threat; and though he exercises will power and makes a choice, still, since he is making it under threat, his servitude is called "involuntary." And one who obeys some compulsory requirement of the law in order to avoid a penalty is likewise making a choice. If he has physical power to disobey, his obedience is not a matter of physical necessity, but of choice. Yet no one would deny that the requirement of the law is a compulsory one. It restricts his liberty to act out of conformity to it. (Hale 1943, 606)

Government has power to compel one to choose obedience, since it can threaten disobedience with death, imprisonment, or seizure of property. Private individuals are not permitted to make such threats to other individuals, save in exceptional circumstances, such as self-defence. But there are other threats which may lawfully to be made to induce a party to enter into a transaction. In the complex bargains made in the course of production, some parties who deal with the manufacturer surrender a portion of their property, others their liberty not to work for him, in order to avert his threat to withhold his money, while he, in turn, surrenders some part of the money he now owns, or some part of his right to keep from them money he may obtain in the future, to avert their threats of withholding from him their raw materials or their labor. And he may have surrendered property in the past, and the freedom to abstain from labor, in order to attain his position as owner of the plant and its products, and so to obtain the money with which to avert the threats of the owners of the things he wishes to consume, to withhold those things from him. *In consenting to enter into any bargain, each party yields to the threats of the other.* (Hale 1943, 605–606 emphasis added) Hale's work has been particularly welcomed by Critical Legal scholars (Dalton 1985: 1029–1030), because he goes on from the theoretical point outlined here to show how contract can therefore be exploitive in spite of the choice involved in its creation. This is the point missed by *all* liberal analysis whenever it is limited to models which assume the status quo, as in microeconomic analysis, for example, with or without the addition of transaction costs as normally used.

Once Hale's basic point is taken, it becomes apparent that exchange—whether economic, social, or the interactive process of mutual influence in politics—is the application of unilateral power. Whether a prisoner is tied up and carried somewhere by burly guards, walks there in fear of the guards' whips, or walks there because given a cigarette, he moves in response to the application of unilateral power. In the first case it is the actual application of sheer physical power, in the second the power to ship or to refrain from whipping, and in the third the power to keep the cigarette or turn it over to the prisoner. But there are important differences. The trussed-and-carried prisoner has no unilateral power to avoid going where he is taken. But the prisoner in the other two situations does have unilateral power, to walk or not to walk. Moreover, whether he walks to avoid the whipping or to gain the cigarette, he exercises unilaterally his power to walk. The fact that walking is done in exchange for no whipping or in return for a cigarette does not magically convert two unilateral exercises of power by the guards and the prisoner into non-unilateral exercises of power.

Thus those who insist respecting the political arena that the exercise of power is a unilateral act are correct, not only respecting particular sequences of events that everyone might agree involve unilateral acts, but also respecting sequences of events which indisputably constitute exchanges. This is an extremely important point. It puts the initial focus where it belongs, on the relative power positions of those involved, rather than on the exchange itself as if it could sensibly be examined free of consideration of the unilateral power positions giving rise to it.

But it is also incorrect to equate the exercises of two unilateral powers in an exchange to two independent one-way exercises of unilateral power. They are interdependent, each being motivated by the other, and neither can be properly analyzed, indeed even understood, without considering the other. Moreover, they cannot be understood without understanding the solidarity which permits their interdependence—the prisoner above will not walk unless he has at least a glimmer of hope of avoiding a whipping if he does; the guard will not give the cigarette unless he thinks the prisoner will walk. Such solidarity does not occur in the absence of some relationship. The significance of this is immense in countless ways, summed up by Baldwin's term "interactive process of mutual influence." One can, at least in theory, shoot a person without thinking about interaction, but one cannot exchange with him without doing so.

Chapter 5

The Nature of Contract and the Contract Norms

5.1. "Barriers to the Idea of Relational Contracts" (Macneil 1987a, 45)

5.2. *The New Social Contract* (Macneil 1980c, 1–35)

5.3. "Values in Contract: External and Internal" (Macneil 1983b, 346–356, 357, 357–373, 373–382)

The three selections in this chapter are a very brief synopsis of the relational theory of contract taken from "Barriers to the Idea of Relational Contracts", and excerpts from its two principal later statements, *The New Social Contract* and "Values in Contract: External and Internal". As has been mentioned in the "Preface" to this book, the decision has been taken to completely omit the principal paper which those familiar with Macneil's work might well expect to see here, "The Many Futures of Contract". Ian Macneil has said the following in explanation of this omission: "This was Macneil's seminal article developing systematically the ideas of relational contract theory, which he has substantially called essential contract theory (see 10.1. in this book). "The Many Futures of Contract" is, to use the jargon, a thick study and hence book length. Its ideas have been summarised and extended in *The New Social Contract* and "Values in Contract: External and Internal". Due to the length of "The Many Futures of Contract" and the restatement of its central ideas in these later works, it is not excerpted here. Its full original version is of interest now primarily for the manner in which it shows the deep foundations of modern contract not only in the evolution of human societies but also in primate behaviour".

5.1   Barriers to the Idea of Relational Contracts

People producing, distributing, and using material wealth invariably do so in a welter of complex relations, here called material relations. Material relations always incorporate elements external to the humans directly involved in them. At a minimum these include language and learned capacities for communication and affirmative cooperation, social and legal support for some degree of peace and control of capital, social and legal support of obligations generated in the relations, and usually the use of money. But this is the irreducible minimum, and usually there is much more, such as custom and interpenetration with quasi-external bureaucracy. In addition, material relations generate their own internal elements of great complexity, ranging from unspoken custom to detailed elements of bureaucratic planning and conduct, which define and redefine the relations.

The most prominent feature of all material relations is reciprocity, the idea of at least a two way movement of material wealth. Equally omnipresent, but not always as prominent, is solidarity, the trust necessary for the relations to exist. Reciprocity in material relations may sometimes take the form of quite discrete exchanges. But no truly discrete exchanges, completely free of external relations, ever occur, and even relatively discrete exchanges turn out on careful examination to be far more embedded in relations than may at first glance appear.

The structure of the principles of general contract law, instead of reflecting material relations as they actually exist, is based entirely on the nonexistent discrete transaction. Other forms of reciprocity, dominant in the real world, have been eliminated. And solidarity has been reduced to narrow legal remedies.

This general contract structure omits vital aspects of real life material relations, and distorts the rest. With rare exceptions, however, the consequence has not been the development of legal theories of material relations. Rather, competing social and legal principles simply supersede the general law of contract. In addition, specialized law has developed respecting particular types of material relations, such as corporations, families, and industrial relations. Nevertheless, all of this other law depends in part, but nonetheless fundamentally, on the general law of discrete contracts.

126

5.2 The New Social Contract

An Inquiry into Modern Contractual Relations

1 The Nature of Contract

PRIMAL ROOTS OF CONTRACT

SOCIETY. We shall start at the beginning. In the beginning was society. And ever since has been society. This surely must be the most forgotten fact in the modern study of contracts, whether in law or in economics. This lapse of memory we deliberately impose on ourselves in both disciplines by our heroin-like addiction to discrete transactions. And I use that simile advisedly, for surely it is some kind of madness—the image flashes to mind of the mad scientist of movie and television—to carve out of the body of society its economic heart, yet expect to examine it as an independent and functioning organ. For nowhere in human history or prehistory has there been only Adam or even Adam and Eve, but always there has been human society.

If we wish to understand contract, we must return from our self-imposed intellectual isolation and absorb some basic truths. Contract without the common needs and tastes created only by society is inconceivable; contract between totally isolated, utility-maximizing individuals is not contract, but war; contract without language is impossible; and contract without social structure and stability is—quite literally—rationally unthinkable, just as man outside society is rationally unthinkable. The fundamental root, the base, of contract is society. Never has contract occurred without society; never will it occur without society; and never can its functioning be understood isolated from its *particular* society.

SPECIALIZATION OF LABOR AND EXCHANGE. The second primal root of contract is specialization of labor and exchange. You know what specialization of labor is. To paraphrase Adlai Stevenson: We all do God's work, but you do it in your way, and I do it in His. Quips aside, specialization of labor is something we seem unable to overlook in our daily lives. We cannot so much as tell a story about a cab driver, or say

127

that we are studying to be lawyers, or discuss farm subsidies, or complain about the reluctance of auto manufacturers to install anti-pollution devices, without constantly calling specialization to our attention. And yet we can and do overlook it; even when we see it we are blissfully able to ignore it. Until the women's movement, or even since, how many people consciously recognized the housewife as a highly specialized laborer within the family unit? And even when specialization is obvious enough, its ramifications hardly jump to our comprehension, as we shall see.

But what of exchange, that shadow of specialization? Is it so easily recognizable? Partly because the word is used in so many different ways, the answer is no. Moreover, the concept of exchange has become a field for political and social warfare, revolution and reaction; its shifting meanings are thereby obscured even further by the smoke of battle.

One form of exchange, the measured reciprocal exchange—in which we engage every time we go to the supermarket—is clearly an exchange under anyone's definition. But discrete exchange is *not* the primal root of contract. While it has far deeper historical and prehistorical antecedents than is sometimes recognized, discrete exchange is but one of the subspecies forming the exchange part of this second primal root. The broad generic concept of exchange traceable far back into history and prehistory simply recognizes that specialization requires some process of reciprocal distribution of product for the specialization to be worthwhile. Indeed, in extensive specialization where individuals do not produce for themselves everything needed to continue living and producing, each *must* receive the product of others to continue specializing. *How* such exchange occurs is irrelevant to this foundation notion of the concept and to understanding it as a basic root of contract. Exchange can happen in countless ways other than measured reciprocal exchange, ways such as following custom, the Pharaoh's feeding of the pyramid-building slaves, a socialist centralized rationing system, or the intricacies of complex employment relations. But whatever the particular technique of exchange, without it the system of specialization will come to a grinding halt. Everyone will then become unspecialized subsistence farmers, or, more likely, small group hunters and gatherers.

Thus, as we examine the conceptual nature of contract, we must plant in the earth of society the two-pronged root of specialization of labor and the inevitable exchange accompanying it.

CHOICE. The third primal root of contract is a sense of choice, the concept of some freedom to elect among a range of behaviors. In its absence, speaking of even rudimentary contract is futile despite the existence of specialization of labor and exchange. The social insects, particularly ants, rather than humans, clearly are the world's leading contractors if choice is omitted from the concept of contract. Without freedom of will—real, imagined, or postulated—contract becomes conceptually indistinguishable from their genetically programmed specialization of labor and exchange of product. Note, however, that a concept of contract does not require that choice be real, only that we act as if it is.

AWARENESS OF FUTURE. The rudiments of contract exist in a society with specialization and exchange, coupled with a sense of choice. But it is not until addition of the fourth root, conscious awareness of a future, that contract can come into full bloom. Once mankind has this awareness, and with it an increasing sense of himself as a choosing creature, the potentiality for a full development of contract comes into being. Now, specialization of labor and exchange, a sense of choice, and a consciousness of the future, all completely embedded and intertwined in a society, make contract possible.

PROJECTING EXCHANGE INTO THE FUTURE

It is all very well to speak of these four roots of contract without more precise definition of the term. But contract is a word of a thousand meanings—it means something different in *Hadley v. Baxendale* than in *The Godfather*; it means something different in Durkheim than in Restatement (Second); it means something different to an economist than to a lawyer. One could go on dichotomously at length, and in most, if not all, examples, the four roots would fit. More precision is needed.

By contract I mean no more and no less than the relations among parties to the process of projecting exchange into the future. This projection emanates from combining in a society the other three contract roots. A sense of choice and an awareness of future regularly cause people to do things and to make plans for the future. When these actions and plans relate to exchange, it is projected forward in time. That is, some of the elements of exchange, instead of occurring immediately, will occur in the future. This, or rather the relations between people when this occurs, is what I mean by contract.

Let me compare this with a more traditional definition, that in Restatement (2nd) (Contracts sec.1): "A contract is a promise or a set of promises for the breach of which the law gives a remedy, or the performance of which the law in some way recognizes as a duty." Now,

129

this is a definition not of contract-in-fact, but of contract-in-law. Under it, any relation, no matter how full of exchange, not potentially giving rise to *legal* remedies or *legal* recognition of duties is not a contract. In our law-ridden society—and I agree with Pashukanis (1978) that any society ridden with exchange will be ridden with law—this limitation of the contract concept is in some ways less serious than it might seem. Most of our exchange relations do in fact give rise to legal rights. But in Britain, for example, collective bargaining is in theory outside legal enforceability. And there exist in our society exchange relations, of which marriage is but an extreme example, where much occurs to which the law does not, in any practical sense, extend its remedies or recognize legal duties.

More important than possible omission of particular relations from the domain of a law-oriented definition of contracts is the bias it gives our thinking. While law may be an integral part of virtually all contractual relations, one not to be ignored, law is not what contracts are all about. Contracts are about getting things done in the real world—building things, selling things, cooperating in enterprise, achieving power and prestige, sharing and competing in a family structure. Thus, even if a law-oriented definition encompasses every contract included in an exchange-oriented definition, it will inevitably be perceived as narrower because it immediately tells us to think about law. If we wish to understand contract, and indeed if we wish to understand contract law, we must think about exchange and such things first, and law second.

But an even more serious hindrance to understanding is the limitation of contract to "a promise or a set of promises." Promise is an illusive concept, but the Restatement (sec. 2) tries to put us on the right track by defining it as the "manifestation of intention to act or refrain from acting in a specified way, so made as to justify a promisee in understanding that a commitment has been made." Unfortunately this seems merely a Gertrude Steinian "a promise is a promise is a promise."

Those of us who try to define promise may be under eternal sentence to do so in Steinian terms, but hope is as eternal as the sentence, so let me try something else. Since many of the important applications of promise in contracts have to do with exchange, I shall limit this discussion of promise to its role as an exchange-projector.

The idea of promise is an affirmation of the power of the human will to affect the future. It affirms that an individual can affect the future now. But a promise is made *to* someone. Thus, the first two elements of promise in its contractual context are the wills of *two* or more individuals with beliefs in the power of one to affect the future—subject to the linkage of the social matrix essential to exchange.

A third element of promise is the doing of something now to limit the choices otherwise available to the promisor in the future. This is part of the notion of commitment encompassed in the Restatement definition. For example, a person entering an agreement to sell a house no longer may choose to sell it elsewhere without suffering the consequences of breaching his promise. These may be as intangible as a loss of reputation or as concrete as a judgment awarding damages.

Two other closely linked elements of promise as an exchange-projector must now be added: communication and measured reciprocity. Communication is required by the division between "you" and "me" postulated by the existence of separate wills. Finally, the separation of selfish "you" from selfish "me," together with the existence of commitment, and communication, all go to guarantee that promise-based exchange-projection will indeed encompass *measured* reciprocity, the fifth element.

We have thus five elements of promise in exchange, always to be viewed in their particular society. These are: (1) the will of the promisor and (2) the will of the promisee; (3) present action to limit future choice; (4) communication; and (5) measured reciprocity. These may be more conveniently summarized in this definition of promise as an exchange-projector: "Present communication of a commitment to engage in a reciprocal measured exchange." This extraordinarily powerful mechanism for projecting exchange into the future is the essence of discrete contract.

But *we* are seeking to understand contract as the relations among parties to the processes of future exchange. Only if promise as defined is the *sole* way exchange can be and is projected do we stop with it. And, of course, it is not. Indeed, in many circumstances promise is neither the most effective nor the most important exchange-projector in contractual relations.

Nonpromissory exchange-projectors—those lacking one or more of the elements of promise—come in a great many forms. In all societies, custom, status, habit, and other internalizations project exchange into the future. In some primitive societies these may be the primary projectors, with promise relating to exchange playing only a very minor role, if that. Moreover we err if we fail to recognize that such non-promissory mechanisms continue to play vital parts in the most modern and developed of societies. Even kinship, a form of status which plays major roles in so many societies, is by no means absent as an exchange-projector in ours, although it may now be overshadowed by class or other structures with partially related roles.

More dynamic nonpromissory exchange-projectors than these are positions of command, vital not only in many simple societies but even more so in immensely complex societies. The internal hierarchies of corporations are a modern example. (Macneil 1975b, 629–631) Complicating this pattern in complex structures is the existence of bureaucracies which, while in theory merely tools of higher commanders, in fact develop self-interests inevitably both affecting and effecting exchange-projection.

Finally, the very existence of ongoing contractual relations creates expectations that future exchange will occur, and in partially predictable patterns, simply through the dynamics of the existing relations whether or not hierarchical. For example, the existence of an ongoing market for a product creates, without hierarchical command, expectations that production for that market may be worthwhile. Such markets remain among our most important relational exchange-projectors, even though the relational web they create may be highly impersonal.

Thus we find a great range of nonpromissory exchange-projectors. Key ones include custom, status, habit and other internalizations, command in hierarchical structures, and expectations created by the dynamics of any status quo, including markets.

These nonpromissory types may be and often are accompanied by promises. But more important to understanding contract is the other side of the coin: promissory projectors are *always* accompanied by nonpromissory projectors. This emanates from the interplay of the always present social matrix with the nature of promises themselves. Promises are inherently fragmentary. The human mind can focus on only a limited number of things at the same time, and, for reasons of efficiency in fact focuses on even fewer than it can. Thus, promises can never encompass more than a fragment of the total situation. (Farnsworth 1968, 870) At least as fundamental, the amount of information available about the future is always only partial, and promises, however sweeping, can be understood only against the background. All this is part of what Herbert Simon (1997, 88) calls bounded rationality. Moreover, promises are further narrowed by the need to fit them into symbolic forms required for communication. The latter narrowing is aggravated by the effort required to transform promises into communication symbols; effort is a cost, and therefore not everything that *can* be transformed into promises will be. For all these reasons, promises are inescapably but fragments of any contractual relation or even transaction, no matter how discrete.

A second factor in the inevitably limited role of promises is overt or tacit recognition that the promise made is never exactly the same as the promise received. Every promise is always *two* promises, the sender's and the receiver's. The resulting nonmutuality ranges from subtle to gross differences in understanding. These differences can be resolved only by bringing into the picture something other than the promises themselves. This something, whatever else it may be, is a nonpromissory projection of exchange into the future.

Partly because of the foregoing factors, both individuals and societies always view promises as less than absolute. Much promise breaking is tolerated, expected, and, indeed, desired. This is true not only respecting the parties, as demonstrated, for example, by Professor Macaulay's (1963a; 1963b) studies of the behavior of manufacturers, but also respecting the rest of society, including the legal system. Were it not, we would find legal contract remedies to be real guns, ready for hire at low cost, rather than expensive cap pistols.

Once promises are viewed as less than absolute, other exchange-projectors inevitably must come into play. Thus throughout the realm of contract, albeit in greatly varying degrees, we find promise always accompanied by significant nonpromissory projectors of exchange. This fact gives rise to troublesome questions concerning the relations between the promissory and nonpromissory aspects of any given contractual relations.

In the 1961 Rosenthal Lectures Harold Havighurst (1961, 15) said that in certain primitive societies "Contract . . . is only a ripple upon the great sea of custom." In contrast the systematics of a neoclassical contract law, such as that of Restatement (Second), treats custom and other nonpromissory exchange-projectors as "only a ripple upon the great sea of promise." In modern society, neither of these conditions obtains; there are two deep ocean currents, the promissory and the nonpromissory; the ripple—no, the waves, even storms—come wherever these cross.

DISCRETE AND RELATIONAL CONTRACT: PRIMITIVE AND MODERN

Discrete contract is one in which no relation exists between the parties apart from the simple exchange of goods. (Goldberg 1976, 49) Its paradigm is the transaction of neoclassical microeconomics. But as will be seen, every contract, even such a theoretical transaction, involves relations apart from the exchange of goods itself. Thus every contract is necessarily partially a relational contract, that is, one involving relations other than a discrete exchange.

The differences between discrete contract on the one hand, and two kinds of relational contract on the other, will be explored in this section. The first kind of relational contract includes all the intertwined exchange behavior of a primitive community. Such a community enjoys an independent economy with relatively little specialization, relative stability, and little fundamental change. The other type of relation is the modern contractual relation, intricately interconnected with a larger society of great complexity, involving extremely elaborate specializations, and subject to constant change.

These two kinds of relations result in *two* sets of axes. Both start at the same point, the discrete transaction. But one runs from there to the primitive community; the other runs to the typical modern contractual relation. Use of these two axes will reveal some important differences between the two kinds of relations. If the modern world is drifting toward neotribalism, it is *neo*, not old, tribalism; if we are in a new world of status and dead contract, it is not the status of Henry Maine or the torts of Grant Gilmore but phenomena quite different from both. (Rehbinder, 1971) But our understanding of modern contractual relations can nevertheless be enhanced by first examining primitive relational contract.

Discrete Transactions and Primitive Contractual Relations

Both ends of this first set of axes involve fictional constructs. The description of the primitive contractual relation is a highly generalized and therefore largely fictional summary of anthropological studies of widely disparate primitive communities, widely disparate both in space and in time. Even more important, at the other end of the spectrum the discrete transaction is *entirely* fictional. There we postulate specialization and choice-determined projections of future exchange in the total absence of any society whatsoever. Even in the modern mythical world of neoclassical microeconomic theory such conditions do not exist.

Since exchange in any meaningful economic sense is impossible outside a society, even the purest discrete model necessarily does postulate a social matrix. It must provide at a minimum: (1) a means of communication understandable to both parties; (2) a system of order so that the parties exchange instead of trying to kill and steal; (3) in typical modern applications, a system of money; and finally (4) in the case of exchanges promised, an effective mechanism to enforce promises.

In the purest of discrete transactions, those of neoclassical micro-economics, we have a kind of neutral external god providing these social benefits for no apparent reason and demanding no return. In real life no external disinterested god does these things, but rather the society in which the transactions take place, and societies are notorious interferers. Moreover, social interference creates relations among the parties whether they like it or not. In fact, even within the strictly theoretical neoclassical model itself, tensions exist which prevent us from speaking sensibly of the truly discrete transaction. This complicates our discussion—we find ourselves in a kind of never-never land of a theoretical construct which cannot exist even in theory. It in turn is confused in our minds with real life contracts with many discrete characteristics.

Were this confusion purely one of analytical constructs it could be avoided. But it is not. Humans *do* think both discretely and relationally at the same time, and thus think irrationally. To put it another way, we are at the same time selfish individuals and integral parts of a social unity. (Passmore, 1970) The result is an inherent lack of clarity in the concept of discrete transaction.

A second artificiality in this first set of axes is that the closest real life analogues to discrete transactions have substantial economic significance only in societies with high levels of specialization. But the primitive contractual relations occur in simple societies with low levels of specialization. We are thus treating in the same spectrum two different kinds of societies.

A third and final difficulty of comparison is that each discrete transaction by its very nature can involve only a small part of the total economy of any community, whereas the primitive contractual relation is in a very real sense a description of the exchange relations of the entire community over an indefinite period of time.

In spite of these difficulties, I believe that understanding of modern contracts can be enhanced by starting with this somewhat unrealistic spectrum running from the discrete transaction to the primitive contractual relation. It consists of eleven factors.

1. *Personal relations.* In relational contract personal relations are what the sociologists call primary relations. (Broom *et al.* 1981, 126–127) They involve the whole person, are unlimited in scope, are unique, and are

nontransferable. Communications in such relations are extensive and informal as well as or instead of formal. Communication is not limited to linguistics but involves all senses. The participants derive complex personal noneconomic satisfactions and engage in social exchange, as well as what an outside observer might call economic exchange. In a modern context, marriage would be the most obvious illustration. In a primitive context the whole communal structure is involved in these primary relations, although they are most intense in the nuclear family, the next most intense among other close kin.

Discrete transactions on the other hand are nonprimary relations. They involve only a small part of the personality, are very limited in scope, are nonunique in personal terms, and hence can be transferred readily. Communications in discrete transactions are limited, linguistic, and, if of any length, formal. If they are formal, they are only formal. The satisfactions derived are limited to the narrow economic exchange being accomplished. Buying gasoline for cash at a busy self-service station in a strange town is a fairly good modern example.

2. *Numbers.* The next factor, the number of persons involved, is closely related to the first. The ideal discrete transaction has only two parties. Primitive contractual relations, however, have many, because over time the whole community is involved in the exchanges and other aspects of the relation. Increased numbers tend to increase primary relations. Thus, as is true of many factors discussed, this one tends to resonate with one or more of the others.

3. *Measurement and specificity.* In the discrete transaction the subjects of exchange will be money on one side, and a commodity with monetary market value on the other. They will be carefully measured and specified. This is the paradigm of measured reciprocal exchange. In primitive contractual relations the most important subjects of what an outsider might call economic exchanges will have no measurable monetary market values. Amounts and relative values are likely to be vague. And the remainder of the relation and obligations arising from it are likely to be very diffuse, and hence unmeasurable. In short, calculation in the self-interest sense may be present, but calculation in the reckoning sense is muted.

4. *Sources of contractual solidarity.* The next factor concerns contractual solidarity—the social solidarity making exchange work—that at a minimum holds the parties together enough so that they will not kill and steal in preference to exchanging. In the discrete transaction, apart from the immediate gains each party sees in exchanging, no contractual

136

solidarity exists except for that external god providing social stability, enforcement of promises, and other basic requirements. Within these rigid confines the parties are free to maximize individual utilities to their hearts' content.

The primitive contractual relation also has solidarity from external reinforcement, but not from any disinterested god. Rather its solidarity derives from the society interpenetrating all exchange. As Marshall Sahlins (1974, 185–186) so neatly puts it: "A material transaction is usually a momentary episode in a continuous social relation. The social relation exerts governance: the flow of goods is constrained by, is part of, a status etiquette." In such circumstances it is difficult, indeed perhaps foolish, to try to separate internal reinforcement from external. The parties themselves are so embedded, in external relations, such as kinship, as to make all relations between them simply part of larger relations. For example, how do we separate internalized norms—the deeply rooted, personally felt, sense of what is right and proper—from the society generating them? Nevertheless, no society is so completely communal that differentiations and intensifications in relations fail to occur. The clearest illustrations of this in primitive societies are relations arising from sexual specialization of labor. Specialization within a close ongoing relation such as marriage creates an interdependence between those parties not to be found elsewhere, even in their relations with other close kin.

In sum, unlike discrete transactions, the primitive contractual relation is shot through with reinforcements integrated with exchange itself, reinforcements constituting the basis of contractual solidarity.

5. *Commencement, duration, and termination.* Everything about the discrete transaction is short—the agreement process, the time between agreement and performance, and the time of the performance itself. The discrete transaction commences sharply by clear, instantaneous agreement and terminates sharply by clear, instantaneous performance; sharp in, sharp out. Should a breach occur it will be clear, and the external god will promptly and clearly supply the equivalent of performance at the expense of the breacher.

The foregoing is in marked contrast to the primitive contractual relation. The relation itself has no beginning and no end, constituting as it does the nuclear family, kinship relations, and indeed, the whole community. The individual's participation in the economic web of the community starts at birth and ends at death; religious beliefs may extend the individual's participation to periods even before birth and after death.

137

Of course, specific exchanges will punctuate these complex relations, but since they are always deeply imbedded in the relation, they can never enjoy the discrete characteristics such as sharp in, sharp out.

6. *Planning.* In the discrete transaction planning is complete, specific, and binding. It is achieved by explicit consent of each party at the time of commencement, with no further planning anticipated. Because of the zero-sum aspects of bargaining, discrete transaction planning is heavily laden with overt conflict of interest. More needs to be said about planning of discrete transactions, but it will fit better in the discussion of modern relational contract than here.

In primitive contractual relations, planning is largely the result of an accretion of customary behavior over long periods, with choice playing a subsidiary role. At least tacitly it is recognized that, as the future unfolds, adjustments will have to be made to deal with new circumstances. The processes of custom will tend to keep conflicts of interest in planning more hidden than in the isolated bargaining of the discrete transaction. And where they are recognized, custom will push exchanging parties in the direction of sacrificing some of their immediate self-interest from the exchange in favor of other goals.

7. *Future cooperation.* In the discrete transaction almost no future cooperation will be required. Each party simply produces either the commodity or the money at the time and place promised. But in primitive contractual relations cooperation is likely to be required in performance, which may very well consist of joint efforts, such as two men cooperating in the hunt. Moreover, since adjustment in the relation is endemic, cooperation in that process is also required.

8. *Sharing and dividing benefits and burdens.* Closely related to this is the incidence of benefits and burdens. In a discrete transaction benefits and burdens are sharply divided; each party has his benefits, all his, and his burdens, also all his. In primitive contractual relations, however, undivided sharing of both benefits and burdens is common. All, for example, participate in the hunt, sharing the risks of failure, and all share in the benefits of the kill.

9. *Obligations.* Obligations undertaken differ in three ways: sources of content, sources of obligation, and specificity. In the discrete contract the content comes from the promises of the parties, but the obligation comes from the promise-enforcing external god. In the relational contract, however, both the content and the source of the obligations come from the relation itself, out of slowly evolving patterns of custom and law, with only modest input from individual promise. Thus in the primitive

relation the sources of obligations tend to be the same as the sources of content of the obligations. The separation of source of content from source of obligation in the discrete contract leads to great specificity, whereas obligations in primitive contractual relations lean toward the diffuse and ill-defined.

10. *Transferability.* Both discrete transactions and contractual relations constitute wealth, the value of which is often enhanced by transfer. Thus transferability is to be expected unless something inhibits it. In the case of the discrete transaction nothing exists to inhibit transfer of either rights or obligations, except ultimate responsibility for not performing. Only respecting that ultimate responsibility is the identity of the promisor important—in fact a relational burr under the discrete-transaction saddle. But primitive contractual relations involve primary relations heavily dependent on the identity of participants. They lack measurability of content, duration, and the like. They require much future cooperation, involving sharing of benefits and burdens, and require much trust. They are woven into special structures such as kinship. All of these militate against simple transferability.

11. *Attitudes.* The final factor is a collection of attitudes of the participants toward the transaction or relation. Four subjects are particularly pertinent: awareness of conflict of interest, unity, time, and expectations about trouble.

Awareness of conflict of interest. The very nature of the discrete transaction brings intense awareness of the fact that exchange is occurring, that exchange has zero-sum aspects, and that each party is trying to maximize his gain at the expense of the other. Thus, the discrete transaction tends to focus on the divisiveness and selfishness inherent in exchange, rather than on its cohesive and cooperative aspects. Relations following customary patterns, on the other hand, permit exchange to occur without such sharp and conscious individualistic focus. Awareness of conflict of interest is thereby considerably muted, and, when perceived, is recognized as something to be kept under strong control.

Unity. Closely related to the foregoing is the extent to which participants in exchange view their relation as a unity. In the past I approached this issue in terms of perception of altruism, but that is too narrow and likely to be misleading. The question is how much the participants view their individual interests as coextensive with the interests of the over-all relation. This involves interdependence in the sense of perceiving selfish interest as served through the interest of other participants, or in the ultimate psychological sense of not seeing any difference between selfish interest and the interest of the other participants. It also involves social unity in the sense of desiring individually to serve the relation against competing external interests, for example, hiding food for the nuclear family in periods of famine against competing claims of more remote kin. Whether these attitudes reflect altruism, and what is the nature of altruism, I shall leave others to debate. For my purposes, the question is the extent to which the participants perceive the contractual relation as a unity of which each of them is a part.

Obviously, in the discrete transaction there is no sense of unity whatsoever; it is a case of me and him, in that order, and strangers evermore. In primitive contractual relations, however, there is much evidence of behavior and attitudes reflecting awareness of unity. This is especially so respecting close kin, but to lesser degrees extends further in the community. Moreover, considerable evidence exists that the process of exchanging goods and services is often aimed at least as much, if not more, at enhancing social unity as it is at enhancing individual economic utilities. (Sahlins 1974, ch.5)

Time. Another important attitude to be explored is that relating to time. The ultimate goal of parties to a discrete transaction is to bring all the future relating to it into the present or, to use a rare word, to presentiate. They can then deal with the future as if it were in the present; incidentally, this is precisely what the neoclassical microeconomic model regularly purports to do. Only 100 per cent complete and binding planning can do this. Presentiation thus does not occur—or to be more accurate, can occur only very partially—in a primitive contractual relation. The incompleteness and lack of precision in planning for the future resulting from custom in a primitive society leave the future where it is; waiting to happen. It can be prepared for, but not conquered. Obviously, the difference in viewpoint is likely to affect the way people respond to what the future actually brings.

Trouble. The fourth attitude of concern relates to trouble. Discrete transactions are not supposed to get into trouble; indeed, if the concept is carried to its extreme, they cannot get into trouble, since every conceivable contingency is entirely planned. In contractual relations on the other hand, trouble is expressly or tacitly expected as a normal aspect of life—everyone in our primitive community knows that cattle may die of disease, an event that obviously may affect an obligation to deliver the next newborn calf to a cousin. In an ideal discrete transaction that contingency would be precisely planned for, and moreover, the risk of its happening would have been taken precisely into account in the purchase price. In relations, on the other hand, if the parties have thought at all beyond the point of remembering the ever-present and fickle gods of mishap, they would wait to see if anything bad does happen, and if so, what. Then they would deal with the problem with the whole range of community processes available for hard times.

★ ★ ★

Thus, we find a great range of differences, among a large number of factors, between discrete transactions on the one hand and, on the other, relational contracts in a relatively primitive society. But what has that to do with modern contracts? That query brings us to the concluding part of the chapter, in which I shall focus on modern contractual relations, intimately interconnected with a larger society of great complexity, involving extremely complex specializations of labor and product, and always subject to constant change.

Discrete Transactions and Modern Contractual Relations

These relations are so diverse—the direct result of incredibly high levels of specialization—that you may well question lumping them together in one category. How can one sensibly place in a single grouping a childless marriage and IBM, the UAW's relations with General Motors, the Lockheed—Defense Department relation, a McDonald's hamburger franchise and a shop in Harlem with two employees, yet still claim to be talking about the same phenomenon? As I hope will soon become apparent, this grouping does make sense. Only one bifurcation is necessary in applying the various factors; at a few key points we do need to distinguish between large and small contractual relations. But we can nevertheless for many purposes treat them together.

We need not here re-examine all the factors we treated respecting primitive relations. For our limited purposes four remain much the same in the modern relation as in the primitive. Primary personal relations are a main characteristic. Modern contractual relations too tend to involve large numbers of people, often huge numbers of people. Even the family and small enterprises of various kinds usually involve more than the two parties of the paradigm discrete transaction. The modern contractual relation too tends toward long life. Many, especially large groupings, have beginnings shrouded in the past—Du Pont, for example, goes back over two hundred years—and more have terminations lying only in the far mists of the unforeseeable future. Many such relations also take on and shuck off new members, some for all their working lives, while the relations themselves continue. Finally, all of these modern relations, large and small, demand future cooperation not only in performing what is planned but in future planning.

The original factors left to explore relative to the modern contractual relation are: (1) measurement and specificity, (2) sources of contractual solidarity, (3) planning, (4) sharing and dividing benefits and burdens, (5) obligations, (6) transferability, and (7) attitudes. In dealing with these the stress will be on differences from primitive relations. But it is necessary to remember that *all* of the characteristics of primitive relations may be and often are found in modern relations. For example the latter, just like primitive relations, require solidarity and hence a degree of trust, of faith in others, to work successfully.

The four omissions noted above do not leave us entirely ahead, since it is necessary to add a new factor—power, hierarchy, and command—when we deal with modern contractual relations. While these are by no means absent in primitive contractual relations, for our purposes they can best be developed in the modern context. Thus eight factors require further exploration.

1. *Measurement and specificity*. Unlike the primitive relation modern contractual relations are ridden with measurement and specificity. This is true not only of the money side of the exchange but also the goods and services side. Indeed, the presence of cash as one side inevitably tends to cause careful measuring and specification of goods and services on the other. Where the difference between paying $1,000 and paying $1,100 for something is so hard and clear, measuring of the "something" becomes important also. Relational allocation techniques, such as trust arising from social solidarity, or reliance on future command, will still be used. Indeed, they may assume increased importance. But measurement on one side permits measurement on the other, and where measurement is viewed as the better technique it will be used. Thus we find labor precisely measured in hours or quantity of production; we find amounts of products to be delivered precisely measured reciprocally with price. Marriage or other similar relations are probably the only modern economic arrangements commonly marked by an absence of significant precise measurements.

Moreover, modern technology demands extremely high levels of specification of products and services, and hence immense specificity is required in modern relational exchange. This is one of the most important distinctions between primitive and modern contractual relations. It is the direct result of the unbelievably intricate specialization of the technological era.

Nevertheless, the modern contractual relation does not become simply a bunch of discrete transactions. Quite the contrary, the very complexity of modern technology calls for processes and structures tying even the most specific and measured exchanges into ongoing relational patterns. (Macneil 1978a) Moreover, any modern relation also involves a great deal of exchange that cannot be or is not measured. For example, the difference between a poor and a very good white-collar worker may be neither measured nor measurable on either the pay or the output side. In addition, social exchange and other facets commonly present in contractual relations are entirely or largely unmeasured and unmeasurable, as are such important psychic satisfactions as prestige and personal power.

2. *Sources of contractual solidarity.* This factor is similar in some respects in modern contractual relations as it is in primitive relations. In both it has internal and external sources. In both the basic internal sources are the complex webs of interdependence created by the relation itself. In both, internal customs and laws are generated. But—marriage and family aside—internal regulation of modern relations usually has a large, precise, legalistic element, such as management directives or a detailed collective bargaining agreement. This is a direct result of high levels of measurement and specificity, and is in sharp contrast to the more diffuse regulation of primitive contractual relations. This is not, however, the only distinction between primitive and modern contractual relations respecting sources of solidarity. The modern relation is in many ways more separate from its overall society than is the primitive—a separation symbolized, for example, by the high wire fences surrounding many industrial plants. For this reason, the external and internal sources of contractual solidarity may more readily be distinguished in our minds. We can see a difference between the web of interdependence holding together the stockholders and creditors of a corporation and the sovereign law of contracts ultimately governing their rights, the former internal to the relation and the latter external. Nevertheless, internal and external are closely interwoven, as may be readily seen if one analyzes arbitration under a collective bargaining agreement in juxtaposition to an analysis of NLRB unfair labor practice proceedings, one putatively internal and one putatively external. (Covington 1978) Moreover, as will be seen when we examine the contract norms, the very dichotomy of

internal and external—a dichotomy apparently so clear respecting the discrete transaction—is far fuzzier than at first appears.

3. *Planning*. It hardly need be stated that in modern contractual relations much will be planned in measured and specific terms, a sharp contrast to primitive contractual relations. But there is far more to modern contractual planning than its use respecting measured and specified performance. Partly because of the complexity of planning, a direct comparison of the planning of discrete transactions with planning in modern contractual relations is required. In this comparison, because large relations pose the greatest differences from primitive contractual relations, I shall concentrate on them, omitting smaller contractual relations such as the nuclear family.

Substance-process. The primary, often exclusive, focus of planning a discrete transaction is on the substance of the exchange. How many dollars for how much of what good? In relations, however, the primary focus is bifurcated into planning the substance of exchanges and planning the structures and processes. Although the former is usually important, major emphasis must be placed on the latter, for example on the operating relations of a franchisor and franchisee. Moreover, specific planning of the substance of the exchanges to take place in the future can occur, except early in the relations, only in limited ways. For example, the amount to be paid for common stock shares at the inception of a corporation can be planned initially. But the amount and terms of a *future* common stock issue cannot. Instead it is recognized that future planning of such substantive issues will occur through the structures and processes being established at the beginning. Moreover, even those must be subject to future change. For example, in establishing a corporation it is necessary to recognize the possibility of mergers in which the whole governing structure will be altered.

Completeness-specificity. The nature of the discrete transaction leads to very complete and specific planning: in theory it is totally complete; in actuality it may encompass everything except unforeseen contingencies. In relations, planning of the substance of future exchanges is, as already noted, necessarily incomplete, although techniques of flexibility, such as price indexing, may increase specificity. Planning of structure and processes for future operations, for example, corporate charters and bylaws, may be complete in a constitutional sense but never in a day-to-day operating sense. By its very nature such planning constitutes a confession that many specific substantive courses of action cannot be planned in advance.

Tacit assumptions. One important aspect of incomplete planning in relations is the tacit assumption. The late Lon Fuller, whose term it is, exemplified the tacit assumption by the absent-minded professor reading a book as he steps out into the hall from his office: he tacitly assumes that the hall floor is still there, without consciously giving any thought to the matter. Discrete transactions have no room for tacit assumptions, other than the tacit assumption that out there somewhere is the external god who will prevent theft, enforce promises, and such like. In relational contracts as in all human relations tacit assumptions abound, and constitute a significant aspect of the planning of those contractual relations. Such assumptions may range from general ones such as trust to the highly specific, such as assumptions about particular and precise trade usages.

Participation. Mutual participation in planning differs between discrete transactions and contractual relations. In the discrete transaction planning consists of mutual consent to price in a sale of a good produced for a market by unilateral plan of the seller. There is, thus, an element of adhesion respecting the product, and often respecting the price, whether set by market forces or by the seller partially free of market forces.

The picture respecting the contractual relation is more complex. First it is necessary to distinguish between planning of the relation and planning respecting the admission of new participants, for example, new employees. Consider the creation of a large new relation, such as a business consortium. Its complexities will inevitably require a great deal of mutual participation in planning, rather than unilateral planning acquiring mutuality only by adhesion of the other party. In the case, however, of admission of a new party to an existing relation, that may not be so; by and large the new employee of IBM is handed a plan of the employment relation which he has little power to modify. Or so it seems at the time.

Post-commencement planning. The last cryptic sentence—"or so it seems at the time"—reflects the fact that in contractual relations, unlike discrete transactions, planning continues after formation of the relation and after entry of a new person into the relation. Post-commencement planning by its very nature tends to be mutual, even in strongly hierarchical organizations. Thus the new IBM employee will in fact play a role in planning what happens within IBM; the nature of employment is such that it cannot remain, even though it starts out as, a complete relation of adhesion.

Post-commencement planning of relations is far too complex a subject to do justice to here. But certain characteristics should nevertheless be noted. Since it is embedded in the relation, post-commencement planning is obligational; that is, it is subject to constraints imposed by the relation. (Wachter and Williamson 1978) This is in sharp contrast to the planning of discrete transactions where each party is free to go ahead with a deal or not with no ties to the other before or beyond the prospective deal. Second, post-commencement planning blends off from the very specific to the less specific to the very general. Similarly, it fades off from deliberate to somewhat inadvertent to no planning at all beyond mere incrementalism in which the day-to-day course of the relation develops the future as it goes along. And finally, post-commencement planning in modern contractual relations is immensely affected by the complex processes of administrative-bureaucratic behavior. The importance of this latter factor is highlighted by the recent award of a Nobel Prize for economics to Herbert Simon (1997), an astute student of this subject.

Bindingness. Planning of the discrete transaction is intended to be entirely binding. Some planning in relations is very similar on this score. Both workers and management at Ford, for example, usually think of the wage scales as immutable during the period specified in the collective bargaining agreement. But even mutually agreed planning among participants in contractual relations is often subject to change with circumstances. In addition, much planning in contractual relations is not the result of mutual agreement, but is by command within a hierarchy. And in theory any command is subject to revocation by the commander, as those who have served in the armed forces or other large bureaucracies are all too well aware. In practice, of course, many factors may constrain decision makers in hierarchies from revoking their commands, but the possibility always exists of unilateral revocation.

4. *Sharing and dividing benefits and burdens.* You will recall that, in marked contrast to the primitive contractual relation, the discrete transaction sharply divides benefits and burdens into parcels, each allocated exclusively to a particular party. Most modern relations tend to include *both* sharp divisions of benefits and burdens *and* a sharing of them. Employees, for example, have precise wages and quite precise work assignments—examples of divided benefits and burdens. But employees may share prosperity with management and shareholders through bonus schemes, more comfortable working conditions, more overtime, and the like. And they may share hard times through layoffs, for example, while management and shareholders suffer, respectively, reduced or even terminated incentive bonuses and smaller profits or even losses. This

146

combination of sharp dividing *and* sharing of benefits and burdens parallels the use and non-use of measurement in contractual relations.

5. *Obligations.* Modern contractual relations tend to combine kinds of obligations associated with the discrete transaction with those associated with primitive contractual relations. Thus the sources of the content of the obligations are both the promises of the parties and those arising otherwise from the relation itself. So too the sources of the obligation arise both from the relation and from the external society which provides a structure for carrying on the relation, including the enforcement of promises. But it is a society much intertwined with the relation. Moreover, the underlying obligations of modern contractual relations are both specific and general, and sanctions are likely also to be both very specific and of an ongoing accommodating nature. For example, an unpaid employee has a right to a judgment for wages, but one with a grievance about discipline may well find himself in an arbitration process in which preserving future harmony in the plant is as important as his rights. Thus, we again find a merger in modern relations of characteristics of discrete transactions and primitive contractual relations.

6. *Transferability.* I am not sure whether the same may be said of the next factor. In many ways transferability takes on a whole new characteristic in the large modern contractual relation. You will recall that little or nothing stands in the way of the transfer of a discrete transaction. But primitive relations, dependent as they are on primary, whole person relations are not, because of the uniqueness of each individual personality, simply transferable. Being helped by Woody Allen in hunting elephants is just not quite the same as being helped by Tarzan. In many modern contractual relations, especially small ones, nontransferability remains the case. Being married to A is just not the same as being married to B; any effort of A's spouse to trade off partners with B's spouse without the consent of A and B is quite likely to reveal that fact. Moreover, many of the other relational factors, such as lack of measurement, contribute to make simple transfer not feasible.

But increased size of modern relations tends toward increased depersonalization of participants. It remains true that Employee Jones cannot send Smith as a substitute for a week unless the employer consents, and that Employer Brown cannot assign his contracts of employment when he sells his business to Green. But in effect transfers take place in other ways. For example, suppose Employer Small is a little corporation controlled by a little parent company; the parent company transfers its interest in Small to a giant conglomerate. The effect, for

147

many purposes, is to transfer all Employer Small's contractual relations, whether employment or other kinds, from the first parent company to a giant conglomerate. And you may be sure that that will affect those relations in a number of ways. Similarly, the replacement of one supervisor upon retirement by another supervisor is, for the supervised employees, in many ways like a simple transfer of their employment contract. Thus, although the process is more complicated and the results hardly identical, in many ways some modern contractual relations are as transferable as discrete transactions.

7. *Attitudes.* When we come to the last subject we treated earlier, attitude of participants, we meet again a merger—as we did respecting obligations—of the characteristics of discrete transactions and primitive contractual relations. But the resulting vector differs from that of a simple merger.

Awareness of conflict of interest. In this respect, consider awareness of conflict of interest. The measurement of performance, the often high levels of precise planning, both of substance and structures, and the presence of a sharp division of benefits and burdens, all greatly enhance a constant awareness of conflict of interest in modern contractual relations. This is not to say that all modern contractual relations create the same levels of awareness—they do not—but most, especially large ones, have higher levels than does the typical primitive contractual relation.

Unity. What is the effect of this on attitudes toward unity? The heightened awareness of conflict of interest found in large modern contractual relations might on first glance be expected to turn them into no more than a group of discrete transactions. Such transactions have only an externally imposed unity in constant clash with the individual goals of the parties. But many of the factors found in relations—for example, the need for future cooperation—create high levels of interdependence in which the interests of each party become the interests of other parties. A labor union, for example, generally gains nothing by pushing wages so high by strikes that the employer is forced out of business. Awareness of unity inevitably results from this. And the unity is also against outsiders. Witness the alliance of management and unions in the defense industry against protest opposed to the Vietnam war.

Exploration of the nature of awareness of unity in modern contractual relations would require a major work all by itself. Suffice it for now to say, therefore, that factors such as high consciousness of conflict of interest make this modern awareness a markedly different phenomenon from the sense of unity to be found in primitive contractual relations. Among other things it may be, and often is, perceived in hostile terms: an attitude of "Oh my God, just think, those bastards and us in the same boat!" Nevertheless, interdependence, and with it a sense of unity, may occur with little love lost.

Time. Time is viewed in modern contractual relations both as presentiated and as not presentiated. The more carefully measured and planned parts of the relation may be viewed as having virtually occurred long before they happen. In a sense this is illustrated by the ready market for corporate bonds not payable for years or decades. Other parts of the relation are viewed as preparing for the future when and if it happens in particular ways as, for example, elaborate provisions for handling defaults in corporate bonds. Still others are viewed simply as open to what happens, to be worried about as events occur. We thus have considerably more differentiated and diverse attitudes toward time than in either a discrete transaction or primitive contractual relations. Moreover, even the most fully presentiated aspects of the relation differ from a fully presentiated discrete transaction. The parties are always at least dimly aware that the remainder of the relation might develop in such a way as to change even those parts.

Trouble. Modern contractual relations, like primitive ones, create an awareness that trouble—the final attitude concerning us—may arise, indeed in large long term relations it is well known that trouble *will* arise. This awareness, coupled with modern planning capabilities, often leads to extensive planning to deal with trouble when it occurs. This is planning beyond simply following internalization of norms, existing customs, existing laws, and the like. This contrasts with the discrete transaction, supposed to be trouble-free. And I use the word "supposed" both to mean believed to be and in its colloquial sense of should be.

8. *Power, hierarchy, and command.* The omission of power, hierarchy, and command in the earlier discussion of primitive contractual relations should not be understood as implying their absence from such relations— a primitive Eden where all are always truly free and equal. Rather the omission is purely one of convenience; waiting till now to juxtapose these subjects respecting discrete transactions with contractual relations will, I believe, lead more easily to understanding them in both primitive and modern contractual relations, as well as in discrete transactions.

By power I mean the ability to impose one's will on others irrespective of or by manipulating their wishes. Power is, of course, an immensely complicated subject, and I intend to focus only on some peculiarly contractual aspects, and particularly on dependence as a source of power.

Specialization and the exchange necessary to make it viable inevitably create dependence, each specialist depending upon other kinds of specialists for essential goods and services. To the extent that specialists exercise significant control over their products they acquire power to prevent those dependent on them from taking the product at will. Consider, for example, truck drivers and trucking companies. The drivers own their own time, and the companies own capital. Property and personal rights inhibit seizure of either of these assets by the other group, thereby conferring on both drivers and companies power over each other. An opportunity is provided, however, for exercising power beyond simply the negative power of preventing seizure. Each can exercise power by insisting upon particular terms of exchange, the drivers demanding, for example, $25 an hour, the companies demanding an hour's work for $10. When they finally agree on $15 an hour, while each is doing something that on balance it wants to do, the power created by dependence has nevertheless caused it to reach a result worse than it preferred. The exchange resulted from a vectoring of both willingness and unwillingness producing an affirmative balance in favor of willingness.

It should be obvious that, other things being equal, the terms of the exchange will depend upon relative balances of dependence. (Cook and Emerson 1978; Eisenberg 1976) If, for example, the companies are unorganized and the drivers form a united front, the latter are, for practical purposes, relatively independent, and the power of the companies is relatively modest, although not nonexistent or even insignificant. Indeed, although it is fashionable in some circles to speak, for example, of the powerlessness of consumers or of unorganized workers, they are always far from powerless, far from total unilateral dependence. They are only relatively less powerful, because they are relatively more dependent.

The exchange we have been discussing is a bilateral exercise of power. It does not, therefore, ordinarily create a hierarchy or command position, by which I mean power exercisable unilaterally. For either drivers or companies to exercise their power *so as to gain thereby* they must convince the other of the desirability of permitting the exercise. Nevertheless, contracts also create unilateral power. Indeed, that is true even of the discrete transaction whenever exchange is projected into the future, in other words, whenever there is anything at all to the exchange besides the present bilateral transfer of goods. And, of course, there always is—

for example, in a supermarket sale if the steak is tainted or the money paid is counterfeit we soon see some future aspects to what looked like a simple present exchange. Suppose the meat *is* bad, and the customer is made seriously ill; the customer now has the power, by threat or actual use of legal process, to command the supermarket to pay damages, whether it desires to do so or not.

Thus, even in a discrete transaction, unilateral power exists between the time when promises are made and when they are kept. This is a commonplace to lawyers, but one often subtly evaded in economic models. During the period of unperformed promises whoever is owed performance is indeed in a position of command and the relation can thus be one of hierarchy. Indeed it will be whenever only one party remains obligated, or whenever one party desires not to proceed while the other party wants performance. Whether the command is a potent one or a weak one will depend upon the sanctions available. With the external god assumed by the standard neoclassical microeconomic model the sanctions are, of course, totally effective, and the command position is therefore not just strong, but invincible.

Modern contractual relations create unilateral command powers, not only directly through promises but also through hierarchical structures. For example, a corporate board of directors can direct expenditures of millions of dollars, and no one—employee, stockholder, or creditor—may be able to say them nay. But in addition, contractual relations constantly generate masses of dependence and interdependence. And these in turn create masses of power, the affirmative exercise of which is done bilaterally through the processes of exchange.

What differentiates bilateral exercise of power in contractual relations from that of the discrete transaction is its dynamic quality. The relative balance of dependence in the discrete transaction is a static phenomenon; it is a given. But the balance of dependence in relations is in significant measure a product of the relations themselves. For example, a young welder about to go to work for an industrial plant has, as a result of numerous existing factors, a certain balance of interdependence with prospective employer, and the terms of employment acceptable to both sides will reflect that relatively static situation. But twenty years later countless changes in the employment relation itself will have created a totally different picture of interdependence. Aging, for example, may have made the welder far more dependent on the employer than he was at the start. But the change need not be only in such a direction; unionization may, for example, have made the employer far more dependent on the employee, since dealing with him involves dealing with the whole labor force.

The foregoing phenomenon is by no means limited to circumstances which we may be prone to consider as relatively unbalanced. It is also so common in the industrial and financial world among relative equals that Wachter and Williamson (1978) have coined a new phrase to describe it: obligational market contracting. A neat term that; it captures nicely the vectoring of willingness and unwillingness mentioned earlier, as well as the dynamic dependence of ongoing relations, together with a hint of the command and hierarchy also so very common in contractual relations.

This discussion of power may be summarized as follows in terms of the axes between discrete transactions and modern relational contract. In the discrete transaction bilateral power is exercised initially at the time the deal is made, the exercise being affected by whatever the power status quo is then. Between then and complete performance one or both parties may have unilateral power. Thus while power may be assumed away in theoretical models of the discrete transaction, (*e.g.* Alchian and Demsetz 1972, 777) in fact it is always present and important.

In contractual relations similar bilateral and unilateral power is also regularly present, but the status quo is dynamic, and power relations are always in a state of flux. Given also the presence of continuing command and hierarchical structures, coupled with ongoing conditions of dependence, power becomes a far more complex phenomenon internally. Power of this kind is a dominant feature of modern contractual relations.

5.3   Values in Contract: Internal and External

Values in Context: Contract Behavior and its Internal Principles and Rules

The New Social Contract sets out three classes of contract norms common contract norms, discrete norms, and relational norms. These norms constitute "an abstract summary of the varied and specific norms appearing in myriad varieties of contracts." (Macneil 1980c, 39)

The common norms are essential to *any* behavior we might be willing to call contractual and they become, by conversion of is to ought, principles of right action as well. Similarly, *given a discrete transaction*, the discrete norm reflects both behavior and the oughts growing out it, just as, *given relational contracts*, the relational norms reflect both behavior and the oughts emerging from it. So stated, however, these norms appear to be ahistorical. To the extent the appearance reflects reality, they can have only circumscribed analytical value, of one believes, as I do, that norms and values cannot sensibly be discussed in any ultimate or global sense outside a particular historical context.

Given the intertwining of these norms in behavior, principle, and rule, they encompass the two merged value-arenas of contract behavior and internal principles and rules. The common contract norms are then, in my view, *the* values in the internal (as opposed to external) arenas of contracts whether the contracts are discrete or relational. It is therefore necessary to describe them here briefly and also to suggest some modifications from their earlier statement in *The New Social Contract*.

A. COMMON CONTRACT NORMS

The ten common contract norms are (1) role integrity (requiring consistency, involving internal conflict, and being inherently complex), (2) reciprocity (simply stated as the principle of getting something back for something given ("mutuality" in Macneil 1980c, 46)), (3) implementation of planning, (4) effectuation of consent, (5) flexibility, (6) contractual solidarity, (7) the restitution, reliance, ("procedural justice" in Macneil 1978a, 898; 1980c, 70) and expectation interests (the "linking norms"), (8) creation and restraint of power (the "power norm"), (9) propriety of means, and (10) harmonization with the social matrix. Although all the common contract norms are essential elements of contract behavior and constitute the values of such behavior, two of them call for special notice: contractual solidarity and reciprocity.

As students of man in society, we are faced with an illogicality. Man is both an entirely selfish creature and an entirely social creature, in that man puts the interests of his fellows ahead of his own interests *at the same time* that he puts his own interests first. Such a creature is schizophrenic, and will, to the extent that it does anything except vibrate in utter frustration, constantly alternate between inconsistent behaviors—selfish one second and self-sacrificing the next. Man is, in the most fundamental sense of the word, irrational, and no amount of reasoning, no matter how sophisticated, will produce a complete and consistent account of human behavior, customs, or institutions. Two principles of behavior are essential to the survival of such a creature: solidarity and reciprocity. Man, being a choosing creature, is easily capable of paralysis of decision when two conflicting desires are in equipoise. The two principles of solidarity and reciprocity, neither of which can operate through time without the other, solve this problem. Getting something back for something given nearly releases, or at least reduces, the tension in a creature desiring to be both selfish and social at the same time, and solidarity—a belief in being able to depend on another—permits the projection of reciprocity through time.

While all the contract norms operate in the behavior and in the internal principles and rules of all kinds of contracts, some assume special importance in discrete transactions and others assume special importance in contractual relations. In addition, a contextual transformation or merger of some of these norms may occur. For these reasons, analysis of the differences between discrete transactions and contractual relations is aided by outlining the common norms constituting the basis of the discrete norm and those constituting the bases of the relational norms.

B.   Common Contract Norms and the Discrete Norm: Enhancing Discreteness and Presentiation

As will be seen, the discrete norm is the product of the intensification of two common contract norms: implementation of planning and effectuation of consent.

> Discreteness and presentiation are themselves not the same phenomenon, in spite of their merger in discrete contracts. Discreteness is the separating of a transaction from all else between the participants at the same time and before and after. Its ideal, never achieved in life, occurs when there *is* nothing else between the parties, never has been, and never will be. Presentiation, on the other hand, is the bringing to the future into the present. Underlying both is the ideal of 100 percent planning of the future. (Macneil 1980c, 60)

The closer the parties are to behaving and governing themselves in accordance with this discrete norm, the more they will choose planning that is completely binding (or as close to completely binding as they can get), thereby bringing the future into the present as much as is humanly possible.

C. COMMON CONTRACT NORMS AND THE RELATIONAL NORMS

The relational norms of role integrity, preservation of the relation harmonization of relational conflict, and supracontract norms are also intensifications of particular common contract norms. These are primarily role integrity, contractual solidarity, and harmonization with the social matrix. In addition, relational contexts affect the nature of other common norms. For example, flexibility in relations is at least partially an internal, rather than an entirely external norm as it is (in theory) in discrete transactions. Hence, flexibility comes into partial conflict with the planning and consent norms in ways not occurring in discrete transactions. Reciprocity also becomes an important internal matter lest the relation break down. Power also is an important internal matter in relations.

D. COMMENTARY

The level of values I have been discussing—values of contract behavior and of internal principles and rules—is an extremely important one. It is also one too often partially or entirely overlooked in contract scholarship, which tends to focus either on the next level—the response, especially the legal response, of external society to contract—or on only the discrete transactional aspects of this level. The importance stems from the fact that this is the real operating level—the real life level of exchange relations. Consequently, this is the level at which complementation of values undoubtedly has by far the greatest impact upon the lives of the participants and everyone affected by their activities. The norms generated internally in billions of contractual relations are the most important in determining the value patterns of the overall society in which they occur. A more complete analysis of those norms is therefore, appropriate before considering the next value-arena.

1. *Common Contract Norms.*—It should be noted that since the common contract norms are present in all contracts, they give rise to whatever values emerge from all contract behavior and our assessment of it. Those norms and their interplay permit the widest possible range of

"successful" human activity and interaction.

The only time these norms are not present and therefore do not give rise to oughts is when contract is not operating. Nevertheless, they do not necessarily blossom fully in all contractual relations at all times. Contractual relations fall along a "success spectrum." Those contractual relations operating effectively will reveal the common contract norms in robust condition, while those in varying degrees of trouble will reveal the common contract norms in varying degrees of disarray both as they affect contract behavior and as they affect the internal rules and principles of that behavior. Uganda, both before and after Idi Amin, offers an excellent example of how contract norms disappear as a large contractual relation—the nation and its economy—falls apart; at a more microcosmic level, most any failure of a marriage will illustrate the point.

Lest the foregoing be taken as unthinking adoption of an exclusively consensus theory a comment concerning conflict versus consensus is in order here. In a review of the *New Social Contract*, Foster says:

> As political theory, the book is flawed by its Durkheimian premise of social solidarity. The state as an instrument of class domination and control, or as a bureaucratic organization resting on legitimated domination are theories pushed to one side. Like Durkheim, Macneil appears to see the State as representing the collective organ of moral conscience. Conflict is then a disfunctional disruption of this collective morality. The law's function is to restore the harmony of society. This may be a defensible theoretical position but it needs more explicit argument than Macneil offers. His political values slip into the book as if they were non-problematic and shared by everyone; a not unusual error of consensus theorists (Foster 1982, 147)

The relational contract theory set out in the *New Social Contract* is far from incompatible with theories of the state as an instrument of class domination and control or as a bureaucratic organization resting on legitimated domination. Indeed, I accept such theories of the state to a considerable extent myself. Those theories are incompatible with the theory of "the State as representing" *a* "collective organ of moral conscience" *only* if one believes that a conflict theory and a consensus theory must be incompatible. This I do not believe. Nor do I view conflict as entirely dysfunctional, as Foster implies. A propensity for conflict is a fact of human nature and no more dysfunctional than any other limiting factor in our nature, such as our inability to understand completely both ourselves and the world around us or our restricted range of ways to communicate with one another. In this sense, out propensity to conflict is simply something to which we accommodate ourselves, just as is our propensity to cooperate. Whether actual conflict is functional or dysfunctional in any given circumstance cannot be answered abstractly. Nevertheless, I would have thought that it is a truism that uncontrolled conflict is the antithesis of continuing social behavior. In this sense, wherever there is continuing social behavior among a particular group, the very existence of the group shows that consensus is resolving the problems raised by conflict sufficiently to allow that existence. Elsewhere, I have discussed the fact that this kind of consensus is only a tension between conflict and cooperation. (Macneil 1986) It does not eliminate conflict in some magical way, as Foster seems to imply.

It is Gurvitch, I believe, who has captured most clearly the spirit of the relation between conflict and consensus in contractual relations:

> The jural bond established by a contract consists simultaneously of (a) a convergence of wills of the contracting parties with a view to establishing a mutual obligation valid in the future (*rapprochement*) and (b) the opposition of two or more wills seeking exactly opposite aims and establishing opposing duties (to give something or to receive it, etc.: separation). Again, the contracting parties are in a harmony of rights and interests in so far as execution of the contract is concerned (*rapprochement*) and in a conflict of rights and interests insofar as material clauses and manner of carrying them out are concerned (separation). That is why it is impossible to characterize unequivocally, as has often been erroneously attempted, the contractual relationship, whether as a *consensus* of wills and duties (Durkheim), or as their conflict and delimitation (Tonnies). The secret of contractual bonds, as well as of exchanges in general, various sorts of obligations and the like, lies in the intercourse of *rapprochement* and separation. (Gurvitch 1947, 172–173)

Both the possibility of high conflict levels in contractual relations and the vast range of character of successful, that is surviving, contractual relations mentioned earlier raise questions about the usefulness of the "oughts" arising out of the common contract norms. These norms seem to provide so little basis for moral discrimination among such a wide range of behavior that few would be content solely with the resulting broad-brush naturalistic morality they suggest.

Nevertheless, we should not sneer at norms purporting to reflect nothing more than successful social behavior. The brute social human may not provide all the norms of our higher aspirations, but what be provides is much more than the normative zero that the mythical Hobbesian individual human provides. What social man provides is also in many ways more useful for analysis than more controversial higher levels dependent upon greater ideological consensus. It is true that ideology will affect agreement and disagreement about the content of such naturalistic norms, but surely less so than for norms starting from liberal idealism or Marxist determinism. If, for example, reciprocity is accepted as a fundamental norm for all social behavior, we can move some distance towards establishing quite a decent social morality. I do not, however, want to press the morality of the common contract norms too far at this point. I am still talking about *internal* behavior and norms, and it is therefore not yet necessary to deal with problems relating to the interface of given contractual relations with some larger society and its moralities.

A significant difference between the discrete and relational norms and the common contract norms should now be stressed. I have claimed that contractual behavior cannot exist without the common contract norms. Relative dearth of the discrete or the relational norms does not destroy contractual relations. Rather, dearth of the discrete or relational norms causes, respectively, the relation to become less discrete (more relational) or less relational (more discrete).

2. *The Discrete Norm.*—What does the existence of the discrete norm at the level of behavior and internal principles and rules imply about the values underlying that behavior? You will recall that the norm calls for enhancing discreteness and presentation. I have described it in that way in a deliberate attempt to strip from it as much value as possible. Nevertheless, some of its values, at least, are immediately apparent.

a. Values of the Discrete Norm.—First, the discrete norm is a norm of precision, a focusing norm. It enables people to deal precisely with one thing at a time—to keep their eyes on the ball—a vital factor in much human endeavour." (Macneil 1980c, 63) It is a value that everyone resists in some aspects of life, and that some people resist in all aspects of life to the extent it is possible to resist the value and still survive. It is, thus, far from "neutral" or universal.

158

Secondly, where the norm governs, "following through" on planning utespective of the consequences is what matters. Although *pacta sunt servanda* usually is thought to mean that choice-generated consent is binding, it must never be forgotten that it means equally *planning est servanda*. This planning value is both enhanced and limited by the other intensified common contract norm, that of implementing consent; consenting, where the norm of discreteness and presentation operates, means what it says—the consenter is well and truly stuck. The emphasis on consent, however, is also a limiting factor, because together the participants can consent to change; thus, the norm of enhancing discreteness and presentation does not prevent the parties from creating a new and different discrete presentation any time they wish. Thus, the norm as it works in discrete transactions contains the seeds of its own destruction.

Thirdly, discreteness "fits very well the concepts of efficiency developed in the neoclassical microeconomic model. Indeed, that is a tautology, since the discrete transaction is the basis of the model." (Macneil 1980c, 63 citing Goldberg 1976) Thus, whatever are the values of patterning real contracting on the efficiency paradigm also are values of the discrete norm. I am not at all sure that these values differ in any respect from the other values discussed here. Nonetheless, given the prevalence of efficiency theory in economic analysis of law, this "efficiency value" should be mentioned.

Fourthly, because the discrete norm is, in part, a great intensification of the norm of consent, and because of the origin of consent in choice, the discrete norm appears to promote the value of freedom of individuals to choose. This is what Charles Fried (1981, 8) calls the liberal ideal, the ideal which "makes what we achieve our own and our failures our responsibility too." But, the appearance that the discrete norm promotes the value of the autonomy of individuals—that is, the purported value of what Professor Fried calls the promise principle—is misleading.

Placing value on allowing people to make choices—to act free of restraint—leads to placing value on not freeing persons of the consequences of their choices. Freeing them of such consequences would undo the choice and in significant ways would retroactively deprive them of the power of choice.

It does *not*, however, automatically follow that placing value on effective choice leads to placing value on consent to bind oneself in the future. Indeed, on the face of it, the individualistic premise suggests the opposite. The only way an autonomous individual *can* bind himself in the

159

future is by invoking the power of the society of which he is a member—that is, by calling upon it to bind him, to deprive him of choice in the future. Even though the individual may have asked society to deprive him of his future choice, this social tying down of the individual appears to conflict with placing value on choice.

Charles Fried, sets out the only justification for enforcing promises—for converting choice into consent—consistent with the value of autonomy: "The restrictions involved in promising are restrictions undertaken just in order to increase one's options in the long run, and thus are perfectly consistent with the principle of autonomy—consistent with a respect for one's own autonomy and the autonomy of others." (Fried 1981, 14)

Professor Fried's argument is one based on empirical consequences, not a deduction from the principle of autonomy. As such, it is always subject to challenge on the ground that in various particular circumstances the claimed increase does or does not, will or will not, occur.

It certainly is not correct that surrendering autonomy by asking the legal system to add sanctions to the surrender will always increase options—sometimes it will and sometimes it will not. To the extent promises do in fact "increase one's options in the long run," giving effect to consent may be consistent with placing a value on free choice. To the extent that promises reduce one's options in the long run, giving effect to consent is clearly inconsistent with placing a value on free choice.

Because planning merges with choice in consent, and because both planning and consent are important in the discrete norm, the question whether the discrete norm places value on choice in any given circumstances depends on whether the consent has a net overall freeing effect or a net overall enslaving effect. This is not something that can be ascertained by ahistorical abstract analysis of the kind adopted by Professor Fried, but only by examining particular circumstances in their historical context.

Fifthly, in one sense the discrete norm is conservative; it "presupposes the status quo and goes on from there." (Macneil 1980c, 64) But this is only part of its effect. Discreteness involves sharp focusing, it is consent-oriented, and it is related to efficiency in the technical sense; therefore, continual following of the discrete norm may be the path of great social and economic change. Indeed, the common view, accurate or not, of the putative heyday of discreteness in contract—the early-middle of the industrial revolution in Great Britain and America—is that dependence on the discrete norm led to significant social and economic change. Because of the opposing effects of the discrete norm on social change, however, we are again unable to make sound conclusions in the abstract about the values actually implemented, but must instead depend upon empirical study of particular historical contexts.

Sixthly, the discrete norm looks equalitarian because choice appears to dominate. That appearance, however, is deceptive; the discrete norm is inequalitarian in its immediate effect to whatever the degree the status quo is inequalitarian, and generally more so. By presupposing the status quo, the discrete norm

> inevitably aids the already powerful and tends to make them more powerful ... The norm also aids the powerful in capturing a larger part of the exchange-surplus than the less powerful, ... [It is important] that we recognize the existence of this power bias of the discrete norm and not pretend an equality in it that does not exist (Macneil 1980c, 64)

This immediately inequalitarian character of the discrete norm has stimulated many attacks on the norm on many intellectual, social, and political fronts. Nevertheless, the same comments may be made here that were made respecting the consent principles and conservatism. Whether, in a macro sense, the internal governance of contracts by the discrete norm is any more equalitarian than more relational alternatives is a matter for empirical historical investigation, and cannot be determined by abstract reasoning.

Seventhly, and finally, the discrete norm requires the sacrifice of relational values of many kinds, because it focuses sharply on money and other easy-to-quantify subjects of exchange, it ignores the identity of the parties, and it uses precise promise as a touchstone. All of these aspects of the discrete norm not uncommonly conflict with such particularly relational values as preservation of the relation and harmonization of relational contract. Furthermore, they may conflict with role integrity as it appears *in relations*, as well as with various supracontract norms.

b. Relationship Between Values of the Discrete Norm and Values of the Other Common Contract Norms.—Although the discrete norm reflects the great intensification of two of the common contract norms— implementation of planning and effectuation of consent—the other eight do not—indeed, cannot—disappear if the contract is to be viable. Thus, everything that has been said about the values of the discrete norms must be read against a backdrop of the other common contract norms, but a backdrop itself vitally affected by the presence of the discrete norm. What follows is a brief discussion of the other eight common contract norms as they relate to the discrete norm.

In the face of discreteness, role integrity is maintained by each participant's "operating within rigid rules of property and law under which he will maximize his utility, but only to the extent that the other consents." (Macneil 1980c, 65) Reciprocity is served by the *mutual* consent process leading to the formation of the deal. After that, reciprocity drops out. Where discreteness prevails, however, there is theoretically no "after that" because the whole approach to the transaction is complete presentation. Flexibility is achieved, not within the discrete transaction, where all is rigid presentiation, but outside it, in the repeated use of numerous discrete transactions. Contractual solidarity is maintained only through external forces, such as the law of contract, implementing the presentiated discrete transaction. The linking norms are served by equating restitution and reliance with expectation, and by the protection of expectation by the external forces fostering solidarity.

In addition, propriety of means is established where the discrete norm prevails by whatever the parties consent to in the agreement process. Where the agreement process does not explicitly deal with means, the discrete norm calls for whatever means are effective to accomplish the substantive results agreed upon. The free use of the full force of positive law in the event of backsliding clearly falls within this norm where discreteness prevails. The power norm is served by the existence of enforceability of the terms consented to as well as the limitation of all enforcement to such terms. There are no open-ended obligations.

Finally, the discrete norm must be harmonized with the social matrix, since it can be implemented only if the larger society in which it occurs is either willing to have it implemented or is unwilling to have it implemented but is unable to prevent implementation. The latter pattern cannot occur respecting any projection of the discrete transaction into the future, since such projection is dependent on the larger society's providing enforceability, the discrete transaction's version of contractual solidarity.

From the foregoing discussion, it is apparent that the intensification of the planning and consent norms in discrete transactions affects the other common contract norms, often drastically. While this brief treatment of this interplay fails to show any need to add to or change items in the list of discrete values, it does sharpen the relief respecting some of them. For

162

example, the fact that contractual solidarity exists in the discrete transaction only because of external force brings into sharp focus the questions raised earlier concerning the antichoice characteristics of the consent (promise) principle.

3. *The Relational Norms.*—The five norms of enhanced importance in ongoing contractual relations are role integrity, preservation of the relation, harmonization of relational conflict, propriety of means, and supracontract norms. Once again it should be stressed that, except to the extent that they are also common contract norms, the relational norms are not essential to contract behavior, they are simply essential to *relational* contract behavior, just as the discrete norm is essential to discrete transaction behavior. Their disappearance from any given contractual relation thus may or may not end all contract behavior among the parties to the contract. All contractual behavior between the participants is in danger of ending only if the relational norms are so eroded that the common contract norms underlying them are unfulfilled.

a. Values of the Relational Norms.—Role integrity, a common contract norm, becomes a very complex value in contractual relations involving as it does intricate linkings of habit, custom, internal principles and rules, social exchange and other social principles, dependence, expectations, and much else. Moreover, relational roles tend to be long term and to involve primary relations and diverse obligations. Role integrity becomes "more than simply keeping the rule honest; ... maintaining its integrity in the sense of keeping it together in a coherent piece is a major job of social engineering. Particularly is this so it the face of ... internal conflicts in roles." (Macneil 1980c, 66 footnote omitted)

The norm of preservation of the relation "is an intensification and expansion of the norm of contractual solidarity ... [It] involves preservation of particular memberships in relations—individual preservation—as well as preservation of the larger relation—collective preservation." (Macneil 1980c, 66) (Preservation of the larger relation and individual preservation of membership can easily come into conflict.)

The peaceable value, harmonization of relational conflict, is almost distinguishable from its underlying role of preserving relations peace is valued in its own right. One reason for its importance in modern contractual relations, at least, is that conflict exists between the need for measurement and specificity, for precision and focus, and for adherence to planning, and the need for flexibility to meet countless kinds of changed circumstances.

An aspect of harmonization of relational conflict is the necessity of dealing with whole persons, since contractual relations are characterized by whole person—primary—relations. Thus, unless it is possible simply to eliminate someone from a contractual relation, harmonization of relational conflict involving that someone necessarily requires harmonization with the whole person. The disgruntled employee, for example, is a potential or actual saboteur. This type of conflict is very different from conflict in a discrete transaction, where only the particular discrete dispute needs resolving and only for its own sake.

Propriety of means, also a common contract norm, becomes very complex in contractual relations. Every social relation generates norms concerning the ways by which ends may be achieved and the ways by which ends, no matter how legitimate may not. The more complex the social relation, the more complex such principles and practices of decorum become. Thus, just as role integrity becomes complex in contractual relations, so does propriety of means.

Finally, since the scope of supracontract norms is open-ended, it is not feasible to deal with their values in the Article, except to stress again their importance in keeping relational contract theory from being a closed, a historical system of analysis.

b. Relationship Between Values of the Relational Norms and Values of the Other Common Contract Norms.—Just as the discrete norm must be analyzed against a backdrop of the other common contract norms, so must the relational norms. Since two of the relational norms—role integrity and propriety of means—are themselves common contract norms, examination of this interplay of common contract norms with relational norms has, in effect, already started.

Because contractual relations cannot continue without reciprocity, the preservation norm requires continual maintenance of adequate reciprocity, There is no magic formula, such as promise in the discrete transaction, to resolve the reciprocity issue for all time. The question, "What have you done for me lately?" is always in the background, if not the foreground, of ongoing contractual relations. The relational norms are relatively neutral respecting implementation of planning and effectuation of consent. As will be seen in the discussion of the values of relational norms relative to the discrete norm, these common contract norms may be intensified or weakened depending upon the nature of the relation. Flexibility—adaptability to change—in no way conflicts with the relational norms. Indeed, it is essential to implementing all of them. Relations cannot be preserved, nor conflict in relations harmonized, without adequate attention to the demands of change. Furthermore, roles cannot survive with total rigidity. Finally, various supracontract norms very often require adaptability to change.

The connection between contractual solidarity and the relational norms is that one of the relational norms—preservation of the contractual relation—is simply the intensification of the common contract norm of contractual solidarity. In contractual relations, the linking norms—restitution, reliance, and expectation—do not necessarily collapse into one, as in the discrete transaction. They may therefore come into conflict with each other, thereby calling into play the relational norms of preservation and conflict resolution to harmonize the conflicts. In addition, since no relation can endure without both the creation and the restraint of power, and since those two aspects of the power norm are in internal conflict, the relational norms of preservation and conflict resolution are necessarily consistent with this common contract norm. The relational norms are also consistent with the common contract norm of harmonizing with the social matrix. Roles, for example, that do not fit adequately within the social matrix simply will not work. For similar reasons, preservation of the relation and harmonization of relational conflict require adherence to the supracontract norms prevailing in the internal relation and the larger society.

In sum, relational norms are always consistent with the common contract norms. Indeed, relations being a more open social approach to exchange than discrete transactions, relational norms often tend to harmonize more with human relations than does the more refined norm of discreteness and presentiation.

c. Are the Values of the Relational Norms Contrary to the Values of the Discrete Norm?—The answer to the question whether the values of the relational norms are contrary to the values of the discrete norm varies with both context and the value in question. Nothing in the relational norms necessarily precludes precision and focus. Consider rigidly disciplined organizations such as crack military outfits; they achieve very sharp precision and focus within very relational frameworks. NASA with its space shots is another example. Yet, nothing in the relational norms themselves requires a great deal of precision and focus, as many a successful marriage attests.

Planning, too, may or may not be elevated to extremely high levels in relations. "The greatest blossoming of discreteness and presentiation the world has ever seen is not to be found" in private contract "at all either in the past or in the present. Rather it is alive and well—or perhaps alive and malignly sick—in the detailed rules of bureaucracies whether private or public." (Macneil 1980c, 77) On the other hand, unlike the discrete norm, the relational norms do not require such extensive planning, again a fact that many families illustrate.

On the face of it, the relational norms appear to be contrary to notions of economic efficiency; but the basic failure of the microeconomic model to take always-present relational factors into account renders such conclusions highly suspect. (Macneil 1981b, 1041–1063)

The relational norms often operate contrary to the value of autonomy, at least autonomy viewed as of any instant. The relational norms may, for example, lock people into relations that they wish to escape, as in a conscript army. On the other hand, people may voluntarily observe the relational norms, as in the case of a student adapting to the many norms of university life. Certainly voluntary, but even involuntary, adherence to relational norms may increase long run options, an assumption underlying required grade school education, for example. Thus, the impact of relational norms on the choice-value is equivocal, as was true of the impact of implementing consent. The impact of neither norm on the autonomy of the individual can be stated abstractly but can be determined only by examining particular circumstances in historical context.

The relational norms, like the discrete norm, are equivocal in their effect in creating or preventing change. They may operate either to bring about or to stifle change, depending upon the particular circumstances in their particular historical setting. For an example of relational norms effecting social change at the macro-level, consider early Maoist China where all the relational norms, including the supracontract norms of Maoism, dominated every interaction among individuals. Since these norms were operating in a revolutionary society, they were norms of great change. The same norms (other than some of the Maoist supracontract norms) operating in a period of social stability in China, as certainly has happened in the past, would strongly favor the status quo.

The relational norms also have an equivocal effect on the sixth value discussed relative to discreteness: equality. Just as it is not possible to decide abstractly whether discreteness fosters or impedes equality, neither is it possible to decide abstractly whether the relational norms foster or impede equality. Once again, we must examine the circumstances in an historical context.

Virtually by definition, the relational norms have an opposite impact from that of the discrete norm on relational values: the relational norms foster relational values while the discrete norm does not. Probably the

166

only exception to this statement is that short-term discreteness is sometimes beneficial to long-term relational patterns. Nonetheless, one is forced to use rather extreme circumstances to illustrate the latter situation. For example, when a group of soldiers scatters in the face of unexpected incoming artillery fire, each soldier typically is reacting in an extremely selfish, discrete manner. Nevertheless, if the soldiers did not scatter, the whole unit—that is, the contractual relation—might be destroyed.

In sum, the relational norms are equivocal respecting all of the first six values discussed in relation to the discrete norm, whereas two of those values—precision and focus and adherence to planning (presentiation)—always are present when the discrete norm prevails. But both kinds of norms—discrete and relational—are equivocal respecting the other four of those six values—economic efficiency, choice, status quo as opposed to change, equalitarian values. Thus, the only clear, ever-present clash between relational norms and the discrete norm concerns the seventh value discussed in relation to the discrete norm: the sacrifice or nonsacrifice of relational values.

Summary. At the level of contract behavior and internal principles and rules, all common contract norms are essential to the processes of projecting exchange into the future; no exchange activity can continue for long absent any of them. Nevertheless, some of these norms may become exaggerated relative to others, as occurs inevitably in discrete transactions and very often in relations; such exaggeration also may considerably alter the nature of other common contract norms.

Values in Context: External Social Responses

A. INTRODUCTION

1. *Internal-External; Sovereign-Nonsovereign.*—Although a distinction between internal and external social response to contracts causes relatively little trouble for traditional analyses of contract, it causes problems for relational contract theory. Since all contracts are linked horizontally and vertically with other exchange relations until the entire world economy is encompassed, there is no such thing as an external social matrix, nor are there social values external to any contract. All values are internal. Thus, there is never any point at which separation of

the internal from the external can be other than partially arbitrary.

Nevertheless, in many circumstances it may be very helpful to say: "This is the end of the inside of the relations between the parties, and this is where the external society begins." The nuclear family is illustrative. Because of the deep core of relations among mother, father, children, and other members of the immediate household, it is feasible and useful to think in terms of the bounded nuclear family. We then can consider as external the parents' employment and other economic and social relations, and the children's school and other economic and social relations, as well as the family's relations with other family members, friends, church, and government, even though all are really integral aspects of the nuclear family. As long as we remember that our separation of the internal from the external is somewhat artificial and arbitrary, we can proceed with caution to speak in such terms. We can then logically consider the subject of external social values.

Before turning to the substance of values in external social responses to contracts, it should be stressed that such values may originate not only in the positive law of the sovereign, but also from many other sources, of which only one source is conceptualizing about contract. Thus, an exhaustive examination of external social values would by no means be limited to the positive law of the sovereign and conceptualizing about contract. It would also have to include private law, such as that imposed on professional football teams by league rules, on businesses by trade associations, on colleges and universities by the American Association of University Professors, and on family life by churches. Furthermore, it could not stop with relatively hierarchical or vertical impositions such as those listed. It also would have to deal with more horizontal imposition of external values, such as those arising from customs—not only those customs of closely related people or groups, such as customs of a trade, but also customs of broader origin, such as those of civilized intercourse in the particular society.

One Article cannot discuss imposition of external social values by all the important horizontal and nonsovereign sources. The following discussion will thus be limited to imposition of external social values by a sovereign, or, in other words, to sovereign positive law. Considerable danger lies in such limitation. Beginning and ending with the traditional subject creates the potential for a vastly distorted picture, not only of contract, but also of the sovereign positive law itself when it is erroneously perceived as the *only* imposer of external social values. The danger is unavoidable, however, if the Article is not to be prolonged unduly.

2. *Prohibition, Nonintervention, and "Total" Control.*—One sovereign norm governing contracts may be that particular contracts ought not to exist. Under Nazi laws, for example, a Jewish-Aryan marital relation was anathema. To the extent that a sovereign prohibition is successfully implemented, there is, of course, no contract left to be subjected to sovereign values. While such restrictions on forming or continuing certain kinds of contracts raise a host of questions. I do not intend to explore those questions here. To the extent the sovereign prohibitions succeed, there is no interaction to discuss. To the extent they are only partially implemented, the values of the sovereign "prohibition" are transformed into different kinds of values than the value of absolute prevention (even though the desire for prevention may remain the motivating force).

Thus, the following discussion assumes that, whatever else is involved, the sovereign is not actually stamping out the pertinent contract. Having made this assumption, a broad range of possible postures by the sovereign remains, reflecting a wide spectrum of values. At one end of the spectrum is complete nonintervention. The value reflected by nonintervention is total autonomy of the internal participants. A noninterventionist sovereign imposes externally none of the contract norms—common, discrete, or relational.

At the other, end of the spectrum is as complete sovereign control of the relation as possible. When this end is reached, however, the external and internal merge so much that separating them at all may make little sense, or may make sense for only very limited purposes; examples of such extensive mergings are socialist state enterprises, our complex public-private space program, and military procurement. Examples falling short of such a merger are wartime price, quantity, and quality controls, or perhaps the extremely close regulation of employment relations in some Western mixed economies.

The common contract norms impose limits on how far the sovereign *can* go in imposing total control over contractual behavior. Sovereign prevention of the operation of those norms will destroy contract, just as does their disruption by internal forces. One example of how sovereign prevention of the common contract norms destroys contract is the generally conceded inefficiency of slave labor camps; the levels of reciprocity in such camps are simply too low for effective contractual relations to exist.

The class of sovereign norms that will now be treated is identical to the internal norms of contract behavior, principles, and rules discussed earlier. Furthermore, we are interested in their imposition (or nonimposition) by the sovereign only to the extent that such imposition for nonimposition) does not result in such great erosion of the *internal* norms of contract behavior, principles, and rules, as to cause the disapperance of contract.

B.   EXTERNAL SOCIAL RESPONSES: VALUES IN SOVEREIGN POSITIVE LAW

1. *Values of Nonintervention*—The value reflected in complete non-intervention by sovereign positive law is total autonomy of the internal participants. The noninterventionist sovereign imposes externally none of the contract norms—common, discrete, or relational. The effect is to separate the sovereign altogether from the contractual relation in question. An example of sovereign non-intervention is the great reluctance of American courts to interfere in any way at all in the internal affairs of churches. (U.S. Const. Amend. 1) Another example results from the doctrine of *pari delicto* when applied to illegal contracts. To the extent such a value prevails, it is as if the relation were occurring in some other society.

Because of the confusing nature of the term "freedom of contract," it is important to note that the value of sovereign nonintervention is not the same as the value of freedom of contract. Freedom of contract is almost always used to mean freedom to bind oneself by contract—that is, to cause the sovereign to confer power on the other contractor to enforce the contract against one's self. This is sovereign intervention not sovereign nonintervention.

2. *Transformation of Norms When Imposed.*—Sovereign imposition of norms on contract, in contrast to their generation within the contract, results in a transformation of the contract's values. That is the values of imposing contract norms—whether common, discrete, of relational—are not identical to the values reflected by their internal generation. Not only is an imposed norm theoretically different—respecting consent, for example—but it will be practically different as well.[1]

The foregoing may be illustrated by *Edward G. Budd Manufacturing Cof*

---

[1] One of the most delightful examples is *Everet v. Williams* (Exch. 1725), in which one highwayman sued another highwayman for breach of an agreement to split the loot of their past endeavours. Not surprisingly, the court would have none of it.

v. NLRB, (138 F.2d 86 (3d Cir. 1943) where the National Labor Relations Board (NLRB) ordered reinstatement of an employee whom the Board found had been fired because of his work on behalf of the CIO union complaining in the case.

> The case of Walter Weigand is extraordinary. If ever a workman deserved summary discharge, it was he. He was under the influence of liquor while on duty. He came to work when he chose and he left the plant and his shift as he pleased. In fact, a foreman on one occasion was agreeably surprised to find Weigand at work and commented on it. Weigand amiably stated that he was enjoying it. He brought a woman (apparently generally known as "Duchess") to the rear of the plant yard and introduced some of the employees to her. He took another employee to visit her and when this man got too drunk to be able to go home, punched is time-card for him and put him on the table in the representiatives' meeting room in the plant in order to sleep off his intoxication. Weigand's immediate superiors demanded again and again that he be discharged, but each time officials intervened on Weigand's behalf because as was naively stated he was "a representative" [of a company union]. In return for not working at the job for which he was hired, the petitioner gave him full pay and on five separate occasions raised his wages. [Only one of these was a general pay increase given other employees.] (*Id.* at 90 (citation to record omitted)

When the employer suspected that Weigand had joined the CIO union, a fired him. In spite of the foregoing description of Weigand, the Court of Appeals enforced the NLRB's order of reinstatement. One may either be outraged at the imposition of such an employee on a business, or think the order served the employer right, or both. But it a clear that the NLRB's and the court's imposition on the employer of Weigand as an employee reflects very different values from the employer's original retention of him. The upper management originally viewed him as supplying services sufficiently valuable to warrant his retention, thereby satisfying the norm of reciprocity as they saw it. Once Weigand "joined the other side" and hence no longer served his therefore useful function for management, they, entirely correctly, as longer believed that any individual reciprocity would be achieved While the voluntary retention of Weigand reflected the reciprocity norm as applied to a single employee, the sovereign imposition of Weigand as an employee reflected at least three, and perhaps four, norms These were the reciprocity norm applied collectively, the contractual solidarity norm, the restraint of power norm, and perhaps some unidentified supracontract norms. The result, however, unless Weigand mended his ways or was successfully fired for not doing so, was not a contractual relation between the employer and Weigand as an individual. Rather, it was a private welfare scheme imposed on the employer as a means of policing the National Labor Relations Act.

The foregoing is merely illustrative. It is not feasible to deal as length here with all the transformations that contract norms—whether common, discrete, or relational—undergo when those norms are imposed by government compared to internal generation. Instead, only sovereign imposition of the discrete norm and limited aspects of the imposition of other norms will be explored, and those relatively briefly

3. *Imposition of the Discrete Norm.*—Sovereign reinforcement of discreteness and presentation, through classical and, to a lesser extent neoclassical contract law appears to elevate consent to a position of high value. But this appearance is deceiving. Professor Fried has recently done contract scholarship the great service of recognizing—from the standpoint of an advocate of the will or consent theory of contract— the limitations of consent. Unlike earlier advocates of the objective theory of contracts such as Williston, Professor Fried is more than willing to recognize gaps in contracts and then refrain from trying to cram those gaps into the promise principle. (Fried 1981, 57–73) Since, however, classical contract law did far overstep the promise principle in the imposition of discrete values, (Macneil 1974b) it is apparent that sovereign law following the objective theory was, in considerable measure, either anticonsent or neutral respecting it. Rigorous application of the parol evidence rule appears to be a good example of how sovereign law following the objective theory can be anticonsent. (Calamari and Perillo 1967) Nonetheless, it is often difficult to well whether sovereign law implements consent or not. It is possible to argue, for example, that a rigorously exclusionary parol evidence rule prevents perjury and will more often lead to implementing consent than a looser rule leaving perjury a lively possibility.

Another example of an apparently anticonsent doctrine that never-theless possibly implements consent is found in Uniform Conmoirial Code § 2–302, which provides relief from the enforcement of unconscionable provisions in contracts for the purchase and sale of goods. The word "unconscionable" appears to allow relief from terms to

172

which consent has been given. Nevertheless, the first official comment to the section suggests something else: "The principle is one of the prevention of oppression and unfair surprise . . . and not of disturbance of allocation of risks because of superior bargaining power." Thus, the relief is given when the appearance of consent is a false one, when consent to the terms is not "real." To the extent section 2–302 is so applied, it does not frustrate consent at all. Indeed, it implements what the court views as genuine consent.

It may be noted how the *imposition* of the discrete norm, as distinct from its *internal* growth, may transform it. For example, as between parties to a relatively discrete transaction, the norm of discreteness may be served by their implementing promises made over the telephone, even though those promises might be contrary to the formal documents exchanged between them. The parties thereby implement the norm of consent. On the other hand, where there is a dispute, the norm of consent may be disserved when the discrete norm is imposed by government, because the sovereign lacks information available to the participants—for instance, whether the alleged telephone conversation— actually took place.

The common difficulty of ascertaining whether imposition of the discrete norm is proconsent, neutral, or anticonsent adds to the difficulty of ascertaining whether that imposition is prochoice, neutral, or antichoice. Consent originates in choice coupled with the chooser's own invocation of society's enforcement of his choice. Provision of such enforcement by society, however, might or might not have the long run effect of implementing the value of choice. Thus, when the sovereign value is anticonsent, when freedom of contract is not allowed to prevail, no general conclusion can be reached about whether this value is prochoice or antichoice over any substantial period of time. Nor does a proconsent position necessarily mean that a prochoice value is being implemented. Each set of circumstances must be examined to ascertain whether the anticonsent position "has a net overall freeing effect or a net overall enslaving effect."

4. *Imposition of Reciprocity, the Power Norm, Preservation of the Relation, and Propriety of Means.*—Much of the Western nations imposition of sovereign values on contract has concerned four values, two of them common contract norms, one a particularly relational norm, and one which is both. These four values are reciprocity, creation and restraint of power, preservation of relations, and propriety of means. Two aspects of sovereign imposition of these values will be explored their relation to

choice, and their bureaucratic effect.

a. Relation to Choice—Once again, it is not possible to make valid generalizations about the ultimate effect of sovereign imposition of these values on choice. One could argue, for example, that the federal government's increasing intervention into every kind of contractual relation over the past forty years, including its intervention through all its macroeconomic policies, has been a vital factor in a mind-boggling proliferation of choice relating to employment, consumption, and lifestyle. One could also counter that such intervention has helped set the country on a largely technologically-determined historical course in which all such choices are highly superficial; one could counter further that such patterns have gone far to erode the availability of significant choice. Rather than engage in such highflown discussion, however, this section will simply examine some key values the sovereign has sought to impose and their relatively immediate effect on choice.

Reciprocity. A vast array of legislative, administrative, and judicial law of the last 50 years is aimed at imposing levels of reciprocity other than those it is believed would occur in the absence of that law. Nowhere is this more evident than in the area of employment. The government has, for example, imposed the minimum wage, protected and encouraged labor monopolies to raise wages of selected workers, levied social security taxes, and prohibited discrimination respecting wages (and other conditions of employment) on a wide variety of grounds, including race and sex.

Such sovereign efforts to impose reciprocity are intended to limit the choice of one participant in contract, the one whose share in the fruits of the contract are being reduced. It should also be noted, however, that the imposition of reciprocity often deprives other participants of choice as well, since they might well choose *not* to have the reciprocity adjusted in their favor because of various costs to them of doing so. For example, payment of Social Security taxes is mandatory in very considerable measure because many workers, as well as employers, would opt out if given the chance. Furthermore, such opting out would not be limited to the workers least favored by the system. Proponents of the system argue that workers in general place insufficient utility on saving for old age compared to spending their wages immediately. The minimum wage also illustrates that imposed levels of reciprocity restrict choice, of employees as well as of employers. Even if the widespread view that the minimum wage laws eliminate hundreds of thousands, perhaps millions, of jobs is incorrect, every evasion of those laws proves that they aim to limit choice

174

of participants on *both* sides.

Power. To put this norm in context, it should be recalled that the most fundamental sovereign *creation* of power affecting contracts is first, sovereign enforcement of liberty and property rights among the populace and their organizations, and second, sovereign enforcement of contracts. While such creation of power carries with it built-in restraints, over the past century or so sovereign restraints on liberty, property, and contract-enforcement power have become increasingly specific. While relatively little of such regulation seems to be aimed at changing the fundamental nature of liberty, property rights, or contract-enforcement power, its total effect has been to change them drastically. (Atiyah 1979, 727–728)

As it did for sovereign imposition of reciprocity, employment law provides a good example of sovereign imposition of the power norm. Since the power norm operates both to create and to restrain power, it is necessary to deal with both aspects.

Much regulation aims to restrain the power of employers over their employees. Other legislation, such as the National Labor Relations Act, (29 U.S.C. ss. 151–169 (1935)) aims largely to increase the power of employees over their employers. A restraint of employer power obviously reduces the employ*er's* choice, at least in the short run. It may also reduce the employ*ee's* choice, just as happens when the sovereign alters levels of reciprocity. To the extent, for example, that employment safety regulations force marginal employers out of business, they deprive existing or potential employees of a choice to work for those employers, albeit under less safe conditions. Those regulations also may deprive employees, who continue on the job, of choice. Just as employees may not like the form that enhanced levels of reciprocity takes, they may not like the results of every sovereign restraint of employer power even though they retain their jobs. Employ*ee* disregard for safety practices, for example, is an endemic problem in industry. In addition, anti-discrimination legislation such as title VII of the Civil Rights Act of 1964[2] poses the special problems of restraining employer power and restraining the power of some, but not all, employees. The most vigorous opponents of title VII have probably not been employers, but employees organized into trade unions, particularly in the construction industry.

---

[2] Civil Rights Act of 1964, tit. VII, P.L. 88–352, 78 Stat. 241, 42 U.S.C. ss 2000a–2000d (1981).

When the sovereign creates countervailing power, it also reduces the choices available to the parties. For instance, the NLRA's good faith bargaining requirements reduce the choices of both the employer and the union, the exclusive bargaining agent of the employees. Such requirements, taken out of context, seem intended to affect both parties equally. In context, however, their purpose is to increase choice on one side of the relation—the worker's side—by improving its bargaining position. In many respects they achieve this effect, but only by substantially reducing and transforming worker choice. The system requires both a monopolization of the labor supply and a monopolization of the bargaining process by the union. Such monopolies cannot exist without depriving employees and potential employees of choice. Even in the short term, however, the processes of collective choice replace in altered form some of this reduced individual choice.

Preservation of Relations. Much sovereign imposition of values has effectuated the relational norm of preservation of the relation. Some of this has been done indirectly, as has often been the case respecting employment, but some has been done directly, as in the case of the Automobile Dealer's Day in Court Act.[3] Nevertheless, at the same time that such increased impositions have occurred in employment and franchising, very considerable reductions in the imposition of this norm have occurred respecting family relations. (Glendon 1981)

The contrast between the decreasing sanctity of marriage and the increasing sanctity of franchises as reflected in the government's imposing continuation of the relation over the objection of one party is interesting in-terms of choice. In the case of franchising, the reduction of choice is one sided; regulations restricting the freedom of franchisors to terminate dealerships do not reduce choice for all participants. Rather, franchisees generally welcome the imposition of the norm on the relation, because it increases their choice. On the other hand, marriage is an area where sovereign regulation in favor of preservation of the relation would often reduce the choice of all the internal participants.

Propriety of Means. A great deal of government intervention in contractual relations has taken the form of changing the means by which the parties conduct themselves, rather than the substance of their conduct. This type of intervention frequently takes the form of imposing

---

[3] 15 U.S.C. ss. 1121–1125 (1981). This Act restricts the freedom of automobile manufacturers to terminate dealerships.

procedural requirements. These requirements have generally been of the "due process" nature, which presumes a high adversarial level among the participants. These impositions may come about in a range of ways. Perhaps most common are those following automatically from the creation by law of substantive rights—in other words, the imposition of legal duties—where none existed before. Such substantive legal rights carry with them the full panoply of judicial, and often administrative, enforcement replete with rights to due process, often to the highest of constitutional requirements. Imposition of due process requirements may also be created specifically, as in the Wisconsin Dealership Practices Act which requires ninety days' notice of termination by the franchisor, regardless of the validity of the franchisor's cause for terminating.[4] Due process requirements also may be imposed indirectly, as in the case of labor laws protecting collective bargaining, since collective bargaining invariably leads to formalized grievance procedures, usually (in the United States) including arbitration if all other procedures fail.

The effect of due process on choice is clear enough respecting the party upon which it is imposed, at least in the short run: it curtails choice whenever that side would not have introduced such process on its own initiative, which is commonly the case. The long run curtailment is not, however, always so clear; in labor relations, for example, many employers may come to prefer grievance procedures as an effective way of curbing the discretion of lower-level managers—for example, foremen. Once again, choice may also be curtailed in the group for whose benefit the procedures are putatively required. Certain kinds of costs are inherent in the shift from less formal to more formal means—costs in reduction of trust and in flexibility, for example. Not everyone in a protected group would necessarily choose to incur those costs in order to secure the often uncertain benefits of "due process." For example, under the National Labor Relations Act, a union may, if it acts in good faith, refuse to take a grievance to arbitration, and in doing so, the union may deprive the grieving employee of the right to judicial relief that might have been available in the absence of grievance-arbitration provisions in the collective bargaining agreement.[5]

In sum, the effect on choice, even immediate choice, of sovereign

---

[4] Wis. Stat. Ann. ss. 135.04 (West 1973). The statute allows fewer than 90 days' notice for a limited number of causes.

[5] *Vaca v. Sipes*, 386 U.S. 171 (1976).

imposition of these four values is immensely complex. The sovereign often intentionally reduces choice of a party which is reciprocating too little, is too powerful, is terminating relations, or is following arbitrary or other procedures viewed as inadequate by the sovereign. By doing so, however, the sovereign also may consequentially reduce the choice of the putative beneficiaries of the enhanced levels of reciprocity, the redressed power balances, the preserved relations, and the due process. Sovereign imposition of these values also may transform the nature of choice from, for example, individual choice, to choice exercisable only through group political processes and structures. For a complete understanding of the impact of such impositions on choice, it is necessary to look at long run effects as well as immediate restrictions and transformations.

b. Bureaucratization—Transformation of the Propriety of Means—
One of the most important effects of sovereign imposition of the four values discussed—reciprocity, the power norm, relational preservation, and "due process"—is that it bureaucratizes the relations affected. This is especially so in relations which otherwise would be relatively little bureaucratized. Consider, for example, what has happened to many small, originally nonunionized businesses in the last fifty years or so. Ownership and management were initially vested in the sole proprietor, one or more intermediate levels of management may or may not have existed between the proprietor and the employees engaged directly in production. Division of labor could be quite complex, as in a machine shop, with lathes, drill presses, punch machines, various cutting tools, and so on, but an individual laborer did not necessarily always work at the same task or machine. Obviously, such an organization had many bureaucratic elements; in particular, it had extensive division of labor and rational planning and execution of functions. Moreover, the authority structure was based not on traditional or feudal notions, but on the concept of property, of ownership. The reification of human authority into modern property rights was itself a move away from feudal relational patterns toward more discrete social patterns. It was also a step on the road to the concept of authority being legitimized by substantive detailed rules and the correct following of detailed procedures, the mature bureaucratic pattern. Nonetheless, modern property rights are far more general than bureaucratic rights and confer legitimate arbitrary power on their holder—in this case, to direct, to hire and fire, and to determine levels of reciprocity, who will or will not exercise power and what that power will be, and how long relations shall continue.

Now consider the same business in a modern context. It is still a sole proprietorship, with the same levels of intermediate management and division of labor, but now it is subject to the national or state labor relations act, and, as a result, it is unionized. It must comply with complex income tax laws, including obligations to withhold taxes, and Social Security laws. In addition, it must comply with ERISA and OSHA, among much other regulation. All other things being equal, this business is inevitably far more bureaucratized than it was in 1933. Completely apart from technological changes, the division of labor will be far sharper and more permanent than before unionization, not only because of job classification and restrictive work provisions common in collective bargaining agreements, but also because of the mores and personal psychology arising from the existence of such bureaucratic requirements. Rational planning and performance of work will be far more extensive now, partly because of the increased sharpness and permanence of the division of labor. Also, the multiplication of goals in conducting the work increases the need for rational planning and performance; whereas the firm's original goal was to produce the final product and sell it at a profit, now it must add the goal of following the additional rules of the game. These rules are not general principles of safety, for example, but are detailed ways of behaving safety. Further, a change has taken place in the source of legitimacy of authority. Although the sole proprietor remains endowed with the general authority arising from rights of ownership, that authority is now hedged about with a host of rules—both substantive and procedural—arising both from the collective bargaining agreement and from sovereign regulation. His authority is thus a combination of "dos" and "don'ts" very similar to those of more prototypical bureaucrats in large organizations—public or private.

In addition to the foregoing factors, the policing of business needed to ensure compliance with regulation increases bureaucratization. By and large, norms can be imposed by large bureaucratic organizations, such as government, only by detailed rules. Detailed rules require administration not only by the ruler, but also by the organization being ruled. Such internal administration adds to the need for rational planning and performance respecting activities collateral to what once appeared to be the sole function of the organization—producing and selling the goods or services it produces.

The example of the machine shop reveals how a theretofore small, relatively unbureaucratic organization has, by virtue of the sovereign imposition of these four norms, merged into larger bureaucratic organizations—union union and government—and has thereby become heavily bureaucratized.

Where the contractual relation upon which government imposes these norms is heavily bureaucratized from the start—for example, General Motors—the imposition will generally increase the degree of bureau-cratization, unless a saturation level of bureaucratization, if there is such a thing, already exists. In any event, the imposition will add new levels in the bureaucracy. This occurs both internally and externally. For example, sovereign imposition of affirmative action programs results not only in the creation of agencies in the sovereign to enforce the policy, but also in the appointment by the institutions subject to the regulation of their own affirmative action officers. Large employers may even create whole affirmative action offices.

Thus, whether we like it or not, one set of values of sovereign imposition of such norms in a modern technological society inevitably is the value of conducting affairs bureaucratically and of multiplying levels in bureaucratic structures. To the extent this occurs, there is a marked change in what means are proper and what means are improper; nonbureaucratic means of conduct no longer are proper. This is significant not only respecting the means considered purely as means, but also, as the foregoing discussion suggests, in terms of the effect the change in the standards of means-propriety has on the various substantive norms.

Chapter 6

Presentiation and Adjustment Along the Spectrum of Contracts

The five selections in this chapter set out Macneil's analysis of the forms of contract. Macneil has typically been read as contrasting relational to discrete contracts, and there is some warrant for reading him this way. However, his more profound contribution has been to show that all contracts have a relational element (described in chapter 5 of this book), but that there is a spectrum of contracts appropriate to particular forms of exchange, from the relatively discrete to the relatively complex. Discrete contracts place heavier reliance on the contract planning technique of "presentiation" (and on the contract norms supportive of this). Complex contracts place heavier reliance on the contract planning technique of adjustment (and on the contract norms which facilitate this). When properly interpreted, Macneil's work on the spectrum of contracts is the most interesting and robust framework for an integrated understanding of the range of contract action.

181

61. Restatement (Second) of Contracts and Presentiation

To presentiate: "to make or render present in place or time, to cause to be perceived or realized as present." (8 *Oxford English Dictionary* 1306 (1933)) Presentiation is only a manner in which a person perceives the future's effect on the present; but it depends upon events outside the individual psyche, events viewed as determining the future. Presentiation is thus a recognition that the course of the future is bound by present events, *and* that by those events the future has for many purposes been brought effectively into the present.

Although we are surrounded by this phenomenon, its name was described as rare even 40 years ago. (*Id.*) Thus it is not surprising that the term was never employed in a traditional contract theory implicitly requiring total presentiation of each contract relation at the time of its formation through offer and acceptance. This commentary explores presentiation in traditional contract law and the limitations on its usefulness in relational contracts and relational contract law. It then explores the responses of Restatement Second to the demands respecting presentiation that relational contracts impose on contract law.

A remark made by Anthony Quinn while playing an Eskimo in *The Savage Innocents* (1961) illustrates further the concept of presentiation. One of the two white men with Quinn had fallen through the ice in the midst of a raging blizzard, and Quinn and the other had quickly pulled him out of the water. The victim was freezing to death in spite of the efforts of his friend to slap circulation through his body. Watching the frantic efforts, Quinn said, "Your friend *is* dead." It was a perfectly sensible statement even though the doomed man was still breathing, his heart still beating, and his limbs still moving. All the events had occurred which would cause his death, and there was not the slightest chance of avoiding that event.

Seldom is recognition of a present binding of the future so intensely certain that we use the present tense to describe something sure to happen, but yet to happen. Recognition of a present binding of the future, particularly verbalization of that recognition, inevitably lags behind the extent to which the future is in fact bound. No human mind can know all the causes effecting results in any complex sequence of events. Because of limitations on knowledge of causes and effects, our ability to presentiate is always a limited one. Moreover, overt or tacit recognition of those limits causes us to think more of projecting the present into the future than of bringing the future backwards into the present. Normally, our thoughts are of how the present will affect the future, rather than of how present events have now fixed the future. We constantly speak in terms of planning, of prediction, of expecting, and in a myriad of other terms tacitly recognizing the limitations of our present knowledge of the future. The result is that while presentiation is an ever-present phenomenon, it is often likely to occur at relatively low levels of consciousness.

In view of the conceptual dominance of projecting the present forward over bringing the future back into the present, it is reasonable to question whether presentiation is a useful concept of contract analysis. An affirmative answer follows from the fact, explored below, that traditional contract systems are among the greatest intellectual expressions of presentiation. Therefore, presentiation is a useful conceptual platform from which to examine Restatement Second.

Because presentiation depends upon recognition of the binding of the future, anything preventing either binding of the future or recognition of that binding frustrates presentiation. Such an impediment is the existence of choice. To the extent that people have choice and we do nor know how they will exercise it, the future remains unbound, and cannot be presentiated.

It is in connection with choice that the manifestation of mutual assent upon which Restatement Second is primarily founded becomes so important to our need and desire to presentiate. Since before recorded history we have been developing the notion that certain kinds of manifestations of assent, promises, can be used to reduce future choice and enable us to presentiate. When we conclude that a manifestation of mutual assent to a future exchange and to a method for effectuating that exchange is a promise, when each party binds himself not to change his mind and fail to carry out the exchange, then the future has been bound and presentiation has been accomplished.

The importance of ability to presentiate by mutual assent cannot be overemphasized. It forms the basis for the entire credit structure. We trade accounts receivable with as much facility as we trade dollar bills, and we trade them as present, not just future, wealth. This is but an example of the role of mutual assent in presentiating future human behavior so that people may rely upon that behavior now even though it will not occur until later. The ability to act now on the basis of something which we know will not come into being until the future is one of the most productive human tools. Mutual assent in contracting is one of the most important ways we exercise this ability.

Traditional Contract Law and Presentiation

Several generations ago the German legal scholar, Kohler (1914, 136), said, "It is the province of the law of obligations to draw the future into the present." This is precisely what traditional contract law was designed to do, by adding legal sanctions to the bindingness of mutual assent. This aspect of traditional contract law, most highly developed in this country by Williston, was a truly ingenious intellectual creation. Primarily through manipulations of the notion of consent, traditional contract theory created a legal structure which in theory attempted to presentiate not just part of the relation between contracting parties, but virtually all of it. When a subjective meeting of the minds became too narrow a concept upon which to base complete presentiation, the contract structure shifted to an objective theory of contracts, reinforced by such doctrines as the parol evidence rule. Unfortunately, sometimes consent, even objective consent, was too vague in commitment or content to serve as a basis for total presentiation. The relation created by such vague consent was excluded from the realm of contract altogether, leaving the parties with only the legal reinforcement they might find in the law of quasi-contract or torts. Since this was often undesirable, the designers of the structure went to great lengths to infer consent to such things as reasonable times or prices, or to imply conditions and other terms. Faced with inevitable problems of mistakes, impossibility, or other frustration of original goals, the theory utilized implied conditions in an attempt to preserve the facade of initial presentiation by mutual assent. When consent was stretched as far as it reasonably could be or, some would say, farther, then the gap-filling Corpus Juris Contractus took over directly, exemplified by Williston's analysis of impossibility.

The aim was to establish, insofar as the law could, the *entire* relation at the time of the expressions of mutual assent. Total presentiation through 100 per cent predictability was sought as of the time of something called the acceptance of an offer. When possible, the law accomplished this through the form of giving legal effect to party presentiation as demonstrated by party manifestations of mutual assent. When the guise of such consensually formed law was not possible, for example in the case of legal remedies which the parties commonly fail to articulate at all, the

184

system filled the gaps by supplying presentation in the form of predictable and theoretically precise rules.

The dominant characteristics of a typical contract legal system aimed at creating complete presentation at the time of mutual assent may be summarized as follows: As much as possible of the content of the relation, both structure and detail, is forced into a pattern of mutual assent expressed at some instantaneous point of time; content necessary to achieve presentation, but which cannot sensibly be rationalized into a pattern of instantaneous mutual assent, will be supplied *eo instante* by the legal system in a form as precisely predictable as possible. Throughout this commentary these characteristics will serve as a touchstone for evaluating the extent to which a contract legal system adheres to or departs from a total presentation approach.

No one was ever so naive as to believe that contract law could indeed achieve total presentation, but there are some kinds of contracts where close approximations may be possible. Complete presentation is most likely to lead to useful outcomes in contracts properly described as discrete transactions. These are contracts of short duration, with limited personal interactions, and with precise party measurements of easily measured objects of exchange, for example money and grain. They are transactions requiring a minimum of future cooperative behavior between the parties and not requiring a sharing of benefits or burdens. They bind the two parties tightly and precisely. The parties view such transactions as deals free of entangling strings, and they certainly expect no altruism. The parties see virtually everything connected with such transactions as clearly defined and presentiated. If trouble is anticipated at all, it is anticipated only if someone or something turns out unexpectedly badly. The epitome of discrete contract transactions: two strangers come into town from opposite directions, one walking and one riding a horse. The walker offers to buy the horse, and after brief dickering a deal is struck in which delivery of the horse is to be made at sundown upon the handing over of $10. The two strangers expect to have nothing to do with each other between now and sundown, they expect never to see each other again thereafter, and each has as much feeling for the other as has a Viking trading with a Saxon.

A high degree of presentation is possible in truly discrete transactions, because it is possible to approach complete mutual planning and to do so at one point in time. This completeness and unity of planning creates a situation where it is reasonable for the parties to bind themselves to stick rigorously by the planning. That in turn permits the application of the

185

legal reinforcing structure of traditional contract law. Because of the close connection of traditional contract law with discrete transactions, it is appropriate to refer to it as transactional contract law.

Relational Contracts and Presentiation

Few economic exchanges occur entirely in the discrete transactional pattern. Virtually all economic exchange takes place in circumstances characterized by one or more of the following: The relations are of significant duration (for example, franchising). Close whole person relations form an integral aspect of the relation (employment). The object of exchange typically includes both easily measured quantities (wages) and quantities not easily measured (the projection of personality by an airline stewardess). Many individuals with individual and collective poles of interest are involved in the relation (industrial relations). Future cooperative behavior is anticipated (the players and management of the Oakland Raiders). The benefits and burdens of the relation are to be shared rather than divided and allocated (a law partnership). The bindingness of the relation is limited (again a law partnership in which in theory each member is free to quit almost at will). The entangling strings of friendship, reputation, interdependence, morality, and altruistic desires are integral parts of the relation (a theatrical agent and his clients). Trouble is expected as a matter of course (a collective bargaining agreement). Finally the participants never intend or expect to see the whole future of the relation as presentiated at any single time, but view the relation as an ongoing integration of behavior which will grow and vary with events in a largely unforeseeable future (a marriage, a family business).

In circumstances such as the foregoing each exchange no longer stands alone as in the discrete transaction, but is part of a relational web. Since most actual exchanges are at least partially relational, most contracts could be called relational. It is, however, more useful to think of transactional and relational characteristics as creating a spectrum ranging from such extremes as the highly transactional horse selling epitome to the highly relational nuclear family or commune. As one moves towards the relational end of this spectrum presentiation plays a relatively smaller role, since increasing aspects of the relation must be left to future determination. This fact poses problems for contract law.

186

Partially Presentiated Relations and Transactional Contract Doctrine

Any legal doctrine founded on both freedom of contract and the concept of *total* presentiation at some single temporal point, such as the acceptance of an offer, will encounter special difficulties if applied to relational contracts. The difficulties arise both from the incompleteness at any given time of the presentiation and the continuously evolving nature of that presentiation. How many thousand partial presentiations occur in a lifetime of employment with IBM? Every notice about parking spaces, every notice of promotion, every notice of a pay or even a social security withholding change, every request granted for a day off, every granted request for a transfer, every relatively involuntary transfer, every alteration of job patterns, every routine assignment of work, even a movement to a desk in a more desired location, constitutes a partial presentiation of the relation. As time goes by, these partial presentiations supersede earlier ones and previous aspects of the relation, and are in turn eroded and modified. It would require a multidimensional and multi-sense movie projector to present presentiation in such circumstances. Any contract law structure based on concepts of total presentiation at a particular instant in time must necessarily use a slide projector with but a single slide.

Faced with the realities of relational contracts and existing transactional contract law, the possible responses of law makers and law restaters are somewhat limited. One response is simply not to apply that law. A second is or continue to try to force relational contract patterns into the mould of total legal presentiation. A third is to modify the details of transactional contract law so that total presentiation is no longer the actual goal, but to leave total presentiation the apparent goal of the heoretical structure. A fourth response is to develop an overall structure of contract law of greater general applicability than now exists and to merge both the details and the structure of transactional contract law into that overall contract structure.

6.2   Contracts: Adjustment of Long-Term Economic Relations Under Classical, Neoclassical, and Relational Contract Law

Introduction

This article concerns the constant clash in modern economic structures between the need for stability and the need to respond to change.

The range of the conflict is, of course, immense. This article is aimed at but one segment of the problem: that centered around contractual ways of organizing production and distribution of goods and services. It focuses initially on the relation between classical and neoclassical contract law and the organization of production and distribution in flexible patterns that stress discrete transactional characteristics. It then treats the changes in planning and dispute resolution techniques required where the need for flexibility and change exceeds the dispute-resolving capabilities of a system of neoclassical law.

Variations of the following four questions form the core of the article:

1.   How is flexibility planned into economic relations and what is the legal response to such planning?

2.   How is conflict between specific planning and needs to adapt to subsequent change in circumstances treated?

3.   How are contractual relations preserved when conflicts arise?

4.   How are economic activities terminated when they have outlived their usefulness?

The first section focuses on these issues in a system dominated by discrete transactions, the second on a system with substantial infusions of relational patterns. The third section deals with highly relational patterns, where the first three questions tend to merge, and contains a separate discussion of the fourth question.

Discrete Transactions: Classical Contract Law

THE NATURE OF DISCRETE TRANSACTIONS

A *truly* discrete exchange transaction would be entirely separate not only from all other present relations but from all past and future relations as well. In short, it could occur, if at all, only between total strangers, brought together by chance (not by any common social structure, since that link constitutes at least the rudiments of a relation outside the transaction). Moreover, each party would have to be completely sure of never again seeing or having anything else to do with the other. Such an event could involve only a barter of goods, since even money available to one and acceptable to the other postulates some kind of common social structure. Moreover, everything must happen quickly lest the parties should develop some kind of a relation impacting on the transaction so as to deprive it of discreteness. For example, bargaining about quantities or other aspects of the transaction can erode discreteness, as certainly does any effort to project the transaction into the future through promises.

The characteristics of entirely discrete transactions, if they could occur at all deprive them of any utility as social tools of production and distribution of scarce goods and services. That fact by no means, however, renders the construct useless as a tool of economic or legal analysis, because some discreteness is present in all exchange transactions and relations. One must simply not forget that great modification is required before the model can represent a reasonably accurate picture of actual economic life. (Unfortunately, this kind of forgetfulness is an endemic problem in both economics and law.) When so modified, the construct will no longer represent an entirely discrete transaction, but will retain substantial discreteness while nevertheless remaining relatively realistic.

We do find in real life many quite discrete transactions: little personal involvement of the parties, communications largely or entirely linguistic and limited to the subject matter of transaction, the subjects of exchange consisting of an easily monetized commodity and money, little or no social (Blau 1964) or secondary exchange, (Parsons and Smelser, 1956) and no significant past relations nor likely future relations For example, a cash purchase of gasoline at a station on the New Jersey Turnpike by someone rarely traveling the road is such a quite discrete transaction. Such quite discrete transactions are no rarity in modern technological societies. They have been and continue to be an extremely productive economic technique both to achieve distribution of goods and to encourage their production.

Thus far we have dealt only with present exchanges of existing goods. Such exchanges can, however, play but a limited role in advanced economies. Advanced economies require greater specialization of effort and more planning than can be efficiently achieved by present exchanges through discrete transactions; they require the projection of exchange into the future through planning of various kinds, that is, planning permitting and fostering the necessary degree of specialization of effort. The introduction of this key factor of futurity gives rise to the question: what happens to discreteness when exchanges are projected into the future?

The answer is that a massive erosion of discreteness occurs. This is obvious when projection of exchange into the future occurs within structures such as the family, corporations, collective bargaining, and employment, structures obviously relational in nature. Similarly obvious are various relational ways of organizing and controlling markets, for example, the guilds of the feudal era or the planning described by Professor Galbraith in *The New Industrial State* (1985, ch. 3). But this erosion of discreteness occurs even when the projection is by direct and fairly simple promise and where the subject of exchange, if transferred immediately, would permit high levels of discreteness.

Discreteness is lost even in the simple promise situation, because a basis for trust must exist if the promise is to be of any value. Trust in turn presupposes some kind of a relation between the parties. Whether it is that created by a shared morality, by prior experience, by the availability of legal sanction, or whatever, trust depends upon some kind of mutual relation into which the transaction is integrated. And integration into a relation is the antithesis of discreteness. (Lowry 1976)

In spite of the great leap away from pure discreteness occurring when exchange is projected into the future, promises themselves inherently create or maintain at least a certain minimum of discreteness. A promise presupposes that the promisor's individual will can affect the future at least partially free of the communal will, thus separating the individual from the rest of his society. Such separation is an element of discreteness. Promise also stresses the separateness of the promisor and the promisee, another element of discreteness. Moreover, some specificity and measured reciprocity is essential to an exchange of promises—no one in his right mind promises the world. This, again, results in an irreducible level of discreteness.

190

The foregoing can be seen in the following definition of contract promise: present communication of a commitment to future engagement in a specified reciprocal measured exchange. Thus, the partially discrete nature of promise permits the retention of a great deal of discreteness in transactions where promise projects exchange into the future. Where no massive relational elements counterbalance this discreteness (as they do, for example, in the case of collective bargaining), sense is served by speaking of the contract as discrete, even though the contract is inevitably less discrete than would be an equivalent present exchange.

The combination of exchange with promise has been one of the most powerful social tools ever developed for the production of goods and services. Moreover, discreteness in transactions so projected has its own special virtues. Just as a system of discrete transactions for exchanging present goods may be an effective way to conduct business free of all sorts of extraneous social baggage, so too may discrete transaction contracts serve this function. With this background we can now turn to the questions set out above as they relate to a system of discrete transactions.

ADJUSTMENT AND TERMINATION OF ECONOMIC RELATIONS IN A SYSTEM OF DISCRETE TRANSACTIONS

An economic and legal system dominated by discrete transactions deals with the conflict between various needs for stability and needs for flexibility in ways described below. (The treatment following deals both with present exchanges of existing goods and with forward contracts where exchange is projected into the future. But the latter are assumed to be of a fairly discrete nature, e.g. a contract for 100 tons of iron at a fixed price, delivery in one month.)

Planning Flexibility into Economic Relations—Within itself, a discrete transaction is rigid, there being no intention to achieve internal flexibility. Planning for flexibility must, therefore, be achieved outside the confines of the transaction. Consider, for example, a nineteenth century manufacturer of stoves who needs iron to be cast into stove parts but does not know how many stoves he can sell. The required flexibility has to be achieved, in a pattern of discrete transactions, by keeping each iron purchase contract small in amount, thereby permitting adjustments of quantity up or down each time a contract is entered. Thus, the needed flexibility comes from the opportunity to enter or to refrain from entering the market for iron. This market is external to the transaction rather than within it. The epitome of this kind of flexibility is the purchasing of needs for immediate delivery, rather than using any kind of a forward contract for future delivery. Such flexibility is reduced by use of forward contracts; the larger and longer they are, the greater is the reduction.

Dealing with Conflict between Specific Planning and Needs to Adapt to Change Arising Thereafter.—Only rarely in a discrete transaction will the items contracted for become useless before the forward contract is performed or become of such lessened value that the buyer either will not want them or will want them in greatly changed form. To put this another way, only rarely will there be *within* the transaction a serious conflict between specific planning and changed needs. To return to the stove manufacturer as an example, seldom will the demand for iron stoves drop so much that the manufacturer comes to regret that he contracted for as much iron as he did.

The discrete transaction technique does not, however, produce a paradise of stability for economic activity; the conflict between specific planning and the need to adapt to change arising thereafter still remains. In those relatively rare cases of difficulties arising while the contract remains unperformed, the conflict exists but is resolved entirely in favor of the specific planning and against the party desiring flexibility. Moreover, outside the discrete transaction, planning must go on; *e.g.* the seller earlier built an iron smelter in order to sell in the iron market to organizations like the stove manufacturer. Except to the modest extent that the iron producer can shift the risks to the stove manufacturer and other buyers by forward contracts, the risks of change remain with the iron producer. If the demand for iron decreases greatly, the capital invested in building the iron smelter may be largely or entirely lost. Thus, in an economy built on discrete transactions, the risks of change remain but in large measure are not shifted by the transactions. When they are shifted they are shifted totally; *e.g.* the stove manufacturer bears all those risks to the extent of the quantity for which he contracted. In effect, the contract system does not provide planning for changes; it leaves that to the internal planning of each firm.

Preserving Relations When Conflicts Arise—Where the mode of operation is a series of discrete transactions, no significant relations exist to be preserved when conflicts arise. Inside the discrete transaction all that remains is a dispute. Outside the discrete transaction no relation (other than legal rights arising out of the dispute) exists to be preserved. Thus, all that remains is a dispute to be settled or otherwise resolved. The existence of the market that the discrete transactional system presupposes eliminates the necessity for economic relations between the firms to continue in spite of the disputes. That market, rather than continued relations between these particular parties, will supply their future needs.

Terminating Economic Activities Outliving Their Usefulness—This economic need is simply a particular aspect of the need for planning flexibility into economic relations, the ultimate example of which is to scrap the specific planning altogether. If sheet steel becomes the only technologically sensible substance with which to make stoves, then the stove manufacturer simply makes no more contracts to buy iron. The iron manufacturer continues to produce iron if remaining markets make it worthwhile, or he shifts his production facilities to their next most valuable use. In extreme cases that may mean selling the facilities for scrap or even their abandonment.

★ ★ ★

The foregoing description of the responses of the discrete transaction system to the conflict between needs for stability and needs for flexibility may be summarized as follows. Except interstitially, such a system does not shift the risks of loss resulting from such conflicts. Such losses are left to fall largely on the suppliers of goods and services. To the extent that shifting does occur it is total shifting, not a sharing of risks. Given this format, minimizing of risk through planning comes in the *internal* planning of firms, not in *mutual* planning between them through contract. Thus, the iron manufacturer plans for its concern about a declining demand for iron by building a smaller smelter, repairing rather than replacing on old one, etc. It will try, of course, to shift as much of that risk as possible through forward contracts with buyers like the stove manufacturer, but prevailing patterns of relatively short discrete transactions preclude much shifting by that method. In any event, there will be no planning or dealing with the conflicts or possible conflicts through cooperative risk sharing between the iron manufacturer and stove manufacturer.

CLASSICAL CONTRACT LAW AND DISCRETE TRANSACTIONS

Any contract law system necessarily must implement certain norms. It must permit and encourage participation in exchange, promote reciprocity, reinforce role patterns appropriate to particular kinds of exchange relations, provide limited freedom for exercise of choice, effectuate planning, and harmonize the internal and external matrixes of particular contracts. A contract law system reinforcing discrete contract transactions, however, must add two further goals: enhancing discreteness and enhancing presentation.

Presentation is a way of looking at things in which a person perceives the effect of the future on the present. It is a recognition that the course of the future is so unalterably bound by present conditions that the future has been brought effectively into the present so that it may be dealt with just as if it were in fact the present. Thus, the presentation of a transaction involves restricting its expected future effects to those defined in the present, *i.e.* at the inception of the transaction. No eternal distinctions prevent treating the contract norm of enhancing presentation as simply an aspect of the norm of enhancing discreteness. It is, however, such an important aspect of the projection of exchange into the future in discrete contracts—to say nothing of microeconomic theory—that separate treatment aids analysis significantly.

A classical contract law system implements these two norms in a number of ways. To implement discreteness, classical law initially treats as irrelevant the identity of the parties to the transaction. Secondly, it transactionizes or commodifies as much as possible the subject matter of contracts, *e.g.* it turns employment into a short-term commodity by interpreting employment contracts without express terms of duration as terminable at will. Thirdly, it limits strictly the sources to be considered in establishing the substantive content of the transaction. For example, formal communication (*e.g.* writings) controls informal communication (*e.g.* oral statements); linguistic communication controls nonlinguistic communication; and communicated circumstances (to the limited extent that any circumstances outside of "agreements" are taken into account at all) control noncommunicated circumstances (*e.g.* status). Fourthly, only limited contract remedies are available, so that should the initial presentation fail to materialize because of nonperformance, the consequences are relatively predictable from the beginning and are not openended, as they would be, for example, if damages for unforeseeable or psychic losses were allowed. Fifthly, classical contract law draws clear lines between being in and not being in a transaction; *e.g.* rigorous and precise rules of offer and acceptance prevail with no half-way houses where only some contract interests are protected or where losses are shared. Finally, the introduction of third parties into the relation is discouraged since multiple poles of interest tend to create discreteness-destroying relations.

Since discreteness enhances the possibility and likelihood of presentation, all of the foregoing implementations of discreteness by the classical law also tend to enhance presentiation. Other classical law techniques, however, are even more precisely focused on presentiation. (Macneil 1975b, 592–94) The first of these is the equation of the legal effect of a transaction with the promises creating it. This characteristic of classical contract law is commonly explained in terms of freedom of contract, providing maximum scope to the exercise of choice. Nevertheless, a vital consequence of the use of the technique is presentiation of the transaction. Closely related to the first technique is the second: supplying a precise, predictable body of law to deal with all aspects of the transaction not encompassed by the promises. In theory, if not practice, this enables the parties to know exactly what the future holds, no matter what happens to disrupt performance. Finally, stress on expectation remedies, whether specific performance or damages measured by the value of performance, tends to bring the future into the present, since all risks, including market risks, are thereby transferred at the time the "deal is made."

In summary, classical contract law very closely parallels the discrete transactional patterns described in the preceding section. Such a legal system, superimposed on economic patterns of such a nature, constitutes the stereotype of interfirm (or firm and consumer or firm and employee) contracting of the laissez faire era.

Summary

A system of discrete transactions and its corresponding classical contract law provides for flexibility and change through the market outside the transactions, rather than within them. This enables the system to work while the transactions themselves remain nighly discrete and presentiated, characteristics preserved and enhanced by classical contract law.

A system of more relational contract and its corresponding neoclassical contract law remains theoretically structured on the discrete and classical models, but involves significant changes. Such contracts, being more complex and of greater duration than discrete transactions, become dysfunctional if too rigid, thereby preventing the high level of presentiation of the discrete transaction. Thus, flexibility, often a great deal of it, needs to be planned into such contracts, or gaps need to be left in the planning to be added as needed. The neoclassical system responds to this by a range of techniques. These run from some open evasion of its primary theoretical commitment to complete presentiation through initial consent on to the more common techniques of stretching consent far beyond its actual bounds and by fictions to squeeze later changes within an initial consent framework.

Somewhere along the line of increasing duration and complexity, trying to force changes into a pattern of original consent becomes both too difficult and too unrewarding to justify the effort, and the contractual relation escapes the bounds of the neoclassical system. That system is replaced by very different adjustment processes of an ongoing-administrative kind in which discreteness and presentation become merely two of the factors of decision, no the theoretical touchstones. Moreover, the substantive relation of change to the status quo has now altered from what happens in some kind of a market external to the contract to what can be achieved through the political and social processes of the relation, internal and external. This includes internal and external dispute-resolution structures. At this point, the relation has become a minisociety with a vast array of norms beyond the norms centered on exchange and its immediate processes.

TRANSACTIONAL AND RELATIONAL AXES

CONCEPT	EXTREME TRANSACTIONAL POLE	EXTREME RELATIONAL POLE
1. Overall relation type	Nonprimary	Primary
A. Personal involvement	Segmental, limited, non-unique, transferable	Whole person, unlimited, unique, non-transferable
B. Types of communication	Limited, linguistic, formal	Extensive, deep, not limited to linguistic, informa in addition to or in lieu of formal
C. Subject matter of satisfactions	Simple, monetizable economic exchange only	In addition to economic, complex personal non-economic satisfactions very important; social exchange; non-exchange
2. Measurability and actual measurement of exchange and other factors	One side of exchange is money; other side is easily monetized; both are actually measured; no other aspects	Both exchanges and other factors are relatively difficult to monetize or otherwise measure, and the parties do not monetize or measure them
3. Basic sources of socio-economic support	Apart from exchange motivations themselves, external to the transaction	Internal to the relation, as well as external

4. Duration	Short agreement process; short time between agreement and performance; short time of performance	Long term; no finite beginning; no end to either relation or performance, except perhaps upon death of parties
5. Commencement and termination	Sharp in by clear agreement; sharp out by clear performance	Commencement and termination, if any, of relation likely to be gradual; individual entry into existing relation often gradual, as may be withdrawal; individual entry may be by birth, and withdrawal by death
6. Planning		
A. Primary focus of planning	Substance of exchanges	Structures and processes of relation; planning of substance of exchanges primarily for initial period
B. Completeness and specificity		
(1) Possible when planning occurs	Can be very complete and specific; only remote contingencies (if those) are beyond reasonable planning capacity	Limited specific planning of substance possible; extensive specific planning of structures and processes may be possible
(2) Actual planning accomplished	Very complete and specific; only the practically unplanable planable (of which there is little) left unplanned	Limited specific planning of substance carried out; extensive planning of structures may or may not occur
C. Sources and forms of mutual planning		
(1) Bargaining and adhesion	Specific consent to price of a good produced unilaterally by seller; short bid-ask bargaining, if any	Adhesion without bargaining unlikely except in case of entry of new members into existing relation; otherwise extended mutual planning merging imperceptibly into ongoing relation being established; a "joint creative effort"
(2) Tacit assumptions	Inevitably present, but inherently relational and anti-transactional	Recognized aspect of relational planning, without which relations cannot survive
(3) Sources and forms of post-commencement planning	No post-commencement planning	Operation of relation itself is prime source of further planning, which is likely to be extensive; may or may not be extensive explicit post-commencement planning

D. Bindingness of planning	Planning is entirely binding	Planning may be binding, but often some or all of it is characterized by some degree of tentativeness
E. Conflicts of interest in planning	Enterprise planning can be expressed only through partially zero-sum allocative planning, hence all mutual planning is conflict laden.	Enterprise planning may be separable at least in part from allocative planning, and hence relatively low in conflict; merger of non-allocative enterprise planning with allocative planning may occur in ways muting conflict and providing nonnegotiational ways for dealing with it.
7. Future cooperation required in post-commencement planning and actual performance	Almost none required	Success of relation entirely dependent on further cooperation in both performance and further planning
8. Incidence of benefits and burdens	Shifting or other specific assignment of each particular benefit and burden to one party or the other	Undivided sharing of both benefits and burdens
9. Obligations undertaken A. Sources of content	Genuinely expressed, communicated and exchanged promises of parties	Relation itself develops obligations which may or may not include genuinely expressed, communicated and exchanged promises of the parties
B. Sources of obligation	External to parties and transaction expect for their triggering it by manifestation of consent	Both external and internal to the relation; same as the sources of content of the obligation as to internal element
C. Specificity of obligation and sanction	Specific rules and rights specifically applicable and founded on the promises; monetizable or monetized (whether by mutual party planning, *i.e.* promissory or otherwise, *i.e.* by rule)	Nonspecific; nonmeasurable, whether based on customs, general principles or internalizations all arising from relation or partly from external sources; restorative unless breach results in termination, then may become transactional in nature

10. Transferability	Entirely transferable with the sole exception of an obligor's ultimate liability for nonperformance	Transfer likely to be uneconomic economic and difficult to achieve even when it is not impossible
11. Number of participants	Two	May be as few as two, but likely to be more than two and often large masses
12. Participant views of transaction or elation		
A. Recognition of exchange	High	Low or perhaps even none
B. Altruistic behavior	None expected or occurring	Significant expectations of occurrence
C. Time-sense	Presentiation of the future	Futurizing of the present, *i.e.* to the extent past, present and future are viewed as separate, the present is viewed in terms of planning and preparing for a future not yet arrived.
D. Expectations about trouble in performance or among the participants	None expected, except perhaps that planned for; if it occurs expected to be governed by specific rights	Possibility of trouble anticipated as normal part of relation, to be dealt with by cooperation and other restorational techniques

6.3   A Primer of Contract Planning

TABLE OF CONTENTS

II. LAWYER FUNCTIONS: THE PROCESSES OF PERFORMANCE AND RISK PLANNING

  A. ASCERTAINING THE FACTS
  B. NEGOTIATION
  C. DRAFTING: REDUCING PLANNING TO MEDIA OF MUTUAL COMMUNICATION

    1. *Audience*
    2. *Environment*
    3. *Organizing and Composing*

        a. *Organizing*
        b. *Composing*

  D. APPLICATION OF LEGAL KNOWLEDGE

III. PERFORMANCE PLANNING

  A. ECONOMIC REGULATION AND PERFORMANCE PLANNING
  B. STANDARDIZED SPECIFICATION OF PERFORMANCE PLANNING— HEREIN OF USE OF FORMS
  C. PROVIDING FOR FLEXIBLE OPERATING RELATIONS

    1. *Techniques of Flexibility*

        a. *Use of standards*
        b. *Direct third party determination of performance*
        c. *One-party control of terms*
        d. *Agreements to agree*

    2. *Adjusting Existing Contractual Relationships*

IV. RISK PLANNING

  A. LEGAL CONSEQUENCES OF INCOMPLETE PLANNING
  B. INDEMNIFICATION, INSURANCE, AND SURETYSHIP
  C. PLANNING FOR DISPUTE RESOLUTION

    1. *Planning Self-Help Remedies*

        a. *Planning for refraining from performance*
        b. *Planning to keep ahead of the game: security and forfeitures*
        c. *Planning for the uncertain-duty-risk*

2. *Planning Processes of Dispute Resolution*

    a. *One-sided dispute resolution*
    b. *Negotiation and mediation*
    c. *Arbitration*
    d. *Judicial processes*

3. *Planning Substance of Dispute Resolution*

    a. *Planning litigation content: looking forward to the courts look backward*

       (i) *Recitals*
       (ii) *Battle of the forms*

    b. *Substantive stimulated remedies*

V. ADMINISTERING THE FINAL AGREEMENT PROCESS

CONCLUSION

A poem would need to be well made, in view of the number of bunglers who'll be at it.
                Neil Gunn

This Article is offered to those who may wish to explore the principles and processes underlying what is surely the largest single segment of the business of the American lawyer: planning contractual transactions and relations. After an initial exploration of the nature of horizontal and vertical organization of economic enterprise and the fundamental characteristics of contract planning processes, lawyer functions in contract planning will be examined. The concepts of performance planning and risk planning necessarily introduced in considering lawyer functions will then be treated in more detail. Finally, there is a short description of administering the final agreement process.

1. Introduction to Contract Planning

A. VERTICAL AND HORIZONTAL ECONOMIC ORDERING

No complex economic system can operate without vast amounts of coordination of economic activity, coordination requiring extensive planning. Oversimplifying, it may be said that such coordination and its planning can be achieved vertically, horizontally, or in a combination of the two. Vertical coordination is command coordination: subordinates are instructed in the details of coordinating their activities to achieve goals desired by the commander. Horizontal coordination is exchange coordination: relative equals make arrangements to coordinate their activities in order to achieve mutually acceptable goals through exchange of effort or property.

Contractual transactions and relations are the techniques whereby horizontal coordination is accomplished. The focus of this Article is, therefore, upon the planning of horizontal economic relations. Before that subject is treated in more detail, however, it should be noted that coordination between enterprise units is by no means an entirely different type of process from some of the coordination occurring within a single unit. True, much coordination within a unit is achieved by vertical orders from higher levels to lower, but coordination horizontally is is also a vital aspect, and the horizontal coordination, combined with vertical coordination, may look very "contractual." For example, suppose that in a large company the manager of the Widget Department of the Production Division receives a directive from the Production Division manager to produce 1250 widgets during November. This is vertical control of the production process. It will result in planning by the manager of the Widget Department, and in further vertical control—he must decide what machines to use, which men to assign, what overtime will be needed, etc. But in addition he will require materials and supplies which he must secure from the Purchasing Division, a portion of the enterprise not under his command. He sends to the Purchasing Division a requisition form duly filled out and signed. ("Offer"). The Materials Supervisor of the Purchasing Division determines that the items can be available, and returns a copy of the requisition to the manager of the Widget Department with his initials on it, thereby indicating that the Purchasing Division will supply the items at the times called for in the order. ("Acceptance"). If the Materials Supervisor had foreseen difficulties in securing the items, or if the market or other conditions had made substitutions advisable, he undoubtedly would have called the manager of the Widget Department and together they would have tried to get things straightened out. ("Negotiations" and "Counter-offer"). So too, if a hitch occurs after returning the requisition form, the Materials Supervisor and the manager of the Widget Department undoubtedly will attempt to iron out the matter between themselves. ("Mutual

202

adjustments"). In case of insuperable difficulties at any time the discussion will no doubt be carried on to higher levels. ("Grievance procedures"). If the difficulty is not resolved by these discussions, it will sooner or later reach someone in the line of command in a position to issue orders to both divisions, Production and Purchasing, and he will do so after hearing both sides. ("Arbitration" and "Specific Performance"). The similarity between this kind of process and contractual relationships is quite marked. Because all these steps occur within one enterprise unit, there is of course a direct vertical control of the process that may be lacking when two separate enterprise units are coordinating with each other. Nevertheless, in many respects the relationships of the subdivisions are not much different from what they would be if each subdivision were a separate enterprise unit coordinating its activities via contract. The reverse is also true: horizontal coordination by contract may not differ greatly from coordination by vertical control, a fact well recognized in the anti-trust field.

A solid understanding of the nature of horizontal ordering of economic activity through contract is essential to successful contract planning. Many avenues lead to such understanding: much of the law school curriculum is devoted to various aspects of contractual ordering, and inevitably lawyers develop a sophisticated, if perhaps unarticulated, understanding through the day-to-day practice of law. One should not, however, overlook the insights to be found not only in the many academic overviews of contract, but also often in the nooks and crannies of more directly practical works on particular kinds of contracts.

B. DISCRETE AND RELATIONAL AGREEMENTS

Contractual ordering of economic activity takes place along a spectrum of transactional and relational behavior, a spectrum which justifies distinguishing the discrete transactions lying at one end of the spectrum from the contractual relations lying at the other.

> [Discrete transactions] are contracts of short duration, with limited personal interactions, and with precise party measurements of easily measured objects of exchange, for example money and grain. They are transactions requiring a minimum of future cooperative behavior between the parties and not requiring a sharing of benefits or burdens. They bind the two parties tightly and

precisely. The parties view such transactions as deals free of entangling strings, and they certainly expect no altruism. The parties see virtually everything connected with such transactions as clearly defined and presentiated. If trouble is anticipated at all, it is anticipated only if someone or something turns out unexpectedly badly. The epitome of discrete contract transactions: two strangers come into town from opposite directions, one walking and one riding a horse. The walker offers to buy the horse, and after brief dickering a deal is struck in which delivery of the horse is to be made at sundown upon the handing over of $10. The two strangers expect to have nothing to do with each other between now and sundown, they expect never to see each other thereafter, and each has as much feeling for the other as has a Viking trading with a Saxon. (Macneil 1974b, 594)

Contractual relations, being more diverse in nature than the well-honed discrete transaction, are more difficult to describe concisely, but the following typical characteristics will convey the concept:

The relations are of significant duration (for example, franchising). Close whole person relations form an integral aspect of the relation (employment). The object of exchange typically includes both easily measured quantities (wages) and quantities not easily measured (the projection of personality by an airline stewardess). Many individuals with individual and collective poles of interest are involved in the relation (industrial relations). Future cooperative behavior is anticipated (the players and management of the Oakland Raiders). The benefits and burdens of the relation are to be shared rather than divided and allocated (a law partnership). The bindingness of the relation is limited (again a law partnership in which in theory each member is free to quit almost at will). The entangling strings of friendship, reputation, interdependence, morality, and altruistic desires are integral parts of the relation (a theatrical agent and his clients). Trouble is expected as a matter of course (a collective bargaining agreement). Finally, the participants never intend or expect to see the whole future of the relation as presentiated at any single time, but view the relation as an ongoing integration of behavior which will grow and vary with events in a largely unforeseeable future (a marriage; a family business). (Macneil 1974b, 595)

A great deal of contractual planning takes place within already existing contractual relations. Much of the detail and perhaps all of the general principles discussed in this Article pertain, albeit with modifications, to relational planning of this kind. Such relations often present many occasions for extensive and highly transactional planning, for example, collective bargaining, which is punctuated periodically by the extremely sharp transactional focusing involved in negotiating a "new" contract. But in this Article the focus is on contract planning in the transactional context, a context in which the separateness of the parties and discreteness of the contract necessarily force concentrated attention upon the planning of specified and dichotomous rights and duties such as those to be found in a commercial loan or a single sale of goods.

C. Fundamental Processes and Characteristics of Contract Planning

Two processes are essential to contract planning: determining goals (along with related costs of their attainment) and communication. Two fundamental characteristics of contract planning are a constant interplay between planning and non-planning and a distinction between performance planning and risk planning. Since these four aspects of contract planning constitute the base upon which the remainder of the Article is founded, they will be explored briefly in the following pages.

1. Determining Goals and Ascertaining Costs

Although in theory determining goals and ascertaining costs are two separable processes, outside the Garden of Eden they are entirely interrelated—a fact inherent in exchange. Thus, the very act of agreeing to a transaction constitutes a determination by each party that what he will receive (his goal, the other's cost) exceeds in value *to him* what he will surrender (his cost, the other's goal). An aspect of this process is ascertaining facts relating to alternative ways of achieving the goals and meeting the costs of achieving the goals, either through the transaction in question or by some other route.

2. Communication

Communication, like goal and cost determination, is an integral facet of any exchange. Anyone planning an exchange must always communicate in some fashion with the other party to accomplish the exchange. This process is not simply additive or sequential to determining goals and ascertaining the costs of attaining them; it is interwoven with those processes and affects them as they affect it. Even the party acting entirely alone, who plans his goals and ascertains their costs, has to take into account the effect that his desires will have on the other potential party; he is thereby engaging in what might be called anticipatory communication. And, of course, far more active mutuality of planning often occurs in which much actual communication shapes both parties' goals and costs. Finally, some kind of communication will be used in determining that the parties are in some degree of harmony on the allocations of those goals and costs. Even passive receipt of the adhesive planning of someone else constitutes a form of mutual communication in such circumstances.

3. Planning and Non-Planning

A friend who has practiced law for many years wrote in a personal letter not long ago:

> My experience has been of the person struggling to draw the maps of "territories to be" with all the attendant frustrations and anxieties imposed by the assumption that the perfect contract anticipates and disposes of all possible future problems and questions.

The perfect contract to which he refers is, of course, always impossible of achievement, even in the simplest and most transactional of situations. That it may serve as an appropriate goad to the planning lawyer to do his best should not be permitted to obscure the idealistic and unachievable nature of the goal. Every contract is necessarily partially unplanned, not only because of the nature of planning, but also because of the nature of one of the major tools of planning—promises.

Thus, generally speaking the unexecuted portion of every contract contains two parts: the planned and the unplanned. The unplanned part of a viable contract consists of at most an anticipation, vague or otherwise, of future cooperation or lack of it in taking the future actions necessary to make the contract work out satisfactorily, with all of the superstructure of hopes, worries, fears, ids, egos, and Freudian syndromes ordinarily involved in such anticipation. The more precise this anticipation is, the more closely it comes to resemble planning.

At least four factors complicate any description of the planned portion of the relationship. First, one party may plan the relationship differently than the other party, or else plan in an unsatisfactory manner a portion left unplanned by the other party. The sources of such difficulties are manifold and are potentially present in every contractual relationship.

A second complication in describing planning is that it is not always clear where the unplanned portion of a contract ends and the planning begins. Planning may take the form of establishing frame-works for handling otherwise unplanned aspects of the relationship, such as labor grievance and arbitration structures. But this sort of planning itself may be so vague as to be little more than an expression of hope for future cooperation: "We'll worry about that later and work it out somehow."

A further complication comes from the fact that the human mind focuses on only a limited number of aspects of any given situation at any given time, or even over a range of time. Thus, planning is inevitably interstitial in nature. This interstitiality is increased by the further fact that specification of planning inevitably fails to include all the aspects upon which the parties have focused their minds. As Farnsworth put it:

> [A] second process of selection occurs at the initial stage. Instead of attempting to reduce all of their expectations to contract language, the parties again confine their "limited attention" to a limited number of expectations selected as particularly suitable for inclusion in the contract. (Farnsworth 1968, 869–870)

Finally, all planning is complicated by what Professor Fuller describes as "tacit assumptions." (Fuller and Eisenberg 1972, 804–808) These lie "somewhere between the superficial layer of consciousness and the dark inner recesses of the human psyche probed by the psychoanalysts." (Fuller and Eisenberg 1972, 806) His example of the absent-minded professor reading a book as he steps out of the office demonstrates well what he means by tacit assumptions: the professor assumes that the hall floor is still there, although consciously he never gives any thought to the matter.

Tacit assumptions are as important in contract planning as they are in any other human behavior. Just as people constantly make tacit assumptions while they are eating, driving, playing football, operating a computer, or making love, so too they make tacit assumptions when they are planning contractual relationships.

In light of the foregoing complexities any description of the planned portion of a contract must necessarily be a description of an ideal that actual contract planning may approach but certainly never achieve. That ideal is the complete and exact mapping of all "territories to be," totally understood in precisely the same way by all parties with all details in sharp conscious focus at the same time, with all being entirely unaffected by anything external to that mapping, including tacit assumptions of the parties. Such an ideal is as unobtainable as the Holy Grail.

4. Performance Planning and Risk Planning

Parties enter contracts to achieve particular known goals at the expense of incurring particular known costs. These particular goals and costs may or may not be planned specifically at the time of making a contract. For example, one goes to a doctor for an examination knowing that the doctor's fee will have to be paid, but often not knowing just what the fee will be. Goals and costs of this nature are central to party purposes in making the contract, and planning for them can usefully be called performance planning. A shorthand way of identifying performance planning is to ask: Will what is planned almost certainly have to be carried out if this contract is to go through to a successful conclusion as planned? An affirmative answer identifies performance planning.

Like any other human activity, engaging in contractual behavior involves risks of loss. Sometimes dealing with risks of loss is the central purpose of the contract, as in the case of insurance. Where this is the case, planning for those risks is performance planning. In many circumstances, however, risks of loss exist which are peripheral to the main purposes of the parties in making the contract in the sense that the contract may be carried to a completely successful conclusion without the cost of such loss ever being incurred. Planning for such risks can usefully be distinguished from performance planning and called risk planning. A shorthand way of identifying risk planning is to ask: Is this contract likely to go through to a successful conclusion without what is being planned having to be carried out? An affirmative answer identifies risk planning as that term is used here.

The questions at the end of each of the two preceding paragraphs are not always easy to answer. Just as certainty and uncertainty are part of a single spectrum, so are performance and risk planning. Some risk hovers about even the most certain of human events including the most certain performance planning of contracts, and risk planning *can* often be argued to be central to party purposes. Nevertheless, with these limitations kept in mind, separating the concepts of performance planning and risk planning can be immensely helpful in enhancing understanding of effective contract planning. This is particularly true respecting lawyer functions in contract planning, to which we turn in the next section.

II. Lawyer Functions: The Processes of Performance and Risk Planning

Many a contract is entered into and carried to some kind of a conclusion without having passed before the eyes of any lawyer. Others may involve massive input by lawyers at planning or other stages. Thus it is possible here to do no more than point out the potential functions of the lawyer in contract planning—administering the agreement process and administering contract performance. This leaves open questions of when those functions are fulfilled by lawyers and when by others. The functions are summarized by the following chart.

Since this is an Article on planning, it will follow the lawyer functions only as far as administering the agreement process, omitting any direct consideration of administering contract performance.

A lawyer engages in four processes in risk and performance planning—ascertaining the facts, negotiation, drafting, and application of legal knowledge. Performance planning and risk planning lend themselves fairly readily to separate treatment, but the four processes constituting them do not. Each of those processes is interlinked with each of the others, and it is virtually impossible to carry out one without carrying out aspects of the others. Nevertheless, each contains a nucleus distinguishing it from the others. The following sections focus on both the nucleus and the interplay with the other processes.

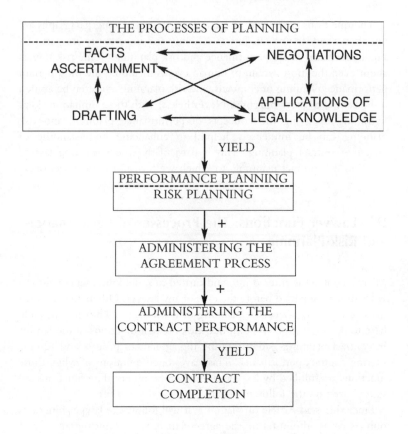

A. Ascertaining the Facts

The first process to be initiated in contract planning is ascertaining the facts. The lawyer must determine two distinct, albeit related, kinds of facts in preparation for drafting any contract transaction or relation. One type encompasses the planning goals of the parties: what is it they seek? The other type encompasses the factual matrix in which the parties' planning goals occur: how will the parties achieve what they seek? Simplistic, but useful, labels for these are, respectively, "goal facts" and "means facts." Thus, for example, if a client asks a lawyer to draft an agreement respecting a business joint venture, the lawyer must ascertain what the client seeks in the way of return, such as allocation of profits—a goal fact. The lawyer must also ascertain what each joint venturer will contribute—both a means fact and a goal fact, not only because in exchanges one person's goal is another person's means, but also because a cost to a party is a "negative" goal, not one desired, but one put up with as necessary to the achievement of other goals. Typically, however, the lawyer must also ascertain much more than goal and means facts as they exist in the minds of the parties if he is to lend realism to the prospects for their realization. Thus, for example, in a joint venture, if one of the other parties is to put up $100,000 cash and a $500,000 line of credit, the lawyer may inquire about the assets and liabilities of that other party to ascertain his capacity to perform, a means fact.

In the process of unearthing both kinds of facts, the lawyer also shapes the facts; he is not simply a computer-like collector of information. This is most obvious respecting the goal facts; the very process of asking a client to explain goals is a shaping process. Often, however, the means facts are also shaped by the lawyer's questions, since focus on them may lead to developing new means, as where a lawyer uncovers shortcomings in prior perceptions of economic reality. These changes in means facts or in the client's perception of them often, of course, change goal facts as well.

Since the lawyer is doing something more in ascertaining the facts than simply ingesting pre-existing and entirely choate information, it is obvious that simply by asking questions he is beginning the representation of his client. He needs, therefore, to be alert, even at this early stage of representation, to possible conflicts of interest among the parties to the contract, conflicts which either preclude his representing everyone, or at least require full notice.

As with other aspects of the planning processes, the ascertainment of facts is a continuing process never safely to be forgotten in any part of planning. While the major portion of the facts may be dug out when the lawyer is first presented with a request to draft a contract, if he sets about his drafting, intelligently and diligently he will soon discover that in all but the most routine transactions he does not know everything he needs to know. Moreover, as he acquires more insight into the proposed contract, he will see additional lines of inquiry to be made as he proceeds with the work of specifying the contract. His ignorance is no reflection on his competence; quite the opposite, it is a sign that he is performing an important function. His quest for information may well reveal that inadequate planning has taken place which may still be remediable without serious difficulty, or at least with less difficulty than if discovered later.

Revelation by the lawyer of inadequate performance planning may not bring joy to the client's heart, and the lawyer must be prepared for negative as well as affirmative reactions. A refusal by the client to plan more carefully may or may not be in harmony with the client's real interests. Precise specification of parts of the relationship may be impossible or undesirable for a variety of reasons. (Macaulay 1963b, 14; Shulman 1955, 1002–1005) Such specification may be too costly (in money or time), or it may jeopardize the prospective relationship between the parties. For example, a couple about to marry may fear the possibly disruptive effect of arms-length negotiations required for specification of performance planning. On the other hand, nonspecification resulting from inadvertence may be undesirable. Examples of that, of course, constitute much of the material in basic contracts casebooks.

Clients may react differently to advice regarding inadequate performance planning than they do to advice regarding inadequate risk planning. The often negative response to the latter may be, as Macaulay (Macaulay 1963b, 14) points out, a reaction against what is viewed as excessive lawyer concern for remote risks—a concern the client sees as threatening the deal itself. Obviously, discovery of either type of omission calls for the lawyer to be tactful, although not so tactful as to neglect to protect his client's interests properly—in short, on occasion he will be walking a knife edge.

B. Negotiation

Two law teachers who conducted a course for third year law students in simulated negotiation observed that because few law students have engaged in extensive legal negotiation and few have had much experience in representing the interests of others, reading descriptions of negotiating technique is pointless. (Moore and Tomlinson 1969) Although this observation is a less than accurate overstatement, it would certainly be accurate as to any summation of negotiation—its techniques, its psychology, its pervasiveness—short enough to include in an Article of this nature. Accordingly, no such summation will be made, but rather merely a suggestion that there is indeed merit in reading about negotiation and a reminder that negotiation is conducted in a constant interplay with the other three planning processes: fact ascertainment, drafting, and application of legal knowledge.

C. Drafting: Reducing Planning to Media of Mutual Communication

Certain common sense principles govern drafting of contractual communications. These principles include paying attention to audience and environment and following certain practices in organizing and composing the contract. Only constant practice will make anyone into a first-class draftsman, but an understanding of these basic principles can help make practice a more effective teacher.

1. Audience

As Dickerson (1965, 19) points out, one of the main elements of the communication process is the audience to which communication is addressed. All too many contracts are drafted with complete disregard of the audience likely to read them. In most contracts which stay out of serious trouble, and that is most of them, the audience that will actually deal with the contract is not one of lawyers. Rather, the audience consists of people who need the contract documents in order to know what they are expected to do and what they can expect from others.

In more complicated transactions, such as a contract for constructing a large office building, numerous types of personnel may need to know what they are expected to do and what they can expect from others. In such cases there are likely to be numerous other communications following the execution of the contract documents. In a construction contract such communications may range in scope from an overall building schedule prepared by the contractor's main office down to an oral direction given by a foreman. At least part of the contract documents themselves may therefore be addressed only to one or a few experts, who in turn will restate the expectations described therein in a form usable by others. In such circumstances, it is, of course, the few experts who are the audience to whom the contract drafter must successfully communicate. Dickerson (1965, 19) gives a good statutory example of this—taxation of individual income under the Internal Revenue Code. The Code itself is neither addressed to nor often read by the people who pay taxes. Information needed by taxpayers is instead communicated to them through such methods as instructions to Form 1040, Form 1040 itself, or through accounting or legal advice. The statute can, therefore, be drafted very differently from the form it would have to take were it necessary for most taxpayers to understand it directly. When similar stages of communication are needed in contracts, the nature of the audience is affected, and with it the drafter's task.

Since any contract may run into difficulties involving intervention of lawyers, judges, and lawyer-like people such as Internal Revenue agents, all contract planning, whether performance planning or risk planning, is potentially addressed in part to such an audience. That fact should never, however, be allowed to obscure the nature of the audience which will have to carry out performance of the contract, nor prevent proper communication to that audience.

2. Environment

The written words a drafter directs to the audience are simply part of an overall environment of circumstances surrounding the contract—its beginnings, its life, and its termination, if any. Just as the drafter runs great risks if he ignores his audience, he also runs great risks if he ignores those circumstances and writes as if the contract were occurring in some kind of abstract and generalized vacuum. For example, drafting a supply contract while in a state of ignorance about customs of the particular industry is an act of utmost foolhardiness. Not only do *all* circumstances surrounding the contract determine the meanings his audience will attribute to his words, but they will determine the unplanned parts of the contract as well—parts intimately intertwined with the drafted specificities.

3. Organizing and Composing

The actual drafting of the document which becomes the contract instrument involves two interrelated functions: organizing and composing. In fact, the lawyer starts performing both functions when he starts inquiring about the facts and thinking about the legal framework in which the relationship will be operating. For instance, the lawyer who, in an organized fashion, has solicited facts concerning a proposed partnership has already purposely or inadvertently gone a long way in organizing the document which will ultimately emerge. (Mulder and Volz 1967, 4–9)

    a. *Organizing*: Statements of principles concerning the organization of contract instruments are likely to be so general as to be useless, or, if specific, inapplicable to many contracts. One general principle, however, is worth always keeping in mind: the best organization of a contract document is that which will lead to the accomplishment of the goals of the client. (Trite, but nevertheless, constantly forgotten.) This generalization simply restates the basic principle of lawyering: the lawyer must constantly urge himself to remember what he is trying to accomplish. Few occupations, with the probable exception of teaching, are as subject to forgetfulness on this point as lawyering.

b. *Composing*: Words used by the drafter should be carefully chosen and arranged to convey with clarity and economy the information he wishes to communicate. A contractual document is not the place to display literary style except active, direct, concise, and, one hopes, graceful use of language. Nor is a contractual document a place to show how much useless legal jargon the drafter has absorbed. *Saids, to wits, thereuntos, aforementioneds*, and *whatsoevers* are the works of ancient devils that must be exorcised if contractual writing is to serve its purpose of clear and concise communication. (Mellinkoff 1963)

Ensuring achievement of clear, concise, and complete communication requires a number of actions of diverse nature. Preceding the writing of the first draft is the creation of an initial drafting plan of organization, normally an outline. After writing the first draft, the lawyer should always revise, a process which, if properly carried out, will normally create many revised drafts. Revision is probably the most seriously neglected stage in drafting, whether through lack of prior training, laziness, sloppiness, or perhaps a false pride of authorship.

The next stage of composition (interspersed with revision) is what Dickerson calls the "across-the-board check." Across-the-board checks are made in recognition of the fact that instruments are drafted initially vertically from top-to-bottom and step-by-step. In the across-the-board check, the drafter reviews his work horizontally; that is, he checks individually each item of significance that is repeated. These include definitions, cross-references, individual words of significance, and repetitive subject matter such as all the provisions relating to notice, arbitration, times of payment, and the like. For example, in a contract for the sale of a business involving two different banks as lending institutions, each with different obligations, the drafter should check the entire instrument to make sure that each bank is correctly referred to at each point. Not only does this process tend to uncover ordinary mistakes, but it may also reveal that in the process of drafting step-by-step the drafter has inadvertently changed the meanings of terms, and with them

215

substantive provisions. Moreover, the horizontal check forces the drafter to look at the work from a series of fresh perspectives that may reveal significant defects in the product of the step-by-step approach.

The next stage of composition is also one many lawyers neglect: having the work reviewed by others. This is a step which should be taken in all but the most minor or routine drafting. Pride of authorship and fear of criticism become the greatest evil if they prevent this step. The best drafted contracts are those reviewed by others. Reviewers are, after all, a trial-run audience. Although they may not be typical of the audience that will use the performance provisions of the contract, they provide at least some check on the success (or lack of it) of the drafter's efforts.

D. APPLICATION OF LEGAL KNOWLEDGE

The processes of performance and risk planning discussed thus far require no knowledge of principles or rules of law. But a lawyer, or anyone performing these lawyer functions, can deal wisely with what his client wants only if he has an intimate knowledge of the legal framework work or milieu in which the contractual relation will take place. This milieu affects fact ascertainment, negotiations, and drafting—*all* the processes yielding contract planning. It also, of course, affects all of the substantive content of the planning, whether it be performance planning or risk planning. This process is so intertwined in the details of the remainder of this Article and lawyers are so alert to this aspect of their functions that nothing further need be said about it here.

Summarizing briefly, four key processes—ascertainment of facts, negotiation, drafting, and application of legal knowledge—constitute the processes of performance and risk planning of contracts. The application of these processes to the preliminary goals and assessments of costs of the parties results in the final substantive content of the particular contract planning. Equally important, it all also affects the substantive content of the unplanned portions of the contract, although by the very nature of non-planning this effect tends to be far less evident to all concerned than in the case of the planned portions.

III. Performance Planning

The most important substantive goal of performance planning is smooth and efficient performance. As noted earlier, a great deal of that kind of performance planning depends upon non-lawyers. If, for example, an architect designs a building satisfying to the owner and capable of being built with a minimum of construction difficulties, smooth performance by both parties to the ensuing building contract is more likely to occur than in the case of design not satisfying these needs of the parties. Nevertheless, the planning processes of the lawyer also may go a long distance in aiding the achievement of such effective performance planning. This part will treat the following key aspects of lawyer planning of processes of performance: economic regulation and performance planning; utilization of standardized specification of performance planning; and providing for flexible operating relations.

A. Economic Regulation and Performance Planning

Complex economics produce complex regulation of economic activities. Complex regulation, in turn, creates needs for careful legal planning of economic activities, including contractual activities. Regulations create a major part of lawyers' work in modern American society, and the major part of that work is contract planning. In areas in which a lawyer is an old hand, he needs little warning of the need for careful performance planning to comply with legal requirements. No Wall Street securities lawyer needs to be reminded that an SEC exists. But the same lawyer might run afoul of Vermont's stringent environmental statutes and local ordinances were he to enter, without benefit of local counsel, a purchase and sale agreement for five acres of land for a summer cottage in the Green Mountains. Even good lawyers can easily stray off the relative safety of the Old Forest Road of their specialities and encounter the dangers of the Mirkwood.

A particularly important aspect of the regulatory matrix in which modern contract planning occurs is taxation. Society does not control or affect contractual behavior solely by restraints. It also channels it by a variety of benefits, such as giving certain kinds of contract behavior preferred treatment under income or other tax laws. These benefits are so pervasive, particularly those under the federal income tax laws, that few, if any, economic enterprises can afford to proceed without constant planning and channeling of all of their behavior, including contractual behavior, to take advantage of preferred tax treatment. The lawyer planning any contract must be constantly aware of the tax impact of what he is doing, even in a relatively simple transaction.

B.   Standardized Specification of Performance Planning— Herein of Use of Forms

A lawyer must also be aware of the nature and optimal use of standardized forms in planning the performance relationship. Forms are but one aspect of the standardization of the specification of performance relationships, a phenomenon always resulting from techniques of mass production of goods and services. A person buying a new automobile is, for example, given a choice of standardized "contract specifications" in the shape of whatever Detroit and its competitors have decided to put on the road in the current year. Supplemental to the delivery of the standardized automobile itself, the purchaser is given standardized contract terms (including some performance terms) in a written form.

For the moment, let us put aside the legal impact of performance planning and consider forms solely in terms of that smooth and efficient performance which constitutes the primary goal of all performance planning. To the extent that performance relationships are standardized, forms describing the relationships tend to develop, *e.g.* bank checks and rules governing deliveries of securities between brokers. These are but an extension into contracting of a rational administrative process for the ordering of standardized economic activities.

Like non-contractual ordering processes, *e.g.* a directive from a vice-president to a division manager, contractual communications must be understood by the recipient as well as by the sender in order to be effective in accomplishing the goals intended. An obstacle to recipient understanding of contractual communications results, however, from one of the factors likely to lead in the first place to the use of contractual economic ordering in preference to vertical organization. That factor is economic specialization. The more one economic activity is differentiated from another, the more likely enterprisers are to develop separate enterprise units to perform each, rather than to perform them under the umbrella of one vertically organized unit. Thus, contractual communications are more likely than vertical orders within an enterprise unit to be addressed to people whose specialized knowledge is more remote from the specialties of others involved in the pertinent economic activity. The upshot is greater difficulty in successfully communicating. This is a problem of any contractual communication, but is especially acute in the case of standardized specifications. Whenever they are drafted without the participation of recipients, their very generality of use is likely to result in the overlooking of differentials in knowledge of various specialized recipents

The intervention of the lawyer, made necessary in considerable measure by the existence of separate enterprise units presupposed by use of the contracting process, creates additional problems. Commonly the lawyer is far less cognizant of operational problems than are the participants in the internal chain-of-command of an enterprise. Moreover, the lawyer's other functions in contract planning may distract his attention from the vital task of ensuring that both parties fully understand the operational aspects of the contract being planned. This particularly is the case where the lure of speed and case offered by standardized forms is great.

Thus, whether the form is standardized or unstandardized, the lawyer (or anyone else) using one wisely will go through all the planning processes discussed earlier—the only difference is that the form can serve either as a starting point or a checking mechanism. The lawyer is justified in using an unaltered form only when he knows from prior experience or otherwise that the proposed relationship will be identical to the one for which the form was designed, and that the form is still well designed for its purpose.

Forms, of course, are often used for legal planning as well as for operational planning. In fact, the natural professional biases of lawyers too often lead them to think of contract planning as meaning only law-of-contract planning. But people do not enter contracts for the sake of the law of contracts. They enter contracts to achieve the goals of their mutual operational planning, e.g. to sell goods for money. A lawyer who uses a form—however good it is from the legal aspect—which constitutes inadequate or inaccurate operational planning is doing his client a great disservice. Conversely, all the operational planning takes place in a situation saturated with law; operational planning, like it or not, is legal planning. The lawyer must, therefore, approach every form both as an operational planning document and a legal framework planning document.

Advantages of forms in legal framework planning itself are obvious: they are convenient and efficient. There is, however, vast variation in the quality of forms. Moreover, using any form can be dangerous. First, the legal framework contained in the form simply may not fit the relationship being planned. In addition, however good the form may be as far as it goes, it may not constitute complete legal framework planning. Finally, a form may have become outdated because of changes in the law.

Every lawyer has to decide for himself on numerous occasions the

219

extent to which he will utilize a form. Few will or should always rise to Dickerson's suggestion that:

> the danger that the form will lull him into a false sense of accomplishment is so great that in other than the most routine situations he is wise to use it mainly as a cross check. (Dickerson 1965, 53)

But the lawyer failing to follow Dickerson's next dictum is no lawyer, simply a hack: "He must not forget that he has been engaged to exercise his professional judgment, not to serve as a mere retrieval system."

C. Providing for Flexible Operating Relations

Since all contracts are necessarily partially unplanned, another key aspect of performance planning is the need for providing flexibility in operating relations. (Weistart 1973; Anon 1950) Effective planning for such flexibility is, however, not easy. Not only is it difficult to provide effectively for a maximum of smooth and efficient operation, but also legal effectiveness is by no means always easy to achieve. (Macneil 1971a, 588–590, 604–736)

It is possible to have so much flexibility in planning of a "contract" that the whole "contract" is largely unplanned. But this is rare. What is common is both the occurrence of gaps in heavily planned contracts and the use of a range of techniques to create flexibility in lieu of either leaving a gap or trying to plan rigidly. These techniques inevitably raise difficulties for any legal system implementing the contract; they raise particular difficulties for any transactional contract law system. One of the key concepts of such a system is the maximization of presentation. The ideal goal of a transactional contract law system is total presentation through 100 per cent predictability as of the time of the acceptance of an offer. In more common language, this means that the contract is in theory fully planned at the time of creation. The following sections deal with two aspects of the difficulties of planning for such a system— difficulties relating to techniques for achieving flexibility and difficulties in adjusting existing contractual relationships in the face of unplanned occurrences.

220

1. Techniques of Flexibility

a. *Use of standards*: The use of a standard which is uncontrolled by either of the parties to plan the contractual relation is very common. One important example is the provision in many collective bargaining agreements for adjustments of wages to reflect fluctuations in the Consumer Price Index. Sometimes questions arise concerning the adequacy of the standard itself as a planning substitute. For example, an agreement to erect an expensive electric sign provided that the price would be "at ordinary industry prices." Should the court assume in the absence of evidence that this was "a standard ascertainable by proof"? The planning moral is to attempt to find standards with sufficient flexibility for the situation but not so loose as to cause unnecessary trouble between the parties. One must be aware of the possibility that a court will let the relation fall apart if the standard is too indefinite.

Trouble can also come if the standard is discontinued or altered in some way. For example, the Bureau of Labor Statistics revises the Consumer Price Index periodically[1] thereby causing problems with respect to escalator clauses in collective bargaining agreements.

The standard incorporated may, of course, be established by third parties not altogether unrelated to the contractual relationship. For example, it is common to find building contracts requiring compliance by the builders with regulations, plans, or standards of the Federal Housing Administration or the Veterans' Administration.[2] Both of these agencies insure mortgage loans, and their regulations are promulgated to deal with mortgages they insure. Thus, although the regulations are drafted with no particular contract in mind, they are aimed at a class of contracts, some of which incorporate them by reference. This kind of planning merges into the technique of using direct third party determination of performance, the subject of the following section.

b. *Direct third party determination of performance*: A good example of direct third party determination of performance is the role of the architect under form construction contracts of the American Institute of Architects.[3] Under those contracts, the architect is responsible for

---

[1] 4 CCH Lab. L. Rep. Paras. 7760, *et seq.*
[2] See *e.g. Helm v. Speith*, 298 Ky. 225, 182 S.W. 2d 635 (1944); Annot., 67 A.L.R. 2d 1017 (1959).
[3] A.I.A. Document A101, Standard Form of Agreement Between Owner and Contractor; AIA Document A201, General Conditions of the Contract for Construction.

221

determining many aspects of the performance relationship, everything from "general administration" of the contract and making final decisions "in matters relating to artistic effect" to approving the contractor's selection of a superintendent. The use of an expert who is relatively independent of the parties to determine contract content is, however, no guarantee of smooth performance; witness the fairly large amount of litigation arising under these contracts with respect to delays, payments, and completion of the work. In spite of the large authority given the architect by AIA articles dealing with these subjects, (A.I.A. A201, Arts. 8–9) litigation is by no means uncommon.[4] A recurrent problem in litigation of this kind is the scope of finality to be accorded to determinations of the third party. (Calamari & Perillo 1970, s. 152; Murray 1974, s. 153)

A particularly important and increasingly used technique for third-party determination of performance content is arbitration. Arbitration is best known for resolving "rights disputes,"—disputes about existing rights usually growing out of existing contracts and always substantially defined by law at the time the arbitration takes place. Planning for the arbitration of rights disputes is an important aspect of risk planning. But arbitration is also being used for filling gaps in performance planning, *e.g.* in industrial relations where the inability of management and labor to negotiate on their own the performance terms of a collective bargaining agreement is known as an "interest dispute."[5] Collective bargaining agreements are not, however, the only agreements where issues relating to future performance are left open. For example, certain joint ventures among design professionals may leave important aspects open to arbitration to provide necessary flexibility. (Aksen 1973, 599)

Interest disputes and hence their arbitration are inherently more open-ended than rights disputes. In the latter, the very notion of "rights"—whether they are based on contract terms or other legal sources, such as the rules of tort law—circumscribes the scope of potential arbitral resolution. In theory, if not in fact, such limits are far looser or perhaps even nonexistent in interest disputes. This calls for particular care in planning arbitration aimed at filling gaps in performance planning, and consideration must always be given to the need to include substantive limits on arbitrator authority. In any event, the planner should be fully

---

[4] See A.I.A., Building Construction Legal Citator (1971).
[5] See National Academy of Arbitrators, Arbitration of Interest Disputes (1974).

aware that identical general language of broad arbitration clauses applied to interest disputes lacks the situational limits usually present when it is applied to rights disputes.

c. *One-party control of terms*: Rather than use external standards or independent third parties, the contract may provide that one of the parties to the contract will define, directly or indirectly, parts of the relation. This may go so far as to allow one party a completely free will to terminate the relation. For example, a party may purchase the privilege of going ahead with a contract or not doing so, an option contract. One-party control of terms in the form of a "deal-no-deal" option is important in certain areas of enterprise such as the financial markets, commercial real estate transactions, some kinds of commercial sales of goods and certain types of consumer transactions.

Whenever a party is not clearly paying for the privilege of retaining a free will not to perform his own contractual "obligations," the contract drafter wanting to give that party such freedom walks a narrow line between rigid planning and the danger that the consideration doctrine will make that party's "rights" unenforceable. To cope with the difficulties created by its own doctrine of consideration, the transactional legal structure has produced, however, a wide range of concepts, provisions, techniques, and other devices limiting the impact of the doctrine. The drafter desiring to achieve workable flexibility must be aware both of the limitations the law imposes on the techniques that may be used and the opportunities it offers.

d. *Agreements to agree*: A flexible technique used more often than one might initially expect is an "agreement to agree." Since parties can almost always agree later to fill gaps in their relation, such an express provision seems pointless, particularly since, if taken literally, it is meaningless. But common human behavior patterns are seldom if ever pointless, and this is no exception. In general, parties probably use the technique because they are not yet prepared to agree on details which will require agreement, but they want to emphasize to each other that resolution will be required and to express a willingness to engage in the processes of agreement at the appropriate time. These processes undoubtedly more often than not lead to future agreement; but when and if difficulty later ensues in trying to reach agreement, a gap in the contract is revealed. The law should treat such gaps quite similarly to other gaps. The cases are legion, however, in which courts have said "an agreement to agree is not a contract" or some such similar bit of doggerel, in circumstances where the court would have held a contract to exist if the gap had occurred in any other manner than a breakdown of an explicit "agreement to agree." Thus, in terms of judicial enforcement, the enunciation of an agreement to agree can be fatal to later securing of gap-filling from the legal system. The planner may avoid this difficulty either by avoiding the technique entirely or by adding an alternative gap-filling technique to come into operation if the parties are unable to agree. Which of these routes is chosen depends at least in part upon how important it is to alert the parties to the need for further negotiation at the appropriate time.

2. Adjusting Existing Contractual Relationships

The preceding section treated the planning of flexibility into contracts so that future adjustments could be made within the original planning framework. This section focuses briefly on problems of adjustments which seemingly alter prior planning. These adjustments may involve further planning for future performance, as where an automobile dealer agrees to change a customer's order for a sports car to an order for a station wagon, with an appropriate change in price. Or they may involve no further planning for the future but rather involve adjustments performed immediately upon agreement. For example, when the customer goes to pick up his new sports car, he spots a station wagon he likes better, and the dealer promptly sells and delivers the latter in lieu of the former. To the extent that the latter adjustments involve no further planning for the future, they may not seem appropriate to the subject of this Article. In fact, they are. At the initial planning stage of any contract, one of the essential considerations must always be the potential need for effectuation of mutually agreeable changes. Planning of flexibility into that process needs to be carried out against a background of knowledge of what happens in the absence of such planning.

Adjustments of existing contractual relationships occur in numerous ways. Performance itself is a kind of adjustment from original planning. Even meticulous performance of the most explicit planning transforms figments of the imagination, however precise, into a new, and therefore different, reality. A set of blueprints and specifications, however detailed, and a newly built house are simply not the same thing. Less explicit planning is changed even more by performance. For example, the vaguely articulated duties of a secretary are made concrete by her actual performance of a day's work. Perhaps this is merely a way of saying that planning is inherently filled with gaps, and that performance fills the gaps

224

and thereby alters the relationship as originally planned.

Events outside the performance of the parties also may effect adjustments in contractual relationships. The $3 per hour promised an employee for his work in 1974 is not really the same when paid in November 1974 as it was when promised at the beginning of the year; inflation has seen to that. More or less drastic changes in outside circumstances constantly effect contractual adjustments, however firmly the parties may appear to be holding to their original course.

Nonperformance by one of the parties without the consent of the other also alters contractual relationships, although in a different way from performance. This is true no matter how many powers are available to the other party to redress the situation.

Another kind of adjustment occurring in any kind of contractual relationship is that based either on mutual agreement or on unilateral concession by one of the parties of a planned right beneficial to him. These alterations, additions, subtractions, terminations, and other changes from original planning may take place at any time during any contractual relationship. This is most vividly illustrated by various processes of collective bargaining, including periodic renegotiation of the "whole" contract. As already noted, such changes may take place with immediate effect, or they may consist initially of further planning of the future relationship. Changes involving planning for the future are subject to all the considerations dealt with in preceding sections of this Article. The fact that such planning happens to come after the relationship is established, rather than in its more formative stages, eliminates no problems of ascertaining facts, negotiation, drafting, and applying legal knowledge. Indeed, these processes are often even more complex at later stages because of the following special characteristics of contractual adjustments.

Adjustments of an existing relationship must always be viewed against the background of that relationship if disputes concerning them are to be handled wisely by parties, lawyers, judges, or legislatures. This fact is merely an example of what has been seen earlier: contract planning is comprehensible only when viewed as part of a whole relationship. Thus the subject of this section is not inherently different from much of the planning and other relational techniques considered heretofore throughout the Article. In adjustment, however, an element of "ongoingness" is *always* involved before or after the adjustment, or both, and with it the special problems of ongoing relationships.

When disputes arise out of contractual relationships that have been adjusted by mutual assent or concession, which governs, the original planning or the adjusted planning? Keeping in mind the exchange element basic to contractual relationships, and various problems the legal system has in dealing with contractual disputes, the answer might seem to depend in any given situation on answers to the following kinds of questions:

1. How sure is it that the adjustment really was mutually agreed upon or conceded?

2. Did one party take improper advantage of the other in securing the concession or agreement?

3. Was the adjustment mutually beneficial, *i.e.* was there an exchange element in the adjustment itself, or was only one of the parties benefited?

4. If the adjustment benefited only one party, was its purpose to alleviate some difficulty resulting from lack of prior planning or unplanned consequences of prior planning?

5. How much had the adjustment become integrated into the relationship when disputes concerning it arose? (Here of unjust enrichment and reliance, among other things.)

No comprehensive doctrinal structure has developed in the common law to answer systematically the foregoing questions. The closest the common law comes to providing such a structure is the doctrine of consideration, which pervades much thinking on the subject. Consideration doctrine, however, by no means deals comprehensively with all the questions. Moreover, consideration doctrine often obscures some, or perhaps all, of them.

Although the consideration doctrine may fail in directing adequate attention to the important issues arising out of disputed adjustments to contracts, it behooves the contract planner to understand its details in order to avoid falling into traps. Moreover, consideration doctrine often provides the knowledgeable with readily available channels, the use of which may preclude successful attack on such grounds as economic duress. "May preclude," not "will preclude," because concepts such as good faith and unconscionability—more direct ways of regulating contract behavior—are increasingly superseding or replacing consideration as a regulatory technique.

The purpose of this part on performance planning has been two-fold: first, to emphasize the importance of keeping the lawyerly eye on the main purpose of contract planning—always the smooth and efficient achievement of performance goals; and second, to examine several key points that are particularly vital and particularly troublesome to lawyerly success in achieving performance goals—economic regulation of contracts, standardized performance specification, flexible operating relations, and adjustments of existing contractual relationships. Only after one has firmly grasped the purpose of the contract being planned, can one understand in its proper context the more familiar lawyerly function examined in the following part—risk planning.

IV. Risk Planning

No matter what activity or inactivity engages him, man is subject to potential losses—losses of life, dignity, health, happiness, wealth, and all else he holds dear. Contractual activities are no exception. Not only may the people or property involved be harmed by mishaps, but the wealth created by the contract or hoped to be created may itself be destroyed, damaged, or prevented from coming into existence. This section is concerned with planning related to losses of this nature that might occur in contractual relationships.

The words "potential," "may," "might," and "mishaps" dominating the preceding paragraph are all words of uncertainty and therefore bring us to the subject of risk. The man-made concept of risk is a recognition that human beings are in a constant state of partial ignorance about the future, including future losses. We know with certainty from past experience that losses of various kinds will occur, but we do not know where, when, how, to whom, or how bad they will be. This state of partial ignorance we call risk. It disappears from our minds as soon as we know for sure either that the loss will occur or that it will not occur, simply because certainty is the opposite of risk. Risk is thus reduced whenever man acquires more certain knowledge about the occurrence or non-occurrence of future losses.

Except to the extent that he may be controlled by negative instincts such as the so-called death-wish, man seeks to avoid both losses and risks of loss. He does many things to try to avoid losses, from brushing his teeth in the morning to fighting massive, if commonly futile, wars. He

227

tries to eliminate risks not only by seeking to eliminate causes of losses, but also by using various techniques to acquire more certain information concerning future losses. Organized efforts along these lines in the world of commerce and family matters have come to be called risk management. Risk planning in connection with contracts is simply one facet of risk management in the economic world.

Like legal framework planning, planning for contractual risks (whether or not they are legal framework risks) calls for special awareness on the part of a lawyer participating in contract planning. Except in specialized contracts such as insurance, contractual risk planning is very likely not to be central to the purpose of the parties in entering the contractual relationship. When risk planning is not a central purpose of the contract, it may be seen by the parties in the same light as any other "trouble" planning, namely something distasteful and disruptive to the relationship, perhaps to be put up with, but never to be liked; in short, it is a lawyer's job. It is not surprising, therefore, that lawyers commonly are involved heavily with contractual risk planning.

A. Legal Consequences of Incomplete Planning

No contract can ever be fully planned; every contract presents the possibility that events will occur for which the planning was incomplete by reason of omission or ineffectiveness, or both. This is particularly true of the risk aspects of the contract. Relative certainties concerning performance often make nearly complete performance planning quite possible; but the element of the unknown in risk reduces the completeness of planning which can occur. Moreover, the degree of completeness of contract risk planning which *can* occur generally *does not* occur. The peripheral nature of risks relative to the central purposes underlying most contracts tends to lead to less completeness of risk planning than is possible. (This peripheral nature also normally leads in any given contract to less completeness in risk planning than in performance planning.) Moreover, the costs in time, money, and danger to successful negotiation of the basic performance planning arising from thoroughness of risk planning may often be too high relative to the gains to be thereby achieved.

Some of the costs of risk planning can often be avoided by recognizing that planning need not always be explicit in order to be well understood by the parties. Prior relationships of the parties, customs, rules of law with which they are familiar, and inferences from their explicit planning may all constitute well understood mutual risk planning without explicit expression by either of the parties. As a general proposition, the legal structure gives similar recognition to such risk planning as it does to performance planning of a comparable nature.

Perhaps the most common and biggest gap in explicit risk planning is the absence of any expression that the contractual relationship is to have legal consequences or is to be enforceable by legal mechanisms. This gap is filled by the legal system without hesitation.

Closely related to the absence of specific reference to legal enforceability is another gap very common in explicit risk planning: the nature of the legal remedies to be afforded when, and if, the contractual relationship lands in trouble. The legal structure provides a gamut of contract remedies even though the parties may never mention the subject.

Legal enforceability and contract remedies are but two of the many risk gap-filling enterprises of the legal system. Others may involve subtle risk gap-filling such as various interpretive provisions found in article 2 of the Uniform Commercial Code, (e.g. U.C.C. ss. 2–202(a), 2–208.) or provisions relating to risks of noncommunication between parties. (e.g. U.C.C. ss. 2–216.) But they also may deal in a direct and straightforward manner with substantive gap-filling such as risks from delegations of performance and assignments of rights, nondetermination of price, warranties, third parties, and countless others.[6]

To summarize, incomplete risk planning is an inherent characteristic of the planning process, with the result that, to be effective, any contract legal system must engage in a very wide range of gap-filling. The successful risk planner must be aware not only of the general nature of this legal gap-filling, but also of many of its details relating to contracts generally and to the specific kind of contract being planned.

In any given situation there may be countless reasons why good risk planning calls for explicitness in drafting, rather than reliance on the gap-filling of the legal structure, even where the terms the legal structure would supply are well understood by all concerned. Among these may be dissatisfaction with the legal allocation, the need for greater explicitness

---

[6] U.C.C. art.2 Pts 2 and 3 are in large measure made up of such provisions. See e.g. U.C.C. ss. 2–210, 2–305 (1)(b)-(c), (3), (4); 2–306(1); 2–306(1); 2–310; 2–311(3); 2–312; 2–314 to −3251 2–327. Similar lists could easily be compiled from other parts of Art. 2 as well as from other articles of the U.C.C.

than is provided by the applicable rules of law, costs imposed by use of the legal system that may be avoided or reduced by specific planning, ineffectiveness of the techniques supplied by the legal system for implementing its risk allocation, inflexibility of the legal rules, or even such things as a need to have the planning spelled out in contract documents in order to insure ready availability if dispute arises. Many of the explicit planning responses to these and other circumstances are far too specific to particular kinds of contracts to justify inclusion in a primer on contract planning, *e.g.*, limitations on implied warranties for the sale of goods. But two categories of risk planning are of sufficiently general utility for inclusion here: the related concepts of indemnification, insurance, and suretyship, and planning for dispute resolution. These form respectively the subjects of the following two sections.

B. INDEMNIFICATION, INSURANCE, AND SURETYSHIP

Net risk of economic loss can be reduced in two basic ways: (1) reducing the causes of losses and (2) insurance. An example of risk reduction by loss reduction is widespread smallpox vaccinations. They not only reduce losses of life from smallpox in the society, but in doing so also increase the certainty for each individual in the society that he will not die from the disease.

The other risk reduction technique, insurance, reduces risk through the insurer's compensation of the insured, even if it fails to reduce not losses. Instead of incurring a *risk* of a *large* loss, the insured sustains a certain smaller loss, namely the premium he pays for the insurance coverage. In large measure, the risk is not simply transferred to the insurer; it is destroyed. Not only is the insured's loss rendered more certain, but the insurer's losses are made fairly certain as well. This phenomenon results from what is sometimes called the Law of Large Numbers. The uncertainly about the occurrence of a loss respecting the property of any single insured does not, of course, change because of the insurance. But the insurance transaction cannot be viewed sensibly as a single transaction. It can only be viewed as one of numerous transactions into which the insurer is entering. And when all of these transactions are taken together, the insurer's expected losses are readily ascertainable. While the insurer is unable to predict with complete accuracy the total losses it will incur, it enjoys far more certainty than would any single insured about his own property. In short, from the insurer's standpoint, most of the losses are simply predictable costs of carrying on the insurance business. Insurance thus reduces the net uncertainty and risk suffered by society, apart from any effect it has in reducing total losses themselves.

Another way to reduce or eliminate risk of loss to an *individual* person or enterprise unit is to transfer the risk to a non-insurer. Such a transfer does not in principle, however, reduce either net losses or net uncertainty to the society as a whole, and does not, therefore, reduce net risk; it simply transfers it from one person or unit to another. For example, suppose that in the absence of agreement to the contrary the builder under a construction contract is legally responsible for restoring any portions of the partially finished structure damaged by fire. If the builder is in a strong enough position at the time he is negotiating a contract and does not want to bear that risk, he may be able to convince the owner to agree to assume the responsibility for such restoration. This is not insurance as the term is used in this Article because the owner's risk of loss remains the same as the contractor's would have been, and, unlike an insurer, the owner will receive no premiums from others to reduce his total risks. Such indemnity or "hold harmless" clauses are a specialized kind of contract in themselves with particular rules governing their interpretation and use. They should not be used (or at least not relied upon) without careful study of the pertinent law.

In applying these methods of risk management, the lawyer deals both with risks inherent in the contractual relationship itself and those which will affect his client after the conclusion of the contractual relationship. For example, a lawyer advising the buyer of a house is concerned with advising his client about fire insurance coverage for the period between the execution of the purchase and sale agreement and the buyer's taking possession of the property. But he should also make sure that the client is aware of the need for fire insurance protection beginning on the day that he becomes the owner of the house. Thus, it is most important to think of the lawyer's role and his professional obligations relating to risks as not limited to the period of, or to those inherent in, the contractual relationship itself. Nevertheless, the kinds of risks inherent in contractual relationships present particular problems for the lawyer, problems worth focusing upon as an integral part of contract planning.

Insurance and indemnity tend to focus on contract risks arising from the property and activities involved in the contract. Suretyship, a technique related to insurance, focuses more on the risks inherent in the nature of contracting itself. Two kinds of surety arrangements are of particular importance in contract planning: payment bonds and performance bonds.

The need for payment bonds arises because numerous statutory provisions create power in suppliers of goods or services to establish liens on property in which the goods or services are incorporated. If the subcontractor or other supplier is not paid by the general contractor or voluntarily by the owner, such a lien when duly perfected will result in the owner's property being used to satisfy the general contractor's obligation to the supplier. Because of possible liens the owner has a very real need to make sure that the contractor pays subcontractors and other suppliers of goods or services incorporated into his property. It is, therefore, very common to require payment bonds from construction contractors. But payment bonds are even more commonly required on government projects where sovereign immunity typically precludes the creation of construction liens. This suggests that another motivation for requiring such bonds is the encouragement of subcontractors and materialmen to contract with the general contractor, thereby facilitating his performance to the benefit of the owner having the work done.

Payment bonds deal with risks closely related, but nevertheless collateral, to the normal performance of the contract. More central to the principal purposes of the contracting parties are performance bonds, in which the contractor promises (again) to perform the contract, and a solvent third party (usually a paid surety company) acts as surety on that promise.

Like indemnity agreements, payment and performance bonds are highly specialized contracts with their own particular sets of governing legal rules, and are used at their own peril by those unknowledgeable on the subject.

While the lawyer can and often should become expert in the law relating to indemnification, suretyship, and insurance, few lawyers can or should become fully competent experts on subjects such as the kinds of coverage available, the costs of various coverages, the pitfalls of various kinds of insurance, the "best buys," and the like. They should, however, know enough about these matters to know when and how to consult and use the expertise of qualified insurance and risk experts.

The subject of the following section—planning for dispute resolution—is one upon which lawyers can and do become expert, not only respecting the applicable law, but also concerning the "commodity" being purchased by their planning, namely dispute resolution in forms most beneficial to their clients. Indeed, as a class, lawyers are probably the leading group of experts on this subject.

C. Planning for Dispute Resolution

The ideal technique of dispute resolution is avoiding the dispute in the first place. Everything that has gone before in this Article *could* be viewed as instruction in dispute resolution by avoidance. If, however, anything can be learned from what has gone before, it should be that no planning is ever so perfect that disputes cannot arise. Recognizing that conflict and dispute are possibilities inherent in every contract, it may be and usually is incumbent upon the contract planner to give thought to planning ahead for their resolution. This section deals with a variety of techniques for doing so, focusing on planning for self-help remedies and planning for the processes and substance of dispute resolution.

1. Planning Self-Help Remedies

The best possible remedy a party can have for non-performance is very often some form of self-help. Self-help may take the form either of doing nothing,[7] or doing something affirmative. A right of a secured creditor to sell the property held as security exemplifies affirmative self-help. Many techniques, not themselves clearly self-help, may have a self-help effect by making defense of litigation so fruitless that the non-performing party will simply capitulate to demands which he might otherwise fight. For example, actual damages from non-performance may be minimal, but there may be a liquidated damages clause which the courts of the jurisdiction would enforce. The legal system itself creates or supports a great volume of self-help remedies, even without much, if any, planning of them by the parties or their representatives.

Planning by the legal system may or may not fit the needs of one or both parties to a contractual relationship, and self-help planning is no exception to this general proposition. It therefore behooves the lawyer engaged in contract planning to know what the legal system supplies and if and how he can improve on that planning from his client's standpoint. At the very minimum, improvement may take the form of spelling out in contractual documents what the law provides anyway, simply so that the

---

[7] See, *e.g. Nolan v. Whitney*, 8 NY 649 (1882), where progress payments made under a construction contract were so much smaller than the value of the completed work that upon contractor's breach the owner was content simply to sit tight, keeping the benefit of the work done refusing to pay the balance of the contract price.

parties can easily refer to it. But improvement may be of far greater scope. In this section, emphasis will be divided between the importance of comprehending what is the law's planning of self-help remedies in a given situation and the importance of engaging in supplemental or superseding planning of such remedies. Needless to say, no complete survey of the law of such planning is feasible; only some of the techniques and pitfalls can be mentioned here.

Planning self-help remedies so as to ensure effectiveness in accomplishing the preventive and remedial purposes for which they are intended is only half of the planning task. Less obvious, but of almost equal importance, is reducing the risks of utilizing self-help. This principle, important enough respecting any remedy, is particularly important in the area of self-help because of the ease with which parties often may exercise self-help. The caution which may be forced or otherwise induced when a remedy is available only by invoking legal process may be completely missing when a remedy is available simply by saying: "I won't!" Minimizing the dangers at the planning stage is, therefore, particularly vital.

Three closely interrelated categories of planning constitute the core of planning self-help remedies: planning for refraining from performance; planning to keep ahead of the game—security and forfeitures; and planning for the uncertain-duty-risk.

a. *Planning for refraining from performance*: The law often confers on a party the right to suspend, refuse, or stop his own performance in the face of nonperformance by the other party. While such rights are by no means unlimited and sometimes run into countervailing policies and legal rules effecting such policies,[8] courts have often broadened the self-help remedy of nonperformance by allowing explicit contractual terms to supersede countervailing policy considerations and legal rules. In view of this permissiveness of the legal system, it is incumbent upon those concerned with planning remedies for nonperformance to give close attention to broadening and specifying a client's rights to refrain from performance in the face of breach.

Good planning of the refraining-from-performance remedy always contains three elements: explicit conferring of rights on a party to stop his own performance; precise specifying of the events giving rise to those

---

[8] For example, many rules reflect society's distaste for forfeitures. See *e.g.* U.C.C. ss. 2–718(2)(3).

rights; and dealing with further remedies and other related matters.

b. *Planning to keep ahead of the game: security and forfeitures*: In planning self-help remedies the lawyer may often advantageously utilize the forfeiture or security root or basis of legal reinforcement of contracts. This root, to be distinguished from the enforcement-of-promise root, traces historically to the giving of hostages or property as assurance that an expected, although not necessarily promised, performance would occur. (Llewellyn 1931, 714) The purest modern example is probably the pawning of goods. Although there is no promise by the borrower to repay the loan, if he does not do so the goods pawned are forfeited. The working principle of the security-forfeiture root may be said to be keeping ahead of the game. When it is working at its best from the viewpoint of the protected party, that party is always ahead, or at least not behind, no matter what the other party does about performance. For example, an owner who has contracted to have a building erected on his property under a contract with no progress payments typically is increasingly ahead of the game as the contract is performed. Should the contractor stop performance, the chances are often excellent that the value of the partially completed building will equal or exceed any loss the owner may suffer because of nonperformance. The consequences of such an arrangement are manifold. Because the forfeiting of the security is within the control of the beneficiary, the arrangement constitutes a form of self-help remedy available in the event of nonperformance. Thus the beneficiary of the forfeiture-security arrangement need rely less on the promise root of assurance. And the arrangement may result in the beneficiary being left after nonperformance by the other party with more than is needed to protect any of his restitutionary, reliance, and expectation interests.

c. *Planning for the uncertain-duty-risk*: A constant risk of contractual relationships is the uncertain-duty-risk—the need to act or refrain from acting in the face of uncertainty concerning the duties of the parties. We associate this risk most often with disputes, but it also exists even in the absence of a present dispute. A party often has to act on his interpretation of performance obligations at the peril of being held wrong in the event of a subsequent dispute. Nevertheless, the uncertain-duty-risk is most likely to be serious where a dispute has arisen or seems likely to arise. In such circumstances parties often find themselves having to act or refrain from acting at considerable risk that their premises for action will subsequently be held erroneous.

It is impossible through planning of contractual relationships to avoid uncertain-duty-risks completely. Nevertheless, such risks can be drastically reduced in many ways through prior planning. Good performance planning, for example, reduces the uncertain-duty-risk by reducing the likelihood of a dispute arising at all. Moreover, good performance planning leads to clarity in the performance relationship, so that in the event of trouble it is often clear who is right and who is wrong. Much, if not all, the risk planning dealt with in this Article reduces uncertain-duty-risks. A valid liquidated damages provision, for example, eliminates the risks inherent in disputes about how much a party has been hurt by the other's breach.

Nowhere is the uncertain-duty-risk greater than when a party undertakes a self-help remedy. Unlike a typical litigation remedy, where the remedy award coincides with resolving the dispute, the self-help remedy is used *before* the dispute is resolved. Moreover, as noted earlier, parties often can easily utilize self-help remedies without legal advice or assistance, whereas such advice and assistance generally has to be sought respecting litigation remedies. The absence of this kind of restraint enhances risks from hasty action whenever duties are uncertain. It is therefore desirable in the planning of contracts to reduce uncertain-duty-risks by clarifying ahead of time when and how a party may use self-help remedies. Effective self-help planning, as noted earlier, is intended to accomplish this purpose as well as to confer on one of the parties self-help rights to achieve particular substantive gains. Good planning aimed at particular substantive self-help remedies, such as rescission, thus also aims at reducing the uncertain-duty-risk, sometimes more than at gaining any particular substantive advantage. Sometimes these "remedies" are integral parts of performance, while sometimes they are rather more clearly directed at dispute situations. But in either case they make it clear what one may or may not properly do if disputes should arise.

2. Planning Processes of Dispute Resolution

Self-help remedies illustrate processes of dispute resolution, such as sitting tight while ahead of the game, as well as substantive dispute remedies, such as the forfeiture which one can gain from sitting tight while ahead of the game. As in so many other areas of law, substance and process are inevitably intertwined in dispute resolution, and a planner cannot plan wisely the one without at the same time planning the other. Nevertheless, in developing an understanding of the intertwined

236

combination, we may usefully separate the two for analytical purposes.

a. *One-sided dispute resolution*: Planned processes of one-sided dispute resolution often arise somewhat inadvertently from one-party control of performance terms or from performance itself, *e.g.* self-help remedies resulting from security strategies of various kinds. Only under extreme pressure is a person contemplating a dispute willing to allow the adverse party a completely free hand in resolving the dispute. Nevertheless, people do put their heads in the mouths of hungry lions, as the prevalence in some jurisdictions of cognovits (confession of judgment provisions) suggests. Many performance or other substantive risk provisions, such as warranties, may be no more than veiled one-sided dispute provisions. Moreover, one suspects that most consumers are resigned to the fact that most of their disputes with persons supplying them with goods and services largely depend for resolution on the discretion of the supplier.

Just as a great many one-party controls of substantive terms are hedged with restraints, such as that of good faith, so too are many one-sided dispute resolution processes. These restraints may take many forms. One form is limiting the scope of the one-party control. For example, in a contract for the sale of goods, the U.C.C. s. 2–712 permits the buyer to establish the amount of damages to which he will be entitled by covering, but this discretion is limited by such standards as honesty and reasonableness. Another form of restraint is limiting the circumstances in which a party has a free hand. A seller may, for example, be willing to give a buyer complete Ieeway to return goods if dissatisfied for any reason, provided the return is accomplished within a fixed period. Procedural requirements may also be imposed. For example, the party with power to decide may be required to provide a hearing upon disputes before being free to decide, as is the case with disputes arising in federal government contracts. For such procedures to be of much value, however, it is necessary to move from true one-party control of the dispute resolution to circumstances where the person resolving the dispute is in some respects at least partially independent of the interested party. Examples include government contracting officers and the members of the Board of Contract Appeals who are employees of one of the parties to government contracts, but who nevertheless have at least some, and perhaps a very great deal, of independence. Another example is the architect who is "the Owner's representative during construction," but who is called upon to "exercise his best efforts to insure faithful performance by both the Owner and the Contractor" and not to "show partiality to either."[9] Independence of the employees and agents of one of the parties of the foregoing kinds not only makes procedural requirements such as hearings more significant as limitations on one-sided dispute resolution, but also is a significant move away from one-sided resolution itself toward third-party resolution.

In summary, planning of one-sided dispute resolution requires careful delimitation because of the great power such resolution can put, perhaps inadvertently, into the hands of one of the parties. This power, when misused, may divert the whole contractual relationship from its original purposes.

b. *Negotiation and mediation*: Negotiation is undoubtedly the most common technique for resolving disputes and avoiding them as they begin to arise. Since, however, negotiation involves only the two parties to the contract and since they are free in any event to negotiate whenever a dispute arises, one may be easily tempted to reject the need for prior planning for such negotiation. Falling prey to this temptation is, however, the height of folly; negotiations are extremely difficult human activities at best, and dispute negotiations are particularly difficult because they always involve disappointments and tensions. Any planning of processes, scope, limits on force to be used, and the like, which may case the course of negotiations, enhances the likelihood of their success. We have already seen one example, "the agreement to agree," but it was so simple as to do little more than create a sense of anticipation of cooperation. Collective bargaining agreements supply far more complex examples, many such agreements providing for processing of grievances through as many as four stages before reaching the stage of bringing in an independent arbitrator.

Typical collective bargaining grievance procedures also introduce the concept of mediation, a process in which a third party edges both sides towards adhering to existing or newly created and mutually acceptable norms. At the first stage, the employee and supervisor may battle out the dispute solely between themselves; this is pure negotiation. Even at this stage, however, a union representative may be present. This presence may or may not introduce an element of mediation. Succeeding stages of grievance-resolving procedures may include appeal to the department superintendent who meets with the union grievance committee, then an

---

[9] A.I.A. A201, Art.2. The architect's need to preserve his professional reputation is an important factor in his dispute resolutions.

appeal taken to the personnel director of the company, who meets with an international representative of the union, with or without the grievance committee. At all these stages, those representing the employee and those representing management may maintain entirely negotiational stances as battlefield champions of the employee and supervisor respectively. On the other hand, either or both may take on mediational roles in trying to get the disputants (who often are not the union and management but the employee and a supervisor) to agree to settlement.

Planning ahead for mediational processes may be quite desirable in certain kinds of situations, as it may ease the entry of a mediator onto the scene. Moreover, mediation itself, like negotiation, is a complex human process likely to benefit from prior planning.

c. *Arbitration*: Arbitration is extremely complex in many ways, as the following summary of what the lawyer should know about arbitration suggests:

> In advising a client whether to use or to consent to use arbitration or in drafting an arbitration clause, he must know the nature of the process, its areas of utility, the character of the agency administering the arbitration and of its rules, the type of controversy made arbitrable by the legislature and courts, and the formal requirements of statutes and court decisions. When a dispute has arisen under an agreement purporting to make it arbitrable, he must also know the procedure whereby arbitration may be compelled or prevented. When the proceeding is undertaken, he must know the method by which the arbitrator is selected, and how to prepare for, and participate in, the hearing. Lastly, when the award is made, he must be familiar with the practice for confirming, vacating or modifying it, and the problems involved in its enforcement. It is only with this knowledge that the lawyer can serve most effectively.[10]

Planning of arbitration takes place against a peculiar legal background: a common law history displaying little enthusiasm for but not outright opposition to arbitration and a mosaic of arbitration statutes in various jurisdictions providing varying degrees of legal enhancement of the

---

[10] Ass'n of the Bar of the City of New York, An Outline of Procedure under the New York Arbitration Law 8 (1965).

arbitration technique. Always present is the possibility that the United States Arbitration Act[11] is applicable to transactions one might initially assume to be governed by state law.[12]

For arbitration to approach its potential as an effective dispute resolution technique, the applicable law must provide the following reinforcements:

1. irrevocability of any agreement to submit future disputes to arbitration;

2. power of a party, pursuant to a court directive, to compel a recalcitrant party to proceed to arbitration;

3. provision that any court action instituted in violation of an arbitration agreement may be stayed until arbitration in the agreed manner has taken place;

4. authority of the court to appoint arbitrators and fill vacancies when the parties do not make the designation, or when arbitrators withdraw or become unable to serve during the arbitration;

5. restrictions on the court's freedom to review the findings of facts by the arbitrator and his application of the law;

6. specification of the grounds on which awards may be attacked for procedural defects, and of time limits for such challenges. (Domke 1968, 20–21)

Arbitration statutes generally are held not to have preempted the subject of arbitration, (Sturges and Reckson 1962) with the result that in most states two legal systems respecting arbitration coexist. One system, the statutory, is often a reasonably well-articulated and cohesive legal structure. The other, the common law, is a potpourri of historical relies, reflecting in large measure 19th-century and earlier resolutions of conflicting policies—resolutions made largely obsolete by the statutory system itself. Thus arbitration agreements not complying with the local general arbitration statute are in a kind of legal limbo, the nature of which varies from state to state. They may be given effect as common law agreements to arbitrate (with all the common law limitations); they

---

[11] 9 U.S.C. ss. 1–14 (1970).
[12] See *Prima Paint Corp. v. Flood & Conklin Mfg. Co* 388 U.S. 395 (1967).

may be held to be completely unenforceable; or the more pro-arbitration climate of modern times may result in changes in the common law itself. Moreover, even when an agreement does comply with the local general arbitration statute, a question can arise whether the parties intended it to be governed by statutory or common law rules, and if the latter, whether they are free to make such an election.

The existence of two systems of arbitration in one jurisdiction may call for careful planning to ensure that the more effective system will apply, if the parties so desire, as they normally will. In the absence of explicit planning, the courts can come up with strange results, such as those occurring in Pennsylvania, where the presumption that the parties intend the common law to apply is hard to rebut.[13]

One of the most important questions to be answered in the planning of arbitration is: what issues do the parties wish to have subject to arbitration? This question is important primarily to avoid inadvertent narrowing or broadening of the arbitrator's role contrary to the desires of the parties at the time of the planning. Such provisions must be drafted with care and with particular consideration of the judicial attitude toward the scope to be given to arbitration provisions.

Another matter of importance in many contracts containing arbitration clauses is the obligation of the parties to continue with performance while a dispute is in the arbitration process. Is the arbitration clause to serve, like the disputes clause in federal government procurement contracts, as a substitute for discontinuing performance in the face of disputes, or may a party stop performance while the dispute is being settled, albeit at the risk of being in further difficulty if he loses before the arbitrator? A provision such as that contained in an AIA form[14] is a good start on such planning: "The Contractor shall carry on the work and maintain the progress schedule during any arbitration proceedings, unless otherwise agreed by him and the Owner in writing."

An entry-of-judgment provision should be a part of every arbitration clause in order to eliminate any danger of a holding such as that in *Cueroni v. Coburnville Garage, Inc.*[15] The agreement in that case provided only that "any finding made by the arbitrators shall be final and binding on each party." The court held "nothing further was contemplated after

---

[13] *La Vale Plaza, Inc v. RS Noonan, Inc*, 378 F.2d 569 (3rd Cir. 1967).
[14] A.I.A. A201 Art. 7.10.3
[15] 315 Mass. 135, 52 N.E.2d (1943)

the arbitrators should make their award." That being the case, the clause was not a "reference" under the arbitration statute then in effect in Massachusetts and thus was not enforceable under the statute. While this result would probably not obtain under many other statutes, it is pointless to run unnecessary risks by omitting an entry-of-judgment provision in the agreement.

More complex than the entry-of-judgment provision is the planning of provisions relating to jurisdiction of particular courts, both with respect to subject matter and personal jurisdiction. Some of these matters are likely to be provided for by the applicable statute. Nevertheless, one should not rely on the statutes entirely, as they seldom if ever deal with everything which should be planned.

Aspects of jurisdictional matters may also be dealt with through institutional rules incorporated by reference in the arbitration agreement. For example, the American Arbitration Association (AAA) Construction Industry Arbitration Rules specify that parties agreeing to arbitration also agree that service by mail satisfies all jurisdictional requirements, provided that reasonable opportunity to be heard is granted.

The final aspect of arbitration planning requiring special mention is planning of arbitration procedure. Arbitration is a form of mini-judicial dispute resolution; while its relative informality and consensual character free it from many of the more complex procedural needs of a full-blown judicial system, countless questions do require prior planning. Who will be the arbitrators? How is arbitration initiated? How are issues framed? How are hearings held? What remedial processes are available to the arbitrators? These are but a few needing answers.

Planning of arbitration procedure is greatly simplified by the likelihood that it will be desirable to incorporate institutional rules into the contract by reference. Incorporation of such procedure, however, presents many of the same dangers as does the use of mass-produced forms. For example, the planning may be incomplete in some respects, as in the case of the AAA Construction Industry Arbitration Rules which do not specify time limits for initiating arbitration but defer to time limits, if any, specified in the contract.

"Form" planning of arbitration through incorporation of institutional rules may be deficient not only in leaving gaps but also in providing unwanted planning. For example, incorporating arbitration association rules by reference might inadvertently bring in the association as administrator, thereby committing the parties to sizable arbitration fees.

In addition to containing too little or too much for the particular

242

situation, rules incorporated by reference might also deal with a particular matter differently from the manner in which a party would otherwise prefer to have it handled. Thus, incorporation of institutional rules calls for the same kinds of general astuteness, knowledge of content, and understanding of the needs of the parties as does the use of any other kind of form.

d. *Judicial processes*: The American legal system gives contracting parties broad latitude to vary by agreement judicial processes otherwise applicable to their disputes. It is, therefore, incumbent upon the contract planner to take this permissiveness into account in seeking to achieve the goals of his client. For example, he may include cognovit provisions to give his client superior power if a dispute arises; he may effectively shorten the statute of limitations to encourage speedy resolution of disputes; he may provide for assignment of wages as a good to performance and security in the event of nonperformance; he may add to or limit the forums in which an action can be brought for any number of reasons, of which economy of dispute resolution is only one; and he may waive jury trials and alter rules of evidence. Unlimited freedom of contract is by no means the rule respecting such planning, however, and the planner needs to be fully familiar with the particular restraints pertinent legislatures and courts may have imposed.

3. Planning Substance of Dispute Resolution

a. *Planning litigation content: looking forward to the court's look backward*: Litigation content is quite different from the content of an untroubled viable contractual relationship. The court is engaged in conducting an autopsy on a corpse, not in examining an ongoing relationship in which exchange and other motivations create a mutual need for cooperation. Instead of constituting a way of satisfying such motivations—as does a viable contractual relationship—the contractual relationship in litigation has become simply a tool for securing or avoiding damages. Inevitably the contract's contents are no longer the same once mutuality of exchange motivations has disappeared, since the most important single element of a viable ongoing contractual relationship commonly is the mutual desire to make it succeed. The court thus is always looking backward at the contractual relationship to see what it once was.

In planning litigation content, the lawyer should keep in mind two fundamental aspects of the court's look backward. One is that the court

243

can view the relationship only indirectly through documents, witnesses, etc., and also only through the procedural and evidentiary filters constituting integral parts of its operating techniques. The court can never, therefore, even at best, view the contractual relationship as a whole; it must make its decisions on only part of the facts viewed from a distance and with inevitable distortion.

The second fundamental aspect of the court's retrospective look at contracts in litigation is the relative narrowness of its possible responses compared to the range of adjustments available to parties to a viable ongoing relationship. The court can, after all, generally do little more than convert the content it finds into a money judgment. Even granting of specific performance is limited to situations where the spirit of cooperation is relatively unimportant to the relationship. In order to award damages or grant specific performance, the court must, by judicial fiat, often make certain aspects of the relationship definite and concrete which, in a viable situation, would have remained flexible or subject to negotiation and accommodation.

Although the primary focus of contract planning is on performance rather than on trouble in the relationship, any aspect of any contractual relationship is potentially subject to litigation. For that reason all contract planning is intimately related to litigation content regardless of whether the planner is conscious of that fact or whether he actively takes into account the possibilities of litigation in his planning.

Although not all litigation planning is also performance planning, much of it is, and this fact gives rise to inherent conflicts. (Macaulay, 1963b) Planning for an autopsy on the corpse of a contractual relationship in the judicial mortuary may harmonize poorly with planning for the living relationship. When this is the case, the planner often must balance risks from undesirable litigation planning with risks from undesirable performance planning.

It has been seen earlier that the law can and does fill gaps in the explicit performance planning of the parties. This is true as well of certain aspects of litigation planning, whether they also constitute performance planning or whether they are directed primarily or exclusively toward litigation. Indeed, if performance planning is sufficiently complete to avoid problems of indefiniteness, the legal structure will supply *all* of the rest of the litigation content. It provides rules of evidence, interpretation, gap-filling, procedure, remedies—in short, the whole spectrum of litigation content.

Much of the litigation content supplied by the legal system will depend at least in part upon the specific performance planning in which the parties engage. But even to the extent that litigation content is independent of specific planning for performance, the parties, simply by entering a contractual relationship, have brought into it the whole range of litigation content the legal structure will supply in the event litigation occurs or potential litigation is ever a factor in the relationship. Thus, a lawyer who is unaware of the existence, nature, and substance of this massive infusion of litigation content drafts a contract at his client's— and his own—peril.

Since experienced lawyers are very much aware of the foregoing, in many instances conscious or tacit planning of litigation content may occur even though nothing expressly appears in the contract relating to the subject. On the other hand, the absence of express provisions on the subject may be indicative of inadvertent or ignorant planning. Moreover, merger or similar clauses are such common boilerplate that their presence in an agreement is by no means necessarily an indication of thoughtful planning for litigation.

Much of the litigation content of contracts consists of law applicable to non-contract litigation as well, such as most procedural rules and most rules of evidence. Much of the content is related to specific kinds of contracts, such as implied warranties in sales of goods. But a large body is pertinent primarily, or even exclusively, to contractual relationships, and to wide varieties of them. It is, however, unnecessary as well as impossible in an article of this nature to give a summary of such general contract litigation content. Virtually every contract course in law school, to which virtually every law student or lawyer has been or is being exposed, is a course in general contract litigation content. Thus, the primary function of this section is the modest one of suggesting a planning perspective in which to place the great knowledge of general contract litigation content known to every reader.

The key to understanding litigation content from the standpoint of contract planning is recognition that no matter what the contract planner writes or otherwise expresses, the litigation content of a contract will ultimately be what the court—judge or jury—says it is. A fundamental tool of the planner must, therefore, be a thorough understanding of the principles of interpretation applied by the court. This should include an understanding of limitations on the effect given to expressions of intent and everything else a judge or jury might do concerning the contract, ranging from actions appearing to be based on party meaning or purpose to open limitations on freedom of contract.

The lawyer should also be aware of the importance of litigation content planning in preventing litigation and bringing about settlements: the better the planning of litigation content, the clearer will be the predictable outcome of litigation. The more clearly counsel for both parties can predict the outcome, the easier it is to settle disputes and thereby avoid actual litigation. Indeed, in many instances disputes may never arise simply because one of the parties who is unhappy with something realizes that he would have no hope of winning the issue in litigation.

The foregoing remarks lose considerable force when the issue is whether a provision is illegal, unconscionable, or the like. Even the clearest drafting near the verge of such social control may result in unpredictability of litigation outcome. But even in such cases, clear drafting tends to reduce uncertainty about how the court will interpret the provision in issue.

A caveat is in order concerning the consequences of drafting to the brink of legal unenforceability. It is a double-barreled caveat, one barrel having to do with the client's interest and the other with the lawyer's soul. Respecting the former, as long as the only sanction for drafting past the brink of legal unenforceability is refusal of courts to enforce the "illegal" aspect of the agreement, the client suffers no loss from drafting that overreaches, and such a sanction therefore has little impact on drafting. Perhaps next up the ladder of severity is simple unenforceability of the offending provision itself. This sanction may have an impact on planning, since overreaching can result in loss of a benefit that could have been achieved by a narrower legal clause. The inclusion of a clause resulting in the whole contract being held unenforceable can cause an even higher price to be paid, particularly if the law permits the other party to retain any benefits received under the contract. Other punitive results are also possible, such as statutes permitting recoveries against usurers of three times the amount of the usurious interest. Sanctions not running in favor of one of the parties, such as criminal sanctions and loss of rights to do business, may be viewed as very high prices exacted by society for improper contract planning and performance.

The second barrel of the caveat is that the realities of the regulatory structures within which contracts are planned and performed produce ethical problems for lawyers whenever the transactions skirt close to regulatory limits. *The Code of Professional Responsibility* provides that a lawyer shall not counse or assist his client in conduct that the lawyer

246

knows to be illegal.[16] This seems to provide a great deal of leeway, even when read in conjunction with another part of the Code *permitting* a lawyer to refuse to participate in arguably legal conduct that he believes to be unlawful.[17] It would be a rare situation, however, where rules such as these would limit a lawyer's planning recommendations before they were already inhibited by consideration of the legitimate interests of the client. Whether stricter standards than these rules govern the actual or desired conduct of the bar will have to be decided elsewhere, every lawyer planning contracts constantly faces such questions personally.

The primary function of this section has been to give an overview of the planning of litigation content. Before closing it, however, two particular aspects of that kind of planning should be mentioned. One is a specialized technique for supplying litigation content, the recital; the other is a conflict inherent in exchange which is carried on by forms drafted individually by each of the parties, the so-called battle of the forms.

(i) *Recitals*: Most contract clauses are what linguists call directive language. Recitals are a different species typically starting with a linguistically peculiar word—"whereas." Two uses are the setting out of facts ("Whereas ABC is the owner of Blackacre ...") and setting out purposes of the parties in making the agreement ("Whereas the parties wish to establish a partnership for the purpose of engaging in the business of landscape architects ..."). Such clauses may be useful, but they must be used with care to avoid undesired results. A provision intended to set out one of the explicit agreements between the parties should never be introduced by the word "whereas" or otherwise set out as a recital because of the risk that a court might give it less than full effect. On the other hand, a recital of purposes of the parties and of circumstances surrounding the relationship may be considered by a court for the purposes of interpretation, construction, or possibly even contradiction. To the extent that a recital constitutes party agreement on relevant facts, it may be unnecessary to offer other proof of those facts in the event of litigation. Moreover, agreement on the facts in the recital may bar a party from proving facts to the contrary. Even if it does not, it puts him in the bad tactical position of having to contradict his prior agreement on what the facts are.

Whether he is thinking of a fact recital or of a broader background-

---

[16] A.B.A. Code of Professional Responsibility DR7–102(A)(7) (1969).
[17] *Id.* DR7–101(B)(2).

purposes recital, a drafter needs to think through very carefully the answers to questions such as: Who is likely to be using this recital and for what purposes? What effect would any court likely to hear the case give to this recital? Would it treat the recital identically to an "agreeing" provision? Would the court refuse to consider it altogether? Would it consider the recital for limited purposes, and if so, for what purposes? Are the uncertainties revealed by these questions so great that the dangers of using such a clause exceed its possible benefits?

(ii) *Battle of the forms*: The term "battle of the forms" has come to be applied to the common practice in which each party to an agreement uses its own forms. Since each is drafted with the interest of the user in mind, this very commonly leads to agreements being made and performed with very different terms in the two forms. When trouble occurs, the question arises: whose form governs, if that of either? Engaging in a "battle of the forms" can be detrimental to both performance and risk planning.

Performance terms are ordinarily controlled by exchange motivations of the parties. Each party's attempt to get the best possible deal out of negotiations is inherent in the exchange motivations underlying contracting. Dickering about price, credit terms, product quality, inspections, transportation terms, quantities, wage rates, working conditions, and countless other performance terms is, therefore, standard practice in economic life. But out of this dickering generally comes agreement, not just objective or apparent agreement, but a reasonable degree of actual mutual harmony on questions of who is to get what and who is do to what. Such harmony occurs because of exchange motivations: each wants what the other offers, and the only way he can get it is by achieving very real and substantive agreement on the essentials of the relationship.

In ordinary economic intercourse, relatively little is likely to be gained by trying to slip past the notice of another party his obligations relating to the essential performance terms of that relationship. To do so simply puts obstacles in the way of that party's return performance, the return performance constituting the very reason one enters the relationship in the first place. There is less danger to the self-satisfaction of exchange motivations if the other party is unaware of the exact nature of the performance to be rendered to him. But even there, disappointment on the part of that party may jeopardize in a variety of ways his performing as planned. On the whole, therefore, "slipping one by" the other party at the "deal" stage is somewhat dangerous or even self-defeating, whenever

248

what is slipped by has to do with essentials of performance.

Turning from the mutual planning of basic performance relationships to planning for risks collateral to those relationships, a very different picture emerges. In risk planning, exchange motivations no longer necessarily tend to deter deliberate creation of mutual misunderstanding. Suppose for example that the question is whether a buyer of goods can hide from the seller the fact that the fine-print paragraph 82 of the contract subjects seller to all risks of loss of the goods in transit. The only time anyone will have occasion to look at paragraph 82 is when the goods have been lost in transit. If that happens, the problem will shift from concern for getting performance to the allocation of losses resulting from nonperformance. Exchange motivations do not lead a buyer planning for such an event to make sure that the seller knows what the planning is. Telling him after the loss occurs will be just dandy as long as seller is legally bound by paragraph 82.

The discussion above is deliberately overdrawn to make a point. In fact, genuine mutuality of risk planning may be very important to the parties. Not only is a party knowingly assuming a risk more likely to cooperate in handling a loss, but he is also likely to have more ability to perform such duties because he has prepared for the risk, e.g., by purchasing insurance. Moreover, the prevailing business ethos may frown on slippery bargaining of various kinds that might result in lack of mutuality of risk planning. Nevertheless, the fact remains that once the parties leave the performance essentials of the transaction and deal with risk planning, the economic motivations to achieve genuine mutual understanding are likely to be far weaker. The "battle of the forms" therefore tends to center on risk planning where the costs of winning the battle may be low and the rewards great.

b. *Substantive stipulated remedies*: Substantive stipulated remedies are provisions establishing what one party will owe the other in the event of breach. The most common clearly-denominated substantive stipulated remedy probably is the liquidated damages clause—a provision for a stipulated amount of damages payable in the event of breach. Also very common are provisions for attorney fees or other collection costs that will be incurred in the event of breach. Less common are provisions for specific performance.

Virtually any substantive stipulated remedy *could* logically be viewed as a provision for an alternative performance rather than as a remedy for breach. This may cause difficulties since the common law system distinguishes rather sharply in its treatment of substantive performance planning and planned remedies for breach. Respecting the former, notions of freedom of contract make courts reluctant to interfere with the planning of the parties. On the other hand, the legal system, not the parties, is the source of the legal remedies available in the event of nonperformance, and stipulated remedies are therefore viewed as an incursion into the judicial realm. Courts tend to be far more willing to question the validity of such remedial provisions than they are to question provisions viewed as substantive planning. The upshot of the foregoing is that planning of substantive remedies invokes a significant specialized body of law which must be well understood before one can successfully engage in it.

It should be noted that use of substantive stipulated remedies by no means necessarily eliminates the need for insurance planning. The is evident as to the party to whom such clauses shift risks of loss. But a party attempting to shift risks to or leave them on the other also needs insurance planning. Not only may the terms of the planning deliberately leave some risks with that party, but also a risk always exists that the legal system will not give effect to the effort to shift risks or leave them on a particular party. Moreover, even if the legal system does in theory effectuate the planning, the party legally subject to the risk may be unable to protect the other from a loss falling initially on the protected party, as, for example, when a party having a duty to pay damages under a perfectly good liquidated damages clause has no assets.

Among the purposes of this part on risk planning have been to bring home the inherent-incompleteness characteristic of the planning process, to develop an understanding of the different kinds of risks faced by parties to contracts, to describe various planning techniques for reducing or shifting those risks, and to promote understanding of the wide range of methods available for planning dispute resolution. These methods have included establishing self-help techniques of various kinds, developing processes for handling disputes, and planning the substance itself of the resolution of future disputes. The emphasis in this and the preceding part on performance planning has been on the substantive content of planning, whereas the emphasis in the two parts preceding these was on the processes of planning. Together the four parts constitute an overall primer of contract planning, lacking but one thing: a brief discussion of how it is all put together. This is the subject of the final part.

V. Administering the Final Agreement Process

The final agreement process may range from someone on the telephone saying "OK" in response to the question "Is it a deal?" to a series of acts involving so many actions by so many people that a dress rehearsal of the real thing is required to ensure that everything is done properly. Administering such processes is an important function of the lawyer and often comes as a considerable surprise to young lawyers unaware of the processes and their complexity. Because of the great range of complexity and the idiosyncrasies of particular contracts, only general principles can be outlined here; the details involved in each kind of transaction must be learned elsewhere, mainly in practice.

When properly carried out, the final agreement process is really two processes: final review of all prior planning and effectuation of the processes of agreement itself. The two, however, are often intertwined and reinforce each other.

Whenever the final agreement process is the least bit complex a schedule should be prepared of all the steps required to execute it. The schedule serves not only to ensure that the right people, documents, and so forth are available when needed, but also later as a checklist to ensure that everything required has in fact been done. Preparation of the schedule will, among other things, cause the planner to focus on making sure who the parties are and to what they are agreeing. This should be clear from the early planning processes, but a late focus on this key question may reveal weaknesses and avoid later embarrassment, or worse, real trouble. Preparation of a proper schedule also requires the lawyer' to ascertain who will engage in the agreement process on behalf of any party not an individual person—e.g. a corporation, partnership, or government agency—and the authority of persons acting as agents to bind such a party to the terms of the contract.

Further, a complete final review of all documents and other aspects of planning for accuracy, completeness, and the like should be performed. This is often a time for making sure that the parties themselves are aware of what they are getting into, and the reading or explanation of documents is often an integral aspect of the process. Such reading and explanation may also have important additional preventive consequences, since it is likely to make more difficult later attacks on grounds of mistake or misunderstanding.

Additionally, the lawyer must be certain that whatever formalities are required are in fact observed. "Required" in this sense means not only such legal requirements as those of the Statute of Frauds or notarization where required by law, but also practical evidentiary requirements, such as having initials on alterations in documents and making sure that all counterpart copies are fully executed.

Part of the agreement process includes post-execution activities, such as recording of documents or filing with various public agencies. In addition, disseminating copies of documents to clients or others for the purpose of their administering the contract or for record-keeping is an integral part of the lawyer's function in the agreement process. It constitutes, as well, the start of the administration of performance.

When the agreement process is an ongoing one, or one occurring in stages, the processes described above must necessarily also be carried out on an ongoing basis or repeated at the various stages. For example, the typical real estate transaction consists of at least two stages—the purchase and sale agreement and the closing of the sale itself. The former requires administration as described above. The latter, although it constitutes "performance" of the purchase and sale agreement, also involves substantially similar activities and requires substantially similar adminis-trative processes.

In summary, administering the final agreement process is a kind of martialing of all that has gone before into a coherent package to serve as the foundation for administering performance itself, as well as a tying of all the knots required to achieve the goals of the planning preceding it.

Conclusion

What has thus far been described is by no means the end of a contract; it is just the beginning. But the administration of contract performance ultimately yielding fulfillment of the contract relationship is beyond the scope of this Article. It is an activity generally involving less lawyer participation than does contract planning. Speaking very generally, only in the relatively rare event of serious trouble arising in that administration (or lack of it) do lawyers once again come on the scene. And when they do, their roles have changed from that of creative builders of contracts to resolvers of disputes. While in ongoing contract relations the resolver of disputes may also be the builder of further relations, in transactional contract, upon which this Article has primarily focused, this is commonly less true; the job of the lawyer in such circumstances is one of picking up as many of the broken pieces for his client as possible. Exploration of that function is adequately accomplished in many a law school classroom and needs no assistance here.

6.4 Economic Analysis of Contractual Relations: Its Shortfalls and the Need for a "Rich Classificatory Apparatus"

I. Introduction

The paradigm for the conduct of exchange in the neoclassical microeconomic model is the discrete transaction. Victor Goldberg (1976, 45, 51) summarizes this point:

> The paradigmatic contract of neoclassical economics ... is a discrete transaction in which no duties exist between the parties prior to the contract formation and in which the duties of the parties are determined at the formation stage. Prior to their contract. Smith has no duty to Brown; at the time they enter their agreement, in a single joint exercise of their free choice, they determine their respective duties to each other for the duration of the agreement; completion of the promised performance terminates that party's obligations ...
>
> ... [T]he elegance (and, to be sure, practical merits in many contexts) of analytical models based on choice has led economists to suppress the relational aspects of contracts.
>
> ... [E]conomists have treated all private sector exchange as presentiated discrete transactions; firms equate marginal cost to marginal revenue, and how they do this is of no great concern to the analyst.

The contract of neoclassical economics may thus be viewed, as Todd Lowry put it in a letter to the author, as "nothing more than a sale with a time lag, a sale of futures, or, as Morris Cohen once put it, a system for distributing risk."

Goldberg's description reveals that even in very discrete transactions, relations are present apart from the exchange itself, apart from the "sale with a time lag." For example, if *no* duties exist prior to the contract formation, then theft by the stronger party is more likely to occur than is exchange. (Lowry 1976, 4–5; *cf.* Hobbes 1968, ch. 14) Nor can the parties "determine their respective duties to each other for the duration of the agreement" unless some relation exists between them, such as a system of law, to keep each from doing as it pleases during the period, irrespective of the agreement. Nevertheless, transactions as described by Goldberg are discrete indeed compared to the relational ways in which most exchange is conducted in the modern world, for example, through employment and other exchanges between firms, through long term supply contracts, through consortia—the list is endless.

The present paper focuses on these more relational patterns. After an introduction to the interplay of neoclassical macroeconomics, transaction costs, and contractual relations, it reviews briefly some of the important distinctions between discrete transactions and modern contractual relations. This is essentially description, not analysis; if one prefers, this section is definitional. There then follows an analysis of the problems such relations pose for neoclassical microeconomic analysis.

II. Neoclassical Microeconomic Model, Transaction Costs, and Relational Contract

The term "neoclassical microeconomic model" is limited in this paper to the basic textbook model of the consumer and the firm. The consumer is accordingly assumed to be a self-interested utility maximizer. This self-interest is expressed entirely through the exchange with other maximizers of the particular goods under examination. Thus the model always deals with interactions among two or more maximizing units. The subjects of exchange must be sufficiently identifiable so that the user of the model can tell what the choice or choices concern. Normally this means that those subjects must be relatively simple (or simplified in the mind of the exchangers or the modeler). And for the model to be used to reveal pertinent information the subjects of exchange must be quantifiable in some manner. Assumptions respecting the firm are similar, except that the utility the firm maximizes is profit, the difference between revenue and cost. So far as I know, this is the only model upon which are based technical descriptions of economic efficiency, and by which efficient behavior may be predicted.

Since the famous article of Coase in 1960, increasing attention has been paid to the problem of transaction costs in the neoclassical model; now a substantial body of scholarship focuses on this problem. (Williamson 1986, 101 n. 1) Arrow's (1983, 134) definition of transaction costs, "costs of running the economic system," may be paraphrased for present purposes as "costs of running the contractual relation."

Because it is impossible to conduct exchange without transaction costs, and since they are variable, they are as much a factor of production as are capital and labor. Any sensible application of the neoclassical model requires the inclusion of these costs whenever they are variable, affect other factors, and are significant. This usually will be the case. Nevertheless, as Oliver Williamson (1996, 101) points out, many economists still commonly view transaction cost analysis with suspicion. Undoubtedly many factors cause this suspicion, but I suspect that one of them is the fact that analysis of transaction costs is often *not* neoclassical microeconomic analysis of transaction costs. As will be seen, Williamson's (1986, ch. 7) excellent 'Transaction-Cost Economics: The Governance of Contractual Relations' illustrates this. A key element in neoclassical microeconomic analysis is exchange *between* maximizing units. In his discussion of transaction costs and their effect on choice of contract governance structures, Williamson treats the parties not as separate exchangers, but as if they comprised a *single maximizing unit*. For example, he states: "The interests of the principals in sustaining the relation are especially great for highly idiosyncratic transactions." (1986, 113) This, according to Williamson, leads in such circumstances to the parties making arrangements for either trilateral governance, such as contractual enforcement in courts, or to unified governance—the firm. (Williamson 1986, 112–117) This is not neoclassical microeconomic analysis, since there is by hypothesis no exchange transaction to analyze. It is simply an argument that in cases of idiosyncratic transactions the maximizing unit of buyer-and-seller will find costs lower if it adopts a governance structure likely to sustain the relation than if it does not, just as a firm might find costs lower if it uses coal, rather than oil, in production. The analysis tells us nothing of exchange, or of allocation of risks or costs *between* buyer and seller, a key aspect of neoclassical analysis.

That Williamson is treating buyer and seller as a maximizing unit and not making a neoclassical analysis of their separate individual choices of governance structures, may be obscured by the nature of their (and his) concern: the prevention of their *subsequently* acting as separate maximizers, the limiting of opportunism. But his treatment of transaction costs and contractual governance in a non-neoclassical manner bears out a point made by Lowry in his communication to the author concerning relational exchange: in relations there can be present a "sense of productive increase from the relationship which can dwarf variations in expectation, or of long-term anticipations of mutual benefit that dwarf variations in shares received by the parties." This anticipatory, commonly held "sense" of the parties may virtually obliterate any present separation as maximizers, thereby making them effectively a single maximizer for many purposes, including, for example, the selection of governance structures. This tendency will be intensified by ignorance at the time of decisions about future division of the economic pie. Thus, boundedness of rationality is an important factor in Williamson's proper disregard of neoclassical analysis. At the time of decision about which governance structures to adopt, the parties will often have very limited information about the substantive effect of alternative structures on the future division of the pie to be produced by their efforts. For that reason, their individual interests are best served by presently paying little attention to how the pie will later be divided and a great deal to how it will be made.

The foregoing discussion implies that transaction cost analysis of some kind is essential to any useful economic analysis of contractual relations, a conclusion further justified by Section IV of this essay. It implies, however, no conclusion whether the neoclassical model, modified by transaction cost analysis, even of the non-neoclassical type, is *sufficient* for useful economic analysis of *all* contractual relations. But before considering whether the model, even so supplemented with non-neoclassical analysis, is always a sufficient tool, some of the important distinctions between discrete transactions and modern contractual relations will be briefly reviewed.

Conclusion

The existence of relations in all real-life transactions raises theoretical problems for the neoclassical microeconomic model founded on the discrete transaction. Even putting aside the theoretical difficulties, however, a range of practical problems precludes effective, simple application of the model to contractual relations of any complexity. At the very least this includes a large percentage of real-life contractual relations. Only repeated application of such a unitime model can purport to be accurate, and then only if careful account is taken of changes *between* each pair of applications. The alternative is to tear out relatively small pieces of the relations and treat them as if they were discrete. But that is not analysis *of the relation*, and it can make few claims to useful positive (or normative) analysis in terms of the overall relation. The process of repeated unitime analysis, coupled with accounting for change between the unitimes, necessarily becomes so complex and so full of unfounded assumptions as to raise serious questions of accuracy whenever any extensive contractual relations is involved. The use of transaction cost analysis is a recognition of these limitations and addition of non-neoclassical transaction cost analysis, such as that of Williamson, expands the area of effectiveness of the model markedly. But there are serious limits even with these modifications. When these limits are reached, those who seek accuracy are thrown back on other far more complex models with far richer classificatory apparatuses than that offered by the neoclassical microeconomic model.

6.5 Relational Contract: What We Do and Do Not Know

The relational contract dimensions are first, the everyday working of exchange relations and transactions, or contract behavior (the behavioral dimension); secondly, the positive law of the sovereign relating to that behavior (the legal dimension).

I. Contract Behavior

To have even a glimmer of hope of understanding relational contract we must overcome the impact hundreds of years of history have had on our minds. We must start with exchange viewed broadly. By now, we are so brainwashed as to be almost unable to conceive of exchange except in terms of markets and discrete transactions. But exchange is not the product simply of social relations so organized. Rather, exchange is the inevitable product of specialization of labor, however that specialization of labor may occur. Whether in a factory, in a commune, within a corporation, between discrete entities in markets, or within a family,

257

exchange will occur as long as specialization exists. Understanding this is the first step towards freeing ourselves of the Hobbesian and utilitarian intellectual blinders which prevent us from understanding contract behavior and with it relational contract.

In the second step, we must recognize that discrete exchange which itself is the product of particular kinds of social relations, such as markets permitting and encouraging it—can play only a very limited and specialized function in any economy, no matter how market-oriented that economy may be. That function is the transfer of control of capital and labor, *i.e.* goods and services, between quasi-independent entities, either individuals or collectives of individuals. That transfer of control of goods and services is one economic function essential to the production of goods and services goes without saying. (But such transfer may or may not be discrete exchange between quasi-independent entitites.)

That discrete exchange can never be the *only* economic function essential to production, distribution, and final consumption of goods and services should also go without saying. But it must be said because the so-called science of neoclassical economics presumes a model treating discrete exchange as the sole economic function essential to production, distribution, and final consumption. And this model or other less sophisticated Hobbesian alternatives dominates the conventional wisdom of Western economic thinking.

But what about the actual tasks of physical production, distribution, and final consumption of goods and services? These discrete exchange cannot accomplish. They occur in only one of two ways: (1) one person applies his hands and mind over time to available tools and materials to change them to more economically useful forms, or (2) a number of people working together do the same. The former is not exchange at all, and the latter is not discrete exchange, but relational exchange. Consider, for example, Adam Smith's famous example of pin-making:

> One man draws out the wire, another straights it, a third cuts it, a fourth points it, a fifth grinds it at the top for receiving the head; to make the head requires two or three distinct operations; to put it on, is a peculiar business, to whiten the pins is another; it is even a trade by itself to put them into the paper; and the important business of making a pin is, in this manner, divided into about 18 distinct operations, which, in some manufactories, are all performed by distinct hands, though in others the same man will sometimes perform two or three of them. (Smith 1976, 14–5)

Nowhere is the actual production of the pins conducted by discrete exchange. Since, however, exchange obviously does and must occur in the process, it necessarily is relational exchange. Smith's reference to manufactories (and his subsequent discussion) makes plain that relational exchange among the workers through their contributions to the common enterprise is an essential aspect of the production he describes.

To summarize: when discrete exchange occurs, it does so at interfaces between quasi-independent entities, and is not in itself *physically* productive. Instead, it is productive only because the exchange per se—virtually by definition, and certainly in effect—is expected to enhance the value of the items exchanged. In the discrete exchange the control transferred is usually that described by those seemingly definite, but in fact extremely indefinite terms: ownership or property. (Becker 1983; Cohen 1982) While discrete exchange is commonly a prelude to further physical production, and while it enhances value by itself, it does not achieve physical production. This is not to minimize its importance or to denigrate its social value, but to recognize its nature.

We take the third step in understanding the behavioral dimension of relational contract when we recognize the obvious: discrete exchanges are always relatively rare compared to patterns of relational exchange. But why? The answer lies in the two ways resources gain value: their conversion into goods and services and their transfer to people to whom they are more valuable than they are to the transferor(s). Except where a single person consumes without exchange what he produces, *both* processes must occur for goods and services to achieve anything close to their potential value. What, for example, could the individual maker of pinheads do with the 48,000 pinheads Adam Smith discusses if he could not exchange them in a way to secure a share of the value of the finished pins? Not much. Discrete exchange will always be a comparatively rare phenomenon because it performs only the transfer of control function and is only minimally related to physical production of goods and services. (Its closest relation to the latter is in the transport of the goods or services from one place to another). Relational exchange also serves the function of transferring control, but it is in addition closely integrated with all aspects of the physical production of goods and services, thus, relational exchange will always be far more common in any given productive system than discrete exchange.

Our final step in understanding relational contract behavior lies in assessing the significance of discrete exchange in the production of the value of goods and services relative to physically productive activities

259

occurring in patterns of relational exchange. There are a number of ways to do this. One is to look at its impact on social, political, and intellectual arenas. Such impact may be immense, as it is in our own society. Another is to assess its importance in the two ways of creating economic value— physical production and exchange, separating the latter into the categories of relational and discrete. This could be done directly only by comparing the value of final output in the production of which no discrete exchange has occurred with that in which some has occurred. Since some relatively discrete exchange probably occurs somewhere in the course of production of most goods and services in Western societies, this will tell us only that discrete exchange adds some value to the final product. It will, not, however, tell us how much value was contributed by each of the three kinds of activities—physical production, relational exchange (whether as part of or in addition to physical production), and discrete exchange.

Comparisons based on costs, however, are possible. We can ascertain the costs of labor and capital going into physically making and physically distributing the various components of the pertinent goods and services, including any relational exchange connected with those processes. We can determine the costs of transfers of control—relational or discrete— required to achieve the ultimate acquisition of the goods and services by the final consumer. We can then compare the costs of the discrete-exchange-transfers of control with all the other costs. That will enable us to compare input costs of discrete transfers of control to those of physical production and relational exchange in the the overall production of, for example, pin-value in that operation and society.

Were we to acquire such information on a large scale, we would surely find that even in those societies most heavily dependent on discrete exchange, the bulk of resources used in productive efforts go into the physical production and distribution of goods and services and relational transfers of control over those goods and services. In contrast, only a relatively small proportion of resources could conceivably go into discrete exchanges between quasi-independent entities.

To help understand why only a small part of capital and labor will be devoted in any given society to conducting discrete exchange, consider the nature of the most discretely organized economy imaginable. Each productive person is a specialist, each is a solo owner-worker, each acquires all the goods and services needed for production through discrete exchanges, and each produces a good or service which can be disposed of through discrete exchanges with other specialists. There must

260

be enough specialists of each kind so that the discrete exchanges remain discrete and do not slip into relational patterns through repeated exchanges. Of course, no employment is possible, nor forward contracts, nor services involving relations that cannot be divided into discrete transactions, nor countless other relations to be found in every real economy, including those created by sovereign law, monetary systems, and the like. The denizens of such a mythical discrete economy would be mighty busy exchanging things, and the costs in labor and capital of those discrete transactions might rival or even surpass the costs of physical production itself. Consider, for example, Adam Smith's pinmakers. In this mythical discrete economy the process he described could have been carried out by A's purchase of metal from which to draw the wire, his drawing it in his own one-man plant and then selling the drawn wire to B, who straights it in his own one-man plant, and then sells it to C, who cuts it in his own one-man plant, and then sells it to D, who points it in his own one-man plant, etc. through eighteen individual efforts and sales. But, to be discrete, each sale would have to be conducted through markets with enough similar sellers, *e.g.* pin wire cutters, and similar buyers, *e.g.* pin pointers, so that relations between individual sellers and buyers did not convert repeated transactions of this kind into complex ongoing relations. Such a discrete economy would have such low productive capacity, such severe limitations on the kinds of goods and services it could produce, and such immense transaction costs, that nothing even remotely approaching it will be found outside the imagination.

In sum, for us to "know" contract behavior (the first dimension of relational contract) we must recognize that physical production of goods and services is not carried out by discrete exchange. Instead, it is done sometimes by one person applying hands and mind to tools and materials, but more commonly by people doing the same in patterns involving relational exchange. We must also recognize that the sole function of discrete exchange is the transfer of control of capital and labor, of goods and services. This is a limited economic function, albeit one essential to the physical production itself of goods and services and necessary for enhancing the value of those goods and services. Because of the limited nature of this function and because it can be and is also carried on by relational exchange, discrete exchange is always rare compared to relational exchange; it is inevitably a relatively small part of the overall economic activities of any given society.

Since we shall focus on what we know about relational contract in

American law and scholarship, I should emphasize that no period in American history provides any evidence contrary to what has been said. In the very heyday of laissez-faire, wherever there were sales of wheat in markets, there were banks financing every step from the fields themselves to final delivery, family farms growing the wheat, harvester teams harvesting it, private companies or cooperatives storing it, rail-roads and carters moving it, mills milling it, and baking companies and families baking it. All these entities carried on their operations in internal patterns of relational exchange, most of them including employment relations, not only for physical production, but for both classes of the necessary changes of control—those among individuals within the entities, and those required to accomplish discrete exchanges (when they were discrete exchanges) between the entities. Unquestionably, the many discrete exchanges which did occur between quasi-independent entities had a tremendous impact on America's economy and society. Nevertheless, that impact cannot be allowed to obscure the limited economic functions of those exchanges if we wish to understand relational contract in the real life of the Republic.

II.   Positive Law of the Sovereign

The second dimension of relational contract to be considered is the positive law of the sovereign interacting with the behavioral dimension of contract. I turn now to just a few highlights from one specific place and two specific eras: America of approximately 1865–1933 and 1933 to date. As I have suggested, the America of the first of these periods was inevitably a world dominated by relational contract. But it was one in which discrete exchange was nevertheless commonplace, exercising tremendous influence throughout the society in every conceivable way.

Given such a situation, we might expect to find Leviathan responding with law supportive of both relational and discrete exchange. And so we do. We know that property, the prerequisite of discrete exchange, was the legal fundament throughout the period, followed closely by liberty, at least insofar as the sale of labor was concerned. A well-developed law of discrete contract (including rules concerning sales) existed, although at the beginning of the period it lacked the baroque systemization it was to acquire later, particularly at the hands of Samuel Williston. Its underlying principle of freedom of contract (really power of contract) is an essential

262

element of any law supporting discrete exchange.

At the same time the sovereign's law supported relational exchange. Property law permitted unlimited aggregations of capital (property) by anyone who could lay his hands on it without too egregious violations of certain kinds of criminal laws. The ensuing aggregations inevitably required employment, an extremely relational contract, no matter how strenuously a party attempts to make it discrete. Freedom of contract— that great element in discrete exchange—also extended to relations between such aggregators of capital and everyone with whom they dealt, including their labor forces. Its presence did not convert relations such as employment or corporate control and ownership into discrete transactions, however, but into extremely hierarchical contractual relations. Furthermore, the principle of legally unlimited aggregation of capital was extended to groups of individuals, particularly through the corporation. And the corporation itself is one of the greatest relational contracts ever.

The sovereign aided relational contract in numerous other ways: laws of principal and agent (including master and servant and partnerships); trusts; family law (including inheritance); and the law of associations. These of course were in addition to more obvious forms of assistance such as land grants to homesteaders and aid to hierarchical contractual relationships, especially corporations, through subsidies of various kinds, such as land grants to railroads. And even in those days of relatively limited governmental activity, the government itself constituted extensive contractual relations.

In contrast, since 1933 the increasing intervention of the sovereign into almost all aspects of the socioeconomy, has effected two changes in the foregoing picture. First, the expansion of the sovereign's role has largely eliminated predominantly discrete exchanges. (It would be more accurate to say that, since all exchanges, even the most discrete, are embedded in relations, the intervention reduced the discreteness of all exchanges by introducing the relational element of regulation.) Virtually no type of contract exists in which this has not occurred.

Secondly, increasing intervention has changed significantly the substantive and procedural content of contractual relations. (Macneil 1984–5) This has not necessarily made them any more relational, however. For example, even hourly wage employment was very relational before Leviathan lent its aid to collective bargaining. Corporations have always been exchange relations writ large; thus, legal protection of shareholder rights did not convert them from a series of discrete exchanges into relations, but simply changed the nature of those relations. Indeed, since Leviathan intervenes through positive bureau-cratic law, and since bureaucratic law's specificity creates a type of discreteness, such intervention has actually increased discreteness in collective bargaining and corporate relations. (Macneil 1984)

This account of these periods in American history demonstrates that relational contract law did not magically materialize within the last half-century. Instead, relational contract law was always present; since 1933 the sovereign's intervention has merely expanded its domain to include areas previously governed by discrete contract law, thereby aiding their conversion to relational patterns. Simultaneously, relational contract law has expanded beyond its earlier base—a primarily facilitative law of property, contract and associations, particularly corporations—to a second, rapidly growing base concerning regulation and other sovereign intervention into relations. Again, I do not here claim to present an exhaustive historical account of relational contract, but only a sufficiently clear outline of the essential changes in the American law of relational contract.

Conclusion

We know a great deal about relational contract, yet are quite ignorant of it. We know much more about subject-specific relational contracts than we do about relational contract either as a class of behavior patterns or as a general concept. Our knowledge of the latter is hindered in part by the immense intellectual barriers we put in the way of its acquisition, particularly those created by our addiction to promise. Nevertheless, in spite of these barriers, the struggle to acquire greater knowledge of these essential human social patterns is going forward on many fronts. We can and we shall learn a great deal more about relational contract.

Chapter 7

The Analysis of Remedies

Macneil's relational analysis allows us to integrate our awareness of the limitations of formal legal remedies, and in "Essays on the Nature of Contract" these limitations are summarised. In "Efficient Brach of Contract: Circles in the Sky" and "Contract Remedies: A Need for a Better Efficiency Analysis", the weaknesses of a "simple" view of efficient breach associated with Posner are ruthlessly exposed. Many have made criticisms to similar effect, but Macneil's is the richest, for it does not merely point to inadequacies but shows how those inadequacies may be resolved within the relational theory.

7.1 Essays on the Nature of Contract

Promissory exchange-projecting mechanisms reinforced by law grow out of the individual choice inherent in exchange when "my" and "your" are present. When the respective subjects of exchange are initially within "my" and "your" control, we can give assurance *by promise* that an exchange will be made in the future. By promising we do something now limiting the choices otherwise available to us in the future. The role of law respecting such promises is to add its force to the assurance.

The law can say that if, in return for A's giving B a cow, B promises to

265

give A 20 bushels of wheat next month, mechanisms will be available to make life unpleasant for B if he does not perform his promise. Or it might be able to do even more and make devices available to accomplish the promised transfer, *e.g.* court officers will seize the wheat (if there is any) from B and turn it over to A. Or it might allow A to go after B's property to recoup losses A has suffered because of the breach of the promise. These devices cannot, of course, provide 100 per cent certainty that the promise will be fulfilled by the transfer of the wheat, but they may nevertheless add to the assurance. How much they add varies from one situation to another. *In any case one should never assume that even ironclad legal rights of enforcement will necessarily result in performance of a promise.* Indeed one of the most important recurring questions in contracts concerns the effectiveness of legal contract remedies in a variety of real-life contexts.

It is all too easy to read a rule of positive law such as UCC 2-708 or 2-713 and jump to the conclusion that the law will miraculously put an injured party in an economic position equivalent to performance. In fact, countless obstacles lie between such statements of positive law and what is practically available to an injured party through legal process.

First, the very spirit underlying these remedies is not one of assuring performance or its equivalent. As Professor Farnsworth (1970, 1147) has put it:

> Our system . . . is not much concerned with the question suggested by Frost's lines: How can men be made to keep their promises? It is instead preoccupied with a different question: How can men be encouraged to deal with those who make promises. . . .
> [T]his . . . adds to the celebrated freedom to make contracts, a considerable freedom to break them as well.

Secondly, as a careful reading of almost any selection of contracts cases will reveal, even many "successful" plaintiffs secure only limited recoveries, for one reason or another, *e.g.* because of difficulties with foreseeability or certainty.

Thirdly, is the problem of transaction costs. Litigation costs money, directly in the form of legal and other expenses and indirectly in the form of lost time of participants and disturbance of their normal activities. Nonmoney costs of litigation such as worry are also very high. The American legal system does relatively little to compensate prevailing parties for such costs. It is thus fatuous to think that even the most successful law suit under, for example, UCC 2–708, will in fact put the plaintiff in an economic position equivalent to performance.

Fourthly, litigation is risky. A host of legal and other traps and many burdens of pleading, of proceeding with evidence, and of persuasion lie between a plaintiff and the judgment he seeks. He can never be sure one of these obstacles will not totally or partially block him from securing his putative black letter rights.

Finally, even after winning a judgment, the plaintiff may have little chance of successfully enforcing it. Judgments are not self-executing. Again quoting Farnsworth (1970, 1151–1152).

> The typical judgment at common law declared that the plaintiff recover from the defendant a sum of money, which in effect imposed on him a new obligation as redress for the breach of the old. The new obligation required no cooperation on his part for its enforcement since, if the sum was not paid, a writ of execution would issue empowering the sheriff to seize and sell so much of the defendant's property as was required to pay the plaintiff.

But suppose that the defendant has insufficient or even no property? Or even more likely, suppose that generous debtor-protection laws provide exemptions from seizure of much or all his property? Many a plaintiff has ended up crying all the way to the wastebasket with a judgment for thousands of dollars, but utterly worthless. (Schrag 1969)

The limitations of private remedies in achieving the putative results enshrined in statements of substantive rules, such as those in UCC 2–708 and 2–713, do not, however, erode our overall contract system as much as one might think. To develop this point comprehensively would be a major piece of work: the following three points will have to suffice therefore as a mere introduction.

First, it is a mistake ever to think of law as the equivalent of litigation, or even of potential litigation. Indeed, one might even argue that law is at its most powerful when its invocation through litigation is *most remote* from men's minds. For example, most drivers keeping to the right of a double-yellow line on the highway think not one whit of "The Law", much less of litigation, civil or criminal. Habit and customary behavior and fear of the physical consequences of deviation have long since replaced fear of societal reprisal as the chief enforcement technique. Similarly, many of the "black letter" rules of contract law, including contract remedies, are thoroughly enmeshed in habitual and customary behavior. Such rules are followed with little or no thought of enforcement by litigation. Think, for example, of the restitutionary "remedy" extended customers by virtually all supermarkets and large discount stores. Simply bring back the goods within a reasonable time and your money is returned. Similarly, when a bond series of a prosperous corporation comes due, habit and customary behavior lead to repayment of the bondholders. No one thinks: "If we do not pay, we'll end up with a judgment against us for expectation damages." That is, of course, what would happen, and the fact that it would happen is at least a tacit assumption of financial dealings, but no one thinks of it.

The second reason the limitations of private remedies do not vastly erode our overall contract system arises from the limited role of law in the enforcement of contracts. Parties perform most contracts for the same reason they made them in the first place: they *want* to make the exchanges contemplated initially. This is true even when one party has performed and the other's performance is still due. For a host of reasons we *want* to pay our credit card bills. The reasons have little or nothing to do with the threat of suit if we do not. The reasons involve more fundamental contract *enforcement* mechanisms, namely nonlegal sanctions for breach of promises. If we do not pay our bills, no one will trust us in the future, and we shall have to pay cash for everything, a major disaster in this credit-prone society. We are, in short, very much involved in a huge and pervasive relational contract structure supplying many incentives to perform promises, entirely apart from active intervention of legal contract remedies.

Finally, simple private contract remedies are not the only *legal* mechanisms for reinforcing contract transactions and relations. For one thing, class actions may greatly reinforce contract remedies. Similarly, a statute may provide for allowance of some or all the costs of litigation in certain kinds of cases. An example of the latter is to be found in state statutes allowing costs to the prevailing insured for certain kinds of breaches by insurers. Private remedies may also be reinforced by such techniques as allowance of treble damages for certain kinds of behavior related to contract, although seldom for simple contract breaches.

Even more important than the foregoing, a host of statutes and a vast array of administrative law reinforce contracts by directly regulating them or indirectly affecting them. Some of these are closely related to ordinary contract performance, *e.g.* statutes creating criminal penalties for writing bad checks. Others are more indirectly related, but nevertheless, very significant. For, example, a complex system of bank regulation makes relatively unlikely your bank's insolvency and consequent inability to pay as promised when you seek to make a withdrawal. Even more indirect is the legal reinforcement given to the entire interlocking ongoing relational contract structure of our society—the supplying of corporate forms of organization, legal property rights, full employment policies, and countless others. Consider, for example, Detroit auto workers and their creditors. Full employment in the auto industry is infinitely more important to the creditors than all their private contract remedies put together. By and large, the lenders of Detroit will be paid if the auto workers are working and will not be paid if the auto workers are laid off for long periods of time, UCC 2–708 notwithstanding.

To summarize, habit and custom, other nonlegal enforcement mechanisms, *e.g.* the threat of losing one's good credit rating, and legal mechanisms other than private contract remedies, *e.g.* the system of bank regulation, all lead to contract enforcement. Most often these are of far greater significance than the legal remedies of "contract law." The study of "contract law" and its private remedies often induces myopia obscuring the legal and economic milieu in which "contract law" functions. One should never forget that other forces, usually more vital than "contract law", are at work ordering contract relations. Particularly dangerous to memory on this score is the hypnotic effect of continually dealing with the intricacies of fact and doctrine in litigated "contract law" cases.

7.2   Efficient Breach of Contract: Circles in the Sky

Although the name is relatively new, (Goetz and Scott 1977) the theory of efficient breach has been around for over a decade. (Birmingham 1970) This is a relatively long time as things go in the short but precocious life of law and economics. The doctrine of efficient breach is enshrined in the bible of law and economics, (Posner 1998, 130–40) and has appeared in a number of other discussions. Peter Linzer (1981, 114–117) summarizes the theory as follows

> [E]fficiency theory suggests that promisers who breach increase society's welfare if their benefit exceeds the losses of their promisees. Such failure to perform, the so-called efficient breach

of contract, is illustrated by the following. Assume that Athos owns a woodworking factory capable of taking on one more major project. He contracts to supply Porthos with 100,000 chairs at $10 per chair, which will bring Athos a net profit of $2 per chair, or $200,000 on the contract. Before any work takes place, Aramis, who sells tables, approaches Athos. Although there are several chair factories in the area, only Athos's factory can make tables. If Athos will supply Aramis with 50,000 tables, Aramis will pay him $40 per table. Athos can produce the tables for $25, so he can make a profit of $750,000 if he uses his factory for Aramis's tables. But to do so, he must breach his contract with Porthos. There are other chair factories, and Porthos will be able to get the chairs from one of them—for example, from D'Artagnan's. Let us assume that because of his distress situation Porthos will have to pay D'Artagnan 20% more than Athos's price for comparable chairs, and that Porthos will sustain $100,000 in incidental administrative costs and consequential costs such as damages for delay to his customers. Even with these costs, Porthos will lose only $300,000 because of Athos's breach, and Athos can reimburse him in full and still make $450,000 profit, over twice the profit from his contract with Porthos.

As one might expect, efficiency theorists applaud the Athoses of the world. Thus, Richard Posner sets up a similar illustration and notes that "if damages are limited to loss of expected profit, there will be an incentive to commit a breach. There should be ... The expectation rule thus assures that the product ends up where it is most valuable." Robert Birmingham reaches similar conclusions about a labor contract when the employee is offered a better job.

Although these positions conflict with the notion of *pacta sunt servanda* and with the moral view developed above, they do make some sense. People generally enter into commercial contracts and routine labor contracts for purely economic reasons and can therefore be fully compensated with damages for injuries caused by breach. If we prevent Athos from building tables for Aramis, we force him to waste his resources, with no economic benefit to Porthos. Therefore, while it would be possible to restrain Athos by making his breach of contract a crime, by imposing punitive damages or penalties on him, or by ordering specific performance, the law does not do this ... Thus, despite our concern for holding parties to their word, at least in the conventional market situation that we have illustrated, law, economics, and arguably common sense all condone the deliberate and willful breach.

This is an excellent description of what I shall call the simple-efficient-breach analysis. The modifier "simple" distinguishes descriptions such as this presenting the analysis free of transaction costs from those focusing very specifically on transaction costs.

The present article examines the fallacy in the simple-efficient-breach analysis, focusing on specific performance versus damages, suggests how the rule must be stated to avoid the fallacy, and examines the origin and bias of the fallacy.

I. Fallacy of Simple-Efficient-Breach Analysis

The simple-efficient-breach analysis is fallacious. The assumption that it is economically efficient for Athos to build tables rather than chairs by no means leads to the conclusion that breach is the economically efficient result. Rather, that result is obtained through the *nonperformance* of the contract to build chairs, and the substitution of the contract to build tables. Since breach is far from the only way to avoid performance of the chair contract, no conclusion can be deduced that breach is any more (or less) efficient than other ways of securing the efficient result of nonperformances.

Underlying the simple-efficient-breach analysis is the assumption that the expectation damages rule will lead to the making of tables rather than chairs and that the specific performance rule will lead to the making of chairs rather than tables. Neither assumption is valid. This may be shown by assuming a world in which all relations between the parties can be conducted without transaction costs. They have the usual property and other legal entitlements to start with and can trade them costlessly. Using Linzer's illustration of the Four Musketeers, Aramis's offer of the table contract has created an opportunity for someone to make at least an additional $250,000. Under the expectation damages rule, that someone is Athos. If Athos is subject only to damages in the amount of the $300,000 that Porthos loses from the breach, Athos will breach and pay Porthos $300,000. Under that rule he will make tables, not chairs, and efficiency will be served.

If there are no transaction costs the cause of economic efficiency is served equally well by the specific performance rule. Athos will promptly tell Porthos about the new contract and will agree to pay Porthos something between $0 and $250,000 (over and above his costs of $300,000) for a release from the chair contract. Since this is a world without transaction costs, they will, of course, make a deal. (Once again, while wealth distribution will be different, efficiency will be served.

Free of transaction costs, *neither* of these rules leads to more efficient use of resources than the other in the kinds of situations concerning efficiency theorists. It is, therefore, illogical to conclude that either a right to specific performance or a right to expectation damages will lead to such a result in the real world. Whatever "direction" towards or away from efficiency either of these rules has depends entirely upon the relative transaction costs each will generate.

It is clear then that the simple-efficient-breach conclusion about the inefficiency of the specific performance rule is logically indefensible on the basis of what it purports to be—a deduction from the efficiency model. The conclusion of inefficiency can be defended only on the basis that the transaction costs of securing nonperformance of the first agreement under the specific performance rule are always higher than under the expectation damages rule. Apart from the conclusion based on fallacious use of the model, what we have at most is an intuition about the impact of those rules on how a person behaves when presented with a certain kind of opportunity that might benefit himself and/or others. It is, however, an opportunity that may be exploited by responses ranging from self-help, which places the entire burden of self-protection on the nonbreacher, to a wide range of possible solutions involving acquiescence, including delighted acquiescence, of the other person. Since all these courses of action require the incurring of costs, it is impossible to reach any positive conclusions concerning such behavior without an examination of those costs.

The foregoing analysis of the world of zero transaction costs reveals the dearth of justification for presuppositions about the relative efficiency of the two rules in the real world. Such economic analysis creates no "efficiency burden of proof" for or against either rule. Thus the starting point of analysis for real world events must be neutral; and the analysis must start and end with, not just end with, transaction costs under each rule. Moreover, it must cover all transaction costs of *every* method of bringing about non-performance of the first contract and of entering the second contract. The analysis cannot be limited to transaction costs of breach. Breach is but one possible way of achieving the desired result.

II. Effect of Transaction Costs

Returning from the mythical world of zero transaction costs, we must first exclude from consideration all the circumstances in which *neither* rule will lead to abandonment of the chair contract in favor of the table contract (to return to the Four Musketeers). In such circumstances, whenever Athos's transaction costs of substituting the table contract exceed $250,000 under either rule he will continue to make chairs irrespective of the rule in effect. This will be an economically efficient result.

The other end of the cost spectrum involves circumstances where the transaction costs under *either* rule are so low that the chair contract will be abandoned and tables made. Suppose, for example, that the sole cost to Athos of breach is $25,000 (in damage to his reputation) if he is not later forced to perform (damages rule), and $5,000 if he is (specific performance rule), or $5,000 in negotiating costs if, under a clear specific performance rule, he makes a prelitigation deal with Porthos. Further suppose that the cost to Porthos of securing damages is $0 (because Athos would happily send him a check rather than engage in losing litigation), and his cost of either securing and enforcing a decree of specific performance or negotiating a settlement under a specific performance rule is $20,000. The chair contract will be abandoned and the tables made under either rule.

Under the damages rule Athos will breach, incur the $25,000 loss to his reputation, and pocket a gain of $225,000. Under the specific performance rule, Athos will negotiate with Porthos, and they will make a deal; Athos will incur $5,000 in costs, and Porthos $20,000. The $225,000 net efficiency gain created will be split according to whatever deal they make. Under either rule the tables will be made, and the transaction costs leading to their making will be identical. Efficiency is equally well served by both rules, and only wealth distribution is affected by which rule governs.

The foregoing assumption of equal transaction costs is unrealistic; transactions costs will vary in many ways under the two rules. Thus it is necessary to consider what happens when they are different. Suppose that the damage to Athos's reputation from a breach would be $50,000 under the damages rule, $40,000 if he were to breach and then be forced to perform under a specific performance rule, and that with a specific performance rule in effect it would cost Athos $10,000 to negotiate a deal with Porthos without breaching. Suppose also that Porthos's costs of negotiating a deal with Athos under the specific performance rule would be only $5,000. Now the total transaction costs of achieving the making of tables rather than chairs under the damages rule will be $50,000, as against $15,000 under the specific performance rule. The tables will still be made. But the net efficiency gain under the damages rule will be $200,000 ($250,000 gross efficiency gain minus $50,000 for Athos's loss of reputation); under the specific performance rule it will be $235,000 ($250,000 gross efficiency gain minus $15,000 negotiating cost). The relative efficiency of the result is measured exactly by the transaction costs of the particular rules, not by the substance of the rules, as simple-efficient-breach analysis concludes.

Or suppose under a damages rule that, instead of breaching, Athos gives Porthos $300,000 (Porthos's losses) plus $25,000 in return for release from the chair contract, and Porthos sings praises of Athos all the way to the bank, leaving Athos's reputation in as good a condition as before. And suppose the deal costs each of them $5,000 in negotiating costs. The tables are made, with a net efficiency gain of $240,000 ($250,000 minus $10,000 negotiating costs). Of this Athos has $220,000 and Porthos $20,000. This is $5,000 more efficient than the specific performance rule, but once again the efficiency is measured only by the relative transaction costs of possible ways of proceeding under the rules, not by the substance of the rules.

Now turn to a middle situation. Assume the transaction costs of one rule are such that the chair contract would be continued under that rule, but low enough so that tables would be made under the other rule. These assumptions can be worked into the Four Musketeers hypothetical (although doing so requires assuming very unlikely negotiating cost figures because of the unusually high gross efficiency gains postulated in Linzer's example). To do so, assume that the cost to each party of negotiating a deal under the specific performance rule is $260,000, and that Athos's only costs of breach (above $300,000) is a $50,000 reputational loss, and that there is a transaction cost of $5,000 in paying Porthos for his $300,000 loss.

Under the damages rule Athos will make the tables. He will also pocket the entire efficiency gain of $195,000 ($250,000 gross gain from making tables instead of chairs, less $50,000 reputational loss, less the $5,000 transaction costs of paying Porthos $300,000 for his loss). Under the specific performance rule chairs, not tables, will be made, for a $0 efficiency gain. This appears to suggest that substantive inefficiency of the specific performance rule is preventing the making of tables. In fact, the inefficiency is caused by the relative transaction costs of the rule, not by its substance. The only difference between this and the prior examples is that only *part* of the potential transaction costs of the rule were actually incurred (not directly, but through continuation of the chair contract). The lost net-efficiency gain of $195,000 possible under the damages rule puts a limit on the amount of efficiency loss that can actually result from those high potential transaction costs of the specific performance rule.

In sum, the correct statement of efficient breach in circumstances where a contractor has better opportunities is as follows:

> Whether an expectation damages rule or a specific performance rule is more efficient depends entirely upon the relative transaction costs of operating under the rules. Where, as will most generally be the case, transaction costs under either rule will exceed gross efficiency gains made possible by scrapping one contract in favor of another, each rule is equally (in)efficient. Where both rules will permit substituting a more productive contract for a less productive contract, the difference in efficiency of the rules will be measured exactly by the difference in their respective transaction costs. Where one rule will permit substitution and the other will not, the difference in efficiency will be measured by the difference in respective transaction costs, but subject to an upper limit consisting of the hypothetical net efficiency gain under the rule with the lower transaction costs. None of the transaction costs can be deduced by use of the microeconomic model, but can only be determined inductively from empirical evidence.

The principle of efficient breach also needs to be renamed if analytical error such as that of the simple-efficient-breach theorists is to be avoided; it should be called the principle of *efficient termination-and-remedy*.

I do not intend to make the investigations necessary to reach even slightly definitive conclusions about the transaction costs of the two rules. But the broad scope of the inquiry required before even slightly definitive conclusions could be suggested should be stressed. The pertinent transaction costs cannot be limited to one or two supplemental matters. Rather the inquiry must be addressed to *all* transaction costs respecting each rule. This includes some costs of initial planning in the *first* contract (including negotiations essential to the mutual planning required in contracting), costs of planning (again including negotiations)

275

after the new opportunity comes along, costs of potential or actual litigation (including costs of delay), information costs, costs of inertia, costs of uncertainty, relational costs, such as damage to reputation and loss of future opportunities to deal, and undoubtedly others. All of these may vary depending upon which rule governs.

In addition, two other factors must be taken into account: negative transaction costs and externalities. Negative transaction costs are consequences of a rule which may lessen losses. For example, in the Four Musketeers, Porthos has to pay an added $200,000 to D'Artagnan "because of his distress situation" to enable him to buy substitute chairs. If one of the rules encourages early communication from Athos more than does the other, such distress losses may be reduced by that rule, thereby increasing its efficiency. Relational costs are another type of costs likely to vary a great deal depending upon the rule. If the damages rule encourages breaches without consultation, whereas the specific performance rule encourages consultation and mutually beneficial agreement, relational costs will be lower under the specific performance rule. In the real world it makes a great deal of difference whether a breach occurs, or is even threatened, or whether negotiations are viewed as leading towards mutually beneficial allocations of the increased productivity offered by the new opportunity. Unless the economic modeler explicitly treats this factor, the microeconomic model fails to take into account the difference between negotiating over what is viewed as an allocation of losses, and what is viewed as the allocation of potential gains. And modelers seldom seem to consider the difference.

The other essential factor to consider is externalities. To the extent that whoever decides not to perform the first contract can avoid paying all the costs of that decision, the likelihood of his making inefficient decisions is increased. It is therefore necessary to weigh the two rules (in the wide range of circumstances to which they apply) in these terms. The consequences of uncertainty in measuring damages, of the American rule leaving most costs of litigation on the party initially incurring them, of costs of litigation generally, and of the costs of inertia, may enable the Athoses of the world to shift losses of termination of the first contract to the Porthoses in such a way that significant external costs escape their decision making. One way to limit the effect of this is to require joint decision making concerning termination of the first contract. The bargaining fostered by the specific performance rule in these circumstances seems ideally designed to prevent omission from the decisional calculus of the costs of either party.

276

III. Origin and Bias of the Fallacy

The microeconomic model assumes the existence of very complex relations between the parties—relations established through society generally, language, law, and societal economic organization, as well as those more specifically connected with the transactions being studied. But once such relations are assumed, the impact of those relations on the analysis is typically ignored. *Ceteris paribus* conquers all. Thus, it is extremely easy to introduce selected transaction costs to show that the model "proves" what the modeler wants it to prove, while ignoring countless other transaction costs of equal or greater pertinence in the real world—costs yielding different conclusions. As noted, the model must be used *either* with all pertinent transaction costs excluded, with all the analytical limitations that entails, *or* with all pertinent transaction costs included. Otherwise the analysis reveals nothing about either the real world or about an analytically useful, mythical world. Nevertheless, the ease of slipping in some, but not all, transaction costs is a problem with even the most sophisticated transaction-cost analysis within the model. There is a fundamental intellectual flaw in using a model based on man-outside-society to analyze the behavior of man-in-society. Because economic analysis is analysis of social behavior, economic man is necessarily in society at all times. The particular fallacy of the simple-efficient-breach theory is relatively easy to uncover, but potential fallacy lurks in all social analysis starting from the nonsocial, relation-omitting model of neoclassical economics.

Part of the underlying relational structure enabling Athos, Porthos, Aramis, and D'Artagnan to make the deals described in Linzer's illustration are what law-economists refer to as legal entitlements. These legal entitlements are part of the distributional status quo to which the model is always applied. They are, in short, key parts of the foundations upon which the model always operates. If they vary, then the results produced by the model will vary. For example, that Porthos does not already own a large inventory of chairs is an important factor in the Four Musketeers illustration.

When the model is projected through time it must cope with changes in entitlements, brought about, *inter alia*, by the very transactions being analyzed. The beginning and end are easy for the modelers. At the beginning each party owns things, at the end each owns different things. In the words of Guido Calabresi and Douglas Melamed (1972), at the

THE ANALYSIS OF REMEDIES

beginning and the end the legal entitlements of the parties are protected by "property rules." As it is normally applied, the microeconomic model has no capacity to describe either the beginning or the ending status quo as "inefficient." The original distribution of legal entitlements is simply a given. The ending distribution may have been arrived at efficiently or inefficiently, but once it has occurred the resulting distribution of goods is neither efficient nor inefficient, any more than the original distribution was. The end is simply a new status quo to which anyone who so desires can apply the model again respecting future exchanges.

This characteristic of the neoclassical model causes circularity in simple-efficient-breach analysis. Under the specific performance rule, Porthos *owns* Athos's productive facilities for the purpose of making chairs as soon as he has a legally enforceable contract. But he also owns them for that purpose when his contractual remedy is a fully effective expectation-damages rule. The only difference is that in one case his ownership of those facilities is protected by a property rule and in the other by a liability rule aimed at giving him the exact monetary equivalent of the property rule.

These results are neither efficient nor inefficient, any more than any other property status quo at the beginning or ending of transactions. Efficiency and inefficiency apply only to how the parties got where they are, relative to other ways they might have gotten somewhere else. Once it is admitted that the journey is over, that the parties are "there" (wherever "there" is), "there" is no longer efficient or inefficient. And certainly no a priori reason exists why the parties are not "there" when one of them has an effective right of specific performance, rather than not until he has possession of the goods, or title, or both, or even later. This may be illustrated by the following simple-efficient-breach analysis.

Suppose Athos has completed the chair contract by delivering the chairs to a public warehouse (as agreed in the contract) and has been paid. The chairs now belong to Porthos. Shortly afterwards Richelieu offers Athos $2,000,000 for immediate delivery of 100,000 chairs. Athos, not having any chairs, forges a warehouse receipt, goes to the warehouse, takes Porthos's chairs, and sends Porthos a certified check for $1,250,000. Athos delivers the chairs to Richelieu and is paid, for a net efficiency gain of $750,000. If Porthos's liability for damages is limited to the amount of the check, there will be an incentive for Athos to commit the theft. There should be. To be sure, Athos could have gone to Porthos and negotiated a deal, but that would have involved added transaction costs.

The simple-efficiency theorists would probably consider the foregoing

278

simple-efficient-theft argument a parody. But why? The answer lies in their assumption of efficiency-neutral ironbound property rights at the beginning and end of the changes being studied in the model. Once the magic words "my property" are spoken over the chairs on behalf of Porthos, he is entitled to them, or if they are gone, to their value, which in this case has been demonstrated by the Richelieu deal to be $2,000,000. But that answer leaves the simple-efficient-breach theory in considerable trouble. The magic "his property" can just as well be attributed to the holder of an effective right of specific performance or its true equivalent in damages as to the holder of possession, title, or both.

The very question in issue in the simple-efficient-breach theory is at what time do property rights in the chairs (or in the productive facilities to make them) become ironbound in Porthos? As the foregoing discussion suggests, there is no a priori basis for selecting any particular time or event for determining that the transaction is closed, that new property rights are now established, and that with them a new, efficiency-neutral status quo has been achieved.

But is the foregoing analysis perhaps undone when one considers the complexity of transactions, the fact that transactions of this kind neither open nor shut precisely? After all, they open with negotiations (if not earlier in prior relations), often involve some performance (*e.g.* supplying samples) before a deal is clearly established, often drift through stages when it is difficult to ascertain if neither, one, or both parties are bound in legal or other ways (and if so, how much), commonly involve installment deliveries and various credit arrangements, and go through the noninstantaneous process of acceptance of the goods. Moreover, even after the chairs are delivered and accepted, and the price is paid in full, the transactions are subject to important "tag-ends" involving returns, claims for defective items, and potential warranty claims that may go on for years.

Far from undoing the argument that any a priori selection of one contract remedy as more efficient than another is bootstrapping, the complexity of deals reinforces it. The complexity of even relatively simple deals makes it difficult to move in a clear and simple way from A (ironbound property rights) to B (new and different ironbound property rights). All property rights simply do not change suddenly at one instant. Nevertheless, in legal theory it is possible to create remedies that at some particular event or lapse of time treat the new, final, and complete status quo as occurring with that event or lapse of time, as presentiated. This is possible even though many other events, such as delivery, remain to occur in the actual world. Effective rights of *both* specific performance and expectation damages reflect just such a theory of presentation.

But a presentiated legal doctrine or two, such as specific performance and expectation damages, cannot be considered in isolation. The law governing contracts for the sale of goods such as those in the Four Musketeers does not just jump from offer and acceptance to *either* damages or specific performance (as the case may be), as descriptions of contracts by simple-efficient-breach theorists assume. On the contrary, a review of the law of sales will reveal that just as such contracts themselves "grow," so too the law governing grows with them. And in doing so this law reflects increasing buyer ownership and decreasing seller ownership as the contract follows common courses of development. For example, identification of goods confers on the buyer both a special property and an insurable interest in goods (U.C.C. s. 2–501(1)). In a case like the four Musketears, identification typically occurs when the chairs are "shipped, marked or otherwise designated by the seller as goods to which the [Athos-Porthos] contract refers." (*Ibid.* s. 2–501(1)(b)) Had this happened, Porthos would have acquired a right to replevy the chairs— a recognition of his legal ownership—but, under the U.C.C., only if he were unable to effect cover or could show that an effort to do so would be unavailing.[1] This particular effect of identification might be seen as simply a quirk of Anglo-American legal history, but insurable interest is hardly so easily dismissed, nor is the following buyer's right under U.C.C. § 2–503. Where the buyer has "paid a part or all of the price of goods in which he has a special property" under § 2–502, he may, on making and keeping good a tender of any unpaid portion of the price, recover the goods from the seller if the seller becomes insolvent within ten days after receipt of the first installment on the price. (*Ibid.* s. 2–502.)

Identification and its effects are but one example of how the law reflects the fact that even a simple contract for the sale of goods grows between offer and acceptance and its final complete performance. Others include acceptance of goods passage of title, (U.C.C. s. 2–401.) risks of loss, (*Ibid.* ss. 2–509.) rejection, (*Ibid.* s. 2–601 to 2–605.) cure, (*Ibid.* s. 2–508.) and tender. (*Ibid.* ss. 2–507, 2–508, 2–511.) One point in mentioning these is to emphasize that economic analysis requires consideration not only of final remedies, but also of the complexities of

---

[1] *Ibid.* s. 2–716(3). He could also replevy if the chairs had "been shipped under reservation and satisfaction of [Athos's] security interest in them has been made or tendered."

ownership changes of which remedies are but a part. Another is to stress that a priori conclusions about efficiency have no more validity respecting such complex structures than respecting the simple contract structure presented by simple-efficient-breach theorists.

We thus find ourselves in the in-between mode of complex legal remedies throughout every transaction. In this in-between mode, the issue is not (apart from transaction costs) a matter of expectation damages vs. specific performance, as the simple-efficient-breach theory suggests. It is, rather, a question of rights of ownership, which the model (again apart from transaction costs in the creation of those rights) is powerless to describe as either efficient or inefficient, except in terms of transaction costs. Thus, under the expectation damages rule, Porthos has already acquired many of the rights of ownership of the chairs (and prior to their existence, of Athos's facilities for building them), namely the speculative market risks of such ownership. But the question is, how much ownership? It is perfectly conceivable that a rule of law could give Porthos legal rights in Athos's productive facilities from the time of the contract, but enforceable only by damages, not by specific performance. Porthos would then be entitled to damages equal to the market value of those facilities during the time he is "owner" of them. In the Four Musketeers, that would give him the added $250,000 net efficiency gain from the Aramis table contract. A simple-efficient-breach analyst would, presumably, consider such a result just as inefficient as specific performance.

Thus, it is quite easy to slip into the simple-efficient-breach kind of fallacy in dealing with legal rights in the period between the ironbound (in theory) property rights at the beginning of a transaction and those at the end. During that period of change, which in real life is complex both in behavior and law, legal entitlements themselves are changing in complex ways—various benefits and burdens of ownership and obligation are shifting, but not all at once. In addition *both* property and liability protections of these shifting legal entitlements can be, and often are, at work simultaneously and/or seriatim, as is illustrated by the expectation damages rule itself.

There is a fundamental problem for the economic model here. No way exists to keep the exchanging processes themselves free of the idea of entitlements. Each change in legal rights occurring as the exchanging process goes on is a new set of legal entitlements, with just as much right as the preceding or succeeding one to be considered a new, efficiency-neutral status quo. Nor are the "normal" beginning or ending states of legal entitlements so ironbound and unfuzzy that the in-between stages can readily be distinguished as somehow fundamentally different. The existence of specific performance as a remedy illustrates this, since it can as readily be viewed as establishing a new, ironbound property right as it can be viewed as a remedy in the middle of the exchanging process.

In sum, the economic model provides no basis for an a priori conclusion about the efficiency of passage of ownership at any given stage of a transaction. Moreover, the passage of ownership, a legal entitlement, cannot be separated analytically (except for analyzing transaction costs and the kinds of issues raised by Calabresi and Melamed (1972)) from remedies for breach of contract. Thus, in the complex move from one property right status quo to another that occurs in an exchange, efficiency of particular rules can, once again, be ascertained not by their substantive content affecting ownership, but only by examining their pertinent transaction costs and externalities.

The final question is the nature of the bias of the simple-efficient-breach theory. That bias is in favor of individual, unco-operative behavior as opposed to behavior requiring the co-operation of the parties. The whole thrust of the Posner analysis is breach first, talk afterwards. Indeed, this may be an overstatement of the level of co-operation, since Posner pays singularly little attention to talking afterwards. Although he stresses the transaction costs of negotiations needed to reach efficient results under the specific performance rule, he pays no attention to the transaction costs of talking after a breach. And this is so despite the fact that "talking after a breach" may be one of the more expensive forms of conversation to be found, involving, as it so often does, engaging high-priced lawyers, and gambits like starting litigation, engaging in discovery, and even trying and appealing cases.

The bias against cooperation demonstrated by the simple-efficient-breach theory should surprise no one familiar with the neoclassical model. Such a bias is not limited to this particular fallacy, but is one towards which the neoclassical model inevitably and always tends. That model postulates individuals acting as if the relations in which those individuals exist have no effect on their behavior. Cooperative behavior postulates relations. A model assuming away relations slips with the greatest of ease at any stage into favoring uncooperative and—ironically enough—highly inefficient human behavior.

7.3 Contract Remedies: A Need for Better Efficiency Analysis

Transaction Costs and the Deductive Model

A striking thing about the efficiency analysis of contract remedies is the general acceptance of the need for treating transaction costs. This ranges from Bishop's founding his entire analysis on transaction costs (Bishop 1985, 300) to Rogerson's specific exclusion of transaction costs of *ex post* negotiations for the purpose of eliminating them from consideration in analyzing the effect of various remedies. Nonetheless, much confusion and inadequacy remain in the treatment of transaction costs. The following paragraphs suggest areas where more accuracy is required.

TREATMENT OF ALL PERTINENT AND SIGNIFICANT TRANSACTION COSTS

A few years ago I made the following statement respecting the scope of inquiry required in assessing the relative efficiency of expectation damages and specific performance.

> The pertinent transaction costs cannot be limited to one or two supplemental matters. Rather the inquiry must be addressed to *all* transaction costs respecting each rule. This includes some costs of initial planning in the *first* contract ... costs of planning (again including negotiations) after the new opportunity comes along, costs of potential or actual litigation (including costs of delay), information costs, cost of inertia, costs of uncertainty, relational costs, such as damage to reputation and loss of future opportunities to deal, and undoubtedly others. *All of these may vary depending upon which rule governs.*
>
> In addition, two other factors must be taken into account: negative transaction costs and externalities. Negative transaction costs are consequences of a rule which may lessen losses. For example, ... [if] one of the rules encourages early communication ... distress losses may be reduced by that rule, thereby increasing its efficiency. Relational costs are another type of costs likely to vary a good deal depending upon the rule. If the damages rule encourages

283

breaches without consultation, whereas the specific performance rule encourages consultation and mutually beneficial agreement, relational costs will be lower under the specific performance rule. In the real world it makes a great deal of difference whether a breach occurs, or is even threatened, or whether negotiations are viewed as leading towards mutually beneficial allocations of the increased productivity offered by the new opportunity. Unless the efficiency modeler explicitly treats this factor, the model fails to account for the differences between negotiating over what is viewed as an allocation of losses, and what is viewed as the allocation of potential gains. And modelers seldom seem to consider the difference (Macneil 1982, 957–959, emphasis added).

Bishop later took me to task for this position:

... to avoid misleadingly selective consideration of transition costs (Macneil) tells us, we must refer to all forms of them whenever we state a proposition about the real world application of the model. This is not true. Every purported real world application of a model is predicated on a series of assumptions: that factors other than those considered in the model are unimportant, that every *systematic predictable observable factor* is explained by the model, and that the residual differences are due to the inherent randomness of the world. These assumptions are *never* wholly true, but are often good enough. Selective consideration of (say) negotiation costs for specific performance and damages, without considering possible differences in litigation costs, is perfectly legitimate *provided* litigation cost differences are not systematic. Anyone who thinks they are systematic will decline to be convinced and quite rightly so (Bishop 1986, 319, first and third emphasis added).

Except in one respect. Bishop and I appear to disagree only about the facts, not the principles involved. That is, I believe the costs mentioned are "systematic predictable observable factors" (and said as much), and Bishop, since he excludes most of them from his analysis, obviously does not. This, I would have thought, is self-apparent from the quotation from my article which led to Bishop's comments, as it is from the paragraph following it:

The other essential factor to consider is externalities. To the extent that whoever decides not to perform the first contract can avoid paying all the costs of that decision, the likelihood of his making inefficient decisions is increased. It is therefore necessary to weigh the two rules (in the wide range of circumstances to which they apply) in these terms. The consequences of uncertainty in measuring damages, of the American rule leaving most costs of litigation on the party initially incurring them of costs of litigation generally, and of the costs of inertia, may enable the [deliberate breachers] of the world to shift losses of termination of the first contract to the [victims of breach] in such a way that significant external costs escape decision making (Macneil 1982, 960).

Clear Exposition of Assumptions

The one exception to my agreement with Bishop's principles concerns the proper description of assumptions in models, about which we evidently disagree. I suppose he would agree that the significant assumptions of the model: such as what are not systematic predictable observable factors, should be plainly understood by both modeler and observers of the model. And I doubt if we would disagree on the various ways such understanding may be achieved. One is by shared customs. For example, economists relatively seldom feel the need to repeat some of the fundamental assumptions of the basic efficiency model itself, such as consistency of preferences, presumably because "everyone knows that." (Dangers, of course, lurk in this, because one may be less likely to recognize those occasions where the assumption is wrong if it has not been explicitly stated.)

Surely, assumptions should be expressly stated whenever they are neither clearly established by shared custom nor likely reasonably to be viewed as indisputable by any of those to whom the model is addressed, directly or indirectly. In the case of efficiency analysis of contract remedies that would include not only those in the same school and other interested academies, but most importantly, lawmakers of various kinds. Bishop evidently either does not believe in this standard or is certain that such things as litigation costs of the very remedies he is analyzing could not reasonably be thought to be likely systematic predictable observable factors relating to the efficiency of those remedies. I leave it to the readers of this paper whether either is a tenable position.

Having worked through a number of these complex and often long articles in preparation for this paper, I would say that the standards for setting out assumptions are generally execrably low. Often important assumptions are unstated. Other times they are buried somewhere in lengthy text, sometimes as asides. Sometimes they follow long after very important conclusions have been drawn. In such cases it may be very difficult for the reader to be sure whether the writer took the assumption adequately into account in drawing the conclusions or the degree to which the assumption is a limiting factor on the conclusion. I have yet to find one with its assumptions all nicely lined up like soldiers at the beginning. Yet every paper is based on a wide range of assumptions—by no means the same for all of them—which are absolutely essential to the validity of the conclusions and which are by no means universally accepted as sound. The importance of this failure is immense: as these analyses become (inevitably) more complex and take in more complex contract behavior, the number of and complexity of the assumptions is bound to grow. The models will become virtually useless to anyone unless the assumptions are clearly and efficiently laid out for all to see.

REALISM RESPECTING TRANSACTION COSTS

The existence and extent of transaction costs in particular aspects of contractual behavior are matters of hard facts out in a real world. If one were looking for experts on such matters one would hardly turn to academics, but rather to business people, lawyers, and others professionally engaged in incurring those costs. Yet this empirical aspect of transaction-cost analysis is coming almost entirely from the academy, and from the deductive, not the empirical side of the academy at that. Thomas Ulen provides an example of what this yields:

> In general, the post-breach transaction costs between contractual parties should not be high. After all, they have established a relationship before the breach and the things that make for high transaction costs in other legal contexts are entirely absent here: the parties have identified each other: they have bargained to provide for many contingencies including, possibly, breach: they may have had contact after formation and before full performance to clarify details, report progress, and the like. Thus, if the parties did not provide for some form of relief in the event of breach, the costs to them of dealing with the contingency that has arisen to frustrate the contract should be low (Ulen 1984, 369).

To which one might add additional factors such as: someone has deliberately broken his word, either without consultation or over objection, thereby demonstrating his lack of trustworthiness for the future. In Ulen's terms, someone has betrayed the relationship which is the very source of the low transaction costs he claims.

In Macneil 1982, 968–969 I pointed out that

"talking after a breach" may be one of the more expensive forms of conversation to be found, involving, as it so often does, engaging high-price lawyers, and gambits like starting litigation, engaging in discovery, and even trying and appealing cases.

The reason for such expense is that breach or even serious threat of breach destroys the trust upon which even discrete transactions are built, and with it any desire to cooperate with the other party, except in bilateral monopoly-bargaining conducted with hostility and knowledge of one party that the other does not keep its word. The difficulties and resulting costs of this are aggravated by the fact that most such post-breach bargaining concerns allocation of losses not of gains. Whether Ulen's views or mine are the more realistic I shall leave to the reader, with the suggestion that any reader wishing more enlightenment than we can provide turn to the real world of contract, not to academia, and especially not to the deductive sector of academia.

RELATION OF TRANSACTION COSTS TO THE DEDUCTIVE MODEL.

The efficiency model is a deductive model, that is it starts from assumptions and then draws logical conclusions from them about what would happen in various situations, typically hypothetical. Transaction costs are not automatically a part of the model, and are often assumed not to exist. Such a totally unrealistic assumption has varying effects on the usefulness of the model respecting analysis of contract remedies. In some instances, such as "efficient breach" analysis, omission of transaction costs makes all remedies indistinguishable in efficiency terms (Macneil 1982). At best, omission of important transaction costs limits usefulness of the model to a very tiny arena, if that. For example, Rogerson uses an assumption "that *ex post* negotiations always occur successfully and costlessly." He does this to eliminate the issue of efficient breach, in order to focus on levels of reliance likely to result from various remedial rules (Rogerson 1984). This is an appropriate way of focusing on that issue, but the result is of extremely limited value by itself. The assumption is manifestly false and to draw the conclusions Rogerson does requires a further assumption that *ex post* negotiations *with* transaction costs will not have a systematic countereffect on his conclusions.

There are two alternatives to assuming zero transaction costs. One is to assume or hypothesize particular levels of transaction costs and keep entirely within a deductive model. The other is to introduce them as facts, *i.e.* empirically, thereby attempting to link the model to the real world by something other than assumptions. In the latter case, the value of such effort can, at best be no better than that allowed by the accuracy of the empirical information.

Given the historical origins of efficiency analysis of law, one might have expected that the efficiency analysis of contract remedies would have gone down the first route. Judging, however, from the recent articles discussed in this paper it has not. Instead, either totally or largely ignoring the costs or casual empiricism is the order of the day, with the latter seemingly the prevalent mode. Other examples beside the quotation from Ulen (1984) above include:

> One reason [parties might choose an expectation measure over a reliance measure of damages] is administrative: it is usually easier to establish in court the values of performance than the extent of reliance (Cooter and Eisenberg 1985, 1461).

> Other things being equal simple rules are to be preferred because they generatic lower costs of legal services and judicial administration (Bishop 1986, 307; see also 308).

> [T]here are other reasons to believe that allowing only reasonable reliance will still not guarantee only efficient breach. The most important of these is that determining which reliance expenses were reasonable and which were not is likely to be expensive (Ulen 1984, 359–360; 369).

The defects of the first of these routes—ignoring transaction costs—has already been noted. The problem with the second is that the introduction of these unproved empirical statements, deprives the model of its positivist deductive nature. The accuracy of conclusions can no longer be tested against the assumptions, but depend upon the empirical accuracy of those conclusions.

4. Summary and Conclusion

The efficiency model is too often applied to the analysis of contract remedies without proper attention to its own requirements. Procedurally, there is great and virtually universal failure to make clear what assumptions are being made. This is an extremely serious problem since a very wide range of assumptions. many of them quite complex, are required in the analysis of contract law.

This procedural failing runs over into, and also causes, substantive failings in analysis. These include the following: (1) omission of aspects of contract behavior likely, or even sure, to have systematic effect on efficiency. (2) Failure to recognize the pervasive effect of contract remedies on behavior other than that studied. (3) Failure to recognize that the extremely limited hypothetical situations used in proofs limit the kinds of contracts to which conclusions may properly be addressed, and hence remedies which can be recommended on efficiency grounds. (4) Failure to recognize the limited impact legal rules have on the behavior of participants in contracts. (5) Failure to consider all significant transaction costs likely to have systematic effects on contract behavior and legal remedies. (6) Lack of realism in assessing transaction costs. (7) Failure adequately to recognize that the introduction of real, rather than assumed, transaction costs, into the model deprives the model of its deductive positivist nature and renders it only as good as the empirical demonstrations of the real costs, (8) Confusing the minimum of two times required in the efficiency analysis of contract remedies law so as, at best, to obscure the conclusions reached, and at worst to commit serious logical errors.

Cure of these errors in efficiency analysis of contract remedies can lead only to the following: much greater complexity or conclusions of extremely limited nature or both, and extreme modesty in advocating particular contract remedies on efficiency grounds. This outcome severely limits the utility of efficiency analysis of contract remedies. If such cures are effected, a relational approach to contracts and their remedies in which efficiency analysis is reached only by working to it through the relations, rather than assuming them away *ab initio.* may seem more attractive than it now does as a tool of economic analysis. Such an approach lacks the false clarity and false positivism of the efficiency model as it is currently used in analyzing contract remedies. I believe, however, that it will lead to more realistic and effective analysis of the material and necessarily social aspects of contracts and contract remedies. This I believe also to be the true role of economics, not simply the refined analysis of scarcity.

Chapter 8

Reflections on the Relational Theory

Together with the "Afterword" to this volume, the selections in this chapter cover most of Macneil's responses to criticisms and misunderstandings of the relational theory. Many of the standard criticisms of Macneil will, I think, have to be reconsidered in the light of the wider reception of these responses.

8.1 Reflections on Relational Contract

It took from 1967 to 1971 to produce my first American work in relational contracts a teaching casebook. Macneil (1971a) and until 1974 to produce my first comprehensive synthesis of relational contract theory. Macneil (1974a). So plainly obvious were the things I was writing during those seven years that I was sure someone would beat me to the exposition of a fairly comprehensive relational contract theory. My selfish concern escalated no end when sometime in 1973, I came across Selznick

(1969) There it was! At least, there it almost was because Selznick focused largely on labor relations, with only casual attention to contractual relations generally. But labor relations was just the area from which I expected the insights into contractual relations to arise and so I held my breath until well into 1974.

I have now had over a decade to accept that there never had been any race to a relational theory of contract, nor have the succeeding years seen either widespread acceptance of (or indeed much challenge to) my particular theory or the development of other relational contract theories. This is not to say that contractual relations have failed to attract a great deal of attention in America in the past decades. They always have and always will since contractual relations, not discrete contract, always have and always will be the dominant form of exchange behavior in society (Macneil 1985b). Thus, particular types of contractual relations necessarily give rise to relational ways, including relational ways of thinking about them. Such thinking need, however, go little farther than the bounds of the particular type of contractual relations in questions.

Nor is relational contract conceptualization lacking which nevertheless remains firmly founded on discrete concepts such as those of neoclassical microeconomics, including transaction cost analysis, and neoclassical contract law. Many, such as the series of articles of Goetz and Scou, deal with both subjects, as well as with relational contract law.

Existent also is the work of the critical legal scholars, all of which is necessarily relational in nature. No critical legal scholar has yet produced, however, anything remotely close to a general theory of relational contract and indeed such synthesis may very well be antithetical to critical principles. (Tushnet 1984).

A comment by Foster reviewing my *New Social Contract* (Macneil 1980) also reveals an important omission in relational contract scholarship [Macneil's] relational contract is so wide an analytical category that it loses any power to explain specific legal forms." (Foster 1982, 146). The comment is incorrect, but it does reflect the fact that relatively little has been done to connect relational contract theory to specific legal forms, except from the non-relational perspectives noted above. An exception to this is some of the work of critical legal scholars (although limited by absence of any affirmative overall relational theory), a recent example being Dalton (1985).

Should the dearth of widely accepted relational contract theory or theories be of concern to scholars of contract? The answer is both no and yes. What is essential to any sound theoretical approach to contracts of

292

any kind is a *Grundnorm* recognizing the embeddedness of all exchange in relations. For many purposes this recognition is sufficient for sound analysis of particular kinds of contract without the development of principles overtly dealing with all kinds of contractual relations. That is not true, however, for analysis even of particular types of contracts, purporting to be of a macro social (including most certainly economic) and political nature. Such analysis is at best inadequate, and at worst founders miserably, in the absence of some reasonably coherent understanding of relational exchange as a universal in human social behavior.

Moreover, the best defense against the continued scholarly dominance of theories founded on discrete concepts, *i.e.* concepts which ignore the universal embeddedness of exchange in relations, would be one or more widely accepted theories of relational exchange. In their absence, such tools as neoclassical economics (even with transaction costs) and neoclassical contract doctrine which analyze exchange, rather than relations in which exchange occurs, will continue to dominate the world. (Even critical analysis, or perhaps especially critical analysis, is affected adversely by this dominance. Although critical views of contract are relational in the macro sense, the critique invariably contains large doses of unrealistic neoclassical notions relating to legislation and judicial decision as well as actual behavior in the rest of the economic world. These inaccurate perceptions are bound to continue in the absence of a relational contract theory acceptable to the critical writer.)

Let me hasten to add that both neoclassical economic analysis and neoclassical contract law have proper, although limited, roles in social analysis and social control respectively. (These limited roles are intellectually difficult to deal with, because both are closed systems which deny, yet inconsistently postulate an external social structure in which they operate.) But such roles properly arise only after a recognition in each application that a decision is being made to treat the pertinent aspect of exchange relations as if it were discrete, although in fact it is not in short to ignore the nondiscrete aspects of the relation. This may be justified in positivist economic analysis on the ground that the subject of inquiry is a very limited one *e.g.* what will happen to the demand for petrol if the price rises fifty cents. (There is, of course nothing in such analysis that then permits the conclusion that such a price increase is a "good" or a "bad" thing.) Similarly, application of neoclassical contract law may be justified by a particular or general decision to ignore relational aspects of the exchange in certain circumstances *e.g.* that a commodity trader has serious financial reverses should not be a ground for relieving him from his legal obligations in the commodities market. (Of course relief in bankruptcy is always a limitation on any such discrete neoclassical law.)

When the limits of discrete analysis are ignored, the conclusions reached are not necessarily wrong, they are simply unproven in the case of positivist analysis and unjustified in the case of normative argument. In economic analysis this leads to unproven conclusions about efficiency, conclusions which cannot properly be used normatively to make recommendations—even solely to terms of efficiency itself—for policy or for law illustrating this point is too complicated a matter for the space available here.

In the case of doctrinal legal analysis the use of neoclassical doctrine as the *Grundnorm* where in fact relations significantly affect the situation beyond the capacity of the doctrine to absorb the relational aspects usually leads to one or both the following results.

One result is that the discrete doctrine simply overrides the relational aspects. This may not, of course, differ from the result which would have been reached under a relational approach, where after consideration, it would have been decided that the total relations called for the discrete planning of the parties to override the relational aspects, *e.g.* where a labor arbitrator decides after looking extensively at the whole situation that an explicit provision in the written collective bargaining agreement should supersede a longstanding shop practice. On the other hand such a result may defeat relational aspects which would have governed had they been considered, *e.g.* where a labor arbitrator follows the written agreement without paying any attention to the overall labor relations, but would not have done so had he known what they were. Worse, at least worse from the discrete view of things, such a result may defeat the discrete planning itself, *e.g.* where a labor arbitrator's understanding of the language of the written agreement is wrong in terms of what both management and union meant by it, because, applying standard parol evidence principles, he refused to examine the whole relation in ascertaining what the parties meant.

Neoclassical doctrinal analysis of complex contractual relations may also take the relations into account, but incompletely in various ways. Only some relational aspects may be considered, others being excluded arbitrarily or haphazardly or both. Example: A court favoring arbitration as a matter of good labor relations refuses to examine the particular collective bargaining relation in interpreting a written collective bargaining agreement thereby ignoring negotiations and longstanding past practices of the management and union showing that neither intended a particular kind of dispute to be subject to arbitration.[1]

Moreover, if any thought is given to relational aspects it may be subconscious or at least entirely unarticulated, decisions being made by gut feeling intuition, etc. Or a court may actually take important relational factors into account, but deny doing so. Example: In a dispute over a commercial agreement, the judge steadfastly denied that any contextual inquiry was necessary to ascertain its meaning, but only after making an extensive contextual inquiry upon which he reached that conclusion.[2]

An extremely common technique in using neoclassical contract law is the use of terms such as unfair, unjust one-sided unequal bargaining power, which are so little understood or have such little commonly accepted meaning as to constitute not much more than. "I do not like it." Even terms like unconscionable, duress, good faith, undue influence, all of which have been subjected to a great deal of judicial and scholarly analysis, have such diverse meanings as often to be little more than cliches in many judicial opinions.

Can we do better? Is it possible, while staying essentially within a promise-centric, *i.e.* neoclassical, model of contract, to "reconceptualize contract law so that it consists of a body of principles that are both intellectually coherent and sufficiently open textured to encompass the complex and evolving realities of contract as a social institution"? Eisenberg has made a major effort to do just this in American law (Eisenberg 1979; 1982a; 1982b; 1984). He summarizes the result. "The principles of contract law should be based on considerations of fairness, as determined principally by conventional morality, and of policy, as determined principally by efficiency and administrability (Eisenberg 1984, 1111). Perhaps such broad concepts are all we can hope for once we pass the limits of what can be dealt with satisfactorily by the concept of consent. My own view, demonstrated by the relational theory of contract I have advanced, is that we can articulate more precise, intellectually coherent principles which are nevertheless sufficiently open textured for effective use in the law of modern contractual relations.

---

[1] *United Steelworkers of America v. Warrior & Gulf Navigation Co* 363 U.S. 574 (1960).
[2] *Grumman Industries, Inc v. Rohr Industries Inc* 748 F.2d 729 (2d Cir. 1984).

8.2 A Brief Comment on Farnsworth's "Suggestion for the Future"

I must protest Professor Farnsworth's use of a quotation from a little article of mine, because his ellipsis-and-substitution quite distorts what I said. I wrote:

> I have now had over a decade to accept that there had never been any race to *a relational* theory of contract, nor have the succeeding years seen either widespread acceptance of (or indeed much challenge to) my particular theory or the development of other *relational* contract theories. (Macneil 1985a, 541)

Professor Farnsworth (1987, 209) describes this as "a rather striking statement by the proponent of what may be the most popular new contracts 'theory' of ourtime." This suggests that he fails to see that a widespread recognition—to which I may have contributed—that "relations matter" and an accompanying dissatisfaction with neoclassical contract are not the same as a partly or full-blown relational theory of contract.

Professor Farnsworth excised the emphasized words—the only words that make the sentence of the least academic interest—and replaced them as follows:

> I have now had over a decade to accept that there had never been any race to [*my type of*] theory of contract, nor have the succeeding years seen widespread acceptance of (or indeed much challenge to) my particular theory or the development of other [*similar*] contract theories [emphasis added]. (Farnsworth 1987, 208)

For Professor Farnsworth's immediate purposes—my contradicting the fourth fallacy of his fable—this handling of the sentence may be appropriate enough. But we cannot stop there. The fallacies are part of the fable, and the fallacious fable is the prelude to a cry against theorizing in contracts. And therein lies buried and unrecognized a very important substantive and ideological position.

In the unlikely event that Professor Farnsworth's cry against contract theorizing succeeds, only one theory would survive: neoclassical contract theory. Now Professor Farnsworth's ellipsis-and-substitution becomes of some significance, because neoclassical contract theory seriously slights or even rejects some core principles necessarily underlying any relational theory of contracts:

1. No one can ever understand discrete elements in contractual relations without understanding the relations themselves.

2. If one wishes to understand contracts, including their discrete elements, it is infinitely better to start with whole contractual relations than with their discrete elements.

I believe these principles to be valid whether one is talking about contract behavior, contract law, or contract theory. In contract behavior, there never has been much problem on this score. One does not last long in the real world of contractual relations if one pays attention solely to the discrete elements and ignores the relations in which they occur. Just try bidding at auctions without knowing to which national currencies the auctioneers' figures refer.

In contract law, a greater likelihood exists that the principles will sometimes be ignored with resulting inefficiency and injustice. The likelihood increases in direct proportion to the degree of abstraction involved in the questions asked. The level of abstraction is, of course, affected by many factors. Two important ones are the role of the questioner and the substance of the question. A practicing lawyer faced with a specific question of "contract law" concerning a particular issue in a particular contractual relation is far less likely to miss out on or-misconstrue important relational matters than is an academic writing a law review article on the battle of the forms. An appellate court judge comes somewhere in between.

It is at the level of contract theory, however, that the principles are most apt to be ignored. Consider, for example, microeconomic theory and neoclassical contract theory, each of which is based on fundamental rejections of both principles.

The core principles I have identified are, *inter alia*, what will be thrown out if Professor Farnsworth's suggestion for the future—stop theoriz-ing—is followed. I would not want any quotation of mine to be considered support for such an outcome.

8.3   Barriers to the Idea of Relational Contracts

Wherever we look, human beings who are producing, distributing, and using material wealth, are doing so in a great welter of complex relations. For convenience, I shall call these material relations.

Material relations always incorporate elements beyond those generated by any particular people and activities we may observe. At the very least these elements include the following. First, language and absorbed capacities for communication and for some degree of affirmative cooperation. Secondly, social and legal support of some degree of peace, including peaceful control of capital. Thirdly, social and legal support of obligations generated in the relations. And, finally, almost universally present, is some use of money in the relations.

These are the very least in the way of the *external* elements we see in material relations. But "the very least" is seldom all we see. It is rare, for example, that such relations occur in the absence of multitudinous customs. And, these days, interpenetration with a wide range of quasi-external bureaucracy, up to and including those of the state and of international bodies, is omnipresent.

These material relations generate also their own *internal* elements of great complexity, ranging from the most subtle nuances of unspoken custom among business friends to the most detailed elements of bureaucratic planning and conduct. These constantly define and redefine the nature of the relations.

When we seek common patterns of behavior in any of these relations, one universal element in particular stands out most prominently. That is reciprocity, actions (or inactions) taken to benefit others, but made with the idea that something of value has or will return, directly or indirectly.

Reciprocity is not only always present but also commonly very prominent, as, for example, in a stock exchange transaction. But in some relations, such as the household, reciprocity is often so overlaid with other social phenomena as to be relatively difficult to observe. Indeed, the other social phenomena, such as feelings of love, may lead to the denial by the participants of the very existence of reciprocity. Nonetheless, it is present as long as the relations endure.

Sometimes reciprocity appears in the form of sharp punctuations in the relation, quick, clearly defined exchanges in which This is clearly for That, and That is clearly for This. These are what I have elsewhere somewhat misleadingly called discrete transactions. But these sharp punctuations in relations—the exclamation points of the material world—are parts of material relations, not discrete transactions between atomistic humans. They only seem to be discrete transactions. Very often this is because the relations are structured precisely so that the only active and direct interaction between the parties appears to be highly descrete. An example is a quick exchange of cash for petrol by a foreign traveler. But underlying this apparent discreteness is necessarily a relationship created by a whole panoply of custom, language (even if only sign language), and law, to mention but three of many elements. Indeed the mutual acceptability of the coins or paper as a means of payment itself reflects the existence of a relationship between the parties.

When apparently discrete transactions are removed from the relations in which they occur they are nothing but abstractions, just as exclamation points are nothing but abstractions when removed from a text.

Of equal universality and importance as reciprocity is solidarity—the willingness to trust others to whatever extent is necessary for the relation to continue. It too is always present, else the relation fails. Solidarity, however, may be, and often is, less obvious to the observer, or indeed to the participants, than reciprocity. A businessperson may deal regularly with another whom he would not trust around the corner, and hence, if asked, would deny the existence of solidarity in the relation. Nonetheless, the existence of solidarity is proven if he continues to deal with the other, even though his trust may be based entirely on the belief that the untrustworthy one is terribly fearful of suits for breach of contract.

Reciprocity and solidarity are by no means the only universal elements in material relations, but they are key ones—first among equals—and their mention will suffice for my purposes this morning.

One further word, however, about reciprocity. In the real world of material relations, the exclamation points of very discrete exchange are something of a rarity, compared with the ubiquity of reciprocity utilizing other kinds of exchange. Even the This for That in a supermarket is heavily laden with, among other things, brand name relations, customs of supermarkets, and often, various continuing relations between the customer and a particular supermarket. This is true too in the financial and commodity markets of the world. These markets are systems of extremely complex relations created in large measure precisely to strip individual exchanges of relational characteristics. But this stripping is only for certain limited, albeit extremely important, purposes, as becomes apparent with each new insider trading scandal.

Similarly, the This for That in wage employment at its most discrete is "This 40 hours of my time and efforts—enthusiastic, slothful, refreshed, tired, bright, headachy, attentive, distracted—for That $6 per hour, payable when the time is up." The exchange is half a punctuation point on pay day, but a drawn out Joycean text for the other forty more or less deliverd, and more or less utilized, hours.

But even relations like those in supermarkets, financial and commodities markets, and relatively short term wage employment constitute only a modest part of the material relations we observe in the real world. Consider such agglomerations of capital and people as corporations, franchises, complex long term supply contracts, families, partnerships, leases, and countless other forms of material relations. In them, reciprocity in the form of exclamation points of "discrete This for That exchanges," where any exist at all, are merged with more subtle patterns of exchange complexly spread over time, patterns equalling or outweighing the discrete exchanges in importance. Consider, for example, a quarterly dividend to shareholders. The amount, *per se*, may be of singularly little significance; what matters is how that amount relates to prior dividends, to current earnings, to corporate cash flow, to prospective sales volumes, and much else.

This then is the *real* world of production, distribution, and use of material wealth. It is a world of relations in which reciprocity is everpresent, but truly discrete exchange never is, and relatively discrete exchange only sometimes. Above all, the relatively discrete exchanges, like exclamation points in a text, are always melded with the more subtle patterns of exchange in the relations. And everything is intertwined with solidarity.

I turn now to the abstract world of the law of contract. By this I mean the general principles of contract law purportedly applicable to any relation the law calls contractual, subject to modification only by more specific law. And let me say I am talking about the Anglo-American world of contract law; only some of what I have to say may be applicable to civil law systems. I shall have to leave it to the civilians to decide how much.

What a peculiar world is this law of contract! What has happened to the universe of material relations in this new world? Solidarity has disappeared altogether except in legal remedies. So too, reciprocity is gone except for the discrete transaction. The This for That of atomistic, unrelated humans, nonexistent in the real world, has become *the* lens through which such relations are observed. Contract law thereby boils down to those human atoms, A and B, binding each other in one instant of consent to trade This for That in an entirely discrete transaction. Upon the sands of this abstraction all the other elements of contract law are founded or pretended to be founded. Thus contract law has discarded all the text of human material relations, retaining only the exclamation points! Rarely, if ever, has a major legal conceptualization provided such an incomplete and distorted reflection of the real world to which it relates.

Few today deny the obvious: this abstraction, centered on the exclamation points of discrete exchange, omits vast quantities of the text of the complex material relations in which real people produce, distribute, and use material wealth. And it vastly distorts all the rest. Moreover, the principle of the market and so-called freedom of contract underlying this abstraction regularly gives way to competing social and legal principles. This has happened to such an extent that huge areas of the law of material relations largely ignore, reject, or significantly modify general contract law. In the practice of law and in the courts, these facts are daily bread and butter. It is known even among most academics—a group usually the last to know about such things. Finally, there is widespread recognition that the general contract law abstraction is fundamentally defective as a tool for organizing our thoughts about the law of material relations.

One might reasonably expect in the face of this to find a burgeoning and widespread development among legal scholars of a theory or theories of contractual relations. One might expect that, and one would be wrong. While there is some mild movement of this kind, it is largely limited in nature. Moreover, such affirmative developments are particularly miniscule compared to the constant ignoring, rejecting, and limiting of the principles of existing general contract law which fills the law reviews and books on contracts.

Now, there are a great many reasons for this nondevelopment of theories of relational contract law, and I wish to explore only one facet, barriers to the very idea of contractual relations. Essentially two types of barrier exist: first, conscious rejection of the idea and second, incapacity to understand it. Of the two, I find the second more deeply intriguing, but first a word about why people deliberately reject the very idea of contractual relations in law.

One reason for rejection is a cost-benefit argument which goes something like this: We already have in place a general contract law which in detail, although not in structure and logic, deals extensively

301

with many of the relational aspects of contracts. However internally inconsistent it is, it is nonetheless reasonably adequate to take care of relatively discrete contracts. Where it becomes inadequate in the face of heavily relational contracts, specialized law always has developed and continues to develop to meet the legal needs generated by those relations. True, this specialized relational law necessarily depends in considerable measure upon the general contract law founded on the discrete transaction. Equally true, clashes inevitably arise between the specialized relational law, growing out of the relational needs of the particular contracts, and the discretely modeled general contract law. But a clash between discreteness and other relational elements is an integral aspect of the *real* life of *all* material relations. Thus, some of the clash both within general contract law and between that law and specialized relational law is inevitable to matter how we think about the law of contractual relations. What we have works reasonably well, and we have no assurance that after much expenditure of time and other resources any general law of contract relations we might produce would be better from a practical standpoint. It simply is not worth rethinking contracts and developing general law, or even widely accepted principles, of contractual relations.

In spite of my personal commitment to thinking, teaching, and writing about contractual relations, their principles, and their law, I find this a very powerful argument. Nonetheless, I believe that it often masks very different reasons for deliberately refusing to think about contractual relations as a generic idea important to the law.

These range from the narrow vested interest of lawyers in their intellectual capital in the form of knowledge about any existing law, to the highest—or lowest, depending on your viewpoint—of political and ideological goals. Most commonly we associate tenacious rejection of the idea of relational contract with the market-oriented political right, or I should say, the supposedly market-oriented right. This political sector finds the ideology of the discrete transaction useful in achieving its goals. But I think it fair to say that something not totally different comes from the left in a variety of guises. At the very least, the discrete general contract law is a nice whipping boy for left-liberals—especially nice because it seems to live on in perpetuity. This permit spermanent avoidance of facing up to some key difficulties in the left-liberal position, particularly respecting bureaucracy.

But even the farther left—the Critical Legal Studies movement—has avoided facing up to what it means to incorporate the discreteness universally found in material relations into general principles and law of such relations. They seem most often to prefer pointing out the obvious limitation of the discrete general law of contract only in terms of a limited set of relational concerns.

These are mainly concerns relating to equality and participation of individuals in decisions affecting their lives. As has often been pointed out, Critical Legal Studies has not gone much beyond that in terms of developing theories, whether of relational contract or anything else. Since we must have *some* law dealing with discreteness in contractual relations, even Critical Legal scholars are necessarily left with the existing general contract law. Now let me turn to the more intriguing—and perhaps more fundamental—reason for nonacceptance of the very idea of contractual relations in law, that is the incapacity to understand the idea.

In both conversation and in writing I have regularly come across intelligent, sometimes supremely intelligent, people, knowledgeable in the law, who seem to be simply incapable of conceiving the law of material relations abstractly in any terms other than those of discrete transactions. Professor Charles Fried (1981) is an outstanding example. The very idea of contract as relations rather than as discrete transactions is obscure to such people.

Speak to them informally in such terms, of say the relation of marriage, and the response will be, "Oh, but that isn't contract." You ask: Was it formed by agreement? "Yes, a very formal one." Is there reciprocity respecting material wealth? "Oh yes." Do the parties plan and commit themselves to things? "Of course." Is every other single functional element of contract you can think of present? "Well, I suppose so, but marriage still isn't contract." You can go through the same conversation if you describe a corporation and its many denizens as *a* contractual relation. I have seen legal minds so set in the cement of discreteness as to deny, in essence, that long term supply contracts and leases are really contracts!

Obviously, these same people can and must think relationally about the particular kinds of material relations in which they personally are involved, whether as lawyers or in their private lives. No one could survive professionally or as a person without doing so.

And they can and do think abstractly and relationally about processes pertaining to material relations, such as arbitration. And they can even carry over the relational ideas from one kind of contractual relation, say employment, to another, say, franchises. What they cannot seem to do is think of contractual relations as a species of abstraction, in the same manner they can and do think about the discrete abstraction. What accounts for this?

The most superficial answer is that many people simply never recover from the brainwashing they received at that impressionable period of their lives, the first year of law school. They were then taught the discrete general law of contract, and that is the only general law of contract they have ever been taught. They learned nothing else, and now they can learn nothing else.

Like many superficial answers, there is something to this, but not as much as one might think. Both law students and lawyers are constantly casting off intellectual legal baggage they view as unrealistic. Why not the discrete law of contract? Moreover, my own experience, after 20 years of trying to teach first year law students relational approaches to contract law, is that almost all of them *enter* law school with deeply ingrained discrete views about contract. They are, in American terms, basicly Willistonians. And this seems to be true irrespective of their overall political and social outlook. Not only do they enter my course that way, but in spite of all my efforts for many months, most of these very bright, and in many ways very malleable, young people leave the course without a great deal of change in their discrete mindset. With luck a few acquire a more global picture, but they seem to be the exceptions.

It is true, of course, that in many instances the overall law school experience reinforces the discrete mindset, especially, perhaps, where law-and-economics flourishes. I think we must, however, look to the culture *from* which law students come in order to understand why they so easily slip into thinking of contract law only in discrete terms and so commonly find great difficulty in doing otherwise.

Looking at that culture, we might possibly say that more relatively discrete exchange is embedded in American material relations than is true in many other cultures. We might also note that, like exclamation points, discrete exchanges are always quite noticeable. And we might conclude that law students from any culture—but especially the American one—will simply be drawing on their own experience of contractual relations in accepting the discrete general contract law as the only proper abstraction to treat material relations. But this is a *non sequitur*. After all, equally part of their experience is all the rest of material relations in which those elements of discrete exchange are embedded. While discrete exchange is surely noticeable, so are other elements such as power, solidarity, flexibility, and the importance of proper means of intercourse. Why then, when they come to consider the *legal* conceptions of such

304

relations, should their experience with relative discreteness in real contractual relations drive out their experience of all the rest? The answer must be that it does not, that something else is causing the reaction.

Nor is it enough to say that these students are Americans, living in an economy especially dominated by the cash nexus; America, where the text of life in material relations is more splattered than most with the exclamation points of discrete exchange, exclamation points in the boldest possible print. This may be true, but it is subject to exactly the same comment. However immense its effect, the cash nexus does not, indeed cannot, drive out all the rest of the material relations in which discrete transactions are embedded. Nor does it drive those other elements out of people's minds. So we are left with the same question concerning the ready acceptance of the intellectual dominance of discrete contract law in the face of contrary experience in the real world of material relations.

We cannot thus simply look *directly* to the world of material relations from whence law students come for the source of their acculturalization as discrete contract law theorizers. It may—or may not—be that ultimately material relations dominated by the cash nexus make these students the way they are. The cash nexus itself certainly does not do so directly.

We must instead turn to the culture of the mind from which modern law students emerge. By that I do not mean primarily their formal educational culture, but rather their entire way of thinking while growing up in the *western* world. Nor can we limit ourselves to any present generation, but must consider the residue of literally centuries of thought about material relations among human beings.

No, I do not intend to pin the responsibility for these blind spots on Adam Smith or the later utilitarians, although the similarity between utilitarian models and discrete contract law principles is hardly coincidental. Smith and his countless successors, of both the scholarly and the larger world, have merely been travelers along a road on which Thomas Hobbes set the most prominent signpost.

It is Hobbes's atomistic and entirely selfish individual who not only yields, but absolutely requires, the concept of discrete contract, whether in economic modeling, or law, or in the wider world. The Hobbesian man is bound together with other humans solely be the force of Leviathan. Nothing in the constitution of that selfish atom even permits, much less requires, him to have relations, material or otherwise, with other humans transcending himself. He can—and does—have intercourse with them as long as it is to his selfish advantage as viewed at any given instant or as long as Leviathan compels him so to do. He cannot however have relations constituting anything more than a series of discrete transactions terminable at any time he can and desires to terminate them. Relations transcending terminable series of discrete transactions always entail a concept of individual sacrifice. Such a concept is necessarily unknown to Hobbesian man.

The fact is that no one ever actually lives as Hobbesian man is supposed to live—at least not for very long. Humans are not Hobbesian, but an inconsistent mixture of selfish and sacrificing, not necessarily because they want to be, but because they have to be. They have to be not just because of the exigencies of any given relation, but because of both their biological and cultural nature. We have evolved biologically for many millions of years as social, not solitary, animals. Moreover, as we so evolved we have saddled ourselves increasingly with cultural artifacts ranging from thought and language to the immense residue of physical and psychological capital of the most advanced of modern technology. All of these cultural artifacts force us to remain sacrificing creatures in achieving selfish goals. They are impressed indeliby on our psyches, possibly even on our genes. The most brutish societies remain societies, and their most brutish members remain social animals.

Now, just as we do not live as Hobbesians, but only as half-Hobbesians, we are equally schizophrenic in our thinking patterns, sometimes thinking like Hobbesians, and sometimes not. Many, if not most, of the law students I have seen are far from pure Hobbesians when they think about people hurt in automobile accidents or health care or welfare law or civil rights or consumer protection. In other words, like the working theories of the modern welfare state in which they have matured, they themselves are half-Hobbesian. Nonetheless, when faced with general contract law they commonly slip into the full Hobbesian pattern of discrete thought.

We thus seem no closer than we were before in our quest for the origins of these barriers to the idea of relational contract. But I believe we are. What we see is the incapacity of the liberal mind to generalize *beyond a certain level of abstraction* in patterns other than that of Hobbesian liberalism. *Where* this barrier is located varies with individuals. A few people may be completely unable to translate their experiences of real material relations with contradictory selfishness-sacrifice into any kind of abstract legal model. Such people can escape hardly at all the discrete contract law model. Others may be perfectly able to think of the selfishness-sacrifice contradiction at the levels of abstraction we call collective bargaining relations, marriage, or corporations, but cannot do so at more abstract levels encompassing material relations of all kinds. In either case the individuals concerned have reached a barrier to thought erected by Hobbesian liberalism itself. There are undoubtedly many reasons why this barrier lies where it does in any one individual, but that it exists somewhere in most law students has certainly been my experience.

To pass the barrier, at whatever level of abstraction it appears, requires, I believe, a fundamental revision of our intellectual model for thinking about material relations among people. We must abandon our deepseated conviction that man really is at heart a selfish, nonsocial atom. We must replace it with the conviction that humans are social animals. They are deeply and eternally torn between the needs and desires of direct selfishness, on the one hand, and essential needs and desires to sacrifice, on the other. This conflict is an essential element in the maintenance of relations with others which, in turn, are essential to individual physical and psychic survival. In the very deepest sense individuals can live only through others, while in an equally deep sense others are but obstacles to their own selfish needs.

Material relations as we actually see and live them are the product of these deep conflicts. With varying degrees of selfperception we see and understand these conflicts in our everyday lives. At least we see and understand them enough so that material relations continue to exist and develop.

Our problems come when we try to translate what we see and live into abstractions. As we move from the reality of material relations towards ever greater abstractions while at the same time seeking to preserve in our thoughts the essence of those relations in the real world, we must more and more depend on our intellectual heritage, whatever it may be. The greater the abstraction, the greater the need for a theoretical foundation which fits that heritage. For example, in considering labor relations there is still enough reality to supply the foundation so that many law students can continue to use the contradictory half-Hobbesian of real life, ignoring the inadequacy of the pure Hobbesian model. But as one thinks about contracts in ever more encompassing abstract terms, as is the case with general contract law, most of reality is left behind, and all that remains for the foundation of our abstractions is our intellectual heritage. And our Hobbesian intellectual heritage provides us with only discrete models, whether in law or economics. It provides us with nothing with which to understand an abstraction like general contract principles encompassing all material relations. Only by transcending that Hobbesian heritage can one become comfortable with such abstractions and begin to understand them.

I might add that my own experience suggests that the law students best able to accept intellectually the existence of half-Hobbesian patterns of contradictory selfishness-sacrifice in real life are also best able to understand the abstract ideas of relational contract. Those who view life through very Hobbesian lenses confront the barriers to the idea of relational contract much earlier. So, too, although perhaps for somewhat different reasons, do those who insist that humans are fundamentally altruistic selfsacrificers, if only existing human institutions did not keep them from their true nature.

I have focused my talk today on first year law students, particularly American first year law students. But given my conclusion, they are merely a metaphor for all who are raised in or seriously affected by western culture. Hobbesian atomism affects the fundamental theoretical thinking of us all. In one sense, it always will, because Hobbes was half right: each of us *is* a selfish atom. But he was also half wrong, because each of us is also an animal with deep needs constantly to sacrifice selfish desires in achieving the relations upon which our entire lives depend.

In sum, in our workaday lives all of us behave as half-Hobbesians, and all of us who think about it honestly know that that is how we behave. But when we reach for abstractions for our behaviour, and largely abandon its real texts, the exclamation points of the discrete transaction tend to loom larger and larger. In part this is because discreteness is a very real aspect of material relations, and in part it is because discreteness has dominated abstract thinking in western culture for many hundreds of years.

I do not suppose that at a university which has been the home of both Hegel and Max Weber it is necessary to explain what these barriers to the idea of relational contract have to do with arbitration of long term contracts, a major subject of this conference. Nonetheless, let me briefly suggest some specific connections.

First, the very existence of arbitration as a substitute for sole reliance on Leviathan's laws and remedies is a practical recognition of the relational nature of contract.

Secondly, this practical recognition itself may have only very limited effect in enabling people to comprehend the idea of relational contract. Indeed, I am quite sure that it is perfectly possible to live a lifetime working successfully with arbitration without ever transferring such practical recognition to the realms of abstract ideas, like those of general contract law.

Thirdly, grasping the idea of contractual relations permits those who think about contracts, including arbitration in contracts, fully to accept their inevitable inconsistencies. We always accept those inconsistencies as a practical matter; the idea of contractual relations permits us to accept them as philosophically proper. It is true that this yields only limited peace of mind. After all, the idea of relational contracts is founded only on a tension, the tension between those two contradictory halves of the half-Hobbesian human. Tension it starts, and tension it remains. But the idea of relational contract has the virtue and comfort of being closer to the truth of reality than is the alternative distorted half-truth of the discrete contract idea.

Fourthly, and finally, because the idea of contractual relations is closer to the truth of reality, its recognition provides those thinking about or doing arbitration with a more useful abstract base to help guide them in practical activities.

Many reasons exist for the nondevelopment of relational contract law; only one is explored here: barriers to the very idea of contractual relations. One barrier is conscious rejection of the idea. Reasons for rejection range from arguments that the cost of developing a general relational contract law exceeds the benefits, to the protection of narrow vested professional interests, to the highest of political or ideological goals.

A second reason for nonacceptance of the very idea of contractual relations in law is an incapacity to understand the idea, a common phenomenon. This phenomenon seems a strange one. Those who cannot understand the idea nonetheless perfectly well understand the nondiscrete as well as the discrete aspects of the material relations in which they personally are involved. Moreover, most of them can understand in quite abstract terms the nature of many particular kinds of complex material relations which they observe all around them. Their difficulty comes as they begin to approach the idea of contractual relations as an abstraction pertinent to all kinds of material relations.

The source of this lack of understanding lies in the necessity of relying increasingly on one's cultural intellectual heritage as social abstraction increases and one's real life experience thereby becomes increasingly remote. The cultural heritage brought to bear in western and western-influenced societies is that of Hobbesian atomism.

The sole contract-type Hobbesian atomism permits is the discrete transaction. Hence, in order to think about the idea of relational contract, it is necessary to transcend Hobbesian thinking. It is necessary to recognize that humans are always contradictorily selfish and sacrificing at the same time. They are selfish because of their biology. They are sacrificing because they are social animals who *must* sacrifice to others to maintain the relations, including material relations, upon which their physical and psychological existence depends.

In terms of arbitration, its very existence is a practical recognition of relational contract. But such practical recognition requires no abandonment of Hobbesian atomism at abstract levels of thought. Nonetheless, grasping, the idea of contractual relations permits those who think about contracts, including arbitration in contracts, to accept fully their inevitable inconsistencies, not just practically, but philosophically. Moreover, because the idea of contractual relations is closer to the truth of reality, its recognition provides a more useful abstract guide for the practical activities of those doing or thinking about arbitration.

8.3 Relational Contract Theory as Sociology: A Reply to Professors Lindenberg and de Vos

Recently Professors Lindenberg and de Vos did me the honor of taking my relational contract theory seriously and analyzing it as a sociological theory (Lindenberg and de Vos 1985). Their treatment has helped me better to understand my own work, to clarify the unclear, and to develop further, I hope to improve, relational contract theory. I am indebted to them for these things. Nonetheless, their paper distorted beyond recognition relational contract theory as I have developed it. For that reason a reply is in order to explain this useful way of thinking about exchange relations.

Some of the misunderstanding which lies at the base of the distortion undoubtedly resulted from lack of clarity of expression on my part. Some undoubtedly resulted from a fundamental problem with the basic terminology. I have used in developing relational contract theory, a problem which I hope this paper will illuminate, if not solve. Some might have been avoided had Lindenberg and de Vos had in hand work which I had written but not yet published when they wrote. (Macneil 1985b; 1986)

Misunderstanding arising from such sources is hardly a reflection on Lindenberg and de Vos. But some of their misunderstanding resulted. I believe, from nonreading of and defective reading of language which really is quite clear. A great deal resulted, I believe, from the authors failure to treat the theory as a whole. This contributed, inter alia, to their confusing the basic theory itself with something quite different: my own feelings of affection for community and concern about its position in a world dominated by bureaucracy. And finally, I cannot help but think that a distaste for my ideology favoring community at the expense of what the authors call the "weak solidarity" of the Western democracies, led them too hastily to think that that ideology permeates relational contract theory, when in fact it does not. (This was in spite of my clear differentiation between relational contract theory and my own ideological applications of it in the latter of the two articles on which they based their analysis.

For the reader to understand what is at issue, it is necessary to summarize the essential elements of relational contract theory as heretofore stated.

(1)   The world encompassed by relational contract theory is the world of contract, defined as relations among people who have exchanged, are exchanging, or expect to be exchanging in the future.

(2)   All exchange occurs in relations.

(3)   A number of categories of behavior are required for such relations to exist, two of which, maintaining reciprocity and maintaining solidarity, are first among equals. The others are using roles, planning, consenting, achieving flexibility, protecting restitution, reliance, and expectation interests, creating *and* restraining power, following accepted ways of doing things, and harmonizing the relation with its internal and external social matrix. Obviously these categories of behavior conflict in many ways, but some minimum level is required of *each* of them, else the relations will cease to exist.

(4)   The behavior patterns give rise to norms, a case of an "is" creating an "ought". The norms parallel the elements of behavior, in some cases the behavioral words being satisfactory to describe the norms as well reciprocity and solidarity, again first among equals, role integrity (requiring consistency, involving internal conflict and being inherently complex), implementation of planning, effectuation of consent, flexibility, the restitution reliance, and expectation

311

norms, the power norm justifying both creation and restraint of power, propriety of means, and harmonizing the relation with the internal and external social matrix.

(5) Underlying this structure in my view, but not essential for most of the uses to which it might be put, is the proposition that

Man is both an entirely selfish and an entirely social creature in that man puts the interests of his fellows ahead of his own interests *at the same time* that he puts his own interests first. Man being a choosing creature, is easily capable of paralysis when two conflicting desires are in equipoise. Two principles of behavior are essential to the survival of such a creature solidarity and reciprocity. Getting something back for something given neatly releases, or at least reduces, the tension in a creature desiring to be both selfish and social at the same time, and solidarity—a belief in being able to depend on another—permits the projection of reciprocity through time (Macneil 1983b, 348, rearranged).

(6) Exchange occurs in various patterns along a spectrum ranging from highly discrete to highly relational.

(7) Discrete contracts are characterized by short duration, limited personal interactions, and precise party measurements of easily measured objects of exchange. They require a minimum of future cooperation between the parties. No sharing of benefits or burdens occurs, nor is altruism expected. The parties are bound precisely and tightly. The parties view themselves as free of entangling strings. Everything is clearly defined and presentiated. If trouble is anticipated at all, it is anticipated only if someone or something turns out unexpectedly badly.

Discrete behaviour of this kind gives rise to an intensification in an exchange relation of two of the common contract norms implementation of planning and effectuation of consent. When so intensified they may usefully be labeled as the discrete norm enhancing discreteness and presentation.

Discreteness and presentation are themselves not the same phenomenon, in spite of their merger in discrete contracts. Discreteness is the separating of a transaction from all else between the participant at the same time and before and after its ideal never achieved in life occurs when there *is* nothing else between the parties, never has been and never will be Presentiation, on the other hand is the bringing of the future into the present. Underlying both is the ideal of 100 per cent planning of the future (Macneil 1980c, 60).

(8) Relational contracts.

are of significant duration (for example, franchising). Close whole person relations form an integral aspect of the relation (employment). The object of exchange typically includes both easily measured quantities (wages) and quantities not easily measured (the projection of personality by an airline stewardss). Many individuals with individual and collective poles of interest are involved in the relations (industrial relations). Future cooperative behavior is anticipated (the players and management of the Oakland Raiders). The benefits and burdens of the relation are to be shared rather than divided and allocated (a law partnership). The bindingness of the relation is limited (again a law partnership in which in theory each member is free to quit almost at will). The entangling strings of friendship, reputation, interdependence, morality, and altruistic desires are integral parts of the relation (a theatrical agent and his clients). Trouble is expected as a matter of course (a collective bargaining agreement). Family the participants never intend or expect to see the whole future of the relation as presentiated at any single time, but view the relation as an ongoing integration of behavior which will grow and vary with events in a largely unforeseeable future (a marriage; a family business) (Macneil 1974b, 595).

Just as discrete behavior gives rise to discrete norms, so too, relational behavior gives rise to relational norms. Similarly, these norms are intensifications of particular common contract norms. The norms intensified are primarily solidarity, role integrity and harmonization with the social matrix, especially the internal social matrix.

In addition, relational context affects the nature of other common contract norms. For example, flexibility in relations is at least partially an internal, rather than an entirely external norms as it is (in theory) in discrete transactions. Hence, flexibility comes into partial conflict with the planning and consent norms in ways not occurring in discrete transactions. Reciprocity also becomes an important internal matter, test the relation break down. Power also is an important internal matter in relations (Macneil 1983b, 350–351)

This then is the relational contract theory which was putatively the subject of the Lindenberg and de Vos paper. As suggested earlier, however, the foregoing exposition needs some further clarification. The careful reader will have noticed that "relational" has been used to mean two different things. It is used globally to describe all relations in which exchange occurs, and since all exchange, even the most discrete, occurs in relations, all exchange is thereby "relational". But it is also used to mean the opposite of discrete, that is exchange occurring in relatively intertwined patterns, as for example, much of the exchange in nuclear families and within corporations.

Thus the spectrum of exchange relations is ambiguously described when its poles are labeled discrete and relational. This ambiguity may have some bad effects, even apart from simple confusion. It may, for example, contribute to the erroneous, but extremely common, belief that discrete transactions can and do occur free of relations. For that reason, I propose from hereon to describe the poles of this spectrum of exchange relations as discrete at one end and intertwined at the other. Both, of course, are always relative terms; just as seemingly discrete transactions are in fact parts of relations, and hence intertwined, so too, elements of discreteness penetrate all human relations.

Stripping out this ambiguity also helps show the dual elements of relational contract theory as thus far developed. First, is the description of behavior and norms which I believe to be universal in exchange relations. Secondly, is the dimension of discreteness, from discrete to intertwined. Of the two, the first is more fundamental in the sense that the second makes no sense without it.

Relational contract theory is not intended, as I have elsewhere tried to make plain, (Macneil 1983b, 343) to be a complete theory of human relations, an impossibility in any event. Moreover, that only one analytical dimension is added to the common behavior and norms, vital though it may be to understanding contractual relations, makes this even plainer. It also suggests that the theory might be made into an even richer classificatory apparatus by considering the complexity of some of the behavioral and normative elements. Lindenberg and de Vos, for example, center much of their discussion on two kinds of solidarity, arising from Gemeinschaft and Gesellschaft, a distinction I have always instinctively made and often dealt with, but in limited ways and under different labels. It strikes me that they too may represent ends of a spectrum of solidarity. And are they, spectrum or no, as fundamental within the idea of solidarity or trust, as solidarity itself is to all exchange relations?

Even within the single dimension of discreteness-intertwining there are different kinds and sources of discreteness. The kind I have most commonly looked at is the discrete transaction, the discrete exchange. But precise bureaucratic rules (if expected to be followed) introduce discreteness and presentiation into relations too, yet are not themselves discrete exchanges. And obviously their effects on the relations are different in a great many ways from discrete exchanges. Similarly, there are different kinds of intertwining with differing consequences for the relations in which they occur. Consider, for example, the differences between the intertwining in nuclear families and those in large corporations, at least in the formal kinds of corporate intertwining.

Moreover, it should be evident that the discrete-intertwined spectrum may have many strands in a given relation and the location of each strand on the spectrum may differ from the others. Some may be highly discrete, *e.g.* the hourly wage rates for different kinds of jobs in a collective bargaining agreement, while others in the same relation may be highly intertwined, *e.g.* the personal relations between foremen and workers.

Other aspects also remain largely undeveloped. One is the comprehensiveness of relations. For example, a person who has a live-in housekeeper, a partner in running a shop, and a lover, is likely to have a thinner or less comprehensive relation with each of the three than that of a person whose lover keeps house for them both and is a partner in running the shop. To a degree this parallels the spectrum of discreteness and intertwining, but that spectrum seems inadequate to deal with all of the factors of comprehensiveness.

The same seems to be true respecting another aspect, tightness and looseness of the relation. It is possible to have a great deal of relational tightness in exchange relations also maintaining high levels of relative discreteness, as anyone knows who has been in a highly disciplined bureaucratic organization. Such relations may also be comprehensive in the sense of being all-encompassing of the participants; a military outfit is a good example of this as well as of tightness. But relations may also be relatively noncomprehensive, or thin, as in the case of a close knit, but only once monthly, poker group who seldom see each other on other occasions.

The relation between these other dimensions, which I have yet to develop beyond the above discussion, and the discreteness-intertwined spectrum is too complex to explore further here.

In spite of terminological changes and my belated recognition of other spectra, the discrete-intertwined (relational) spectrum remains the most fundamental adjunct to relational contract theory. It captures much of what I believe to be essential differences between contractual relations. Moreover, it focuses on the primary blind spot in our thinking about contractual relations, a product of our. Hobbesian–utilitarian assumption of man-the-atom, which equates the idea of contract with the discrete transaction.

It may be seen from the above that I view relational contract theory as far from complete, and certainly subject to correction, modification, and change. With this background we can now turn to particular points made by Lindenberg and de Vos.

Lindenberg and de Vos start from exactly the same point that I do, social relations matter. It is, therefore, apparently unnecessary to defend against them my position that the relations in which exchange occurs must be the starting point for understanding exchange. Nor, evidently, need I defend my further view that exchange relations cannot be understood without understanding standing exchange. This is not, however, exactly how they describe the work of Selznick (1969), Hirschman (1970), Hirsch (1978), and White (1983), the group with which they align me. Rather they refer to emphasizing "conditions of exchange, such as norms, status, role etc." Undoubtedly those who are concerned with seeing exchange whole, *i.e.* as an integral aspect of relations, rather than as isolated, emphasize these things. They are, after all fighting a desperate battle against mighty intellectual and other forces favoring analysis based on isolated exchange. But emphasizing them is not the same as slighting exchange itself, which Lindenberg and de Vos suggest by the following statement.

> Durkheim's statement that there is more to contract than exchange, *viz.* the relational aspects, promised that exchange would be studied in the context of relational aspects. *But this did not happen.* Instead, relational aspects and exchange became each the subject of a different discipline (Lindenberg and de Vos 1985, 559 note 2, emphasis added).

They may be correct generally as to the two disciplines, but my own work, which originates in the intellectual discipline of neither sociology nor economics, but of law, certainly belies the implication that the study of exchange "in the context of relational aspects" has not happened. Relational contract theory is full of the study of exchange, albeit not done as "social science". Failure to recognize this is one source of Lindenberg and de Vos's misunderstanding of the theory they were criticizing.

A second source of that misunderstanding is the manner in which Lindenberg and de Vos equated the transactional (discrete) pole of contractual relations with Tönnies's Gesellschaft, and the relational (nondiscrete or intertwined) pole with his Gemeinschaft. It is perfectly correct that what I labeled the "extreme relational pole" in the chart at the end of Macneil (1978b) fits quite neatly, the idea of Gemeinschaft, although I was largely ignorant of Tonnies for many years after I first prepared that chart for Macneil (1974a). It is also true that the "extreme transactional pole" fits very well *part* of *some kinds* of Gesellschaft relations as Tönnies described them. The *part* of the relations it fits is, of course, very discrete transactions embedded in relations. Examples include many kinds of markets and the social, political, and legal institutions supporting them. A major function of the other parts of such relations is precisely to allow and foster discreteness in transactions as long as they remain within their appointed limits. The *kind* of relation is the one just described, those designed to permit discrete transactions to occur. It is one kind of Gesellschaft relation.

The problem is that the "extreme relational [intertwined] pole" in the chart does not describe most modern contractual relations, except some intimate ones. I did, however, develop this point very explicitly in Macneil (1980c, pp. 20–35), which Lindenberg and de Vos did not use in their analysis of my work. Moreover, it is also quite apparent from the first of the articles they did use, the very one in which the chart appears, Macneil (1978b) 887:

> ... presentation will always occur in economic relations, since it tends to follow planning as a matter of course. Nor does a modern technological economy permit the demise of discreteness. Very specialized products and services, the hallmark of such an economy, produce a high degree of discreteness of behavior, even though their production and use are closely integrated into ongoing relations. When for example, an automobile manufacturer orders from another manufacturer with which it regularly deals,

thousands of piston rings of a specified size, no amount of relational softening of discreteness and presentation will obscure the disaster occurring if the wrong size shows up on the auto assembly line. Nor would the disaster be any less if the failure had occurred in an even more relational pattern, *e.g.* if the rings had been ordered from another division of the auto manufacturer. Both discreteness and presentation must be served in such an economic process, whether it is carried out between firms by discrete separate orders, between firms under long-established blanket contracts, or within the firm.

Lindenberg and de Vos state my "thesis" (incorrectly) in this manner:

The similarity with Tönnies's polar types is uncanny, but the conclusions of the two authors are quite opposite. Tönnies saw a development from *Gemeinschaft* (relational) to *Gesellschaft* (transactional) with a possible blending of the two in the future. "*Macneil sees a progression from the transactional to the relational pole since the late 19th century*" (Lindenberg and de vos 1985, 561, emphasis of last sentence added.)

The correct statement of my "thesis" on this particular point is:

Macneil sees a progression from *law* reinforcing discrete transactions as such to *law* reinforcing and regulating modern contractual relations, including their high levels of discreteness, since the late 19th century.

That the *law* has so moved seems beyond dispute I shall not try to justify this statement to any doubters, but simply refer them to my earlier work which has explored these matters extensively.

It should be noted that neither above, nor anywhere else that I recall, have I said that the progress of the law of contractual relations of any kind has been in the direction of *less* total discreteness. This is important to mention because of Lindenberg and de Vos's focus on marriage and the family. As Glendon points out brilliantly in an inadequately recognized book (Glendon 1981), the law of marriage and family relations has moved towards discreteness. At the same time that the law of discrete transactions has gone into a considerable eclipse, the law of contractual relations has in many ways come to reflect the discreteness embedded in modern contractual relations. Once again Lindenberg and de Vos's error comes from ignoring that marriage and family are always highly intertwined relations, and the differences which have occurred in them and in their law the last hundred years, while adding much discreteness, has not turned them into extremely discrete transactions.

My thesis does not describe a change from Gesellschaft to Gemeinschaft as asserted by Lindenberg and de Vos, indeed, I do not believe that the positive law of a modern sovereign could ever be anything except the former. Rather it reflects a change in the forms of Gesellschaft. The older starting point was law favoring the calculating rationality of people within relations created heavily by property and individual rights, law which was aimed at centering everything on the discrete transaction, Gesellschaft. The "progress" is towards law reinforcing the calculating rationality of people within relations with high levels of discreteness of various kinds, including discrete transactions, but always treating the discreteness as an integral part of the relations subject to considerable regulation, again Gesellschaft. But how can discreteness exist as an integral part of relations? There's the rub. But the rub lies not in an incorrect description; it lies in the internal disharmony of human beings and the inherent conflict of such relations.

Since my thesis is that of a move from one type of Gesellschaft to another, and not from Gesellschaft to Gemeinschaft, many of Lindenberg and de Vos's criticisms of relational contract theory, and of my motivations in developing it, simply become irrelevant respecting both, although still inaccurate respecting my views. Two, however, do not become irrelevant, and require further exploration.

The first of these concerns the fifth of the essential elements of relational contract theory mentioned early in this paper, the proposition that the contradictory selfish-sacrificing nature of humans requires both reciprocity and solidarity for survival. Lindenberg and de Vos interpret the effect of this on relational contract theory in the following manner.

> Seen this way, the quest for solidarity and reciprocity is plain human nature and while both are in *in nuce* present in every contractual transaction, they come truely into their own only in extended contractual relations. Thus, human nature itself pushes towards relational contracting.
>
> Macneil even went one important step further human nature is a kind of homing, device that will lead man back into the good natural state. Relational contracts form a sprawling network of

319

solidary minisocieties each operating according to norms it has generated itself [citations]. In short, solidarity is then ubiquitous and not precarious. Neither political institutions nor the factual distributions of goods would need to be looked at on that account (Lindenberg and de Vos 1985, 564–565).

It is hard to know where to start with this. In my view human nature most certainly does push towards relational contracting, because extremely discrete transactions between real strangers are of extremely limited value. They become both much more useful and much more relational. *i.e.* intertwined parts of relations, when they occur embedded in extensive contractual relations. Examples of the latter are the seemingly discrete transactions in 19th century markets, which were in fact embeded in *inter alia*, the contractual relations created by 19th century properly rights and classical contract law. But this reciprocal-solidary human nature most certainly does not lead to the good natural state"—meaning Gemeinschaft. If it did we would never have left that state. Relational contracts do "form a sprawling network of solidary minisocieties each operating (partly) according to norms it has generated itself". That does not mean, however, that "solidarity is then ubiquitous and not precarious". It means that solidarity is ubiquitous so long as those relations are continuing. It, is however, just as precarious as the relations themselves, and no one in their right mind would say that all the myriads of contractual relations in the world are solid and safe. Indeed, in pessimistic moments one might wonder if any of them are. And this means, again *pace* Lindenberg and de Vos, that "political institutions and factual distributions" must, of course, "be looked at on that account."

The second Lindenberg and de Vos criticism requiring exploration is their purported application of relational contract theory to marriage, taking the example of traditional Polish marriages and marriages among Polish immigrants to the United States, citing as their source of information (Thomas and Znaniecki 1958).

Marriage in the traditional Polish village constituted a social unit and conflict, within it was seen as a disruption of the local community the solidarity of which had to be restored. In the United States, marriage was seen as a union and in case of conflict the marriage partners were taken to be adversaries each pursuing his/her own happiness rather than the smoother functioning of the community. In Macneil's terms, the traditional Polish marriage was at the far relational end, while the American marriage was close to the transactional pole. Yet, one could also say that in the traditional Polish case couples were simply forced to suffer the consequences of a partly fictitious initial agreement (never to part again) while the American marriage considered the relationship as it had developed up to the point of conflict. Seen this way, the Polish case is transactional, and the American is relational. Depending on the interpretation of the Polish and American marriage, one can turn Macneil's thesis right side up or upside down. The actual observed historical development cannot help us decide what is right side up and what is upside down (Lindenberg and de Vos 1985, 562–563).

If this were an accurate application of relational contract theory it would be a very damaging criticism indeed, but if is not.

First, Lindenberg and de Vos err in suggesting that "American marriage was close to the transactional pole". Marriage, even in its most discrete forms, is never a relation close to the discrete (transactional) pole, as a casual reference to the characteristics of the two poles set out above will demonstrate. And marriage among Polish-Americans in 1918 (the date of the study cited) was certainly not, compared to much of what we have today, a very discrete form of marriage. The proper question is whether the differences described in these two types of relations— traditional Polish marriage and 1918 Polish American marriage—each heavily intertwined (relational), show a move from lesser to greater discreteness, or whether one can, as Lindenberg and de Vos assert, analyze the shift as being in either direction.

A rundown of characteristics of the "extreme relational pole" in the chart in MACNEIL [1978b], pp. 902–905, from which Lindenberg and de Vos drew their information, readily answers this question. Six of the twelve characteristics come into play in differentially significant ways. All six point to the Polish. American marriage's being more discrete than the traditional Polish marriage.

Measurability and actual measure of exchange and other factors. Because divorce is more feasible, there is a potential for measurement, *e.g.* alimony, child support, division of property, not present in the traditional Polish marriage. This becomes an actuality where divorce happens.

Duration. The Polish-American marriage might terminate by divorce as well as by death, hence possibly earlier than the traditional Polish marriage, a discrete characteristic.

321

Commencement and termination. Here we must consider that the traditional Polish marriage was more of an extension of existing community relations than was the Polish-American. In a very real sense the participants were born into those community relations and marriage was simply an entry into a new phase of the community relations. Commencement by birth is a relational (intertwined) characteristic, as entry, no matter how sharp, into an existing relation is by nature more intertwined than is starting a relation more or less sharply (as in the case of a blind date which develops into a longer term relation). Moreover, termination only by death is a relational (intertwined) manner of terminating relations, whereas the possibility of termination relatively sharply by divorce in the Polish-American marriage is a discrete characteristic, even apart from its effect on duration.

Incidents of benefits and burdens. Sharing of benefits and burdens rather than their division and allocation was more limited in the Polish-American marriage to the extent that a divorce, not possible in the traditional Polish marriage, would typically have the latter (discrete) effect, as, for example, custody and care of children.

Number of participants. As described by Lindenberg and de Vos, the Polish-American marriage was far closer to a two-party matter than was the traditional Polish marriage, where the whole community was much more a part of the relation. Large numbers of participants is an intertwining (relational) characteristic.

Participant views of the transaction or relation. Because both the traditional Polish and the Polish-American marriage are such intertwined relations, only one of the four (out of many possible) participant views of the relation set out in Macneil [1978b] is both especially pertinent and not already dealt with indirectly by discussion of the other characteristics. That concerns expectations about trouble. In both types of marriage the possibility of trouble was undoubtedly anticipated as a normal part of the relation and expected to be dealt with by cooperation and other restorational (often very coercive) techniques. But the Polish-American marriage introduced the expectation that trouble would be governed more by specific rights, those created by domestic relations law, than by the less specific community ways of dealing with marital trouble. This again is a discrete characteristic. In sum, in these two heavily intertwined relations, all factors of increased discreteness lie in the Polish-American relation.

Another way to approach the relative discreteness of these two kinds of marriages is in terms of the intertwining (relational) norms. These are mainly intensified solidarity, role integrity, and harmonization with the social matrix, especially the internal social matrix. The first two need little explanation. The solidarity of the traditional Polish marriage was clearly the greater of the two, since it was expected to, and tended to, continue under conditions much more unsatisfactory to the spouses than was the case with the Polish-American marriage. Similarly, the role integrity required in the former was that of "lifelong spouse", whereas in the latter it was that of "probably, but maybe not, lifelong spouse". Both are heavily intertwining norms, but the former more so.

Turning to harmonization with the social matrix, the more intertwined a contractual relation is the more it requires that such harmonization be active, as distinct from passive. Polish-American marriages, as described by Thomas and Znaniecki (1958) were clearly less actively intertwined with either the larger family or the community outside the family than were traditional Polish marriages.

Thus, whether one focuses on behavior or on norms or on both there simply can be no question that a careful look at relational contract theory shows the traditional Polish marriage to be farther from the discrete pole of contractual relations than is the Polish-American marriage.

We must nonetheless explore further a number of points Lindenberg and de Vos make arising out of the following sentence. "Relational contract law looks at the entire relation as it had developed up to the point in question". (Lindenberg and de Vos 1985, 562). From that they go on to say that in traditional Polish marriage.

> Couples were simply forced to suffer the consequences of a partly fictitious initial agreement (never to part again) while the American marriage considered the relationship as it had developed up to the point of conflict. Seen this way, the Polish case is transactional, and the American is relational.

Taken literally the final sentence is simply wrong. As already noted, neither of these marriage types is transactional (discrete), both are highly intertwined relations. Thus, to avoid being quite senseless this sentence must be read to mean that the traditional Polish marriage, while a highly intertwined relation, is more discrete than the Polish-American one. In the view of Lindenberg and de Vos this is because people and institution (including legal) involved with Polish-American marriages paid more attention to the way the relation had developed and less to the original consent. But that too is incorrect. Both sets of participants and communities looked at relations as they had developed up to the point of conflict. The difference was that one set of people and communities, the Polish-American, saw a change, and the other, the traditional Polish, did not. Because of their belief in lifelong marriage, traditional Polish participants and communities saw a relationship which *had not* fundamentally changed in spite of the conflict. Because of their different beliefs the Polish-American participants and communities saw a relationship which *had* fundamentally changed because of the conflicts. Thus it was the nature of the relationship, rather than the role of consent which made the difference, one, the traditional Polish, being more rigid and durable than the other. And it could afford to be, because the community interests and support made the marriage relation better able to endure, however unpleasantly, in spite of the conflicts. In the absence of such community interests and support similar conflicts would destroy a Polish-American marriage.

Consent, however, did establish both relationships, and in the traditional Polish marriage consent had a more powerful, lasting effect. Does this make the traditional Polish marriage more discrete as Lindenberg and de Vos suggest? The answer is no. Lindenberg and de Vos confuse the importance of the relation with the role of consent in establishing it. Obviously entering the traditional Polish marriage was making a greater commitment than was entering a Polish-American marriage. But that does not make the traditional marriage less relational (intertwined) than the American one. The more intertwined the relation triggered by consent, the more intertwined is the role of the consent, not the opposite as suggested by Lindenberg and de Vos.

Moreover, the consent to both kinds of marriage was, at most, but a trigger, not something that shaped the relation. *Both* the lifelong permanence of the traditional Polish marriages and the lesser permanence of the Polish-American marriages came from the communities in which they occurred, not from variations in the terms of consent. Both were on that score what we might now call contracts of adhesion, although the "standard terms" were supplied by the community rather than by one of the immediate parties. Thus, even if one takes the—to my mind somewhat perverse—view that consent to a less discrete relation is somehow more discrete than consent to a more discrete relation, that increase in discreteness must be weighed against all the other countervailing, less discrete facets. Such a weighing still leaves the Polish-American marriage markedly closer to the discrete pole (albeit still a heavily intertwined relation) than was the traditional Polish marriage.

324

Conclusion

Lindenberg and de Vos misunderstood the nature of relational contract theory, and hence inaccurately attributed to it a Gemeinschaft character. Whether they would consider it of interest as a sociological theory without that character I do not know. Their misunderstanding also led to their misapplication of the theory, and to the finding of faults in it which do not exist. What faults they might find in it properly understood again I do not know.

8.5 Contracting Worlds and Essential Contract Theory

Privatization runs rampant, sweeping even the most traditionally "sovereign" governmental functions into "private" hands. "Free markets" conquer the globe, along with globalization of "private" financial and corporate institutions under the domination of which the "free markets" operate. These "private" institutions are delocalized, being almost totally mobile. Many dwarf half the "sovereign" countries of the world. By their power over money, information and communication they can and do manipulate and control even the largest of "sovereigns". To whatever degree the "sovereigns" are democratic, democracy itself is thereby eroded. (Much "sovereign law" is, of course, already created by highly undemocratic bodies like central banks, WTO, IMF and the EU bureaucracy.)

For these dominant "private" institutions, the only measure of success is the "bottom line" of net gain stated in money. To whatever extent they dominate, Carlyle's cash nexus has taken over the universe. In a world where consumption has become the main human preoccupation of virtually religious intensity, this means that the "private" institutions have taken over "more and more social activities—all dominated, of course, by the cash nexus. Although much is in a state of flux due, *inter alia*, to constantly changing technology, in particular the Internet, the basic continuing trend towards worldwide dominance by "private" institutions remains largely unchallenged. (For a pithy summary in the context of WTO and the Seattle riots and including the role of non-government organizations such as Red Cross, Amnesty International and countless others, see Byers, (2000).

Gunther Teubner (2000) founds his article essentially on this scenario; so shall I found my comments.

Essential Contract Theory

ESSENTIAL CONTRACT THEORY DESCRIBED

The world socioeconomy constitutes a monstrously large and complex ongoing relational contract (Macneil 1990). (In my writing, "contract", unless limited in some way, always means relations among people who have exchanged, are exchanging, or expect to be exchanging in the future, *i.e.* exchange relations.) Any worthy relational contract theory should therefore be useful in examining it. In fact the world socioeconomy offers an ideal subject for examination through the lens of essential contract theory.

Essential contract theory is the label that I have recently adopted to differentiate my own particular relational contract theory from others (*cf.* Macneil 2000c). I adopted this label for two reasons. First, I believe that the theory captures the essential elements of exchange relations. Secondly, I believe that analysis of this general kind is essential to full understanding of any contract.

Although the label is new, the initial form of essential contract theory was presented to academia a quarter of a century ago in Macneil (1974a), with supplementation in the following decade in Macneil (1980c) and Macneil (1983b).

Essential contract theory postulates the existence of 10 common contract behavioural patterns and norms in all contracts, however large or small:

1. role integrity (requiring consistency, involving internal conflict and being inherently complex)

2. reciprocity (simply stated as the principle of getting something back for something given)

3. implementation of planning

4. effectuation of consent

5. flexibility

6. contractual solidarity

7. the restitution, reliance, and expectation interests (the "linking norms")

8. creation and restraint of power (the "power norm")

9. propriety of means: the ways relations are carried on as distinct from more substantive matters, including not merely formal and informal procedures, but such things as customary behaviour, often of the most subtle kind

10. harmonization with the social matrix.

ESSENTIAL CONTRACT THEORY AND CONFLICT

This model of analysis is rife with recognition of the conflicts existing in all exchange relations. Conflict is recognized both within and among the 10 common patterns. *Within* the categories, for example, conflict is explicit in the statements of both role integrity and power. So, too, reciprocity is inherently full of conflict (Macneil 1986). *Among* the categories, for example, implementation of planning and effectuation of consent commonly conflict with flexibility; propriety of means acts as an actual and potential restraint on all the others. So, too, harmonization with the social matrix involves actual and potential restraint on all the others.

TEUBNER'S DISTORTIONS OF ESSENTIAL CONTRACT THEORY

With breathtaking disregard of everything I have written, Teubner has distorted this conflict-laden analytical model of contractual relations into the "usual communitarian sense of the word [relational] as a nice and warm cooperative relation between human beings". Having thus completely misrepresented essential contract theory, Teubner goes on to make statements such as the following, as if they had something to do with essential contract theory:

> [R]elational contract creates a wrong juxtaposition between an economic and a sociological interpretation of contract where economics stands for self-interest, rational choice, market exchange and sociology for solidarity, cooperation, community.

327

Since nothing in essential contract theory distinguishes between the intellectual constructs of economics and sociology, it cannot possibly create a "wrong juxtaposition" of this kind. (In my view, economics is simply one aspect of sociology; Macneil 2000b.)

> Like hard cases that make bad law, communitarian engagements make bad sociology.

Very often, but this has nothing to do with essential contract theory since it is not communitarian.

> Relational contracting expresses indeed the romantic yearning for a mediaeval unity of the *buon governo* ...

This is total nonsense in so far as essential contract theory is concerned.

> It is a fatal error to understand the social embeddedness of modern contract simply as communal cooperation and solidarity ... An adequate concept of relational contracting can no longer take recourse to communal norms which unites Concordia with Justitia, ... Relational contracting is out of step with today's reality *if* it is understood as the warm, human, cooperative interpersonal relation which overcomes the cold economic instrumentalism with a communitarian orientation, as market transactionalism with a human face. (emphasis added)

Certainly, and essential contract theory does none of these things.

> Social embeddedness today is not protection by a coherent community but the exposure of contract to a fractured and contradictory multiplicity of highly developed social rationalities. Sociology's legitimate role today is not the academic pursuit of the noble ideal of solidarity, rather the epistemology of many different social practices, ... An adequate concept of relational contracting ... needs to take into account the different colliding epistemes that exist in one society. Therefore, relational does not mean only to relate contract to the requirements of cooperation, adaptation and good faith, but to the often conflictual requirements of different fields of action that are bound together by the institution of contract ... Instead of dreaming of contract as a cooperative

exchange relation between human actors, we should face its reality as a conflictual relation . . .

Indeed, and essential contract theory recognizes and takes all this into account.

Essential Contract Theory and Teubner's Concerns

TEUBNER'S CONCERNS

Teubner's concerns with the worldwide scenario appear to be summarized by his solution:

> Contemporary private law must see one of its main tasks in the protection of the many private autonomies, not only against the repressive state but also against the expansionist tendencies of technology, science and the market. Spheres of individual freedom and dignity, the realm of self-realization of the individual, the discourses of research, art, education, media communication, even the sphere of politics itself need to [be] protected against the monopolization of translation by the expansionist economic and technological discourses.

Earlier Teubner referred to the urgent need for "private law" to get "rid of th[e] monopoly of economic calculation and *get in direct contact with the many other social subsystems* in society that have different criteria of rationality than the economic discourse" (emphasis added). (These "subsystems" are presumably the "private autonomies" and "spheres" referred to in the preceding quotation.)

APPLYING ESSENTIAL CONTRACT THEORY

Analysis of the many "social subsystems" of any contractual relation is, of course, precisely one of key functions of essential contract theory. Each of its 10 elements applies to whatever social subsystems—economic or otherwise—are present in the contractual relation under analysis. Each element, properly used, helps the analyser to "get in direct contact" with all those social subsystems. It also, *pace* Teubner (see below), enables the analyser to move among those interpenetrating social subsystems.

Such analysis may or may not suggest that sovereign law also should get in "direct contact" with some or all of the various social subsystems. For example, a particular employment pattern may involve class, racial, ethnic, gender and experiential social subsystems. The latter might include, for example, military experience, club memberships and old school ties. In harmonizing the employment relation with the norms of a larger society, essential contract theory analysis might suggest the desirability of the law getting in "direct contact" with racial, ethnic, gender and some experiential subsystems, say allowing veterans" preferences. At the same time it might suggest that subsystems of class, club memberships and old school ties need to be approached in other ways than direct legal contact.

TEUBNER AND TOTALLY INDEPENDENT SOCIAL WORLDS

Teubner, however, would almost certainly object to this approach because of his belief in the incompatability and total independence of various social systems. He postulates that one contract is really "at least three projects in different social worlds: (1) a productive agreement; (2) an economic transaction; and (3) a legal promise". He then goes on to say that these

> three diverse projects are not just the result of applying simultaneously competing contract theories from different academic disciplines. Nor are these projects just three different aspects of one and same contractual relation viewed from a [sic] different analytical perspectives. *Rather these are empirical observations about three existing independent projects each participating in a different social dynamic that is operatively closed to others.* (emphasis added)

Certainly, every contract involves "projects" in many "social worlds" including the many "private autonomies" and "spheres" which Teubner enumerates. Indeed one of my most important goals in developing essential contract theory was to keep that fact ever in view. (Teubner's three barely touch the surface.) Certainly, "projects" in different social worlds regularly conflict with each other. (Each social world, however it may be delimited, also regularly conflicts internally.)

There, however, our agreement ceases. That each of Teubner's "projects" is operating independently in a social dynamic so different that it is operatively closed to each of the others is a totally unrealistic view of human interaction. All these social worlds interpenetrate each other. Any assertion that they do not is simply an attempt to carve into pieces real human psyches and interactions to satisfy some agenda of the carver. (In Teubner's case the agenda appears to be the playing of intellectual-linguistic games through the *total* reification of texts as objects entirely apart from human interaction.) Thus, Teubner's last sentence is utter nonsense in so far as it purports to deal with anything to be found in real life. Given the claim to empiricism, it can hardly be justified even as a purely intellectual game.

Essential Contract Theory and Teubner's Solution

Teubner's solution to the concerns that both he and I have about the world socioeconomy is the establishment of constitutional rights for what he calls "freedom of discourses" among the various spheres. Teubner reached his solution through routes involving complete reification of texts, creation of artificial reified intellectual constructs such as water-tight, non-interactive social systems, and focus on discourses rather than on human relations.

In contrast, approaching the problem from the standpoint of essential contract theory, the very first thing that would come to mind is the eighth factor: the creation and restraint of power. Above all else what we are witnessing is a massive power game, and it is being won by the "private" institutions.

In these circumstances, what does it mean to argue in favour of "externally imposed legal-political restrictions on the self-destructive tendencies of expansive social systems"? The would-be external imposers are the self-same "sovereigns" whose powers are being systematically eroded in favour of those "expansive social systems"—the "private" institutions winning ever-increased power in what Teubner characterizes as a catastrophe. Yet Teubner says casually that the "privatization strategies of neoliberal political parties and governments" may be "easily redressed by social democratic governments". Oh? Where do we find such governments these days? Are we likely to see them again? Those key questions would be evoked by application of essential contract theory, but remain unasked by Teubner.

331

Teubner characterizes the situation as "*post*-catastrophic". But it is early times yet and the catastrophe is far from complete. Many sovereigns—and not just in leading western countries—whether national or international like the EU, retain immense regulatory and financial power. The welfare state is badly bloodied, but far from dead. The light of democracy may be flickering, but it is far from out in many parts of the world.

Nonetheless, unless directions change markedly, we will indeed reach a "*post*-catastrophic situation", but only when "free market" globalization is "complete". Then the "sovereigns"—nominally democratic or otherwise—will be so weakened that even the greatest will be unable to offer serious opposition to the "private" institutions. "Free markets"—the last vestige of "democratic" input—will then be at the mercy of "private" institutions to do with as they will.

True, no human institution has ever been all-powerful and completely unfettered. The "private" institutions will remain exposed to manifold and diverse pressures from their subjects. Those pressures and largely unforeseen social and technological circumstances (including genetic manipulation) will undoubtedly lead to massive changes in every aspect of life. But what they may or should be is the realm of science fiction, not of even semi-realistic current legal scholarship.

Some things are, however, quite foreseeable. The "private" institutions will have every reason not to preserve "free markets" when oligopoly and monopoly will enhance both their profits and their power. And they will use their immense powers, including "constitutional" lawmaking capacities, in whatever self-interested directions they may have.

Teubner's word-games permit him to do something the application of essential contract theory would have barred. By ignoring realpolitik power he has failed to address whether there is some hope of stopping the "catastrophe" from happening. If not, ideas like his will have no chance of blossoming, but will suffer premature death at the hands of "private" institutions unfettered by any effective "sovereign" power. His work is thus not only obscured by his analytical methods, but seems as utopian as my world of Post-Technique in The New Social Contract (Macneil 1980c, 112–17). The difference is that Post-Technique was manifestly utopian. Like Lorenzetti's *Il Buon Governo* and Teubner's "solution" it represents an ideal—a yearning—not social reality.

Chapter 9

Comments on Pedagogy in the Light of the Relational Theory

9.1. "The Master of Arts in Law" (Macneil 1965, 424–427)

9.2. "Whither Contracts?" (Macneil 1969b)

9.3. *Contracts: Instruments for Social Co-operation* (Macneil 1968e, 1–4)

9.4. *Contracts: Instruments for Social Co-operation* (Macneil 1968e, v–vi)

9.5. *Contracts: Exchange Transactions and Relations* (Macneil 1978b, xxv–xxviii)

The selections in this chapter set out Macneil's views on how the teaching of contract should be modified in the light of the criticism of the classical law and the acceptance of the relational theory. "The Master of Arts in Law" and "Whither Contracts?" are discussions about the nature of the contract syllabus. Though written over 30 years ago, their direct contemporary relevance is both striking and depressing. The "Introduction" to Macneil's first casebook and the contents pages of both of his casebooks are included to show how he went about designing such a syllabus. Secs. 3–5 of "A Primer of Contract Planning" (5.3. in this volume) is based on the second part of Macneil's second casebook and clearly sets out the organising themes of that part of these contents.

9.1   The Master of Arts in Law

The question remains, however, whether we should not start a second front. The M.A. in Law. would be awarded to students who enroll in law school for one year and who successfully complete the first-year program.

In referring to the first-year curriculum, I have in mind the fairly typical pattern: courses in contracts, criminal law, procedure, property, and torts. In addition, somewhere in that year I would expect to find something, formalized or not, involving legal bibliography and legal research. The rest of the curriculum is more likely to vary from school to school, with public or constitutional law a common item.

I   THE RELATION OF THE FIRST YEAR CURRICULUM TO THE GOALS OF EDUCATING NON-LAWYERS

A number of teachers who have been interested in legal education have with varying degrees of completeness, articulateness and indeed, poetry, formulated the goals to be achieved thereby. In listing the goals here to see how the first year curriculum achieves them, one runs the risk of being redundant, of plagiarizing, and perhaps of hurting someone's feelings. If the following succeeds in achieving all three of these evils, please be assured that it is unintended.

The goals may be divided into two kinds: (1) those which can be achieved only by the study of law, *e.g.* to develop an understanding of the function of law in the social fabric; (2) those which may also be achieved in ways other than the study of law, *e.g.* the development of a capacity for logical thinking. With respect to both kinds it is necessary, if one would justify legal education for non-lawyers, to show that the goal is a worthwhile one. With respect to the second it is also necessary to show that legal education has as much (or more) marginal utility in achieving the goal as do competing educational experiences.

A. Educational goals which can be achieved only by the study of law.

The non-lawyer can achieve an understanding of the following only by a study of law:

1.   The role of law in creating and maintaining the social order.

334

2. Law as a mechanism for preserving freedom while maintaining order.

3. Legal relations as an omnipresent aspect of social, economic and political relations.

4. The capacities and limitations of law as a social instrument.

In addition, stated negatively, only the study of law can relieve the non-lawyer of misinformation and misconceptions about the law which he has acquired. The first-year curriculum appears to be a superior instrument for achieving all of the foregoing goals.

Since achievement of an understanding of the capacities and limitations of law as a social instrument is an absolute prerequisite to the achievement of the other understanding desired, I shall consider that goal first. I suspect that the first-year curriculum has changed over the years as little as it has precisely because it has been such a superb structure for teaching professionals about the capacities and limitations of law as a social instrument. Only an exceptionally dull-witted student can be exposed to courses in procedure, torts, contracts, property, etc. without sensing that the law is not the omnipotent magician he may once have thought. Not only does he learn of specific capacities and limitations, but he sees this lack of omnipotency in such a wide variety of materials and areas that it dawns on him that the specific things the court does or does not, can or cannot, do are the very fabric of law itself.

Granted that the first year develops the needed procedure-sense and remedysense which enable the student to understand the capacities and limitations of the legal system, several questions remain. First, is such a massive dose of basic law courses required? Obviously, the answer is negative as to some gifted students. But any first-year teacher knows that this development is a slow one for most students, even with the massive attack of the first-year curriculum. As a first-year teacher I have grave doubts whether a single course could enable most graduate students to achieve the kind of insight needed. A somewhat less massive attack than the whole first year might, however, do the job for enough students to justify some curriculum modification. There are, however, dangers in such modification, as will be noted below. A second question is, does the first-year curriculum have any special advantages on this point over the second year? Or the third year? Or a potpourri of courses? Or of courses specially designed for non-law graduate students? The answer is that it has advantages over all these alternatives. In the first place, tough though the first year is, it is designed for, taught to, and aimed at beginners. If the non-law student flounders, he will see others floundering too; if he does well, he will know that he has passed the toughest hurdles we put in the way of our professional students. A second advantage is that the non-law student will be associating with students who are trying for professional purposes to gain the same understandings which he wants for collateral purposes. By the second and third year the picture has changed, and the professional students are refining and polishing these understandings while the non-law student would be struggling to achieve understanding of a much more rudimentary nature. A third advantage (over a special course for non-law students) is the association with professionals. One of the best ways to learn about a field is to work with those who are devoting their careers to it. While the professionals in question are just starting on their careers, they are already acquiring the habits and modes of thoughts characteristic of the lawyer. Simply associating with them while they acquire remedy-sense and procedure-sense should assist the non-lawyer in also acquiring those senses.

The function of the first-year curriculum in developing an under-standing of the role of law in creating and maintaining the social order hardly requires explanation. Every first-year course is a study in that subject. Even with the most moribund of teaching by rules, the student cannot help but see the law as an ordering mechanism.

The first-year curriculum less obviously, but probably equally well, shows the law as a mechanism for preserving freedom while maintaining order. The course which first comes to mind is perhaps constitutional law (where it is in the first year curriculum). But the courses in criminal law, contracts, property, procedure, and torts also demonstrate how a social mechanism can preserve a maximum amount of individual responsibility and freedom of choice and still maintain a high degree of order in a society.

The titles of the courses of the first year curriculum may not at first thought suggest that the courses will show legal relations to be an omnipresent aspect of social, economic, and political relations. It is here, however, that the case-Socratic method fills the bill. One of the great, but too often overlooked, virtues of the case method of instruction is the vast amount of factual experience thrust upon the student. A review of the cases covered in the typical first-year curriculum demonstrates a tremendous variety of human experiences, each of which became involved with the law. The student who lives these experiences vicariously through the cases can readily see that law is not a field of human experience separate from other experiences and relations. By the end of the year it should be quite plain that law is an integral part of all aspects of social, economic, and political life.

B. Additional goals which can be efficiently achieved by the study of law.

The following are additional goals which can be achieved efficiently by the study of law:

1. Developing communication skills. In the active Socratic classroom the student has the opportunity to develop his ability to communicate in the most demanding of circumstances. Not only has each active participant this opportunity, but, by empathetic response, so do other members of the class. Moot court, legal writing courses, and other such requirements also give opportunities for developing writing and speaking skills. And by no means least important, the dialogue between law students outside of class is of great value.

2. Developing an understanding of decision-making and acquiring experience in human problem-solving. Decisions are, of course, studied in college and in other graduate programs. But decision-making itself is a more difficult study because of the absence of raw materials. How many places do we find a decision being made with a contemporaneous explanation of the reasons why it was made and even how it was made? One does not have to be an ardent Realist to recognize that the appellate opinion is only a "very imperfect example of such a phenomenon. But imperfect though opinions are, a court (including, of course, an administrative 'court') is one of the rare makers of decisions which tries to give such a current explanation. The law reports are, therefore, nearly unique as a readily available window through which to examine decision-making.

Closely related to understanding decision-making is the practice in problem-solving which a student acquires through case study. If the student's interest is aroused by the facts (and that is one problem we usually do not have with first-year students) he cannot help but think about solutions, to think about how the problem might have been prevented, etc.

Further elaboration is hardly necessary. The first-year curriculum so obviously fits the bill in teaching about decision-making and problem-solving that it might be titled: A Year of Study of Decision-Making and Practice in Problem-Solving.

3. Developing an increased capacity for sustained rational thought. Some of the purposes of the case method were summarized recently as "training students to think clearly and exactly, to analyze and synthesize, to sift the relevant from the irrelevant, to beware of overgeneralizing ..." (Ritchie 1964, 179) I cannot prove it, but I suspect that nowhere else in American education can as sustained, across-the-curriculum demands for this kind of thinking be found as in the first year of law school.

4. Gaining an understanding of values. The first year curriculum helps create such an understanding in two respects. First of all it shows the social values, *e.g.* order, freedom, equality, morality, which are effected by and which affect the law. Secondly, through the vast conglomeration of human experience found in the cases, the student learns a great deal about the values of a great variety of people and organizations. In this sense, the study of law is by its very nature probably the greatest of interdisciplinary studies.

5. Developing a sense of justice. Everyone has concepts of justice whether or not he has ever heard of the law. But in law study those concepts are applied over and over again; every new case demands their exercise and tests their validity. It does not take long to learn that the abstractions conflict in actual cases and that the conflicts must be resolved, at the expense of one or more of the concepts. This process helps the student to refine his concepts, to recognize them as less than absolute, and to develop a sense of feel about them and about their utility.

9.2 Whither Contracts?

Two preliminary questions require answering before determination of the optimum content of any law school course of particular name: 1. Is there any such thing? 2. If there is, is it significant enough to future lawyers to justify spending law school time on it?

In a panel on contracts the first question is, therefore: Is there such a thing as contracts? My friends teaching such courses as Contracts 201 (Sales), Contracts 202 (Negotiable Instruments), Contracts 307 (Creditors' Rights), Contracts 312 (Labor Law), Contracts 313 (Corporations) and Contracts 319 (Trade Regulation) delight in telling me that there is no such thing as contracts. There are, they say, sales contracts, negotiable instruments, secured transactions and bankruptcy, collective bargaining agreements, insurance contracts, real estate transactions, Robinson-Patman provisions and a host of other contract-types, but contracts-in-gross there ain't. Having earlier rejected childhood beliefs in the higher abstractions of Samuel Williston's metaphysics, I almost came to believe them. But a personal vested economic interest in the existence of contracts-in-gross caused me to search further. Since you too share that vested interest you will be pleased to know that I have reached the conclusion that contracts exists.

In view of the large number of books on your desks with the unmodified word "contracts" on the spine, some of you will doubtless be inclined to think that the foregoing paragraph is an overt manifestation of the departure of its author from reality. The accuracy of that reflection I am not qualified to debate. I should warn you, however, that I do not propose to maintain that there is such a thing as contracts simply because large numbers of distinguished legal scholars have organized their work as if there is, nor even because the word "contracts" is an important organizing-indexing tool for a large amount of judicial doctrine and to a considerable extent for statutes and administrative law. To do so would raise similar doubts about my mental stability among the many who believe "that there is no such thing as a 'law of contracts' applicable to all consensual transactions, but rather a variety of transaction-types for which the courts and legislatures are developing sets of specialized rules and exceptions as the need arises."

Accepting arguendo that there is no such thing as a "law of contracts" necessitates looking to something besides the law to support a belief that there is such a thing as contracts. The only place to turn is to the human behavior which in common usage is called contractual. Upon doing this one finds that a vast variety of behavior is encompassed, from a child's purchase of a nickel candy bar to an arrangement to build an SST for the government, from a purchase of stock on a stock exchange where neither buyer nor seller ever see each other, to the continuing close relationship found between employer and employee. Is it possible to find common elements in that array of behavior, or is the ordinary use of the word "contracts" itself a generalization with no basis in behavior? Happily for our future as first year contracts teachers there are common elements in contractual behavior, in fact at least five of them.

First, every time a relationship seems properly to enjoy the label "contracts" there is, or has been, some cooperation between or among the people connected with it. While this observation distinguishes contracts from behavior like murder, solo fast driving and solitary sunbathing, it does not distinguish it from the building of dams by the Army engineers, the collection of taxes or necking in the moonlight. In short there is a great deal of behavior which would not normally be called contractual. And so, a search for other elements is necessary.

The second common element jumps to the fore, more obviously, indeed, than the first: economic exchange. While borderlines may give us trouble, whenever behavior occurs which we are sure we can call contractual there is always an element of economic exchange in it.

Before examining other elements common to contracts, it is probably desirable to examine briefly the apparent conflict between the presence of economic exchange and the notion that contractual behavior is co-operative behavior. We do, after all, think of economic exchange as being extremely individualistic and selfish, rather than cooperative. Looked at historically or anthropologically, it is readily seen that where tradition and custom dominate production and distribution of goods and services the society in question is generally less individualistic and more common in structure, operation and attitudes, than are the societies in which exchange dominates. And in our own century a decline in individualism has paralleled a decline in the significance of exchange as the dominant social mechanism, whether one looks at the modern Western welfare state in its many varieties or at frankly socialistic states. (Conversely, the relatively recent innovations in Russia and Eastern Europe which increase the use of market mechanisms have been hailed, in the Western press at least, as evidence of increasing individualism in those countries.) Moreover, our thinking on this score is also influenced by the deification of exchange by Nineteenth (and Twentieth) century laissez faire political economists, and the counter-vailing consignment of exchange to the works of the devil by Karl Marx and at least some of his successors

Easy to escape in view of the foregoing is the fact that exchange represents a species of human cooperation. In the first place it is a kind of social behavior—the true lone wolf has no one with whom to exchange goods or services. Nor, of course, can the true lone wolf participate in the specialization of labor which both causes and is caused by exchange. Moreover, exchange involves a *mutual* goal of the parties, namely, the reciprocal transfer of values. And this is true however strongly the "economic man"—the "as-much-as-possible-for-as-little-as-possible-in-return-man"—may dominate the motivations of both parties to an exchange.

The core of co-operation which is involved in the immediate exchange of existing goods tends to expand if the exchange is extended over time. Whether he likes it or not a customer who enters a contract to purchase goods in the future enables the seller to plan his activities with a degree of assurance which he otherwise would probably have lacked. The customer is thereby co-operating in the seller's production or acquisition of the goods in a manner which would not have occurred had the customer simply purchased goods already produced. Requirements and output contracts are prime examples of this. They provide a framework for co-operation in the production of goods in some (but not all) respects not unlike that which would occur if the buyer and seller were to merge their corporate identities. Other contracts which simply expand the time for exchange perform similar cooperative functions.

Continuing exchange relationships also are very likely to involve varying degrees of mutual social contacts. These contracts inevitably lead to cooperative behavior, whether or not it is motivated by heavily economic exchange. Employment relationships are one of the more obvious examples of this kind of contractual behavior. In such contracts the cooperative behavior which in the quick one-shot exchange is obscured by selfish economic motives bursts into view as a panoply of continual cooperative behavior. This co-operation is motivated not only by economic exchange motives, but also by social exchange motives and by whatever altruistic or other internal motives cause men to "get along together."

A third element in contractual behavior is that it involves mutual planning for the future. At the very least each party must decide that he wants what the other proposes to give and is willing to give what the other wants in return. Since in some exchanges this happens very quickly it is easy to overlook the element of mutuality in the planning of the parties for the future. But in the contract which more clearly involves more than an immediate exchange of existing goods, this mutual planning becomes obvious. (Man being a talkative animal such planning is to a considerable extent verbalized in some way.) We have, however, all too often obscured the fact that it is mutual planning of the relationship which is occurring by our focus on assent and its binding (or non-binding) nature in terms of legal sanctions. This focus may make practical sense in quick exchanges, but its value diminishes in the case of continuing relationships. We have further obscured the fact that it is planning we are talking about by our emphasis on such legal concepts as consideration, mutuality, the sanctity of written verbalizations of plans, etc. Nevertheless, it is mutual planning for the future which is so involved in such matters.

The fourth element in contractual behavior is that potential sanctions external to the "contract" itself are incorporated or added to give reinforcement to the relationship. We are perhaps inclined to think of these sanctions as being legal sanctions, but they are, of course, not so limited, and non-legal sanctions, *e.g.* business ostracism, are not only significant, but often more significant, than legal sanctions.

The fifth element of contractual behavior is that like all social behavior it is subject to social control and social manipulation which may or may not take into account the interest and desire of those engaging in the behavior.

I am tempted to add a sixth common element, but it is not quite as universal among contractual relationships as the others. A great many contracts, however, acquire the characteristics of property, and in particular the characteristic of alienability. This is bound to happen in a market-credit economy, since the contractual relationship very commonly acquires an economic value of its own and tends to be treated like any other economic value owned by someone.

There are thus, it seems to me, five basic elements of contracts: 1. cooperation, 2. economic exchange, 3. planning for the future, 4. potential external sanctions, and, 5. social control and manipulation. There is also a sixth which is equally basic whenever it is present, the property characteristics of contracts. These conclusions, however, answer only the first of the two preliminary questions posed at the beginning of this paper, namely, whether there is any such thing as contracts? The affirmative answer simply brings on the second question: is contracts a significant enough social phenomenon to justify spending law school time on it?

Given our heavy reliance on a market economy it is not necessary to justify teaching courses relating to important types of exchange relationships, such as distribution of goods and services, collective bargaining, insurance, trade regulation, corporate finance, credit transactions, government contracts, etc. And conceivably a first year law school course could be justified which is no more than a collection of important and representative contract areas, simply to introduce those areas. A strong argument could be made for at least that much of a "contracts" course on the ground that the subsequent curriculum is heavily elective, and that it is desirable for lawyers to be aware of the extent to which economic exchange transactions permeate our economic, social and legal life.

But, can we go farther and justify a course which explores the behavioral elements common to all of contracting? Is it worthwhile to attempt to examine the legal significance of these elements and the varying ways they affect and are affected by the legal system? Since these questions are answered affirmatively in practically every law school curriculum in the United States a great many people may feel that the discussion can stop at this point. But as noted above I agreed not to base my arguments on the position that there is a "law of contracts" in the Willistonian (or perhaps even a Corbinian) sense. Is there, then, any justification for a generalizing first year course in contracts if we abandon, ex hypothesi, a belief in a "law of contracts"?

I am not convinced that the disappearance of a generalized course in contracts from the law school curriculum would be a disaster on the scale of Waterloo. Nor do I think the Western world would collapse if the generalized concept of contracts ceased altogether to be a way of organizing statutes, judicial decisions, administrative action, text-books, legal digests, etc. I do think, however, that we would lose some of our understanding of the functions and techniques of contracting and of contract law in the various transaction-type areas themselves. In short, recognition that the various transaction-types do have common elements of behavior can lead lawyers, judges, legislators, administrators and even law teachers to a better grasp of and better dealing with each transaction-type itself. To the extent that this is true a generalized contracts course becomes justified, not on the ground that there is a "law of contracts" but on the ground that the common elements in contracts-in-gross present problems and challenges for the legal system which widely cut across transaction-type lines.

All right, you say, prove it. It is, of course, impossible to prove it to a group like this or in a paper like this. All that can be done is to present some of the significant challenges to the legal system and to lawyers which do cut across the transaction-types. They are set out below not in order of significance, but following generally the order in which the common elements have been presented above.

Co-operation. The fact that contracts are fundamentally mechanisms of cooperation, and only mechanisms of conflict when things have gone wrong, presents the legal system with special problems. In the first place, contracts get along very well without the law most of the time, or at least

343

without its active intervention. The law thus has to deal largely with pathological cases. This in itself would not be so very troublesome except for the feedback of precedent: the rule of the pathological case governs the healthy contract too. To the extent that contractual behavior is influenced by the law this feedback can have very significant effect on all contractual behavior. At least two primary problems arise from this. First, the law arising from sick cases is not necessarily the optimum law for healthy cases. Secondly, the legal system has only limited techniques and abilities to deal with contracts-in-conflict, and must define the contractual relationship quite specifically in order to do so. In contracts-in-co-operation, however, the most important single ingredient often is an unspecific general willingness to co-operate to achieve mutual success in the relationship. The legal system is thus often in the position not unlike that of a scientist who has to dry out a jellyfish before his instruments of examination can be used on it.

Economic exchange. Many of the consequences of the fact that contracts is a mechanism of economic exchange can better be considered subsequently. Three might, however, be noted at this point. First, the overall impact on the legal system of the exchange-credit economy is something of which no lawyer can afford to be unaware of—so too of the impact of the legal system on the exchange-credit economy. Secondly, exchange-credit is only one of the two major ways in which societies answer basic economic problems, the other being socialist mechanisms which do not depend upon exchange, *e.g.* public schools, taxation for defense, etc. A lawyer needs to be aware of the similarities and differences between exchange mechanisms and socialist mechanisms and of their legal significance in view of the importance of both in our society. Thirdly, and closely related to the foregoing, a profitable study can be made of the borderlines between exchange and other kinds of relationships. We have been doing this for years in contract courses with respect to family gifts and the doctrine of consideration. But there are borderline areas of far more social significance, *e.g.* forced exchanges, such as condemnation of property, the duty to bargain in good faith in the NLRA, duties to enter contracts under the various civil rights laws.

Planning for the future. This aspect of contractual behavior is extremely and directly significant to the practicing lawyer irrespective of the nature of the transaction-type with which he is dealing. First, he must be aware of the fact that the primary purpose of the planning of the parties is to achieve a workable operating relationship for the future. Secondly, as an expert in verbalizing, in questioning, in anticipating problems, etc. the

344

lawyer may be called upon to assist the parties in planning a workable operating relationship. Thirdly, the lawyer as legal technician has two important further planning roles: (a) planning for trouble between the parties, *e.g.* thinking about and preparing for such things as risks of non-performance, changed circumstances, liquidated damages, arbitration, etc.; (b) planning both to avoid illegality, *e.g.* Robinson-Patman, and to utilize the law affirmatively, *e.g.* qualifying the transaction for beneficial tax treatment.

Potential external sanctions. A lawyer needs to know at least the following generalities about this aspect of contracts-in-gross: The most important support for contractual relationships is not a sanction at all, but a continuation of the exchange motivations which led the parties to enter the relationship in the first place. These motivations may continue in effect even after one party has fully performed while the other has not. The motivation causing the debtor in such a case to perform may well be his desire to enter other exchange relationships with the same creditor. Also of great importance are internal command and habit. For example, it simply never dawns on many people not to pay their department store bills on time, or if it does dawn on them the thought is put aside immediately as immoral or otherwise unthinkable. The lawyer needs to know also that informal social and community sanctions are extremely important. So too are non-legal but more formalized community sanctions, as for example, trade association penalties, or mediation or arbitration (even when these are of no legal force). Legal sanctions are but a last resort, however important they may become when in fact resorted to.

Since, when the last resort is reached, the lawyer is practically always involved, it is essential for him to have some understanding of what it is. The kind of development found in the first chapter of Fuller and Braucher, *Basic Contract Law* (1964) is a proper and very desirable foundation for thinking about contract remedies relating to any transaction-type.

Social control and manipulation. The most obvious example of social control and manipulation of contractual behavior is the one most observed, most noted and the nature of which as a social control is most overlooked. That is the fact that the legal system enforces contracts at all. It doing so, of course, represents a conscious or unconscious policy of reinforcing market mechanisms by the law, a policy which goes far beyond simply protecting the changes in property interests which may have been effectuated in a completed contract. This policy is what

345

Macaulay (1966) has called the market goals of contract law and policy. One of the most important pedagogical aims of a course in contracts should be to bring home to the student the fact that these market goals themselves constitute social control and manipulation, the social value of which in particular instances must be weighed against competing goals.

The competing non-market goals of legal policy in contractual relationships are bifurcated rather than unitary. Since contract, especially when reinforced by legal sanctions reflecting market goal policy, can be a wild and dangerous animal, it is often necessary to control it by limiting its power. Such control can be achieved in numerous ways, some obvious and some not so obvious. For example, certain transaction types or certain contractual provisions may be made illegal in a criminal sense, or may be stripped of legal enforcement. These limitations are obvious enough. Less obvious, however, may be such things as rules of interpretation which may subtly prevent certain types of parties from effectively creating particularly undesirable contractual provisions. Moreover, the limited nature of contract remedies themselves represents an extremely important limitation on the market goal policy—the law does not, for example, consider that goal sufficiently important to make a breach of contract an economic crime punishable criminally.

Limitation on contract power, however, is not the only social alternative to the market goal policy. The contracts of its citizens are far too valuable and important in a market society for the society to refrain from using them affirmatively for its own purposes. There is thus affirmative social manipulation and exploitation of "private" contracts which is an extremely important goal competing not only with market goals, but often with limitation-of-power goals as well. In the heyday of laissez faire this type of manipulation and exploitation was somewhat limited in scope, taxation of certain kinds of contractual relationships and subsidies being the most obvious examples. In the modern mixed economy, however, social manipulation and exploitation of contractual relationships abound. Not only has transaction-type taxation, notably the sales tax and the income tax, increased vastly in importance, but many kinds of social goals are being achieved by other kinds of required (or societally encouraged) appurtenances to contractual relationships. Nowhere is this more evident than in employment relationships with such imposed appurtenances as Social Security, unemployment insurance, workmen's compensation, health and safety requirements, etc. But employment is by no means the only example, it is merely one of the areas where the process started early. A more recent entry into the field is the vast amount of legal manipulation of contractual relationships to try to solve racial and religious discrimination problems. Although the focus thus far in the civil rights area has been on preventing refusal to contract, certainly more and more it will also be on preventing discrimination within established contractual relationships, *e.g.* preventing price discrimination by supermarkets in the ghetto or racial discrimination in employee promotion.

Thus, throughout contractual relationships three competing social policies are found: market goals, limitation of contract power and affirmative manipulation and social exploitation. The interplay of these policies cuts across transaction-type lines in such a way that study of them in some transaction-types should aid considerably in understanding them in other types of transactions.

Property characteristics of contracts. Just as society in general may exploit contracts made between its citizens, so too may individual third parties seek to take advantage of them. This is, of course, inevitable in any society in which contracts become a significant form of wealth. At least as long as there is a significant market for the subject matter of a contract there may be third party interests of one kind or another. And since markets are available in a great many transaction-types, such legal matters as assignability, third party beneficiaries, etc. are also a proper subject of a generalized contracts course.

To summarize the answer to the second question which started this paper, all five (or six) of the common elements of contractual relations do present to the legal system and to lawyers problems and challenges which cut across transaction-type boundaries. These problems and challenges could be studied in separate transaction-type courses, and it would even be possible to demonstrate in such courses something of their universality. Nevertheless, their great social and practical-lawyer significance call for a unitary contracts course as the most effective way possible to present the elements and their legal raminfications to the students. In the remainder of the paper I propose to set out some thoughts about the content and structure of a course built around these basic elements.

Contents and structure of a unitary contracts course built on the common contract elements. This is not the proper place to develop a thesis that present generalized contract legal doctrine is vastly deficient as a useful organization of the social and legal problems inherent in contractual relationships. And it certainly is not the place to undertake the task of revamping contracts doctrine to present a theoretical model which corresponds to the basic elements in contractual relationships. And even more it is not the place to try to reconcile such a model with the actual outcome of cases, with legislation and administrative law, with business and other social practice, etc. It is, however, an appropriate place to suggest what should be included in a generalized contracts course in order to bring into the open and to develop the common elements of contractual relationships and the common problems and challenges presented to the legal system by them. So too, the basic organization of the teaching materials is a proper subject for consideration.

The reader who has troubled to arrive at this point will already have inferred some of the purposes and goals of a contracts course built on the common contract elements. Nevertheless, it is appropriate to summarize them at this point:

1. To perform its share (or more) of the development goals of all first year courses: learning to read (and write) and developing other communication skills; developing an increased capacity for sustained rational thought; increasing perception of human values and of how to achieve them; developing a workable sense of justice; developing understanding of decision making and engaging in vicarious practice in human problem solving; sharpening abilities to use legal tools such as statutes and precedent.

2. Broadening perceptions of the significance, consequences, roles and limitations of contractual relations in our society.

3. Acquiring some information about and some understanding of specific and important contractual transaction types, *e.g.* collective bargaining agreements, consumer purchases, franchise agreements, insurance, etc.

4. Developing a general understanding of the interplay of contractual relationships with the legal system, and specific comprehension of contractual legal problems such as dispute settlement, limitations on legal remedies and their effectiveness, those caused by incomplete and flexible planning, by the need of the legal system to reduce cooperative on-going relationships to relatively rigid verbalizations in order to be able to cope with conflicts, by specific social limitations and exploitations of contractual relationships, etc.

5. Developing an understanding of the role of the lawyer in contractual relationships generally, and specifically with respect to the response of the legal system to contractual relationships.

6. Acquiring elemental skills in the "lawyering" of contracts from negotiation and drafting to advocacy and judging in appellate litigation, to legislating, etc.

Goals such as the foregoing may look very nice in a law school catalog or sound good in a teacher's introductory lecture, but we all know that we are lucky to achieve much of anything we set out to do in the classroom. It would perhaps therefore be better to call them directions, rather than goals. And so the question is, if we set out with these directions in mind, what goes into the contracts course and how does it go in?

First, the areas of human behavior from which materials are selected are as broad as the common elements of contractual behavior. This broad area of selection encompasses not only most of the traditional contract areas, but gives full weight to continuing economic exchange relationships which have tended to drop out of contracts courses, *e.g.* collective bargaining and other aspects of employment relationships, mediation, arbitration. Perhaps even more important is that it brings into the contracts fold all of the black sheep transaction-types which have tended to slip away as the academic shepherds of contracts have sought to avoid the doctrinal stresses which otherwise would have been caused by legislative, administrative and sometimes judicial regulation. With the return of such transaction-types comes the regulation as an integral part of the contractual relationship. Robinson-Patman, New York Insurance Law, NLRA, Workmen's Compensation, all seem to be as much a proper study of contracts as is the mailbox rule. Indeed, they are considerably more so since they have some current significance—a comment which brings me to the next point.

Secondly, the subject matter of the materials selected should have some present or future topical significance. This is important to the achievement of almost all the goals enumerated above. Dead problems, however fascinating intellectually, simply do not achieve most of those goals, unless enough history is reincarnated with them so that the student can see them with the full flavor of the social and economic background of their day. This is a pretty tricky thing to pull off with an 1854 English case concerning the well known carriers trading under the name of l'ickford & Co who evidently did not use printed shipping forms.[1] I shall be the first to agree that it is not always easy to tell when a problem is

---

[1] *Hadley v. Baxendale.* For citation try any contracts casebook.

dead and when it is still topically significant—certainly its absence from current reported appellate cases does not conclusively demonstrate its topical demise. Nevertheless, the difficulty does not justify failure to make an attempt. Moreover, I suspect that there would be considerable agreement about what was and what was not topical if a representative group of contracts teachers were to survey current case-books.

Thirdly, non-legal as well as legal aspects of contractual relationships should be considered. I have in mind in part, but only in part, the sort of formal sociological studies which have been done by Stewart Macaulay and others. In addition to such studies, however, legal materials themselves can often yield a great deal of enlightenment on non-legal aspects of contractual relations. For example, cases, while the "spawn of trouble" often nevertheless yield much information about the way people "really" conduct themselves in the real world, even when there is no trouble. Moreover, there is much to be found with respect to "real life" in journals, etc. dealing with areas of contracts such as collective bargaining agreements, government contracts, etc. Nor, in spite of my own relative lack of success in digging out much, am I yet convinced that business school libraries, for example, do not have something for us. And certainly, such genuinely negotiated form contracts as those of the American Institute of Architects are goldmines of information about how the parties plan many of the things which have to be done in connection with the construction of buildings. In short, I do not think that it is either necessary or desirable to wait until the legal sociologists have progressed further before making more diligent efforts to work in considerably more information on contracting in contrast to that on contract law and litigation.

Fourthly, since it is impossible to study the elements of contractual behavior with any degree of breadth without going heavily into areas regulated by statute and administrative law, a considerable volume of statutory law and administrative regulation and decisions will inevitably be included. This, plus the fact that even the traditional area of contract doctrine has now been invaded by the UCC will help the contracts course do its bit towards remedying the present absurdity of a common law first year curriculum in an age of legislative and administrative legal dominance. In addition, such important dispute settling mechanisms as arbitration require treatment with more care than is now generally devoted to them—perhaps even as much as we now devote to some of the topically insignificant aspects of the doctrine of consideration. Thus, if the course is broadened as is herein suggested there will inevitably be a marked reduction in reliance on appellate cases and especially on common law appellate cases, with corresponding increases in other types of legal materials.

Fifthly, it is apparent that a traditional doctrinal organization of the materials, with chapter headings such as consideration, offer and acceptance, puts nearly insurmountable hurdles in the way of achieving the goals of the course. For one thing that kind of organization simply does not fit the functional legal problems created by contracts. For another it causes students to see contracts backwards. They tend to see contractual relations as extrapolations of legal doctrines, rather than see legal doctrines as a response to contractual relations. Whatever validity this approach may have with respect to non-market policies in contract law, it is extremely misleading with respect to market policies, the very area with which traditional doctrines are most at home. The organization should, therefore, be based on assessments of the most effective way of accomplishing those goals, rather than doctrinally.

It is not meant to suggest that even the more abstract legal doctrines can be ignored (except insofar as they have nothing to do with significant modern problems). For example, the doctrine of consideration would be dealt with as it arises in the legal responses to various problems, e.g. in the mutuality questions arising in output and requirements contracts and franchise agreements, in the duress problems arising out of adjustments in existing contracts, in the problems arising from unconscionable contracts, in dealing with the revocation of offers, etc. On the other hand, whether it would be dealt with at all in respect to family gifts would depend upon an assessment of the current importance of the revocability of family gift promises. Or such cases might be included for contrasting the utilization of the consideration doctrines with the handling of similar transactions under the Internal Revenue Code (the latter being a significant and lively current problem).

The foregoing paragraphs outline some of the principles which I think should be applied in order to get into the contracts course what is necessary in order to move it in the direction of the goals argued for earlier. Obviously, however, as soon as we take off from the doctrinal organizations now available, the door is open to a host of possible organizations, selections of topic areas, emphases on types of materials, etc. I am doubtless falling down on the job assigned by the esoteric title which we chose for this panel in failing to be more specific as to the measure of the "mix." My justification is that until someone has in fact attempted to make a mix along the foregoing lines there is not much sense in guessing at the proportions with which he would come up. And so I shall make proper obeisance to the panel title by simply annexing in a footnote the table of contents of a casebook on East African contracts in which I attempted to implement some of the foregoing ideas in the classroom.[2]

9.3 Contracts Instruments for Social Cooperation East Africa

One of the consequences of the design of this book is that its organisation differs markedly from that of a standard text on contract law. There are a number of reasons for this. First, this book deals with contracts, and the standard texts deal largely with law as defined by the outcome of contract litigation, (and by statutes) or more specifically, with the outcome of appellate decisions in contract litigation. Contracts and contract litigation are not the same thing. Nor are they separate subjects, since the former includes the latter. But as will be seen subsequently, the human institution known as contract includes far more than merely law as developed by contract litigation or by statutes.

A second reason for the difference between the organisation of this book and that of a standard text on contract law is that the latter is organised to facilitate finding things in it. The more orderly and systematic the text is the more successfully this purpose is accomplished. This book, on the other hand, is a classroom teaching book, organised to facilitate your understanding of contracts, even at the cost of sacrificing "logical" organisation.

Thirdly, it is not unfair to say that all the standard texts on English contract law reflect a notion that the law of contract litigation is a relatively neat and logical structure of rules. The author of this book believes this idea to be inaccurate, and the book reflects that belief. Contract law is hardly a neat and logical structure of rules, but like all law a social instrument designed to accomplish the goals of man.

Once you see the law as a useful social instrument for accomplishment of human goals you will see clearly why it is not a neat and logical package. It is because neither individuals nor their societies are neat and

---

[2] See 9.40 this volume.

logical packages. Man is full of conflicting motives and conflicting actions. He seeks security and yearns for adventure. He wants companionship and privacy at the same time. He seeks peace and he makes war. He punishes those he loves and weeps over the graves of his enemies. How, except by a denial of human nature, could any legal system devised and used by such a creature be a neat and logical structure?

The basic contradictions of human nature and of human society cannot be wiped out by the law. Instead law makers must examine those contradictions and work out solutions to them which, hopefully, will keep the tensions resulting from them at a reasonable and controllable level. This cannot be done in gross, but only in relatively small pieces. It is very easy to say: "Thou shalt not kill". But does the rule apply to soldiers in war? to the public official who executes a murderer pursuant to a court judgment? to a man saving his own life? to the insane? Does it apply to the man who smokes in bed and unintentionally but foolishly causes his house and his family to burn up? to the manufacturer of any automobile, who is fully aware of the fact that for every million miles travelled by automobiles a certain number of people die? to a politician who votes money for a prudent and long-range development project, money which could have been spent on doctors and medicine to save lives now? Obviously these are all vastly different problems, although they could all logically be subsumed under the rule: "Thou shalt not kill". Equally obviously literal application of that rule will not solve those problems adequately.

If the law is merely a way of solving problems in relatively small pieces, what then are the "rules" which appear in the books? Instead of having rules, why is not each case decided as a unique proposition to achieve a "just" and "workable" solution to that particular problem? Would such an approach not best keep the contradictions of human nature and of human society in a workable balance? Let us examine a legal system in which each case is a law unto itself, and let us further assume that the individuals administering it enjoy the wisdom of Solomon and the patience of Job.

Guides and norms of conduct. In such a system how are the legal norms of individual and social conduct established? What are the guides? Suppose, for example, that there were no legal rule calling upon automobile drivers to keep to the left side of the road? It is no more just and workable to drive on the left side of the road than it is on the right. Nevertheless, much evil is avoided by establishing one or the other as the

353

normal behaviour. (Note that even such a rule cannot be absolute: drivers are allowed to make right turns at intersections which take them momentarily into the right side of the road, they are allowed to pass slower vehicles on the right, etc.)

Prediction and reliance. People often need to predict the future and to be able to rely on their prediction, and this is as true of law as it is of other social phenomens. For example, forgetting for a moment non-legal sanctions, how many loans would be made if there were no legal "rule" that a man who borrows money must repay it? You might answer: "Many, because usually the wise judge would require payment without any rule". But is that not simply saying that rules may grow informally from widely accepted notions of what is just and workable? If the rule which will be applied is known before the moment of its application one can rely on it.

Efficiency. How many disputes could a judge handle in a month if he had to examine all the social and individual elements of justice in each one, unguided by the prior experience of others expressed in "rules"? In a society of any complexity the answer is clear: "Not very many". With no rules the resolution of disputes would require a major portion of the efforts of society—hardly a desirable use of its productivity.

Legal rules must have a degree of certainty, both as to their content and as to their application, if they are to serve the purposes of establishing legal norms of conduct, of enabling people to rely on them and of assisting decision makers in resolving disputes. To the extent that legal rules are ambiguous they do not serve these purposes. To the extent that one does not know whether or not a particular rule will be applied to a given situation it does not serve these purposes. To the extent that rules are changed in unpredictable ways they tend not to serve these purposes. Certainty of rules and their application is, therefore, an important goal of the law.

But the goals served by the notion of certainty are like all other human goals, they too come into conflict with other desirable goals. The need for achieving a result which works well for society generally or for the people most directly concerned may outweigh in a particular situation the goals served by the notion of certainty. This may come about because a rule was ill-conceived in the first place, because it was stated too broadly and therefore encompassed too much human activity, because the facts of life underlying its formulation have changed, etc. No human mind or collection of human minds is capable of considering everything which can occur in the future, or indeed, everything which is occurring currently, even in connection with the simplest rule stated in the simplest manner. Rules will, therefore, *very often* simply not fit a given dispute, just as a square peg does not fit a round hole. If then, we are always to insist upon the literal application of rules, we must recognize that in many cases the specific result will not be one which works well either for society generally or for the people most directly concerned. The only justification for applying the rule in such cases is that the goals to be achieved by certainty are deemed to outweigh the advantage of justice and workability in the particular case.

A host of forces tend to make legislators, administrators, judges and lawyers elevate certainty to an exaggerated level of importance. In doing so other goals are sacrificed. All too often the sacrifice is made unwittingly or by simply invoking in hushed tone the incantation: "It is the law". Tragically sad is the fact that all too often the sacrifice is in vain, and even certainty itself is not achieved. As Corbin has said:

> "... certainty in the law is largely illusion at best, and altogether too high a price may be paid in the effort to attain it. Inflexible and mechanical rules lead to their own avoidance by fiction and oamouflage." (3 Corbin on Contracts, s. 609, p. 689 (1960)).
>
> "Certainty is an illusion; and the 'illusion of certainty' is the mother of injustice and turmoil." (1 Corbin on Contract, 1964 Supp. 3).

The same forces which lead to the sanctification of certainty by others also are at work in the minds and hearts of law students. But in addition, the new law student is suffering from a normal, but nevertheless often acute, lack of confidence in his very new experience. He is, therefore, often desperately anxious to find some life preserver to save him in the sea of human problems in which he is desperately trying to stay afloat. And what could be more solid and reassuring than clearly stated rules? Surely they are friends which will keep him from sinking, if he cultivates them and becomes thoroughly acquainted with them. But the price of friendship is loyalty, and all too many law students quickly become the dedicated defenders of Certainty and The Rules. Instead of predictability and reliability becoming *a* goal of the law, the concept of abstract certainty becomes *the* goal of the law.

The student who wishes to learn how to use law as an instrument for solving human problems must be fully aware of the natural bias of rules in favour of a rigid legal status quo. He must also be prepared to ask himself repeatedly just *what* goal of certainty is being served by applying an established rule to a given problem, and whether it is being served effectively. But he cannot stop there, he must go on and ask himself always whether the achievement of the goal (if it is achieved) is worth the price paid in the sacrifice of conflicting human goals.

9.4 Contracts Instruments for Social Cooperation East Africa

TABLE OF CONTENTS

CHAPTER 3: THE CONTENT OF CONTRACTUAL
RELATIONSHIPS

S.1: Generally—The Role of Law
S.2: Defining Performance Obligations by Standardised
Form Contract
S.3: Supplying Performance Content by Third Persons—
Arbitration

    A.   Arbitration and Dispute Settlement
    B.   Third Parties and Performance Content

S.4: Supplying Performance Content by Legislative and
Administrative Law—Rent Restriction

CHAPTER 4: SOME SELECTED TYPES OF
SPECIALISED CONTRACTS

S.1: Releases: Contracts of Peace
S.2: Wagering: Contracts of Chance
S.3: Insurance: Contracts of Reduce Risk
S.4: Gifts: Altruistic Contracts

CHAPTER 5: CONTRACTS AND THIRD PARTIES

S.1: Assignment and Negotiability

    A.   Wealth and Assignment of Contract Rights
    B.   History of the Law of Assignment in England and
       East Africa
    C.   Conflicting Interests Involved in Transfers of
       Promises
    D.   Involuntary Assignments

S.2: Agency—Undisclosed Principal
S.3: Third Parties Who Deal with Property Which has been
Subject to a Contract
S.4: Other Situations in which Third Parties Seek to
Participate in the Benefit of a Contract

    A.   Statutory Provisions
    B.   The Trust Exception to Strict Privity Notions
    C.   Bankers' Commercial Credits (Letters of Credit)
    D.   The Residue

9.5 Contracts Exchange Transactions and Relations

TABLE OF CONTENTS

PART 3

AFTERWORD

Chapter 10

Relational Contract Theory: Challenges and Queries

10.1. Relational Contract Theory: Challenges and Queries

On January 29, 1999, a Symposium was held in Ian Macneil's honour at the Northwestern University School of Law, where he had taught since 1980. The Symposium was published in (2000) 94 (3) *Northwestern University Law Review*. Macneil took the opportunity to respond to the observations made on his work at the Symposium and this response is published here as an "Afterword" to this volume.

10.1 Relational Contract Theory: Challenges and Queries

Introduction

The purpose of this Article is both to clarify and to extend the work I have been doing with relational contracts since the mid-1960s. The clarifications include making careful distinctions between (1) descriptions of contract behavior and norms, (2) theories concerning such behavior, (3) descriptions of the law governing such behavior, and (4) prescriptions about the law that should govern.

The clarifications also include making careful distinctions between three *levels* of description and/or theorizing about contract behavior and norms: (1) an umbrella theory encompassing all relational contract theories, (2) what I am calling "essential contract theory," referring specifically to my own relational contract theory based on common contract behavior and norms, and (3) the "relational/as-if-discrete" spectrum or axis in terms of which contract behavior and norms can be evaluated.

I. Challenges/Queries

I decided to intersperse my own contribution with un-answered challenges and queries. Both the nature and addressees of these vary. One of their main functions is to separate and thus clarify various aspects of my work which both friend and foe have often melded together where no melding was or is intended.

A. DEFINITIONS

1. *Contract.* In this Article, "contract" means relations among people who have exchanged, are exchanging or expect to be exchanging in the future—in other words, exchange relations. Experience has shown that the very idea of contract as *relations* in which exchange occurs—rather than as specific transactions, specific agreements, specific promises, specific exchanges, and the like—is extremely difficult for many people to grasp. Either that, or they simply refuse to accept that contract *can* be so defined. However difficult such a definition of contract may be, it is that upon which all that follows is grounded. Thus, this Article can be understood only in terms of that definition.

Challenge/Query No. 1: Is there a more useful definition of contract? If so, for what purposes, and at what price?

2. *Factual Description, Not Theory.* Upon starting down the road leading to, among many other things, this Symposium, it did not occur to me consciously that I might be developing a theory. Rather, I was simply exploring and trying to make sense of reality, the reality of what people are actually *doing* in the real-life world of exchange. (Macneil 1974a, 693)

That exploration has delved into many areas: animal behavior, (Macneil 1974a, 693) primitive human behavior, (Macneil 1980c; 1986) feudal society, England and Scotland from the sixteenth to the eighteenth century, modern East Africa, (Macneil 1966; 1968e) traditional and modern Polish marriages, (Macneil 1987b) political exchange behavior, (Macneil 1990) countless areas of modern socio-economic life, and even Utopia. (Macneil 1980c, 111–117) Starting with

366

animal behavior and primitive human behavior I perceived four primal roots of contract: (1) a social matrix, (2) specialization of labor and exchange, (3) a sense of choice, and (4) conscious awareness of past, present, and future. (Macneil 1974a, 696–720)

These roots by themselves, however, were too general to summarize contract in what seemed to be a useful manner. Thus, I tried to distill what I was finding into a manageable number of basic behavioral categories growing out of those roots. Since repeated human behavior invariably creates norms, these behavioral categories are also normative categories.

The ten common contract behavioral patterns and norms are (1) role integrity (requiring consistency, involving internal conflict, and being inherently complex); (2) reciprocity (the principle of getting something back for something given); (3) implementation of planning; (4) effectuation of consent; (5) flexibility; (6) contractual solidarity; (7) the restitution, reliance, and expectation interests (the "linking norms"); (8) creation and restraint of power (the "power norm"); (9) propriety of means, and (10) harmonization with the social matrix, that is, with supracontract norms. (Macneil 1983b, 347) The behavioral and normative categories were not, and are not, intended to be either watertight or overly sophisticated. Nor are they intended to be exhaustive.

Challenge/Query No. 2: Are there more accurate, comprehensive descriptions of contract *behavior*? If so, what are they? What are their relative advantages and disadvantages for gaining insights into contract? Can these descriptions be bettered by eliminations, alterations, or supplementation? What other questions should be asked about the subject of contract behavior and norms?

Challenge/Query No. 3: Are there more accurate, comprehensive descriptions of the norms prevailing in contract? If so, what are they? What are their relative advantages and disadvantages for gaining insights into contract? Can the above descriptions be bettered by eliminations, alterations and/or supplementation? What other questions should be asked about this subject?

Challenge/Query No. 4: The description of common contract behavior and norms presents a more accurate, positivist picture of exchange relations than that presented by formal rational choice theory or game theory.

3. *Theory Added to Description.* Descriptions of common contract behavior and norms can, should, and do stand alone as a subject of

investigation. They do not constitute a theory standing alone, however, but are simply descriptions of facts observed. I have, however, added my own theory to the descriptions of the common contract behavior and norms—this this is the "essential contract theory" treated in Part III.

Now I turn to what is unquestionably a theory, the core propositions of *all* relational contract theories.

II. The Core of Relational Contract Theories

A. FOUR CORE PROPOSITIONS: INTRODUCTION

A relational contract theory may be defined as any theory based on the following four core propositions.

First, every transaction is embedded in complex relations.

Secondly, understanding any transaction requires understanding all essential elements of its enveloping relations.

Thirdly, effective analysis of any transaction requires recognition and consideration of all essential elements of its enveloping relations that might affect the transaction significantly.

Fourthly, combined contextual analysis of relations and transactions is more efficient and produces a more complete and sure final analytical product than does commencing with non-contextual analysis of transactions.

For purposes of this Article, relational contract theory means these four propositions, nothing more and nothing less.

1. *Provability.* It may be noted that the provability of these propositions varies considerably. The first is a virtually indisputable observation of universal human intercourse. The last, particularly the claim to greater efficiency, would be difficult if not impossible to prove empirically, even though much evidence can be marshalled in its support. It thus comes closer to an article of faith than a provable proposition, to be placed alongside other great articles of faith, such as the belief that rational choice theory has more relation to reality than any competing theories. The middle two propositions lie somewhere in between on the scale of provability.

2. *Applicability.* I believe that these propositions apply to any analysis of any contract or any part of any contract. Nonetheless, I shall exclude from the claims made in this Article matters pertaining primarily to the substance of contracts. Thus, the focus here is on what might, for lack of a better term, be called the behavioral aspects of contracts, as distinct from their substance. In particular, these propositions apply to any law, whether sovereign or otherwise, and to any rules or norms, irrespective of their origin, in any way relating in any significant manner to contracts.

3. *Individualistic Analysis and Relational Contract Theory.* Theories founded essentially on the capitalist system as such are likely to be so influenced by individualist concepts as not to be relational in the foregoing terms. Consider, for example, the modern liberal belief that political and governmental institutions can sift through information, make informed decisions, and, where the decisions so indicate, improve on the status quo and market effects by regulation and wealth redistribution. This liberal pragmatism is no less a theory simply because if may seem nontheoretical to legal academics currently steeped in a great variety of esoteric theories.

Although in academic eclipse, at least in American law schools, liberal pragmatism is essentially the theory of democratic government in its modern context. More than that, it is hands down the primary legal theory prevailing in the work of legislatures, courts, executive and administrative agencies, and practicing lawyers. This liberal pragmatic theory is obviously highly relational. Yet it is, as radicals love to point out, founded fundamentally on individualistic, market notions, and hence is not a relational contract theory as the term is used here.

Before going further, it should be noted that relational contracts unquestionably can be and regularly are analyzed by use of nonrelational contract theories. The most common of these nonrelational theories in modern American academia is rational choice theory, which can be applied with or without taking transaction costs into account. Game theory is another such tool. Both rational choice theory without transaction costs and game theory sweep away all relations, except pure competition with the broom of *ceteris paribus (i.e.* "other things being equal"). Transaction cost analysis introduces whatever relational elements the rational choice theorist might discuss. Nonetheless, as its name suggests, rational choice theory remains transactionally based and individually, rather than relationally, oriented.

4. *Relation of the Four Core Propositions to More Specific Relational Contract Theories.* It is certainly possible simply to stop and to go no further with

relational contract theory than the four propositions set out above. These four propositions represent a quantum step from contract approaches based on transactions, agreements, promises, specific exchanges, and the like. Moreover, a strong case can be made for the merit of the four propositions standing alone, irrespective of what further theories may or may not be founded on them.

Nonetheless, these propositions form no more than an overarching theory, only a framework to accommodate more specific relational contract theories. The propositions thus stand on their own feet and do not depend on the validity of any particular relational contract theory that I or anyone else has developed.

B. ANALYSIS OF THE FOUR CORE PROPOSITIONS

1. *Every Transaction is Embedded in Complex Relations.* It is difficult to see how anyone could dispute this first proposition of relational contract theory. Apart from theoretical transactions, such as those of rational choice theory, nonembedded transactions are virtually impossible to find. Exchange of any importance is impossible outside a society. Even the purest "discrete" exchange postulates a social matrix providing at least the following: (1) a means of communication understandable to both parties; (2) a system of order so that the parties exchange instead of killing and stealing; (3) typically, in modern times, a system of money; and (4) in the case of exchanges promised, an effective mechanism to enforce promises. This social matrix is, of course, the minimum necessary for exchange; it takes great imagination to produce examples, in any society, of exchange characterized by only the minimum degree of relationality. (Macneil 1983b, 344)

Challenge/Query No. 5: Does anyone dispute this proposition?

2. *Understanding Any Transaction Requires Understanding All Elements of its Enveloping Relations that Might Affect the Transaction Significantly.* Although this proposition may at first glance appear to be controversial, it is, again, difficult to see how anyone could seriously disagree with it. It is the application of the proposition rather than the proposition itself that is likely to give rise to controversy—that is, one might ask which, if any, elements do affect any given transaction significantly.

It should also be noted that the second core proposition of relational contract theory requires only that the enveloping relations be understood, not that they necessarily be accorded recognition or further consideration in conducting analysis. The latter is the realm of the third proposition.

Challenge/Query No. 6: Does anyone dispute this proposition?

3. *Effective Analysis of Any Transaction Requires Recognition and Consideration of All Significant Relational Elements.* It is with this third proposition that the fur may begin to fly. Before defending the proposition, however, clarification is in order. Recognition and consideration of all the significant relational elements of a transaction does *not* mean reinventing the wheel every time any given transaction or type of transaction is analyzed. Common sense and normal practices of building knowledge on the basis of past experience are as much in order in analyzing contracts as in any other human endeavor.

Consider, for example, an analysis of the effect on demand of relatively small increases or decreases in the price of bananas in supermarkets. Such sales of bananas occur in extremely complicated supermarket-consumer relationships. The sale of any one product is part of an integrated web of sophisticated supermarket management of the sale of all of its products. In supermarket-consumer relationships, among other things, goods are competing with each other for limited and varying display space, limited consumer attention, and expenditure of limited consumer resources. Elements of these relationships are of such a nature that even small changes in the price of a fairly simple product may send vibrations through other parts of the web, vibrations likely to reverberate back.

Thus, even a modest price analysis calls for at least the following: (1) a statement that this is an area of extremely complicated contractual relations; (2) a brief description of these relations with suggestions, where available and appropriate, of further sources of information; (3) an explanation of why the analyst has concluded that the relations will not affect the outcome of his or her narrow price study; and (4) a conclusion that *ceteris paribus* is therefore appropriate in such a case and constitutes adequate consideration of these relational impacts. Stating conclusions (3) and (4) explicitly *empowers* the reader to respond, "Sure," or "Oh Yeah?," or "I'll reserve judgment," or whatever, and to put the analysis in its appropriate place in light of his or her own view of the relational situation.

Such treatment is essential before any discrete analysis can be undertaken or described. It is even more important as part of the conclusions drawn from the analysis, lest they be overstated.

There will always be a question of where to stop with even such modest recognition and consideration of elements of the enveloping relations. Continuing with our example, banana relations are phenom-enally complex. Their sale is entwined in a particularly tangled international marketing and power structure. It involves monopolistic outfits like Chiquita International Brand, a variety of conflicting third-world interests (Latin American countries, Chiquita and Chiquita-lookalike producers vs. small Caribbean island countries, particularly non-Chiquita-like producers), and European vs. American foreign policy, to say nothing of Chiquita as a symbol of American imperialism, environmentally damaging practices, big money polities, the global capitalistic market generally, and Bill Clinton's zipper problems.

These elements are, however, further removed from the effect on demand of small variations in the price of supermarket sales of bananas than is the supermarket-consumer relation. Moreover, the effect, if any, that these elements have on a narrow price question is likely to be mediated through the supermarket-consumer relation. To the extent this is the case, no need exists to go beyond this relation in dealing with the issue at hand. Probably all that can be said generally about where to stop is that those enamored with relational contract theory will probably see important connections, and hence the need for their treatment, where those enamored with discrete analytical methods will not.

It may be argued that there are instances where even such casual recognition of the relations enveloping transactions is unnecessary, that the relations are simply just too well known to bother mentioning them. And in everyday life, that is precisely how we behave most of the time in familiar situations. The problem is, however, that what is simply just too well known is all too often simply just forgotten. This is especially true respecting subjects of mental exercises. Thus, judges, administrators, and academics can ill afford to be so casual. Even in the most clear-cut situations, it is a salutary and cautionary thing for them to remind themselves that it is relations, not just isolated transactions, with which they work. They are like surgeons who need often to remind themselves that it is patients, not just organs that they are carving up.

Such reminders may do far more than provide an appropriate relational tonic. There will be times when the mere recollection of the obvious will suggest that it is not so obvious after all. When this happens, the actor will recognize that some further attention does need to be paid to relations after all. Moreover, in the case of judges, such reminders will have salutary consequences by helping to limit the precedential effect of their decisions to situations where the relations resemble each other enough for them to be properly ignored for purposes of analysis. This, of course, happens in legal theory without the reminders, since precedential effect is always limited to the facts of a case. But, as every lawyer knows, what the "facts of a case" are is always highly debatable. Reminders that the court is focusing only on discrete elements, and ignoring relations, should help future courts better to tease out what were and what were not the "facts of a case."

The foregoing is, of course, the *minimum* treatment that should accompany discrete analysis of transactions. Where recognition of the enveloping relations suggests that they might indeed have some significant impact on any proposed transactional analysis, then relational contract theory calls for more. That impact must be analyzed to whatever extent it is significant, no matter how difficult or messy the task may be. Failure to give such consideration renders any transactional analysis suspect at best and totally defective at worst. No sweeping application of *ceteris paribus* or anything like it in such circumstances is appropriate respecting those aspects of the relations.

Even where there is agreement to the foregoing in principle, there is always room for dispute about when relations are likely to have an impact on particular transactions and where they are not. Unquestionably, "relationists" will often see impact when "discretists," such as rational choice or game theorists, would not. It is in such circumstances that a practice of insisting upon overt recognition of the enveloping relations by both sides of the debate becomes particularly valuable. Such recognition will require discretetists to state clearly that the enveloping relations do not affect the transactional analysis, and this in turn facilitates challenges to such a conclusion. As illustrated by the banana price example, relational contract theory calls for recognition and consideration of all significant relational elements irrespective of the goal of the analysis. Thus, it applies to price and other substantive aspects of contractual relations. Nonetheless, the assertions of this Article are, as noted earlier, limited to nonsubstantive, behavioral aspects of contractual relations.

Recognition and consideration of all significant relational elements becomes particularly essential where the subject of examination is behavioral aspects, such as the structuring of contractual relations in which transactions occur, including all questions of law pertinent to them. This is partly because, unlike such things as dollars and bananas, behavioral aspects are phenomenally easy for most people to overlook. They tend to be taken for granted, taken as given, taken as unimportant, taken as if they were somehow bestowed by nature, taken as free goods—you name it. Nowhere is this more true than in the Queen of the Social Sciences, Economics. Thus, the need for such recognition and consideration is especially important in that branch of study called law and economics.

Challenge/Query No. 7: Defend the proposition that effective analysis of a transaction can be accomplished without recognition and consideration of all significant relational elements.

4. *Combined Contextual Analysis of Relations and Transactions is More Efficient and Produces a More Complete and Sure Final Analytical Product than Does Commencing with Non-Contextual Analysis of Transactions.* Assuming that both enveloping relations and transactions are to be analyzed, two basic ways to go about the analysis are available. One is the relational approach, and the other is to start at the transaction end and work from there into the remainder of the relations.

a. *Relational Approach.*—The relational approach requires three steps: (1) acquiring an overall grasp of the essential relations of which the transactions are an integral part; (2) working through the interaction of the pertinent transactions with the remainder of the relations until the limitations of transactional analysis are firmly established, and (3) engaging in whatever detailed discrete analysis is desired, subject to whatever constraints the first steps suggest. Although the steps need to be taken in the order suggested, in any complex situation they may be repeated many times, whenever each step reveals inadequacies in the information derived from a prior step.

Before considering the relative merits of the relational and transactionend approaches, it should be noted that, as ordinarily applied, neither rational choice theory (when applied without transaction cost analysis) nor game theory is pertinent here. Such applications typically reject the third relational core proposition, and thus deal only with transactions as such, sweeping away all relational elements by express or implicit use of *ceteris paribus.* The points made respecting the fourth core proposition are pertinent to such approaches only in that they further demonstrate the debilitating weaknesses of ordinary applications of rational choice theory and game theory from the viewpoint of any relational contract theory.

This is not to say that rational choice theory and/or game theory *cannot* be applied consistently with relational contract theory. In this they are analogous to classical contract law, which can and often does play a vital role in relations characterized by high levels of discreteness, such as transactions in organized futures markets. But like the application of any kind of discrete contract analysis, theirs too requires to be circumscribed by the relations.

It should also be recalled that, as suggested in the discussion of the third proposition, starting analysis with an overall picture of relations and their interaction with transactions may in some circumstances lead rapidly to the conclusion that the enveloping relations do not affect the transactional analysis at hand. The banana-price question discussed earlier is an example. We are thus here concerned only with those situations where significant interaction between transactions and their enveloping relations is both anticipated and understood to requrie analysis as a part of transactional analysis. The assumption is that before the job is done the essentials of *both* the transactions and the relations must be analyzed, and the only question is how to go about it.

b. *The Transaction-End Approach Transaction Cost Analysis*—The technique typically used when starting with transactions is transaction cost analysis. To be entirely logical, anyone engaging in such analysis would start by looking at the transaction alone and then trying to infer from the transaction itself what kind and amount of information costs, communication costs, negotiation costs, transfer costs, monitoring costs, enforcement costs, renegotiation costs, "external" costs, and so on may be involved. Theoretically, such a process carried out with the utmost of thoroughness would ultimately result in uncovering all significant aspects of the enveloping relations and their interplay with the transactions being studied.

Needless to say, people are generally sensible rather than completely logical. No one engages in such a Herculean task as that resulting from starting analysis free of *all* relational information. Instead, transaction cost analysis normally starts only after the analyst already knows and/or has gathered a considerable but finite amount of information, real or imagined, about the contractual relations in question. Such information channels the analyst both in seeing what transaction costs are likely to occur and in determining which are important enough to examine and which are not.

c. *Comparing the Relational and Transaction Cost Approaches.*—The difference between transaction cost analysis and the three steps of relational analysis is partly, but only partly, one of degree. Thus, transaction cost analysis also requires initial acquisition of some knowledge of the essential relations in order to pick out transaction costs, which is the first step of relational analysis. Since, however, transaction cost analysis starts at the "wrong" end in relational terms, acquiring such knowledge is a practical necessity rather than a theoretical requirement. Thus, the knowledge acquired of the relations can be, and tends to be, casual rather than the systematic overall grasp called for by relational contract theory. Moreover, it involves high risk of omitting major factors.

The second step of relational analysis—working through the interaction of the pertinent transactions with the remainder of the relations until the limitations of transactional analysis are firmly established—tends to be severely truncated in a transaction cost analysis. In transaction cost analysis, once what appear to be the key transaction costs are identified, they take over as surrogates for the real interaction between the relations and the transaction.

The third step is stated the same way in both true relational contract analysis and transaction cost analysis: engagement in whatever detailed transactional analysis is desired, subject to whatever constraints the first steps suggest. The differences in the first steps, however, cause differences in the constraints, and hence differences in results.

Relational contract theory advances the proposition that it is both more efficient and more sure to engage in combined contextual analysis of relations and transactions than to commence with noncontextual analysis of transactions. As shown above, transaction cost analysis adheres in considerable measure, but by no means entirely, to this proposition.

Whichever approach is used there will always be a considerable degree of subjectivity in deciding what needs treatment, and how much, and what needs none. It is also quite possible, if unlikely, that an analyst starting from the transaction end but also blessed with knowledge, common sense, imagination, subtlety, and skill may do both a more efficient and more complete and sure job than an analyst less blessed but diligently following the relational route. Moreover, it is by no means uncommon to find mixtures of the two approaches:

As noted earlier, the final proposition is the least provable of the four core propositions of relational contract theory. The only way to "prove" it would be to survey a very large body of work on contract, most of which would be at least nominally thought to be transaction cost analysis. The survey would be aimed primarily at attempting to establish how complete and sure the various analyses were. As to the efficiency of the various analyses, it could probably only be inferred from conclusions respecting completeness and sureness. In short, proof of this proposition is a virtually impossible task, akin, perhaps to trying to navigate the Suud in a small boat without a compass on a starless, moonless night.

With regard to the fourth core proposition of relational contract theory, then, there is no challenge or query. Believe it or not, as you like it.

III. Essential Contract Theory

A. TERMINOLOGY

The core propositions of all relational contract theories constitute what should appropriately be called relational contract theory. Using the phrase "relational contract theory" as a title for any one such theory not only in effect purloins the title from its many owners, but also may lead to confusion of one relational contract theory with another. For that reason, I propose hereafter to refer to the ideas growing out of my own descriptions of common contract behavior and norms as *essential contract theory*. This label is appropriate for two reasons. First, I believe that the theory captures the essential elements of exchange relations. Secondly, I believe that analysis of this type is essential to understanding contract.

B. ESSENTIAL CONTRACT THEORY DEFINED

Essential contract theory is the proposition that the common contract behavioral patterns and norms described earlier constitute a highly effective vehicle for satisfying the core propositions of relational contract theory. Those patterns and norms supply a checklist for isolating all elements of the enveloping relations that might affect any transaction significantly. They supply a framework both for understanding those relations and for analyzing them. Finally, I believe they provide a highly effective mechanism for combined contextual analysis of transactions and the relations in which they are enveloped.

Essential contract theory also postulates that where the common contract norms are inadequately served, exchange relations of whatever kind fall apart. Note, however, that essential contract theory does *not* postulate that exchange relations should never fall apart. Whether they do or not depends upon whether common behavior and norms continue with sufficient strength, not on whether they should or should not continue for some reason or other.

In essential contract theory there is a somewhat general assumption that typically the law will more or less track the common contract behavior and norms. This should not, however, be overread. There may often be good reasons why the law should not track the common contract behavior and norms.

Finally, essential contract theory appears to fly in the face of the principles of law and economics (without transaction costs), rational choice theory, and game theory. The appearance is, however, deceiving. Essential contract theory eliminates the use of neither of these theories. It merely requires that their principles be applied only interstitially, within the relations rather than as the single analytical tool, either theoretically or practically.

Challenge/Query No. 8: Are there more effective tools for satisfying the core propositions of relational contract theory than use of the common contract behavioral patterns and norms on which essential contract theory relies? If so, what are they? What are their relative advantages and disadvantages in achieving surer and more complete insights into contract? Do responses to Challenges 2 and 3 suggest that the common contract behavioral patterns and norms can be bettered for these purposes by eliminations, alterations and/or supplementation?

The *common* contract behavior and norms are the end of neither the descriptive nor the theoretical story. I also combined these behavioral patterns and norms with something else, namely the idea of two polar types of contracts, discrete and relational. They, too, are descriptive. Both their nature and their relation to theory are discussed in Part IV.

IV. The Relational/As-If-Discrete Spectrum

Probably the most recognized aspect of my work in contract is the use of a spectrum of contractual behavior and norms with poles, labeled relational and discrete, respectively. As with the broader arena, this spectrum too reflects both descriptions of contract behavior and norms and is the basis for a theory emanating from those descriptions.

A. TERMINOLOGICAL DIFFICULTIES

Two terminological difficulties have emerged respecting this discrete-relational spectrum, one for each term.

1. *The Dual Meaning of Relational*. First, use of the root "relation" to

describe two separate things causes confusion. One use, seen above, encompasses all relations in which exchange occurs. Since even the most discrete exchange occurs in relations, discrete exchange is relational in this sense. The other use refers particularly to relational contract, which is found at the opposite end of a discrete-relational spectrum. The confusion arises because contracts labeled relational in the second sense are already relational in the first sense (as are all discrete contracts), although the obvious implication of describing one pole as relational is that contracts at the other (discrete) pole are *not* relational.

In light of the foregoing problem, I decided, in one of my last articles on contract before being diverted to other activities, to refer to the spectrum of exchange relations as being discrete at one end and intertwined (rather than relational) at the other. (Macneil 1987b, 276) This effort has been unsuccessful respecting the work of others, and I have reached several conclusions. One is that it is too late to change. Another is that most often the context will prevent the ambiguity from causing too much trouble. Yet another is that a terminological change at the other end of the spectrum will help alleviate the problem.

2. *As-If-Discreteness.* The word "discrete" too raises a problem. Since all discrete transactions are embedded in relations, they are relational and not truly discrete. To use the label "discrete" to identify that end of the spectrum appears to be a denial of this fact about some transactions. This might not be a serious problem, were it not for the mesmerizing, indeed paralyzing, influence that the idea of discrete transactions has come to have in the Western mind. (Macneil 1987a) Nowhere is this influence greater than in intellectual endeavors. One consequence of this overpowering effect is that people really do act and think as if discrete transactions exist outside of relations. In fact, what we think of as discrete transactions are something quite different: they are the deliberate or habitual treatment within complex relations of certain events *as if* they were discrete transactions.

Our extensive ability to engage in such treatment of events is an extraordinarily powerful and useful economic and social device, one absolutely indispensable in the modern world. Like all extraordinarily powerful and useful things, however, it is extraordinarily dangerous. Not the least danger of the idea of discrete transactions is its amazing ability to capture the intellect completely. When this happens, the "as if" of reality becomes the "is" of intellectual analysis, and the relations in which the as-if-discrete events actually occur disappear altogether.

There are a number of reasons for adding "as if" to the terminology.

One is to achieve consistency among descriptions of common contract behavior and norms, essential contract theory, and the relational/as-if-discrete spectra. More important is to press home at all times the point that there is *no such thing* in real life as a discrete transaction. What makes them appear to exist is that we treat certain events in large degree as if they were discrete transactions. This treatment, at odds with reality, is properly emphasized by including the phrase "as if" as part of the concept of discreteness.

B. DESCRIPTION, NOT THEORY

Just as the common contract behavioral patterns and norms constitute descriptions, so too do the behaviors and norms singled out by the relational/as-if-discrete spectrum.

1. *Common Contract Behavior and Norms.* Because of their universal nature in contract, that is, in exchange relations, common contract behavioral patterns and norms occur all along the relational/as-if-discrete spectrum. Certain of them, however, are intensified at one end and others at the other end. In the case of relational contracts in particular, some are considerably transformed. There is, however, a caveat: like the ends of rainbows, the ends of the relational/as-if-discrete spectrum are mythical.

2. *As-if-Discrete Transactions.* As-if-discrete transactions give rise to an intensification in exchange relations of two common contract behaviors—implementation of planning and effectuation of consent—and hence to an intensification of the norms arising out of these behaviors. When so intensified, these transactions may usefully be labeled as following the as-if-discrete norm, and thus as enhancing discreteness and presentiation.

3. *Relational Contracts.* Relational contracts, by contrast, give rise to an intensification in exchange relations of several other common contract behaviors, and hence to their norms. Primary among these are (1) role integrity, (2) contractual solidarity, and (3) harmonization with the social matrix, especially the internal social matrix.

In addition, relational contexts affect the nature of other common contract norms. For example, flexibility in relations is at least partially an internal, rather than an entirely external norm as it is (in theory) in as-if-discrete transactions. Hence, flexibility comes into partial conflict with the planning and consent norms in ways not occurring in as-if-discrete transactions. Reciprocity also becomes an important internal matter, lest the relation break down. Power is also an important internal matter in relations. (Macneil 1983b, 350–351)

Challenge/Query No. 9: Are there more accurate descriptions of contract behavior and norms differentiated along a spectrum of relational/as-if-discreteness? If so, what are they? What are their relative advantages and disadvantages for gaining insights into this dimension of contract? Can the above descriptions be bettered by eliminations, alterations, and/or supplementation?

4. *The Law of Relational Contracts.* Another observation pertinent to the relational/as-if-discrete spectrum concerns relational contract law, that is, law which takes into significant account the fact that it is treating contracts towards the relational end of the relational/as-if-discrete spectrum, Since the world abounds with relational contract, the world necessarily abounds with relational contract law.

Relational contract law is so all-pervasive that one feels almost foolish in giving examples. A few examples from but one type of contractual relation, employment, will do: workmen's compensation, numerous anti-discrimination laws, social security taxation and benefits, ERISA, OSHA, other workplace regulations, wage and hours legislation. All of these are relational contract law. And all are part of almost any American employment relation. To which needs to be added where collective bargaining is in place, the NLRA, LMRA, and a wide range of law governing unions and other aspects of collective bargaining. Note that the foregoing is an observation, not a prescription.

5. *Other Dimensions?* It has often occurred to me that there are surely other dimensions beside that of relational/as-if-discreteness that could aid our understanding of contract. For example, in *The New Social Contract* I explored this spectrum in both primitive and modern contractual relations. (Macneil 1980c) But what about the dimension of primitive and modern itself? The dimension of feudal-and-guild and modern? Small and large? Informal and formal?

Challenge/Query No. 10: Are there other dimensions besides the relational/as-if-discrete spectrum which could add to our understanding of contract?

C. The Relational/As-If-Discrete Spectrum and Essential Contract Theory

The spectrum of relational/as-if-discrete behavior thus far discussed is entirely descriptive. The spectrum is, however, also an important refinement of essential contract theory as described above in Part III. As noted in Part IV.B, both relational contracts and as-if-discrete contracts are characterized by intensifications of the common contract behavior and norms that are elements of essential contract theory. That being the case, essential contract theory could get along without teasing out the particularly relational and particularly as-if-discrete behavior and norms for special treatment. I believe, however, that separating them out adds greatly to the usefulness of essential contract theory as an application of the core propositions of relational contract theory.

D. Relational Contract Law for Relational Contracts?

So far nothing said about common contract behavior or norms, about essential contract theory, or about the relational/as-if-discrete spectrum has been prescriptive respecting the content of the law governing relational contracts. Nonetheless, the observation made earlier that a great deal of relational contract law exists has been misconstrued so often that clarification is needed as to what it does and does *not* mean.

This observation means that, irrespective of whether one likes or does not like any particular relational contract law, analysis of contracts subject to it cannot safely ignore that law. This observation does *not* mean that relational contracts can never be dealt with by relatively discrete contract law. Indeed, the discrete elements in contractual relations tend to assure that they will be. It does mean, however, that discrete contract law can never be the beginning and the end of the law applicable to relational contracts. Nor does the observation mean that the applicable relational contract law should necessarily *always* track closely the behavior and norms of the exchange relations in question.

Finally, this observation does not mean that relational contract law should always aim to preserve relations, or even should have some presumption that such an aim is the starting point. As noted in the initial discussion of essential contract theory, it contains no such postulate. Whether contractual relations continue or fall apart depends upon whether the common behavior and norms continue with sufficient strength. Where they do not, relational contract law may or may not appropriately step in.

Challenge/Query No. 11: I challenge to a duel anyone who, after this notice, persists in converting my descriptions of relational contract law into prescriptions of what the law should be, particularly prescriptions of some universal application of relational contract law.

Notwithstanding the challenge just offered, in my work I have gone beyond observation and included two types of prescription respecting relational contract law, being very careful to separate each prescription from the other. One is entirely personal to my perceptions of the good life. While those perceptions undoubtedly are partially influenced by my understanding of contractual relations, they are highly personal glosses on essential contract theory and the relational/as-if-discrete dimension. Their merits or lack there of have no place in assessments of the subjects of this Article.

The other type of prescription is not personal, but rather what I have thought of as basically neutral. The most important of these is a general idea that relational contract law should generally track the relational behavior and norms found in the relations to which it applies. I have long recognized limitations on this idea. Nonetheless, it seemed to me a generally sound notion. This idea has come under attack, and more attacks may be in the offing.

Challenge/Query No. 12: Is the idea that contract law should track the relational behavior and norms of the contracts in question ever sound as a starting principle? If so, is it sound just sometimes? Generally? Under what circumstances? If generally, what, if any, exceptions are there?

V. Symposium Postcript

A. WE'RE ALL RELATIONISTS NOW!

The most striking thing to me about the Symposium was the unanimity of recognition among the participants of the relational nature of contract. I had, of course, expected such recognition from Professors Bernstein, Feinman, Macaulay, and Speidel. I had not, however, expected Professor Posner to say that "[t]his, I hope, will be understood as a vindication of the relational contract approach," or that "[t]his is a first step to understanding the role of courts, once we acknowledge that we live in a relational world." (*cf.* Posner 2000, 4) Nor had I really expected Professor Scott to make this comment (though I probably should have):

> The debate that divides the academics who think about these questions is not over the nature of *contract* as an institution. We are all relationalists now. In that sense Macneil and Macaulay have swept the field. Contract, we now know, is complex and subjective and synthetic in every sense of those terms. The debate, rather, is over the proper nature of *contract law*. All contracts are relational, complex and subjective. (Scott 2000, 852)

Moreover, no one disputed the application to "living contracts" of the first three core propositions of relational contract theories. Indeed, it may be said that even the most discretist contribution to this Symposium, that of Professor Posner, reflects all three of these principles insofar as his living-contract hypothetical is concerned. There also appeared to be no overt challenge to the fourth core proposition, although I would hardly go so far as to claim unanimous agreement with it.

For reasons expressed below, I believe that if this about-face respecting relational contract in the tiny Symposium sample of discretist thought is widespread among discretists generally, serious problems lie ahead for the future of academic "discretism."

B. But Not When It Comes to Law

1. *Introduction.* The unaminous acceptance of the relational character of all living contracts, was, needless to say, not paralleled by unanimous acceptance of relational principles for contracts-at-law. In varying degrees those with discretist tendencies plumped for discrete approaches to contracts-at-law.

2. *Definition.* At the definitional level, Professor Scott came down four-square for the most discrete contract law of all, classical contract law. (Scott 2000) The debate is over the proper nature of contract law, and the point, in his view, is that while all contracts are relational, complex and subjective, contract law—whether we like it or not—is not. It is formal, classical (to use that terminology), and simple. The normative issue is whether or not the failure of contract law to be coextensive with our more complex understanding of contract as an institution is a good idea or a bad idea. Professor Scott thus limits his concept of contract law

to the formality and simplicity of classical contract law. Probably most discretists would, however, grudgingly include neoclassical contract law, or at least some of it.

Similarly, Professor Eisenberg views the relational idea of founding contract-at-law in exchange and reciprocity as a "sort of imperialistic view of contract." Instead, he would base contract-at-law on promise: "There are many areas of life where obligations and even legal obligations are properly imposed on the basis of exchange and reciprocity that I simply wouldn't see as contract law." (Eisenberg 2000, 805)

Neither of these definitional positions, of course, necessarily prevents heavily relational approaches to the law of relations involving exchange and reciprocity. All they necessarily do is to separate the law of such relations into the part encompassed by narrowly defined contract law and all the rest of the law applicable to the relations. Justice Frankfurter, for example, took this position in *Lewis v. Benedict Coal Co*[1] respecting the complex multiparty patterns created by national pension funds in the collective bargaining context. For him, there was contract law (heavily classical) and there was all the rest of the phenomenally complex law—the National Labor Relations Act, for example—that governs those relations.

Nonetheless, definitions and the creation of categories matter. Justice Frankfurter's unwillingness to think of the law in relational terms almost certainly kept him from seeing the absurdity of his interpretation of highly discrete contract law and his application of it to the multiparty context of *Lewis v. Benedict Coal Co.*

3. *Analysis and Substance.* Such a rejection of relational principles in contract-at-law, coupled with an acceptance of the relational character of all living contracts, brings us directly to the final Challenge/Query in this Article:

Challenge/Query No. 13: Relational contract law should generally track the relational behavior and norms found in the relations to which it applies. Indeed, I would go further and say that, on the whole, the law must generally do this.

4. *The General Impact of the Discretist Surrender to Relationism of Everything Outside the Law.* Discretists seem to have no idea how much ground they lose when they concede to relationism all the field of living-contract other than its legal aspects. The ramparts of Castle Law standing

---

[1] *Lewis v. Benedict Coal Co*, 361 U.S. 459 (1960).

alone offer pitifully little defense for discretism. Indeed, although surely not so intended, such concessions in effect concede the intellectual war.

More important, the concessions lose the high ground in the contract-at-law war, both theoretically and practically. The concessions in effect recognize that, in theoretical terms, discretist legal theories such as rational choice theory and game theory can be no more than, at best, important elements in some kind of overarching relational legal approach. Relational attacks are thus no longer irrelevant or beyond the boundaries of some theoretical Pale. In practical terms, this leaves any discretist legal analysis particularly vulnerable to attack for omissions and commissions revealed by relational approaches. No longer, as in the past, can such attacks be casually dismissed as ignoring the main point, namely the precepts of whatever discretist model is in use. No longer can the cop-out of *ceteris paribus* be used to ignore essential relational factors. Moreover, classical and neo-classical contract law can be seen as only a part—however important—of any overarching relational jurisprudence.

Bibliography

Complete Bibliography of the Writings of Ian Macneil

Whilst this bibliography was in press, a third edition of Macneil's Second Casebook has appeared: I.R. Macneil and P.J. Gudel (2001) *Contracts: Exchange Transactions and Relations*. 3rd edn., New York (USA), Foundation Press.

Alexander, L. ed. (1991) *Contract Law (International Library of Essays in Law and Legal Theory)*, vol. 1, New York (USA): New York University Press

Bouckaert, B. and De Geest, G., eds. (2000) *Encyclopaedia of Law and Economics*, vol. 1, Aldershot (U.K.), Edward Elgar and Ghent (Netherlands): University of Ghent Press

Burrows, P. and Veljanovski, C.J., eds. (1991) *The Economic Approach to Law*, London (U.K.): Butterworths

Macneil, I. R. (1960a) "Review of H. Shepherd and B. D. Sher, *Law in Society: An Introduction to Freedom of Contract*" 46 *Cornell Law Quarterly* 176–9

(1960b) "Settlement of Personal Injury Claims of Minors: A Proposal" 3 (October) *New Hampshire Bar Journal* 10–7

(1962) "Power of Contract and Agreed Remedies" 47 *Cornell Law Quarterly* 495–528

(1963) "Exercise in Contract Damages: *City of Memphis* v. *Ford Motor Company*" 4 *Boston College Industrial and Commercial Law Review* 331

(1964) "Time of Acceptance: Too Many Problems for a Single Rule" 112 *University of Pennsylvania Law Review* 947–79 (revised in Macneil 1968q, 1395–433)

(1965) "The Master of Arts in Law" 17 *Journal of Legal Education* 423–31

(1966a) *Bankruptcy Law in East Africa*, Nairobi (Kenya): Legal Publications

(1966b) "The Tanzania Hire-Purchase Act 1966" 2 *East African Law Journal* 84–104

(1966c) "You and the Hire-Purchase Act 1966" no 11 *The Nationalist* (Dar Es Salaam) 14–5

(1967) "Research in East African Law" 3 *East African Law Journal* 47–78

(1968a) "Academic Safari in East Africa" 19 (3) *Harvard Law School Bulletin* 12

(1968b) "Acceptance by Silence", in Schlesinger, ed. (1968, 1073–111)

(1968c) "Acceptance or Acknowledgment of Receipt of Offer", in Schlesinger, ed. (1968, 1049–55)

(1968d) "Communication of the Offer", in Schlesinger, ed. (1968, 683–90)

(1968e) *Contracts: Instruments for Social Co-operation—E Africa*, South Hackensack (USA): Fred B. Rothman

(1968f) "Definiteness of Terms", in Schlesinger, ed. (1968, 433–64)

(1968h) "Is Communication of Acceptance Necessary", in Schlesinger, ed. (1968, 1301–7

(1968i) "Late Acceptance", in Schlesinger, ed. (1968, 1549–55)

(1968j) "Means of Declaring and Communicating Acceptance", in Schlesinger, ed. (1968, 1349–58)

(1968k) "Offer or Invitation to Deal?" Schlesinger, ed. (1968, 327–42)

(1968l) "Offers to the Public", in Schlesinger, ed. (1968, 647–53)

(1968m) "Rejection and Return Offers", in Schlesinger, ed. (1968, 1005–12)

(1968n) "Revocable and Irrevocable Offers", in Schlesinger, ed. (1968, 747–63)

(1968o) "Sale at Auction", in Schlesinger, ed. (1968, 391–402)

(1968p) "Time Limit for Acceptance", in Schlesinger, ed. (1968, 1497–506)

(1968q) "When Acceptance Becomes Effective", in Schlesinger, ed. (1968, 1393–433) (includes revised version of Macneil 1964)

(1969a) "Contracts, Bankruptcy and Insurance: Teaching in Tanzania" 10 (1) *Foreign Exchange Bulletin* 3

(1969b) "Whither Contracts?" 21 *Journal of Legal Education* 403–18 (see also 618)

(1970) "Law and Human Values in the Countdown to Environmental Disaster" 22 (4) *Cornell Law Forum* 2

(1971a) *Contracts: Exchange Transactions and Relations*, Mineola (USA): Foundation Press (2nd. edn. Macneil (1978b))

(1971b) Review of A. Sawyerr and J. Hiller, "The Doctrine of Precedent in the Court of Appeals for East Africa" no. 5 *African Studies* 99 (simultaneously published as Macneil (1971c))

(1971c) Review of A. Sawyerr and J. Hiller, "The Doctrine of Precedent in the Court of Appeals for East Africa" 4 *East Africa Law Review* 289 (simultaneously published as Macneil (1971b))

(1974a) "The Many Futures of Contract" 47 *Southern California Law Review* 691–896

(1974b) "Restatement (Second) of Contracts and Presentation" 60 *Virginia Law Review* 589–704

(1975a) "Contracts and the Big, Wide World" 12 (Spring) *Cornell Law Forum*

(1975b) "A Primer of Contract Planning" 48 *Southern California Law Review* 627–704

(1975c) *Report of Director of Priorities Study*, mimeo, Cornell University

(1976) "The Wheel and the Hearth" 12 (Spring) *Cornell Law Forum* (reprinted as Macneil (1977))

(1977) "The Wheel and the Hearth" 29 *Journal of Legal Education* 1–5 (reprint of Macneil (1976))

(1978a) "Contracts: Adjustment of Longterm Economic Relations Under Classical, Neoclassical and Relational Contract Law" 72 *Northwestern University Law Review* 854–905

(1978b) *Contracts: Exchange Transactions and Relations*, 2nd. edn., Mineola (USA): Foundation Press (2nd. edn. of Macneil (1971a))

(1980a) "Envy Not La Salle Street Nor Main Street" no 67 (Fall) *The Reporter* (Northwestern University School of Law) 11

(1980b) "Essays on the Nature of Contract" 10 *South Carolina Central Law Journal* 159–200

(1980c) *The New Social Contract: An Inquiry into Modern Contractual Relations*, New Haven (USA): Yale University Press

(1980d) "Power, Contract and the Economic Model" 14 *Journal of Economic Issues* 909–23 (revised in Macneil (1981b))

(1981a) "Economic Analysis of Contractual Relations", in Burrows and Veljanovski, eds. (1981, 61–92) (revised in Macneil (1981b))

(1981b) "Economic Analysis of Contractual Relations: Its Shortfalls and the Need for a '"Rich Classificatory Apparatus"'" 75 *Northwestern University Law Review* 1018–63 (this paper is formed by the revision of Macneil (1980b) and Macneil (1981a))

(1981c) "Lon Fuller: Nexusist" 26 *American Journal of Jurisprudence* 219–27

(1982) "Efficient Breach: Circles in the Sky" 68 *Virginia Law Review* 947–969 (reprinted as Macneil (1991a))

(1983a) "The Future of the Supreme Court of Canada as the Final Appellate Tribunal in Private Law Litigation: A View from the South" 7 *Canadian Business Law Journal* 426–41

(1983b) "Values in Contract: Internal and External" 78 *Northwestern University Law Review* 340–418 (reprinted as Macneil (1991b))

(1984) "Bureaucracy and Contracts of Adhesion" 22 *Osgoode Hall Law Journal* 5–28

(1984–5) "Bureaucracy, Liberalism and Community—American Style" 79 *Northwestern University Law Review* 900–48

(1985a) "Reflections on Relational Contract" 141 *Journal of Institutional and Theoretical Economics* 541–6

[1985b] "Relational Contract: What We Do and Do Not Know" *Wisconsin Law Review* 483–525

(1986) "Exchange Revisited: Individual Utility and Social Solidarity" 96 *Ethics* 567–93

(1987a) "Barriers to the Idea of Relational Contracts", in Nicklish, ed. (1987, 31–46)

(1987b) "Relational Contract Theory as Sociology: A Reply to Professors Lindenberg and de Vos" 143 *Journal of Institutional and Theoretical Economics* 272–90

(1987c) "Review of H. Collins, *Law of Contract*" 14 *Journal of Law and Society* 373–80

(1988a) "A Brief Comment on Farnsworth's '"Suggestion for the Future"'" 38 *Journal of Legal Education* 301–3

(1988b) "Contract Remedies: A Need for a Better Efficiency Analysis" 144 *Journal of Institutional and Theoretical Economics* 6–30

(1988c) "Contractland Invaded Again: A Comment on Doctrinal Writing and Shell's Ethical Standards" 82 *Northwestern University Law Review* 1195–7

(1990) "Political Exchange as Relational Contract", in Marin, ed. (1990, 151–72)

(1991a) "Efficient Breach: Circles in the Sky", in Alexander, ed. (1991, 329–

51) (reprint of Macneil (1982))

(1991b) "Values in Contract: Internal and External", in Alexander, ed. (1991, 211–89) (reprint of Macneil (1983b)

(1992) *American Arbitration Law: Reformulation—Nationalisation—Internationalisation*, Oxford: Oxford University Press

(2000a) "Contracting Worlds and Essential Contract Theory" 9 *Social and Legal Studies* 431–8

(2000b) "Other Sociological Approaches and Law and Economics", in Bouckaert and De Geest, eds. (2000, 674–718)

(2000c) "Relational Contract Theory: Challenges and Queries" (2000) 94 *Northwestern University Law Review* 877–907

Macneil, I. R. and Schlesinger, R. B. (1968) "Some Comments on the Legal System of the United States, with Particular Reference to the Law of Contracts", in Schlesinger, ed. (1968, 193–209)

Macneil, I. R., Speidel, R. E. and Stipanowich, T. J. (1994) *Federal Arbitration Law: Agreements, Awards and Remedies Under the Federal Arbitration Act*, 5 vols., Boston: Little, Brown

Marin, B., ed. (1990) *Generalised Political Exchange: Antagonistic Co-operation and Integrated Policy Circuits*, Boulder (USA): Westview Press and Frankfurt am Main (Germany): Campus Verlag

Morison, R. S. and Macneil, I. R. (1970) *Students and Decision Making*, Washington DC (USA): Public Affairs Press

Nicklisch, F., ed. (1987) *The Complex Long-term Contract*, Heidelberg (Germany): C.F. Müller Juristischer Verlag

Schlesinger, R. B., ed. (1968) *Formation of Contracts: A Study of the Common Core of Legal Systems*, 2 vols., Dobbs Ferry (USA): Oceana Publications and London: Stevens and Sons

Other works referred to in the text

In this bibliography, I have sometimes referred to versions of works other than those originally used by Macneil in order to avoid making multiple references to the same work and/or to give references to more recent editions. When I have been aware of a later edition of a work cited by Macneil but have been unable to check it against the version he used, I have made a note to this effect.

Adams, J. and Brownsword, R. (1995) *Key Issues in Contract*, London (U.K.): Butterworths
(2000) *Understanding Contract Law*, 3rd. edn., London (U.K.): Sweet and Maxwell

Aksen, G. (1973) "Legal Considerations in Using Arbitration Clauses to Resolve Future Problems Which May Arise During Long-Term Business Agreements" 28 *Business Lawyer* 595

Alchian, A. A. and Demsetz, H. (1972) "Production, Information Costs and Economic Organization" 62 *American Economic Review* 777

Allen, P. (1995) "Contracts in the National Health Service Internal Market" 58 *Modern Law Review* 321

American Law Institute (1932) *Restatement of the Law of Contracts*, St. Paul (USA): American Law Institute Publishing

Anon. (1950) "Business Practices and the Flexibility of Long-Term Contracts" 36 *Virginia Law Review* 627

Arrighetti, A. *et al.* (1997) "Contract Law, Social Norms and Inter-Firm Cooperation" 21 *Cambridge Journal of Economics* 171

Arrow, K. J. (1983) *Collected Papers*, vol. 2, Cambridge (USA): Belknap Press

Arrow, K. J. and Debreu, G. (1983) "Existence of an Equilibrium for a Competitive Economy", in Arrow (1983, 58)

Atiyah, P. S. (1979) *The Rise and Fall of Freedom of Contract*, Oxford (U.K.): Clarendon University Press
(1990) *Essays on Contract*, rev. edn., Oxford (U.K.), Oxford University Press

Beatson, J. (1998) *Anson's Law of Contract*, 27th. edn., Oxford (U.K.): Oxford University Press

Beatson, J. and Friedmann, D., eds. (1995) *Good Faith and Fault in Contract Law*, Oxford (U.K.): Clarendon Press

Becker, C. (1983) "Property in the Workplace: Labour, Capital and Crime in the

Eighteenth Century British Woollen and Worsted Industry" 69 *Virginia Law Review* 1487

Becker, H. S. (1956) *Man in Reciprocity*, New York (USA), Praeger

Belcher, A. (2000) "A Feminist Perspective on Contract Theories From Law and Economics" 8 *Feminist Legal Studies* 29

Bell, J. (1989) "The Effect of Changes in Circumstances on Long-term Contracts", in Harris and Tallon, eds. (1989, 195)

Bennett, C. and Ferlie, E. (1996) "Contracting in Theory and in Practice: Some Evidence From the NHS" 74 *Public Administration* 49

Birmingham, R. (1970) "Breach of Contract, Damage Measures, and Economic Efficiency" 24 *Rutgers Law Review* 273

Bishop, W. (1986) "The Choice of Remedy for Breach of Contract" 14 *Journal of Legal Studies* 14

Black, F. (1989) "How to Use the Holes in Black-Scholes" (1989) 4 *Journal of Applied Corporate Finance* 67

Black, F. and M. Scholes (1973) "The Pricing of Options and Corporate Liabilities" 81 *Journal of Political Economy* 637

Blau, P. M. (1964) *Exchange and Power in Social Life*, New York (USA): John Wiley

Broom, L. *et al.* (1981) *Sociology*, 7th. edn., New York (USA): Harper and Row

Brown, P. A. and Feinman, J. M. (1991) "Economic Loss, Commercial Practices and Legal Process: *Spring Motors Distributors Inc* v. *Ford Motor Co*" 22 *Rutgers Law Journal* 301

Brownsword, R. (1996) "From Co-operative Contracting to a Contract of Co-operation", in Campbell and Vincent-Jones, eds. (1996, 14)

Brownsword, R. (2000) *Contract Law: Themes for the Twenty-First Century*, London (U.K.): Butterworths

Byers, M. (2000) "Woken Up in Seattle" 22(1) *London Review of Books* 16

Calabresi, G. and Melamed, D. (1972) "Property Rules, Liability Rules, and Inalienability: One View of the Cathedral" 85 *Harvard Law Review* 1089

Calamari J. D. and Perillo, J. M. (1967) "A Plea for a Uniform Parol Evidence Rule and Principles of Contract Interpretation" 42 *Indiana Law Journal* 333
The Law of Contracts, St. Paul (USA): West Publishing (now 4th. ed., 1998)

Campbell, D. (1987) "Review of H. Collins, *The Law of Contract*" 21 *The Law Teacher* 212
(1990) "The Social Theory of Relational Contract: Macneil as the Modern Proudhon" 18 *International Journal of the Sociology of Law* 75
(1992) "The Undeath of Contract: A Study in the Degeneration of a Research Programme" 22 *The Hong Kong Law Journal* 20
(1996a) *The Failure of Marxism*, Aldershot (UK): Dartmouth Publishing
(1996b) "The Relational Constitution of the Discrete Contract", in Campbell and Vincent-Jones, eds. (1996, 40)
(1997a) "The Relational Constitution of Contract and the Limit of 'Economics:'" Kenneth Arrow on the Social Background of Markets," in Deakin and Michie, eds. (1997, 307)
(1997b) "Socio-Legal Analysis of Contract", in Thomas, ed. (1997, 239)
(2000) "The Limits of Concept Formation in Legal Science" 9 *Social and Legal Studies* 439

Campbell, D. and Clay, S. (1992) *Long-Term Contracting: A Bibliography and Review of the Literature* Oxford (U.K.): Centre for Socio-Legal Studies

Campbell, D. and Harris, D. (1993) "Flexibility in Long-term Contractual Relationships: The Role of Co-operation" 20 *Journal of Law and Society* 166

Campbell, D. and Vincent-Jones, P., eds. (1996) *Contract and Economic Organisation: Socio-Legal Initiatives*, Aldershot (U.K.): Dartmouth Publishing

Carlton, D. and D. Fischel (1983) "The Regulation of Insider Trading" 35 *Stanford Law Review* 857

Chandler, A. D. (1962) *Strategy and Structure*, Cambridge (USA), MIT Press
(1976) *The Visible Hand*, Cambridge (USA), The Belknap Press
(1990) *Scale and Scope*, Cambridge (USA), The Belknap Press

Coase, R. H. (1986) *The Firm, the Market and the Law*, Chicago (USA): University of Chicago Press

Coase, R. H. (1994) *Essays on Economics and Economists*, Chicago (USA): University of Chicago Press

Cohen, D. (1982) "The Relationship of Contractual Remedies to Political and Social Status: A Preliminary Inquiry" 32 *University of Totonto Law Journal* 31

Collins, H. (1996) "Competing Norms of Contractual Behaviour", in Campbell and Vincent-Jones, eds. (1996, 67)
(1997) *The Law of Contract*, 3rd. edn., London (U.K.): Butterworths
(1999) *Regulating Contracts*, Oxford (U.K.): Oxford University Press

Cook, K. and Emerson, R. (1978) "Power, Equity, and Commitment in Exchange Networks" 43 *American Sociological Review* 721

Cook, K. et al. (1983) "The Distribution of Power in Exchange Networks" 89 *American Journal of Sociology* 275

Cooter, R. and Eisenberg, M. A. (1985) "Damages for Breach of Contract" 38 *California Law Review* 1432

Cooter, R. and Rappoport, P. (1984) "Were the Ordinalists Wrong about Welfare Economics?" 22 *Journal of Economic Literature* 507

Covington, R. N. (1978) "Arbitrators and the Board: A Revised Relationship" 57 *North Carolina Law Review* 91

Cowan, D., ed. (1998) *Housing: Participation and Exclusion*, Aldershot (U.K.): Dartmouth Publishing

Daintith, T. (1986) "The Design and Performance of Long-Term Contracts", in Daintith and Teubner, eds. (1986, 164)
(1987) "Contract Design and Practice in the Natural Resources Sector", in Owen Saunders, ed. (1987, 189)

Daintith, T. and Teubner, G., eds. (1986) *Contract and Organisation*, Berlin (Germany): de Gruyter

Dalton, C. (1985) "An Essay in the Deconstruction of Contract Doctrine" 94 *Yale Law Journal* 997

Deakin, N. and Walsh, K. (1996) "The Enabling State: The Role of Markets and Contracts" 74 *Public Administration* 33

Deakin, S. and Wilkinson, F. (1996) "Contracts, Co-operation and Trust: The Role of the Institutional Framework", in Campbell and Vincent-Jones, eds. (1996, 95)

Deakin, S. and Michie, J., eds., *Contracts, Co-operation, and Competition: Studies in Economics, Management and Law*, Oxford (U.K.): Oxford University Press

Deakin, S. *et al.*, (1997) "Contract Law, Trust Relations and Incentives for Cooperation: A Comparative Study", in Deakin and Michie, eds. (1997, 105)

Dickerson, F. (1965) *Fundamentals of Legal Drafting*, Boston (USA): Little, Brown

Domke, M. (1968) *The Law and Practice of Commercial Arbitration*, Mundelein (USA): Callaghan (now rev. edn., Wilmette (USA): Callagan, 1984)

Durkheim, E. (1984) *The Division of Labour in Society*, London (U.K.): Macmillan

Eisenberg, M. A. (1976) "Private Ordering Through Negotiation: Dispute-Settlement and Rulemaking" 89 *Harvard Law Review* 637

(1979) "Donative Promises" 47 *University of Chicago Law Review* 33

(1982a) "The Bargain Principle and its Limits" 95 *Harvard Law Review* 741

(1982b) "The Principles of Consideration" 67 *Cornell Law Review* 640

(1984) "The Responsive Model of Contract Law" 36 *Stanford Law Review* 1107

(1995) "Relational Contracts", in Beatson and Friedmann, eds. (1995, 291)

(2000) "Why There Is No Law of Relational Contracts" 94 *Northwestern University Law Review* 94

Elliott, M. (1981) "Review of I. R. Macneil, *The New Social Contract*" 44 *Modern Law Review* 345

Farnsworth, E. A. (1968) "Disputes Over Omission in Contracts" 68 *Columbia Law Rev.* 860

(1970) "Legal Remedies for Breach of Contract" 70 *Columbia Law Review* 1145

(1987) "A Fable and a Quiz on Contracts" 37 *Journal of Legal Education* 206

Feinman, J. M. (1983) "Critical Approaches to Contract Law" 30 *U.C.L.A. Law Review* 829

(1987) "Contract After the Fall" 39 *Stanford Law Review* 1537

(1990) "The Significance of Contract Theory" 58 *University of Cincinnati Law Review* 1283

(1995) *Economic Negligence*, Boston (USA): Little, Brown and Co

(1996) "Attorney Liability to Non-clients" 31 *Tort and Insurance Law Journal* 735

(2000) "Relational Contract Theory in Context", 94 *Northwestern University Law Review* 737

Ferlie, E. (1994) "The Creation and Evolution of Quasi-markets in the Public Sector: Early Evidence from the National Health Service" 22 *Policy and Politics* 105

Flynn, R. and Williams, G., eds. (1997) *Contracting for Health: Quasi-Markets and the National Health Service*, Oxford (U.K.): Oxford University Press

Foster, K. (1982) "Review of I. R. Macneil, *The New Social Contract*" 9 *British Journal of Law and Society* 144

Fried, C. (1981) *Contract as Promise*, Cambridge (USA): Harvard University Press

Fuller, L. L. and Braucher, R. (1964) *Basic Contract Law*, rev. edn., St. Paul (USA): West Publishing Co. (now Fuller and Eisenberg, *Basic Contract Law*, 7th. edn.)

Fuller, L. L. and Eisenberg, M. A. (1972) *Basic Contract Law*, 3rd. edn., St. Paul (USA): West Publishing Co. (now 7th. edn., 2001)

Galbraith, J. (1985) *The New Industrial State*, 4th. edn., Boston (USA): Houghton Mifflin

Gilmore, G. (1995) *The Death of Contract*, 2nd. edn., Columbus (USA): Ohio State University Press

Glendon, M. (1981) *The New Family and the New Property*, Boston (USA): Butterworth Publishers Inc

Goetz, C. J. and Scott R. E. (1977) "Liquidated Damages, Penalties and the Just Compensation Principle: Some Notes on an Enforcement Model and a Theory of Efficient Breach" 77 *Columbia Law Review* 554

(1981) "Principles of Relational Contracts" 67 *Virginia Law Review* 1089

(1983) "The Mitigation Principle: Toward a General Theory of Contractual Obligation" 69 *Virginia Law Review* 967

Goldberg, V. P. (1976) "Toward an Expanded Economic Theory of Contract" 10 *Journal of Economic Issues* 45

(1980) "Relational Exchange: Economics and Complex Contracts" 23 *American Behavioural Scientist* 337

Gordon, R. (1985) "Macaulay, Macneil and the Discovery of Solidarity and Power in Contract Law' *Wisconsin Law Review* 565

Gossen, H. H. (1983) *The Laws of Human Relations*, Cambridge (USA): MIT Press

Gottlieb, G. (1983) "Relationism: Legal Theory for a Relational Society" 50 *University of Chicago Law Review* 567

Gouldner, A. W. (1975) *For Sociology*, Harmondsworth (UK): Penguin

Gurvitch, G (1947) *Sociology of Law*, London (U.K.): Kegan Paul, Trench, Trubner

Hale, R., (1943) "Bargaining, Duress and Economic Liberty' *43 Columbia Law Review* 603

Harries, A. and Vincent-Jones, P. (2001) "Housing Management in Three Metropolitan Local Authorities: The Impact of CCT and Implications for Best Value" 27 *Local Government Studies*, forthcoming

Harris, D. and Tallon, D., eds. (1989) *Contract Law Today: Anglo-French Comparisons* Oxford (U.K.): Clarendon Press

Havighurst, H. (1961) *The Nature of Private Contract*, Evanston (USA): Northwestern University Press

Hawkes, K. (1977) "Co-operation in Binumarien: Evidence for Sahlin's Model" 12 *Man* 459

Hayek, F. A. (1976) *Law, Legislation and Liberty*, Chicago (USA): University of Chicago Press

Healey, C (1984) "Trade and Sociability: Balance Reciprocity as Generosity in the New Guinea Highlands" 11 *American Ethnologist* 42

Hegel, G. W. F. (1967) *Philosophy of Right*, Oxford (U.K.): Oxford University Press

Hillman, R. A. (1988) "The Crisis in Modern Contract Theory" 67 *Texas Law Review* 103

Hirsch, F. (1978) *Social Limits to Growth*, Cambridge (USA): Harvard University Press

Hirschman, A. O. (1970) *Exit, Voice and Loyalty*, Cambridge (USA): Harvard University Press, 1970

Hobbes, T. (1968) *Leviathan*, Harmondsworth (U.K.): Penguin Books

Holmstrom, B. (1982) "Moral Hazard in Teams" 13 *Bell Journal of Economics* 324

395

Homans, G. (1958) "Social Behaviour as Exchange" 65 *American Journal of Sociology* 597

Hondegem, A., ed. (1998) *Ethics and Accountability in a Context of Governance and New Public Management*, Amsterdam (Netherlands): IOS Press

Hughes, D. *et al.* (1996) "Contracts in the NHS? Searching for a Model" in Campbell and Vincent-Jones, eds. (1996, 155)

Hunt, A. (1981) "Dichotomy and Contradiction in the Sociology of Law", 8 *British Journal of Law and Society* 44

Keynes, J. M. (1973) *General Theory of Employment, Interest and Money*, London (U.K.): Macmillan

Kingdom, E. (2000) "Cohabitation Contracts and the Democratisation of Personal Relations" 8 *Feminist Legal Studies* 5

Kohler, J. (1914) *Philosophy of Law*, Boston (USA): The Boston Book Company

Kronman, A. (1978) "Mistake, Disclosure, Information and the Law of Contracts" 7 *Journal of Legal Studies* 1

Lakatos, I. (1980) *Philosophical Papers*, vol. 1, Cambridge (U.K.): Cambridge University Press

Lewis, D. (1969) *Convention: A Philosophical Study*, Cambridge, Harvard University Press

Lindenberg S. and De Vos, M. (1985) "The Limits of Solidarity: Relational Contracting in Perspective and Some Criticism of Traditional Sociology" 141 *Journal of Institutional and Theoretical Economics* 558

Linzer, P. (1981) "On the Amorality of Contract Remedies: Efficiency, Equity and the Second Restatement" 81 *Columbia Law Review* 111

Llewellyn, K. (1931) "What Price Contract?—An Essay in Perspective" 40 *Yale Law Journal* 704

Lowry, S. T. (1976) "Bargain and Contract Theory in Law and Economics" 10 *Journal of Economic Issues* 1

Lyons, B. and Mehta, J. (1997) "Private Sector Business Contracts: The Text Between the Lines", in Deakin and Michie, eds. (1997, 43)

Macaulay, S. (1963a) "Non-contractual Relations in Business: A Preliminary Study" 28 *American Sociological Review* 55
(1963b) "The Use and Non-use of Contracts in The Manufacturing Industry" 9 *The Practical Lawyer* 13
(2000) "Relational Contracts Floating on a Sea of Custom? Thoughts About the Ideas of Ian Macneil and Lisa Bernstein" 94 *Northwestern University Law Review* 775

Macaulay, S. *et al.* (1995) *Contracts: Law in Action*, Charlottesville (USA), The Michie Company

Mandeville, B. (1970) *The Fable of the Bees*, Harmondsworth (U.K.): Penguin Books

McHale, J. *et al.* (1997) "Conceptualizing Contractual Disputes in the National Health Service Internal Market" in Deakin and Michie, eds. (1997, 195)

McKendrick, E. (1995) "The Regulation of Long-term Contracts in English Law", in Beatson and Friedmann, eds.(1995, 305)

Mellinkoff, D. (1963) *The Language of the Law*, Boston (USA): Little Brown

Mertz, E. (2000) "An Afterword: Tapping the Promise of Relational Contract Theory—"Real"' Legal Language and New Legal Realism" 94 *Northwestern*

University Law Review 909

Moore, D. R. and Tomlinson, J. (1969) "The Use of Simulated Negotiation to Teach Substantive Law" 21 *Journal of Legal Education* 579

Mulder, J., and Volz, M. (1967) *The Drafting of Partnership Agreements*, 5th. edn., Philadelphia (USA): Committee on Continuing Legal Education of the American Law Institute and the American Bar Association

Murray, J.E. (1974) *Murray on Contracts*, 2nd. edn., Indianapolis, Bobbs-Merrill (now 4th. edn., New York (USA): Lexis Publishers, 2001)

North, D. C. (1990) *Institutions, Institutional Change and Economic Performance*, Cambridge (U.K.): Cambridge University Press

Nozick, R. (1974) *Anarchy, State and Utopia*, New York (USA): Basic Books

Owen Saunders, J., ed. (1987) *Trading Canada's Natural Resources*, Toronto (Canada): Caswell Legal Publications

Pareto, V. (1971) *Manual of Political Economy*, New York (USA): Augustus M Kelley

Parsons, T. (1968) *The Structure of Social Action*, rev. edn.. Glencoe (USA): Free Press

Parsons, T. and Smelser, N. (1956) *Economy and Society: A Study in the Integration of Economic and Social Theory*, Glencoe (USA): Free Press

Pashukanis, E. B. (1978) *The General Theory of Law and Marxism*, London (U.K.): Ink Links

Passmore, J. (1970) *The Perfectibility of Man*, London (U.K.): Duckworth

Paulin, M. *et al.* (1997) "Relational Contract Norms and the Effectiveness of Commercial Banking Relationships" 8 *International Journal of Service Industry Management* 435

Peterson, J (1978) "Hunter-Gatherer/Farmer Exchange" 80 *American Anthropologist* 335

Polanyi, K (1944) *The Great Transformation*, New York, Farrar and Rinehart

Posner, E. A. (2000) "The Theory of Contract Law Under Conditions of Radical Judicial Error" 94 *Northwestern University Law Review* 749

Posner, R.A. (1993) "The New Institutional Economics Meets Law and Economics" 149 *Journal of Institutional and Theoretical Economics* 73
(1998) *Economic Analysis of Law*, 5th. edn., Boston (USA): Aspen

Prattis, I. (1982) "Synthesis, or a New Problematic in Economic Anthropology" 11 *Theory and Society* 205

Rehbinder, M. (1971) "Status, Contract and the Welfare State" 23 *Stanford Law Review* 941

Ritchie, J. (1964) "Legal Education in the United States" 21 *Washington and Lee Law Review* 177

Rogerson, W. (1984) "Efficient Reliance and Damage Measures for Breach of a Contract" *Rand Journal of Economics* 39

Rubin, J. P. (1995) "Take the Money and Stay: Industrial Location Incentives and Relational Contracting" 70 *New York University Law Review* 1277

Sahlins, M. (1974) *Stone Age Economics*, London, Tavistock

Sako, M. (1992) *Prices, Quality and Trust: Inter-Firm Relations in Britain and Japan* (Cambridge (U.K.): Cambridge University Press

Schwartz, A. (1992) "Relational Analysis in the Courts: An Analysis of Incomplete Agreements and Judicial Strategies" 21 *Journal of Legal Studies* 271

Scott, R. E. (1987) "Conflict and Co-operation in Long-Term Contracts" 75 *California Law Review* 2005

(1990) "A Relational Theory of Default Rules for Commercial Contracts" 19 *Journal of Legal Studies* 577

(2000) "The Case for Formalism in Relational Contract" 94 *Northwestern University Law Review* 847

Schrag, P. G. (1969) "Bleak House 1968: A Report on Consumer Test Litigation" 44 *N.Y.U. Law Review* 115

Selznick, P. (1969) *Law Society and Industrial Justice*, New York (USA): Russell Sage Foundation

Shulman, H. (1955) "Reason, Contract and the Law in Labor Relations" 68 *Harvard Law Review* 999

Simon, H. A. (1997) *Administrative Behaviour*, 4th. edn., New York (USA): Free Press

Smith, A. (1976) *The Wealth of Nations*, Oxford (U.K.): Clarendon Press

Smith, J. (1993) *Law of Contract*, 2nd. edn., London (U.K.): Sweet and Maxwell

Speidel, R.E. (2000) "The Characteristics and Challenges of Relational Contracts" 94 *Northwestern Law Review* 823

Sturges, W. A. and Reckson, J. E. (1962) "Common-Law and Statutory Arbitration: Problems Arising from Their Coexistence" 46 *Minnesota Law Review* 819

Teubner, G. (2000) "Contracting Worlds: The Many Autonomies of Private Law" 9 *Social and Legal Studies* 399

Thomas, W. I . and Znaniecki, F. (1958) *The Polish Peasant in Europe and America*, *The Polish Peasant in Europe and America*, New York (USA): Dover Publications

Thomas, P. A., ed. (1997) *Socio-Legal Studies*, Aldershot (U.K.): Dartmouth Publishing

Trebilcock, M. (1993) *The Limits of Freedom of Contract*, Cambridge (USA): Harvard University Press

Treitel, G. H. (1999) *The Law of Contract*, 10th. edn., London (U.K.): Sweet and Maxwell

Tushnet, M. (1984) "An Essay on Rights" 62 *Texas Law Review* 1363

Ulen, T. S. (1984) "The Efficiency of Specific Performance: Toward a Unified Theory of Contract Remedies" 83 *Michigan Law Review* 1363

Ullman-Margalit, E. (1977) *The Emergence of Norms*, Oxford (U.K.): Clarendon Press

Vincent-Jones, P. (1994a) "The Limits of Near-contractual Governance: Local Authority Internal Trading Under CCT" 21 *Journal of Law and Society* 214

(1994b) "The Limits of Contractual Order in Public Sector Transacting" 14 *Legal Studies* 364

(1997) "Hybrid Organisation, Contractual Governance, and Compulsory Competitive Tendering in the Provision of Local Authority Services", in Deakin and Michie, eds. (1997, 143)

(2000) "Contractual Governance: Institutional and Organizational Analysis" 20 *Oxford Journal of Legal Studies* 317

Vincent-Jones, P. and Harries, A. (1996a) "Limits of Contract in Internal CCT Transactions: A Comparative Study of Buildings Cleaning and Refuse Collection in Northern Metropolitan", in Campbell and Vincent-Jones, eds.

(1996, 180)

(1996b) "Conflict and Cooperation in Local Authority Quasi Markets: The Hybrid Organisation of Internal Contracting Under CCT" 22 *Local Government Studies* 187

Vincent-Jones, P. and Harries, A. (1998) "Tenant Participation in Contracting for Housing Management Services: A Case Study", in Cowan, ed. (1998, 41)

Vincent-Jones, P. *et al.* (1998) *Local Authority Contracting for Professional Services: A Comparative Study*, End of Award No R000236416 Full Report for ESRC, available from the British Library (DSC Shelfmark: 3739.0605)

von Mises, L. (1981) *Socialism*, Indianapolis (USA): Liberty Classics

Wachter, M. and Williamson, O. E. (1978) "Obligational Markets and the Mechanics of Inflation" 9 *Bell Journal of Economics* 549

Walker, B. and Davis, H. (1999) "Perspectives on Contractual Relationships and the Move to Best Value in Local Authorities" 25 *Local Government Studies* 16

Walras, L. (1977) *Elements of Pure Economics*, London: Allen and Unwin

Walsh, K. (1995) *Public Services and Market Mechanisms: Competition, Contracting and the New Public Management*, Houndsmills (U.K.): Macmillan

Walsh, K. *et al.* (1996) "Contracts for Public Services: A Comparative Perspective", in Campbell and Vincent-Jones, eds. (1996, 212)

Walsh, K. *et al.* (1997) *Contracting for Change: Contracts in Health, Social Care, and Other Local Government Services*, Oxford (U.K.): Oxford University Press

Weber, M. (1978) *Economy and Society*, Berkeley (USA): University of California Press

Weistart, J. C. (1973) "Requirements and Output Contracts: Quantity Variations under the U.C.C." *Duke Law Journal* 599

Wheeler, S. (1991) *Reservation of Title Clauses*, Oxford (U.K.): Clarendon Press

White, H. C. (1983) "Agency as Control", paper presented at a symposium on *Asymmetric Information: The Agency Problem in Modern Business Practice*, Harvard University

Whitford, W. C. (1985) "Ian Macneil's Contribution to Contracts Scholarship' *Wisconsin Law Review* 545

Wightman, J. (1996) *Contract: A Critical Commentary*, London (U.K.): Pluto Press (2000) "Intimate Relationships, Relational Contract Theory, and the Reach of Contract" 9 *Feminist Legal Studies* 93

Williamson, O. E. (1985) *The Economic Institutions of Capitalism*, New York (USA): Free Press

Williamson, O. E. (1986) *Economic Organisation*, Sussex (U.K.), Harvester Wheatsheaf

Williamson, O. E. (1996) *The Mechanisms of Governance*, Oxford (U.K.): Oxford University Press

Williston, S. (1920) *The Law of Contracts*, New York (USA): Baker, Vooher and Co

Wilson, E. O. (1975) *Sociobiology*, Cambridge (USA): Belknap Press

Wistrich, E. (1998) "Contracting in the Public Services: The Case of Transport in the UK", in Hondegem, ed. (1998, 279)

Wittgenstein, L. (1968) *Philososphical Investigations*, Oxford, Basil Blackwell

Index

75–76
typology of discrete and
relational contracts, 75–
78
contract, law of, 69–74
Feinman, 72
future developments, 81–85
interest across disciplinary
boundaries, 82
policy-driven regulation, and,
84
quasi-market relationships, and,
84
reform of contract law, 82–83
relative values attaching to
common contract norms,
72–73
social interaction where
reciprocity is dominant
element, 73
study of contract behaviour, 83–
84
**Reception of Macneil's work in
USA**, 59–66
analogous body of work, 64
casebook, 64–65
classical contract law, and, 59
classificatory apparatus, 62
distinction between discrete and
relational exchanges, 61
economic gain, and, 62
influence on legal pedagogy,
65–66
multiplicity of values, 63–64
predominance of truly relational
contracts, 61
Primer of Contract Planning, 65
reality of day-to-day
contracting, and, 60
social contexts of agreements,

and, 60
style, 63
substance, 63–64
Uniform Commercial Code,
60–61
vocabulary, 63
Reciprocity
barter, and, 107–109
difference between
individualized and generic
interdependence, 109–110
generalized, 103–104
gift route to solidarity, 103–104
haggling, and, 107–109
high exchange-surplus, organic
route to solidarity, 105–
110
household, and, 106–107
low-exchange-surplus,
mechanical route to
solidarity, 104-105
meaning, 103
nonspecialized, 104–105
sexual division of labour, and,
106–107
size of exchange-surplus, and,
105–106
symbolism, and, 104–105
trading partnerships, 110
types, 103–110
Recitals
litigation planning, and, 247
**Relational/as-if-discrete
spectrum**, 378–383
as-if-discreteness, 379, 380
common contract behaviour
and norms, 380
description, not theory, 380–
381
dual meaning of relational, 379

408

essential contract theory, and,
382
relational contract law for
relational contracts, 382–
383
relational contracts, 380–381
terminological difficulties, 378–
380
Relational contracts, 126, 291–
332
abstract law of contract, 300–
301
administrative processes, and,
18–19
aim of theory, 314–315
America, and, 304–305
arbitration, and, 308–309
barriers to idea, 126, 298–310
capitalist economy, and, 19–20
challenges, 365–386
competition, 20–22
remedies, and, 16
solidarity, and, 16–17
complexity, 15–20
comprehensiveness, 315
contract behaviour, 257–262
co-operation, 20–22
co-operation in identification
of, 9–20
core of theories, 368–377
Critical Legal Studies
movement, and, 302–303
definition of contract, and, 384
definitions, 366–368
discrete contract, 22–25, 312–
313
discrete doctrine, and, 294
duration, 15–20, 321
essential elements of theory,
311–313

exchange, and, 311–312
"extreme relational pole", 317–
318
factual description, not theory,
366–367
Farnsworth on, 296–297
four core propositions, 368–377
analysis, 370–377
applicability, 369
combined contextual analysis
of relations and
transactions, 374
comparing relational and
transaction cost
approaches, 375–377
every transaction embedded
in complex relations,
370
individualistic analysis and
relational contract
theory, 369
price analysis example, 371–
372
provability, 368–369
recognition and consideration
of all significant
relational elements,
371–374
relation to more specific
relational contract
theories, 370
relational approach, 374–375
transaction-end approach
transaction cost analysis,
375
understanding elements of
enveloping relations,
370–371
general theory, 292
Hobbesian theory, and, 305–

306, 308
human nature, and, 320
importance of social relations,
316
law school experience, and, 304
law students, and, 304–305, 308
less total discreteness, and, 318–
319
long-term arrangements, 18–19
looseness, 315–316
marriage, 321
commencement, 322
consent, 324
incidents of benefits and
burdens, 322
number of pariticpants, 322
participant views, 322–323
termination, 322
material relations, and, 298–307
meaning, 17
measure of exchange, 321
neoclassical contract law, and,
293
neoclassical economic analysis,
and, 293
norm in identification of, 9–20
other common contract norms,
and, 313–314
productive increase, sense of,
17–18
queries, 365–386
reasons for rejection of theories,
301–302
reciprocity, and, 298–299, 319–
320
recognition of, 383
reconceptualization, and, 295
reflections on, 291–332
reply to Professor Lindenberg
and de Vos, 310–325

sociology, as, 310–325
solidarity, and, 299, 319–320
sovereign, positive law of, 262–
263
theory added to description, 368
tightness, 315–316
Relational norms, 163–167
autonomy, and, 166–167
economic efficiency, and, 165–
166
relationship with values of other
common contract norms,
165–166
role integrity, 163
values of, 163–164
Relational theory of contract,
3–57
Macneil, and, 3–57
Relational theory of exchange,
46–53
asymmetries of power, and, 49–
50
communication, and, 54
consumer sovereignty, and, 56
contract theory, and, 53–57
discrete contracting as economic
and legal policy, 55–56
"economic exchange", and, 46
exchange as key concept, 50
exchange, meaning, 47–48
generality of concept of
exchange, 48
Grundnorm, 53–54
half-Hobbesian theory, 55
human nature, and, 53
individualism, and, 51, 54
irrationality, and, 51
measured reciprocal exchange,
48–49
"monetised exchange", 46